The Untold Stories of Broadway

By
Jennifer Ashley Tepper

Dress Circle Publishing
New York

Book design by Emily Dew

Dress Circle Publishing
New York, New York
www.dresscirclepublishing.com

For my grandma, Sylvia, who always knew I belonged in the theatre.

And for my grandpa, Stanley, who always knew I could be a writer.

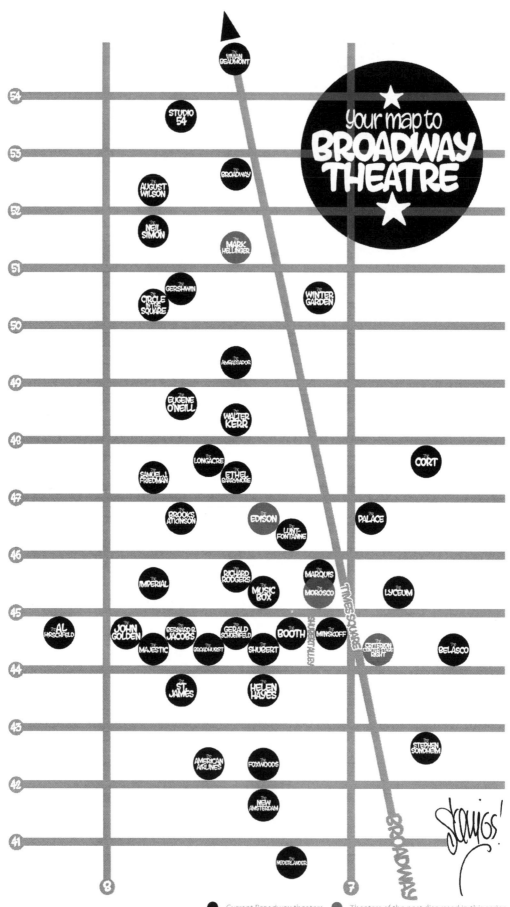

★ your map to **BROADWAY THEATRE** ★

● - Current Broadway theaters. ● - Theaters of the past discussed in this series.
Map illustration ©2013 Justin "Squigs" Robertson • www.squigsonline.com

4

Table of Contents

Introduction

When I was growing up in Boca Raton, Florida, people would ask me: What do you want to be when you grow up? I would often respond:

"I want to be the theatre."

I didn't want to be *in* the theatre. I wanted to *be* the theatre. I wanted to live and breathe Broadway.

I lived 1238.6 miles away from New York City, but I was hell-bent on being a part of it someday. I sat in my humid hometown, listened to cast albums, read Playbill Magazine, and circled all of the shows I would see and places I would go.

I moved to New York City when I was 18 years old, and from the moment I set foot in Times Square, I felt like I was home. As far as theatre was concerned, I was living in the center of the universe. I was the luckiest girl on Earth. I'd take the subway uptown from NYU and spend hours just sitting in front of the Neil Simon Theatre. It was where my favorite musical, *Merrily We Roll Along*, had played. It was my place. Being there made me feel connected to the city, even though I was so new. I felt such a strong connection to these places where shows I cherished from afar had actually played.

Every time I entered a theater—Broadway or otherwise—I was hit by a blast of memories, of history, even though I'd never been there before. I walked into the Imperial Theatre to see *Dirty Rotten Scoundrels* and I knew: *Dreamgirls* was here! And *Fiddler on the Roof*! And *Pippin*! I was now getting to live inside the great theatrical tradition that every inch of New York City was steeped in. Even the restaurants and bars and shops— I knew that they were filled with the footsteps of people who had built our theatrical legacy.

When I was a senior in college at NYU, I worked with the *[title of show]* team and helped get that original musical to Broadway. I spent the summer of 2008 at the Lyceum Theatre assisting director Michael Berresse. It was one of the greatest adventures of my life thus far. My time inside the oldest continually operating theater on Broadway gave me a priceless education and a lot of the experiences I had then greatly informed this book.

Later, while I was working as Broadway director Michael Greif's assistant, we went to see the play *33 Variations* at the Eugene O'Neill Theatre. Michael pointed at the stairs in the back of the orchestra section, and told me a story that had taken place there 25 years earlier during *Big River*, when he had been Des McAnuff's assistant. Experiences like that also planted the seeds for this book.

For three years, I worked for Broadway producer Ken Davenport. Working on the 2011 revival of *Godspell*, I got to spend a lot of time at the Circle in the Square Theatre. That was a very different kind of Broadway house. Spending time at Circle, putting on theatre in the round in a very incredible modern space made me think about the uniqueness of each Broadway theater. That was something I wanted to explore in this book.

This book was inspired by my love, not just for Broadway shows, but also for the beautiful, fascinating palaces where they live, and for the sense of community all around them. In a world where historic places are destroyed every day to make room for the new, New York City has the privilege of having dozens of 100-year-old Broadway theaters where show folk and audiences today do the exact same things they did a century ago.

This book is a love letter to Broadway and all of the people who make shows happen every night, to entertain and enlighten people from all over the world. Just like I craved insight into this world when I was growing up in Florida, I want to provide others who are fascinated by Broadway with never-before-heard backstage/on stage tales. I want to share the history of our Broadway theaters through the personal stories of the people who spend their lives in them.

I interviewed over 200 theatre professionals: actors, directors, writers, producers, designers, stagehands, musicians, box office treasurers, house managers, door men and women, advertising executives, company managers, press agents, stage managers, ushers, and so many more.

I interviewed each person about their memories of every Broadway theater they've worked in, and it was an adventure that I never could have imagined. I took an elevator in Rockefeller Plaza up to legendary Broadway producer/director Hal Prince's office! I went with Lin-Manuel Miranda to one of his favorite restaurants and we ran into his 1st grade teacher! I interviewed Mary Beth Peil, one of my favorite Broadway and TV stars, in her apartment!

I was welcomed into interviewees' homes, rehearsal spaces, offices, their favorite bars. Dozens of interviews took place in Broadway theaters before show time. Dozens of interviews took place on the second floor of Sardi's or the café at the Hotel Edison, where the theatrical community has been dining and drinking since before I was born. Dozens of interviews took place at Worldwide Plaza, the cafeteria of today's Broadway community. I got to see pockets of New York City I hadn't seen, from Harlem to Brooklyn to the Upper East Side. I sat on park benches and on rooftops and in coffee shops with 200 Broadway people and I asked them questions. I laughed a lot. I learned a lot. I cried a couple of times. And the streets that I'd always loved with my whole heart came alive even more than they already had, in ways that I had never dreamed of.

The Untold Stories of Broadway covers over 65 years of our theatrical past. Stories from those who were there begin in 1947! Even though this work covers as many shows and people and events as it does, it is still a representative rather than comprehensive look at Broadway history. If you get a glimpse of stage management and you wish you knew more, go take a stage management class. If you find yourself wanting to know more about *Pacific Overtures*, go buy a book on musicals of the 1970s. I hope that it is a gateway for people to learn more *and* create more theatre.

Our Broadway theaters have been home to thousands of shows. They have borne witness to the best and the worst times of peoples' lives. They have been there for the shows that ran years and the shows that closed in one night. Each theater holds secrets. There are secret rooms and secret doors and energy of secrets from the past swirling in the air. When you sit in a seat at a Broadway theater, you are sitting in the exact spot where thousands before you have sat and watched a show. When you move into a dressing room at a Broadway theater, you are sharing a room with the hundreds of show people before you that smeared grease paint on in that same mirror. The 40 theaters between 41st and 66th Street are where every Broadway musical and play has come to life for over 100 years. While the shows change every year, "Broadway" still stands for people telling each other stories in a handful of large buildings in midtown Manhattan. That sense of continuity creates something very powerful in the center of our city that gives it a special sparkle. Broadway is, and has always been, the heart of New York.

Here are the stories of the Winter Garden Theatre, the Richard Rodgers Theatre, the Marriott Marquis Theatre, the Al Hirschfeld Theatre, the Neil Simon Theatre, the August Wilson Theatre, the Mark Hellinger Theatre, and the Lyceum Theatre, eight Broadway theaters that light up New York City. This is the first volume of a multi-volume work that will include all 40 Broadway theaters, as well as several Broadway theaters that are no longer.

I wanted to chronicle how Broadway, like many types of art, is in the eye of the beholder. One person finds a theater intimate and another finds it cramped. One person loves a show and another hates it. One person thinks backstage is glamorous and another thinks it's a dump. You ask 200 people a question, you get 200 different answers.

But every single person interviewed for *The Untold Stories of Broadway* did have one thing in common: we all love the theatre. The good, the bad, and the ugly of it. The great highs and the bitter disappointments, the opening nights and the lazy Tuesdays, the beginnings and the endings, the moments of drama and the moments of comedy, the tears and the cheers.

And we are all part of it—from the fanciest Broadway legend to the kid in Florida listening to her first Broadway cast album.

Jennifer Ashley Tepper, November 2013

Notes:

For the purposes of this book, "theater" refers to the location, and "theatre" refers to the art form.

While the majority of tales take place in the featured theater, I've left in select excerpts that took place "off site," where I felt they were valuable to a full story. I've also left in some elements of conversational tone that were found in the interviews. As an avid reader, I often enjoy seeing how people truly expressed themselves. Similar to reading a rehearsal script with notes for a now-famous show, sometimes seeing the process adds to the work itself. In that spirit, I wanted you, the reader, to see some of the wheels turning, some of the thoughts trailing...

Each chapter of this book focuses on one Broadway theater and uses personal stories to take you chronologically through the history of that theater. Interspersed with interviewees' stories are my own tales and also some interesting facts and stories that I collected along the way.

The Richard Rodgers Theatre

Built: 1925
Location: 226 West 46th Street
Owner: The Nederlander Organization
Formerly Named: Chanin's 46th Street Theatre (1925-1932), 46th Street Theatre (1932-1989)
Longest-Running Show: *The Best Little Whorehouse In Texas* (1978-1982)
Shortest-Running Show: *Come Angel Band* (closed after two performances in 1936)
Number of Productions: 125

The coolest part is the history that's right there.

You walk those halls, and you walk that stage, and you know that so many of the greats walked them, too. I found out that my dressing room at the Richard Rodgers once belonged to Joel Grey. That was *his* dressing room.

Just to know that you're on that same stage, that those same lights are shining on you, you're looking in the same mirror... all of those elements. And at the same time, you know that those people all grew up wanting to do Broadway too, and one day they had been just as excited to get to the Richard Rodgers Theatre as you are.

-Corbin Bleu, Actor

Introduction: Why Don't You Call The Nederlanders?

Tim Pettolina, House Manager

I always told people that I wanted to work in theatre. When I was in high school, a friend of my dad's worked for the New York Yankees. The Nederlander Organization was involved with the Yankees. He said, "Why don't you call the Nederlanders and see if they have any internships?"

I called, and I got hired. I spent one summer during high school as an intern, for $50 a week. I answered phones. I went through old files and organized. It was tedious, but it was a great way to learn because I got to see so much history! I was around all these professional people, learning from them, and I got to run around to all of the Nederlander theaters, dropping off things, picking up things. The internship had me doing something different every week.

I stayed for a few years. I worked as an usher. I worked in their office. I kept coming back, and eventually, they gave me a management position.

The first theater I worked at was the Marquis, as an usher and then an assistant manager. I would show people the Biltmore or the Nederlander on behalf of the organization. Eventually, I became the house manager at the Richard Rodgers.

I saw *Nine* (1982) here at the Rodgers when I was a little kid, and *Accomplice* (1990) when I was in high school, and *Oh, Kay!* (1990). I would go to TKTS all the time, and see anything I could.

The Rodgers is structured similarly to the Neil Simon, the Nederlander, and the Brooks Atkinson. I know because I've worked in all of those Nederlander houses, too. They were all built around the same time, so they have one side with only a couple dressing rooms and one side with a huge tower of dressing rooms.

What's unique about the Rodgers is that we have a beautiful outdoor balcony above the marquee that looks out onto 46th Street! It's a nice space and we have parties up there. It's also a fire escape, so when we have receptions up there, we also have to rope off the steps. They're steep, and you really only want them used in an emergency.

The other thing that's unique to our theater is that the orchestra has stadium seating! Only the Majestic and the Rodgers have that.

Right now at the Rodgers, we're renovating. We're getting new seats, new carpeting, a complete paint job all over the theater, a new men's room, new backstage, new bathrooms and doors for the dressing rooms. It's almost a complete overhaul of the building. We're getting a new air conditioning system. It's a big project, and we're thrilled to be doing it.

When you're in theatre, renovations have to happen quickly, because you want the theater to be open for shows as much as possible. You don't want to close the theater for a year, because you will put so many people out of work. There are so many people who work at the Rodgers who are on unemployment right now. Our bosses are very good about trying to keep the theaters always open.

We have a bond with the Imperial Theater because it's right next door. Our stage doors are next to each other. During the time of *Billy Elliot* and *In the Heights*, it seemed like everyone got to know someone working on the other show, and we'd go back and forth meeting for dinners and drinks after shows. A lot of us are still friends.

As the house manager, it's always thrilling to have legendary artists and wonderful actors visiting the theater. You get to spend a moment with them, take them backstage, make sure they feel welcome. We've had Prince, Barbra Streisand, Diana Ross, James Earl Jones, Bono... Bill and Hillary Clinton came to *In the Heights* (2008), and the whole place started chanting, "Hillary! Hillary!" And Michelle Obama came to see *Porgy and Bess* (2012) That was unreal. I prepared the visit with the Secret Service; they had to do a whole background check on me! She was lovely and the whole cast was so thrilled to meet her. I got to chat with her and I told her she was beautiful.

During *Movin' Out* (2002), there were always problems with people singing along, because everyone knew all of the Billy Joel songs. One night, there was a group of intoxicated guys who would not stop singing along to *everything*. They were asked to stop, and wouldn't. They were really bothering the family in front of them. During the second act, the teenage son turned around, stood up and clocked one of the guys square in the face! The dance captain ran into the lobby and yelled, "A fight broke out! You have to get in there!" The bartender and I grabbed the guy and threw him out. I have so much sympathy for the people who work on *Rock of Ages*; they have to deal with all of that on a regular basis!

I remember the first preview of *Tarzan* (2006). I was just so happy that it was happening, because it was such a technically difficult show to get up. There was a long tech process to get through! It took six to eight weeks for us to do work in the theater to accommodate the show, and for them to get the show ready, with all of the flying. We felt such relief on the first preview. We did it!

The most exciting first preview was *In the Heights* because it was a brand new, original, thrilling New York show. There have been so many wonderful times. We also had a wedding during *In the Heights* for Bill Sherman, the arranger and orchestrator. He had his wedding on stage, and cast members wrote him songs and performed. That was wonderful.

Then, *In the Heights* closing felt like this gigantic party where the audience sang and screamed throughout the whole thing. It was like a rock concert. Actually, it reminded me of the last performance of *A Chorus Line*, which my dad brought me to when I was 11 years old. I was obsessed with that show and *In the Heights* was like that in that every song got a ten-minute ovation. It was happy and sad.

The box office treasurer, the head stagehands and I are always very much connected about what is going on in the theater. When we're in between shows, we talk on a daily basis about what might come in. We're always very concerned, because we have to plan our lives if we're going to be out of work for three months. Then, we'll usually find out from our bosses what's coming in and what the details are. Right now, we know we have *Romeo and Juliet* coming in August and then a show for the spring that's not announced yet[1]. So, the box office will reopen in July. Sometimes we have to wait for a while and don't know what'll come into our theater, and other times we have to get ready very quickly.

I try not to think about the bad times, but sometimes, they're the ones you can't forget. As for the good times, the best thing of all is that I see people leaving the theater so happy and they thank me and tell me that theatre is so great. Those are the times that remind me of when I was younger and so enthusiastic. I'm still enthusiastic when I go to the theater, but not in the same way. I love getting to see that in other people.

———————

The Richard Rodgers Theatre was built as Chanin's 46th Street Theatre in 1925 by Irwin Chanin, an architect and real estate developer. It was one of the first theaters to utilize a "democratic structure." In other words, those in the orchestra and those in the balcony used the same door to enter.

Chanin once said, "We made a sign when we started that theater: Everybody goes in the same door. Whether you've got a nickel or a five dollar bill, go right inside. No climbing stairs. You're part of the audience—whether you have a million dollars or you borrow money."

Chanin also built other Broadway theaters, such as the Majestic and Golden, as well as buildings like Milford Plaza and Central Park's Century Apartments. Chanin sold the 46th Street to the Shuberts in the 1930s. In the 1940s, they sold it to Robert Dowling, a private owner who would go on to turn the movie theater across the street, the Globe, into a legitimate Broadway theater, the Lunt-Fontanne.

The theater exchanged hands twice more, before landing in the portfolio of the Nederlanders in 1981.

———————

1947: I Remember Everything

Harvey Sabinson, Press Agent

My favorite Broadway theaters, without a doubt, are the St. James Theatre and the 46th Street Theatre, which is now the Richard Rodgers Theatre. I had a lot of hits in those theaters. The first show I ever worked on was *Finian's Rainbow*, which opened at the 46th Street.

I remember everything about *Finian's Rainbow*. I remember every song, every lyric.

I had no theatrical training whatsoever in school, but I was in the army, and when the war was over, I had nothing to do. So I volunteered to produce a show in Germany using talent from the division I was in. When they asked me what qualified me, I said my brother was a Broadway producer, which he was. And I went home and I asked my brother, "How do I get into your business?"

———————

[1] Tim was referring to the new musical *If/Then* which will open at the Rodgers in 2014

I found out that it was heavily unionized, but he wanted me to learn the business from the bottom up because he never had that opportunity. He became a producer by saying one day, when he woke up, "Today I'm a producer." He produced four shows in his lifetime, that was all. But anyway, he said, "I want you to learn the business from the bottom up and work with every department."

The first job he got me was as an apprentice to his press agent, a remarkable guy named Samuel J. Friedman, for whom a theater on 47th Street is now named. It was formerly the Biltmore. And when it was the Biltmore, it housed the longest-running straight play I ever worked on, *Barefoot in the Park*, the Neil Simon play.

Anyway, I began to work as an apprentice to Sam Friedman. I loved that work, and I was good at it. I said, "This is the career I really want." And that's the career I pursued for about 30 years before I became the director of the League of American Theatres, which is now the Broadway League.

Anyway, I really do remember everything about *Finian's Rainbow*. I remember sitting there on opening night next to my father. The orchestra struck up the overture, which starts with the song "How are Things in Glocca Morra?" My father elbowed me and said, "It's a smash!"

He fortunately turned out to be correct.

My memories are so vivid of the original cast. Michael Kidd's choreography was incredible. Michael Kidd was one of my big heroes, and when I was starting out on my own after I had worked for other press agents, later in 1956, Michael was about to produce and direct a musical, and he hired me to be the press agent. It was the first show I handled on my own as a senior press agent, and the reason he hired me was because my brother gave Michael *his* first opportunity to direct a Broadway show—that was *Finian's Rainbow*.

I live in Sarasota now, but the last time I was in New York, would you believe it, I saw a revival of *Finian's Rainbow*.

———————

At the time during the summer of 2013 that I interviewed Tim Pettolina, current house manager at the Rodgers Theatre, the theater was undergoing a renovation, between The Rascals *and* Romeo and Juliet. *Tim took me into the house, which looked otherworldly to me! Other than one sneaky glance in the Hilton stage door when* Spider Man *was being built, I don't think I'd ever seen a Broadway theater without seats in it before! The long shoe box-shaped lobby, the grand proscenium arch, the seating... it was all in a state of reconstruction, with dust and pieces of the building laid about.*

The theater was being renovated to look as beautiful as it did for its first production, The Greenwich Village Follies *in 1925! In the intervening years, a lot of the details of the theater had been painted over, and this refurbishment was meant to return the theater to its past glory. Many Broadway theaters had been built with a certain attention to detail in design, and in the middle of the 20th century, this was considered old-fashioned. During the 1940s and 1950s, many of our Broadway theaters were redone to suit the style of the time. They were made to look modern with coats of paint covering murals, marble, and detailed figures and statues. In fact, the remodelers at the Rodgers discovered halfway into the three and a half million dollar renovation that there was an old proscenium arch* underneath *the current one!*

Under each layer of dust and paint at a Broadway theater, lies decades of secrets. Tim told me that during the renovation, they'd found two interesting things. Under plaster beneath some seats, there was a very old postcard. On the front was a beautiful scene from Rosalinda, *a show that had played the theater in 1943. The back read: "Dear ____, I have just seen* Rosalinda. *_____." Imagine a postcard from 70 years ago, that you could send to your friends to spread word of mouth about a show! A lot of marketing ideas that people think are very "today," are even older than your grandparents.*

The other thing they found was a telegram, lodged in a pocket of the box office wall that had previously been covered. It was a notification that Finian's Rainbow *had closed, and that tickets could be exchanged for the tour or for the theater's next tenant,* Love Life.

These treasures and more had been lurking in hidden corners of the Rodgers for years.

Postcards and telegrams used to be staples of the Broadway experience. In fact, on opening nights, hundreds of telegrams would typically arrive at the stage door! Another tangible artifact that no longer exists is the herald. Heralds were inserts in Playbills that advertised other shows. They could be all different shapes and sizes. For instance, the second show at the theater was Is Zat So? *about a prize-fighting boxer, in 1926. For that show, the herald was a colorful boxing glove that opened up to tell readers more about the show.*

While heralds, postcards, and telegrams of this sort are no longer part of the Broadway we know, they are the ancestors of materials we use today. Broadway advertisements in the shape of fans are a descendant of the herald, and certainly Facebook sharing is a descendant of postcard mailing!

1954: *On Your Toes* At Age 14

Marilyn D'Honau, Actor

My older sisters Dorothy and Lillian went to dance class. I followed whatever my sisters did, so I danced too. We studied in New Jersey.

My father was an artist, and he did a layout for the Dance Congress. A woman there, Lucille Stoddard, said to my father, "Well if your three daughters want to dance, they should come to New York." So that's how we came here. My siblings and I went to Professional Children's School. Then, my older sisters started doing Broadway shows. Lillian was in *Hazel Flagg*. Dorothy *and* Lillian were in *By The Beautiful Sea*. I saw all the shows that they both did. And then I got to do shows too! In fact, when Lillian was in *Lil Abner*, and Dorothy was in *Mr. Wonderful*, I was in *West Side Story* all at the same time. And when Lillian was doing *Destry Rides Again* and Dorothy was doing *Once Upon A Mattress*, I was doing *Gypsy*!

One of the shows that I thought was just great—that *both* of my sisters were in—was *Nowhere To Go But Up!* Wonderful, fabulous choreography by Ron Field.

I made my Broadway debut as a replacement in the ballet line of *On Your Toes* when I was 14. I auditioned on the stage of the 46th Street Theatre. My sister Lillian was in the tap line of that show, and all the girls in the ballet line were Balanchine Ballet Russes dancers.

They needed one girl. Paula Lloyd had left, and she was small, and my sister knew that I was pretty good at ballet. Even though I was so young, I went in and auditioned. I showed that I could do Balanchine's work. So I got that show.

When I did *On Your Toes*, I was assigned to be part of "Slaughter on 10th Avenue". Well I learned it, and when I went on stage, with the garters and everything, I really didn't look quite right at that age, doing such a number! So, my sister was asked to do it in my place.

1955: Open The Show, Then Change It

Harold Prince, Producer/Director

Damn Yankees! That was at the 46th Street Theatre. It opened and it did not get a great review—in fact, not even a *good* review, in the *Times*.

Around five or six in the morning, after opening night, I called writer George Abbott. He said, "I'm up." And I said, "I've been up, waiting to call you. I couldn't wait any longer." He said, "Let's make some changes today. We made some real mistakes. We've got a number in the second act that should be in the first, we should take out another number, we left Gwen Verdon an ugly witch at the end of the show and we should restore the adorable girl that the audience has fallen in love with."

So, we took 15 minutes out of the show. We did all of those things in one afternoon. We went to Dinty Moore's on 46th Street, right next to the theater. We called the authors and they joined us, and everybody divided up the cast. We all made phone calls and, by breakfast, we had gotten the cast to come in. We had a rehearsal and made all the changes that day!

The show ran for over a thousand performances and we never changed another thing.

———————————

Dinty Moore's on 46th Street was a favorite hang-out for the theater crowd. An upper end Irish joint, it was located just next to the 46th Street Theatre, a spot now occupied by the breezeway of the Marriott Marquis.

The owner was James Moore, and the place was first called "James Moore's." Then, restaurant regular George McManus penned the comic strip Life With Father, *featuring an Irish tavern owner named Dinty Moore. James loved this presumable tribute, and changed the name of his venue.*

In the 1920s, Dinty Moore's was the place to go for hooch, as the restaurant paid no mind to Prohibition. Over the years, the place was populated by everyone from Walter Winchell to Will Rogers to Audrey Hepburn to Frank Sinatra to Judy Garland.

Florenz Ziegfeld was so depressed after the audience left the opening night of Show Boat *in silence that he spent the night drowning his sorrows at Dinty Moore's—before returning to the New Amsterdam the next morning to discover lines around the block to buy tickets.*

Legend has it that George S. Kaufman was once kicked out of Dinty Moore's for ordering a hamburger without onions. James Moore was known for booting even the most notable of his patrons, and this time, he hollered, "I don't tell you how to write your goddamned plays, don't tell me how to serve my hamburgers!" In 1932, George S. Kaufman and Edna Ferber's play Dinner At Eight *opened around the corner at the Music Box, with a character uttering a passingly throw-away line: "I've only got a minute. I got a classy dinner date—I've got to meet a hamburger with onions, at Dinty Moore's."*

Not only was Dinty Moore's frequented by the theatrical cognoscenti, Damon Runyon was also a regular. Police raids and unsavory dealings were frequent there during his time, which is especially poignant given that Runyon's Guys and Dolls *would open next door at the 46th Street Theatre, years later.*

Dinty Moore's closed in the early 1970s, shortly after a change in ownership. The last crowd to spend time there was the No No Nanette *cast, after performances next door. Talk about nostalgia.*

———————————

1955: Standing In The Wings

Richard Maltby Jr., Writer/Director

When I was at Yale, all the shows came to town. New Haven was the big out-of-town tryout city. You came to New Haven for a week and then you went to Boston or Philadelphia. I discovered you could usher at the theater and that way, I could see everything seven or eight times.

I met some people every now and then. I knew Richard Adler because my father, Richard Maltby Sr., the orchestra leader, had done a recording with him. The tour of *Damn Yankees* opened in New Haven, so also I met Jimmy Hammerstein who was the stage manager. He said, "Come to New York if you want to watch the show from backstage." That's how I got to watch *Damn Yankees* from backstage at the 46th Street Theatre. That was kind of wonderful.

There's not very much room back there! There was one slot that was big enough for the bleachers, and everything else flew. There was not very much on the floor. I remember that was in the days when you ran light cues by grouping the dimmers together. The stagehands would pull a bunch of dimmers at once and then they'd sit there and read a book or read a magazine—then, the next cue would come and they would get up for that one.

I was standing in the wings and actor Ray Walston came by. That was exciting. The other thing I remember is that the set was just a house with wallpaper, but in order to make the flat walls appear alive, there was a layer of screening in front of them. The wallpaper design was on the screening, so that the wall wasn't flat. The wall had life to it. Who would know?

1955: My Parents Invested

Jamie DeRoy, Producer

My parents had a friend in Pittsburgh named Jimmy, and he was a friend of Harold Prince. I asked my dad once, "How did you become producers? Did you go to backer's auditions?" And he said that they didn't. Jimmy just asked his friends to invest and they did it.

Because of that, I got to see the original productions of *The Pajama Game* and *Damn Yankees* when I was a little kid. I remember getting to go backstage and meet everybody, and getting to stand on the stage and look out at the house, and getting to just be there, seeing the show. I met Gwen Verdon! It was an inspiring, awesome experience and it cemented that I wanted to be part of theatre. My parents didn't put a terribly high sum of money in the show, but it got us there. I'm forever grateful that they did it.

1955/1959: Gwen Verdon

Larry Fuller, Choreographer/Actor

The first Broadway show I ever saw was the original *Damn Yankees*. It was in what was then called the 46th Street Theatre. Gwen Verdon was amazing. I was 18 and I'd just come to the city from St. Louis. Being a dancer, I was of course overwhelmed with her and her dancing. It was right at the peak of her career. It was so memorable to me. Luckily, I got to work with her later in the same theater, in *Redhead*.

About three years later, I was a replacement in *Redhead* at the end of the Broadway run, and then we went on a limited 12-week tour. I didn't really get to know Gwen very well. She worked very hard and she stayed to herself. But she was just amazing. She had eyes in the back of her head. When she was on stage dancing, of course she was always down front—but she would give the dance captain notes to give to the dancers. Because she had been a Jack Cole assistant for years, that was part of her psyche.

————————

Gwen Verdon starred in three successive musicals at the 46th Street Theatre in the 1950s—and won Tony Awards for each of them! Her performances in Damn Yankees, New Girl In Town, *and* Redhead *all won her the Tony for Best Actress In A Musical. She would later return to the theater two decades later, for* Chicago.

————————

1957: I Had To Beg The Audience To Stay

Harold Prince, Producer/Director

New Girl In Town! Gwen Verdon and Thelma Ritter were the stars. The show was okay, but it was not a great show by any stretch. But the star power was extraordinary, so that made it a hit.

When Gwen got sick and then Thelma got sick—and then they both got sick on the same night—I had to stand at the base of the stairs of the 46th Street when the announcement was made and *beg* the audience to go back and see the show with the understudies. Of course, most of them just rushed past me and got their money back.

1960: My Broadway Debut At Three Years Old

Mana Allen, Actor

My earliest memory, which my Dad always called my Broadway debut, was in *Tenderloin*. My Dad was the stage manager, and I was about three years old.

Back then, the musical theater was really like a family—like the circus. You know how the circus kids are always around in the tent? How they learn from the gymnasts, and they're in the back learning everything? It was like that on Broadway when I was growing up.

Tenderloin was about the red-light district. My father was stage managing and calling the show from the wings. He would call it from the downstage wing, so he could watch on stage and off. You were on deck with everybody. Now there seems to be a kind of distance when you call it because of all of the technology, but back then, everybody was right there.

I was standing with my father just off-stage during a performance, and Maurice Evans was singing something about being drunk. Maurice winked at me and I walked on the stage! I thought it was an invitation! The audience was watching a show set in the red-light district and a three-year-old walked out!

The audience saw just my father's arm from the wings, a man's big hand grab me and pull me off. That was my Broadway debut at the 46th Street Theatre!

1961: Playing Show Albums Around The House On Sundays

Joanna Gleason, Actor

The first Broadway show my parents took me to was *Bye Bye Birdie*. We were living in New Rochelle, New York. I don't remember what theater it was in because I was quite young at the time. But the next show they took me to was *How to Succeed in Business Without Really Trying*, and that meant a trip into New York and staying overnight in a hotel! That was with Robert Morse and Michele Lee and Rudy Vallee. And the funny thing is, years later, I got to do a revival of it with Robert Morse and Rudy Vallee, understudying the lead. I was maybe ten or 11 at the time that I saw them in the original production.

My folks would play show albums all the time in the house, usually on Sundays. When I was 11, we moved to California, so when I saw shows, I saw them at what was then the Huntington Theatre, or the Music Center, or the Pantages, or at the Orpheum. I didn't get back to Broadway until I moved back to New York City in the 1970s.

But *How to Succeed* was one of the shows that made me want to perform, definitely. I came back to the hotel where we were all staying that night as a part of our New York adventure and I sang pretty much the entire score into the bathroom mirror.

———————

In talking to people about their first memories of loving theatre, "show albums at home on Sundays" was a common recurrence. Of all the now-defunct traditions of years gone by, this is one of the most important ones to reinstate! Families spending time together on Sundays listening to theatre albums instead of watching television in separate rooms? Yes, please.

———————

1965: A Magical, Mystical Miracle

James Dybas, Actor

When I was 19 years old, I made my Broadway debut in *Do I Hear A Waltz?*

I went to the audition and I sang in Italian for Mr. Rodgers. I was on the stage of the 46th Street Theatre, which is now the Richard Rodgers, *singing* for Mr. Rodgers.

I was cast and I got to work at the 46th Street Theatre. I do remember that backstage. When you walk into a theater that's been around for that many decades, it has a certain smell. I remember walking into the stage door at that theater and climbing these tiny stairs that just went up and up and up. They put me on the top floor with the two little kids in the show.

Elizabeth Allen was in the show and she had been the star of the first show I ever did professionally in Kansas City. Madeline Sherwood was in it, who I had seen in the movie *Sweet Bird of Youth*, and Carol Bruce, who was a hoot and a half. There was a wonderful woman named Fleury D'Antonakis, who played the maid in the show, who I would spend time talking to backstage. There's a photograph of the first day of rehearsal, of everybody on a break, standing around talking to each other. All of those people are in the photograph. And me. And Arthur Laurents, Stephen Sondheim, Richard Rodgers and John Dexter. There we were.

I didn't have a song, since I had mostly an acting part, but I stuck around to watch when Richard Rodgers rehearsed with the singers. He was very specific about performers doing the notes exactly as they were written. When the songs came together, I understood why he did that.

Richard and his wife, Dorothy Rodgers, had a party for the principals in the cast at their home in Connecticut. We spent a wonderful Sunday afternoon there, with Mr. Rodgers playing the piano and people singing around it.

As the show went on, there was a lot of friction about how it was shaping up. Tempers flew a bit, especially when we were out of town in Boston. But all in all, we got to hear that music every night! We called it "No

Horns" as a joke, because Mr. Rodgers had also written *No Strings*, and *our* orchestration had no brass! That score was beautiful to listen to every night. I have goosebumps just thinking about it.

Everything about the experience was magical. I remember that I had my photo with my name in the back of the Theatre World annual book. I had a bunch of those, dating back to the 1940s—and then I was in one.

1965: Second-Acting

Marty Bell, Producer

I second-acted[2] a lot when I was younger! I actually learned about that trick early on, by going to a seminar one day at the Shubert. Richard Barr, who produced all of Edward Albee's plays, was a speaker. He talked about second-acting, which I had never thought of before.

That day, I went and second-acted *Pickwick* at the 46th Street Theatre. Right after the seminar, I just walked around the block and tried it. It worked!

1966: Five Flops In A Row

Red Press, Musical Coordinator

I did a show called *Pousse-Café* at the 46th Street Theatre in 1966. Oh boy, did it run quickly! We closed the first week on Broadway.

I remember a review we got in Toronto: "I can't say that this is the worst show ever done, because I haven't seen every show ever done." *Pousse-Café* happened in this period where I had five flops in a row, some of which closed on the road—and my wife was at home with our new baby. I was trying to make a living!

In 1965, I had done *Drat! The Cat!* which ran less than a week, then I subbed on a show in Philadelphia for two weeks, then I came back to New York for a Broadway show called *La Grosse Valise*, which ran two weeks... finally, after *Pousse-Café*, I got *Mame*.

I stayed at *Mame* for a little while, but then our director, Gene Saks, and his wife, Bea Arthur were doing a new show called *A Mother's Kisses*, and I left to do that with them. That was a great mistake. The show turned out to be terrible. The dance arranger tried to commit suicide in New Haven! We closed out of town.

———————

You know *the show's in trouble when the dance arranger tries to commit suicide in New Haven!*

———————

1969: No Advance

Harvey Sabinson, Press Agent

I knew *1776* was going to be a hit. I loved that show.

It opened in New Haven, at the Shubert. I watched a preview of *1776* and thought: *This show has it; it's going to make it.*

———————————————

[2] second-acted: as a verb, this means to sneak into a show during intermission and catch only the second act

18

I had to get back to New York on Monday morning for work, and I was going to come back to New Haven for the actual opening on Monday night.

My wife and I started to head back to New York, but we couldn't get there. The Connecticut Turnpike was closed. The snow was too heavy. We had to stop and get a motel room. Meanwhile, the show sat up there in New Haven, postponing its opening.

I had been smart enough to leave my apprentice up in New Haven with *1776*. By Wednesday, I got to New York. I called her and said, "When are they going to open?" and she said, "They're going to open it at the matinee today." I said, "You're covering it, I cannot get there."

I couldn't get there because that night we were opening a play in New York that David Merrick produced, by Woody Allen. The play was *Play it Again, Sam*. Although I barely made it back to New York on time, I got there! In those days you wore black tie to the openings. I didn't have a tuxedo. I had the same grungy clothes from the previous Saturday. Imagine how grungy I was!

Merrick looked at me and said, "What happened to you?" and I said, "You don't want to know!"

Anyway, *1776* opened on a Wednesday matinee in New Haven before about 120 people in a theatre that sat almost 2,000. It was still a tremendous smash. By the time we got to Washington, it was pretty obvious that we were going to be a success. But before we opened, we could not build up an advance sale because who wants to buy a show about the signing of the Declaration of Independence? Doesn't sound very sexy.

The morning after *1776* opened on Broadway, I came down to the theater to see if there was a line at the box office. Sure enough, there was a line down the block. I'm standing there and my wonderful producer, Stuart Ostrow, comes up behind me and says, "Isn't this great?"

We're hugging each other, and Alex Cohen, another producer comes up. He looks at the line and he says, "That's the kind of line my shows have *before* they open!"

It was a great success; we ran for three years!

———————————

Eight Best Musical Tony Award winners have opened at the Richard Rodgers—that's more than any other Broadway theater.

Guys and Dolls, Damn Yankees, Redhead, How To Succeed In Business Without Really Trying, 1776, Raisin, Nine, *and* In the Heights *all opened there, and went on to win the big prize.*

The Shubert and St. James have a tie for the next highest number of Best Musical winners: five each.

Then again, the Shubert was home to A Chorus Line *for 25 years, so it was out of the running for quite a while! The longest time any of the Best Musical winners spent at the Rodgers was three and a half years (*How To Succeed*).*

———————————

1971: New Kids In An Old-Fashioned Show

Ed Dixon, Actor

No, No, Nanette at the 46th Street Theatre was amazing. It was such an extraordinary way to make a debut.

I had seen Mary Martin and Robert Preston in *I Do! I Do!* at the 46th Street Theatre the week I ran away to New York when I was just out of high school. I saw an empty seat down front and moved to the very front row! When Mary Martin sang "What Is a Woman", she was literally three feet in front of me, on the lip of the stage. I was 18. Of course, that's the house in which I made my Broadway debut.

No, No, Nanette had Busby Berkeley, Ruby Keeler, Patsy Kelly, Bobby Van, Helen Gallagher... it was a mindboggling event to be connected with historic people like that. And to have Burt Shevelove, who had written with Stephen Sondheim, was an added bonus.

We had been a huge success in Boston and Toronto and Baltimore and Philadelphia. It seemed like a premade hit. No one had done a revival of this magnitude before. It was not commonplace to do revivals in those days and certainly not shows from the 1920s, so everything about it was unusual.

Back in those days, all of the critics came on opening night. It was not spread out over two or three weeks like it is today, so everything depended on one night and the audience was made up almost entirely of critics.

Something devastating happened on opening night: one of our principals came on stage drunk. When she stumbled onto the stage, it became instantly clear that she was very drunk indeed. We knew that we were in this premade gigantic hit, and we thought that it was all going to go down the drain right in front of us. Luckily, it didn't!

I wanted two things when I came to New York: I wanted to be in a Leonard Bernstein show and I wanted to be in a Richard Rodgers show. During the run of *No, No, Nanette*, I got hired by Leonard Bernstein to be a soloist in his *Mass,* which was to open the Kennedy Center. It was an enormous thing.

We had this unbelievably mean-spirited stage manager and she tried to hold me to my contract and not let me go. The union stood up for me and let me out. All of this happened during the course of one performance! I turned in my notice, and I was about to walk on stage and do the "Where-Has-My-Hubby-Gone Blues" with Helen Gallagher. The stage manager walked up to me, shoved my notice back in my hands and said, "I'm not accepting your notice." I walked out on stage and stood behind Helen Gallagher and started crying. I cried through the whole number. Then, after the show, the union stood up for me and got me out of it. I got to open the Kennedy Center with Leonard Bernstein! That was a pretty good day.

There were so many actors in *No, No, Nanette*, more than was normal for a show at that time. There was a very large male chorus and there was a large female chorus. There was a singing chorus and a dancing chorus, which was really old fashioned.

They had to open another dressing room on the seventh floor that hadn't been open since the 1920s! It was just being used as a storeroom. There was no elevator in that theater, and we used to do all of our changes on the seventh floor. We would take the stairs three or four at a time, because we were all in our early 20s and it just seemed normal. We all had fantastic legs.

I'm still friends with numerous people from *No, No, Nanette,* because that was such a life changing experience for all of us. We were all so young. It was a turning point, and it was our first Broadway show.

––––––––––––

Ed Dixon's book, Secrets of a Life On Stage... and Off, *is a terrific tome that tells many more stories of his life in showbiz, from playing Thernadier in* Les Mis *on Broadway while secretly living in his dressing room and in Central Park, to working with legends in his extensive career, which includes 15 Broadway shows.*

––––––––––––

1972: Tap Dancing On The Sidewalk

Eddie Korbich, Actor

The first Broadway show I ever saw was *No, No Nanette*, with the replacement cast. What I remember is first walking up to the box office with my family, and our tickets not being there! We were from Pennsylvania and my mom and dad didn't know what to do, so we went back to the hotel. My mom was sad, but I didn't care; I was eleven, and I just wanted to see the Statue of Liberty!

It ended up that our tickets were actually for the next night, so we went back. I remember Helen Gallagher, and the mass of tap dancers, and all these beach balls. When we walked out of the theater, I remember that I was tap dancing on the sidewalk, holding my dad's hand, and laughing. We were so happy. I didn't know how to tap dance yet, but I acted like I did, and I sang "I Want To Be Happy" from the show in the street.

We were walking, and that's when we saw Richard Nixon coming out of the Winter Garden! He had been seeing *Much Ado About Nothing*. There were all these barricades, and my dad said, "Let's get out of here," because he thought it was a drug takedown at first. But it was Richard Nixon, the president, with his family.

1975: Understudying And All That Jazz

Michon Peacock, Actor

Some of us "Cell Block" girls have been able to stay in touch.

Chita Rivera was kind enough to let me know way in advance—maybe six weeks—that she would be out of *Chicago* for a week. So, I had plenty of time to prepare to go on as Velma—but also plenty of time to stress out about it!!

I owe a great debt of gratitude to Graciela Daniele, who was our dance captain. She was amazing and the other understudies were really great, so our understudy rehearsals were extremely productive. The only thing that was odd was that this was a first-class Broadway show, but I had to go get my own costumes, etc., for when I went on as Velma. I had to make all the arrangements for wig and costume fittings —maybe because the designers were no longer around?

I think that was the reality as an understudy then. Maybe it's better now. Once in performance though, the wonderful wardrobe crew and hair stylists were so helpful, so supportive!

As the Velma understudy, the one thing we could never rehearse ahead of time was the opening of the show. The stage was an ungodly rake[3], and the center had what we called the drum. It was in the basement and could be lifted up to stage level or even higher. The base of the drum had doors that would slide open for a reveal or a scene.

In the opening of the show, Chita started in the basement inside the base of the drum. During the intro, before she started "All That Jazz", the thing moved up in total blackness. No lights on the stage. Just a spotlight. The musicians were on top of the drum and were therefore elevated when the drum hit stage level.

Then, right on "Come on, babe," you had to step out and start walking forward to the edge of the stage. But where was it? You couldn't see a damn thing! Everything's black, and there's just a spotlight!

---

[3] rake: a stage sloped upward, away from the audience

Fortunately for me, the first night I went on, I had a lot of friends in the audience. A friend of mine had sent notes to our friends: "Come see Michon!" So instead of being total silence or a big ol' "Boo!" because Chita's understudy was on— always, she would get raging applause as it would come up—my friends applauded like crazy. That was so great, except I didn't know how to do the first thing! It was like: *Oh God! This is so scary! This was never rehearsed!*

Working with Bob Fosse was a tremendous learning experience for me. I really didn't know how to execute his style. Everybody else did. I didn't know those fine things like how to hold the hat, the spread fingers, the pelvis work. And he'd say, "Let me show you and work with you on that." It was great to work directly with him.

Bob asked me to use a cigarette in the opening number, because he knew that I smoked and he wanted someone to have a cigarette. It was a weird bond. He taught me how to hold it, when to transfer it hand to hand, when it had to be in my mouth because I had to dance. That was amazing. That was all in the first week.

After the first week, he had his heart attack. We had done "All That Jazz" and a lot of "Cell Block Tango" in the first week, and they did "Funny Honey", which I thought was brilliant.

During performances I would always watch Chita do "My Sister and I" from the wings because that was the hardest thing for me to do! She was so good in it—how she worked with Gwen and her incredible energy—it was just amazing.

I did much better with "When Velma Takes the Stand" than I did with "My Sister & I". Chita was a little afraid of "When Velma Takes the Stand". The chair unnerved her a bit. I didn't have any fear with that. I just made a relationship with it, so that piece was easier for me to do.

In 1975 when *A Chorus Line* took everything during the Tony Awards, that was hard.

Of course, *A Chorus Line* was all hopeful and bright and future and accessible and *Chicago* was all death and darkness and depression and criminals. It was like night and day.

It was total craziness being a part of both shows. When we were in Philadelphia, I was calling Nick Dante every night. The hardest thing was that they couldn't figure out who should get the show within *A Chorus Line*. They kept trying different things. Whenever Donna didn't get it, the audiences fell apart. They couldn't handle it. Cassie had to be cast. That was really interesting to me. The audience dictated how the show ended.

Also, the reaction to *Chicago* was pretty tepid. It was way ahead of its time. O.J. Simpson hadn't happened yet. Criminals weren't glorified yet. That was not a frame of mind people were willing to put themselves in. They did, however, relate to "Cell Block", but it was a different reaction every night. You just never knew what to expect.

Sometimes the reaction would be nothing. Like: *I don't know what that meant.* Sometimes it was like: *Yeah, I think about doing that to my husband, too!* Candy would say, "He ran into my knife ten times," and sometimes there'd be a gasp and sometimes there'd be hysterical laughter. Same with my Mormon line. Sometimes there would be hysterics and sometimes it would be: *What? Are you kidding?* It was odd – but it always kept us on our toes. However, the audience always connected with Graciela as Hunyak. She was so marvelous and sympathetic.

––––––––––––––––––

For nearly two years, Chicago *was at the 46th Street Theatre while Fosse's* Pippin *was playing the Imperial next door. A small alleyway connecting the two theaters allowed the dancers to run back and forth and watch each other's shows.*

So many of the theaters on Broadway are connected by hidden tunnels or backstage passageways or secret alleys. The Broadhurst on 44th Street and Schoenfeld on 45th Street have an underground tunnel connecting them, and people at either theater will sneak back and forth to catch glimpses of the other show. The Majestic, Golden and Jacobs share a large stage door alleyway—and the Milford Plaza Hotel shares it too! The catacombs in between the Shubert, Booth, Broadhurst and Schoenfeld are like a secret lair in the middle of bustling Times Square.

Farther uptown, the Barrymore and Longacre Theatres are back to back, as are the Walter Kerr and Eugene O'Neill. With some creative fire-escape-climbing, you get into a friend's window, and surprise them when they get back to their dressing room. With every interview I did, Broadway, with all its secret passageways, seemed more and more like the board game Clue.

1975: I Want You To See It

Fred Ricci, Stagehand

The first show I ever saw was *Chicago*, in what they called the 46th Street Theatre, which is now the Richard Rodgers. I'd just started working for a guy named Freddie Feller, building *Chicago* for the road. He asked me if I had ever seen a Broadway show before. I said no. And so he sent me to the theater. He said "I want you to see it."

A bunch of us who work on Broadway now came up together at the Feller's shop. Gene O'Donovan was the foreman when I was there, and he drove an old, rusted out, Toyota pickup truck. None of us had two nickels to rub together; we were all just struggling to make a buck.

1975: Bob Fosse Did Bob Fosse's Advertising!

Nancy Coyne, Advertising and Marketing Executive

The first time around, *Chicago* was eclipsed by *A Chorus Line*, so it's wonderful to see *Chicago* having the life that it has now. That's what the show deserved.

Working on the original... well, I didn't have much to do with the Bob Fosse version. Bob Fosse did Bob Fosse's advertising!

But I loved it. I remember writing radio spots, and it was a real thrill when Fosse said "That's great." There have been so many people—clients and directors and people in my life—who, when they said, "I love that," I'd just walk around with a glow all day.

Edward Albee on *Seascape*, when I was at Blaine Thompson was another. I wrote a radio commercial he didn't like, and he said "I can write it better." I said, "Oh, that would be wonderful!" A week later he came back and said, "I can't write anything in a minute, that's fine," and I said, "Okay, it's not so easy is it?" We laughed. I felt a little glow there.

1975: Partial View

Christopher Durang, Writer

I moved to New York in the summer of 1975. I went to Yale School of Drama, and then stayed an extra year in New Haven because I didn't have enough money to move to New York yet. After a year, I moved to the city.

Sigourney Weaver and Wendy Wasserstein helped me look for apartments, because they were both there already.

I was always really careful about my money, but the best thing that I would do was wait until 7:15pm to decide if I was going to see a Broadway show that night, and call and ask if there was standing room or partial view. The first time I discovered you could buy something called "partial view" I thought: *This is going to be awful.* It wasn't! I decided to see *Chicago*, starring Gwen Verdon and Chita Rivera and Jerry Orbach, who I had loved since I saw him as a child in *Carnival*.

I sat all the way on house right in a box and yes, if an actor was all the way stage left, I couldn't see them. On the other hand, you could see three quarters of the stage, and you were wonderfully close! It cost me $10 to see *Chicago*, a great Kander and Ebb show. I was really close and could see the faces of that fabulous trio of Verdon-Rivera-Orbach.

1977: Glamorous And Tiny

Kathleen Marshall, Director/Choreographer

When we were growing up in Pittsburgh there was a gal named Lenora Nemetz. She was a Pittsburger and a bit of a star in Pittsburgh. My brother, director/choreographer Rob Marshall and sister, Maura, and I were her fan club.

Lenora was in the original production of *Chicago*. She was the standby[4] for Gwen Verdon and Chita Rivera, and when Chita left the show, she actually replaced her. We saw the show the night that she took over for Chita Rivera. We were there. My parents brought us to see it and she took us backstage.

I remember that was at the Richard Rodgers Theatre which was then, of course, the 46th Street Theatre. That was the first time I ever went backstage at a Broadway theater and I couldn't believe how small the stage was. Of course, in the original *Chicago* the band was on stage and the stage was raked. Remember that?

Lenora took us to her dressing room, which was completely glamorous but also tiny. I remember there was a shelf above her dressing room mirror that had all of her shoes lined up. There were silver shoes and red shoes and black shoes and white shoes—all lined up!

It was just amazing to me how small it was. You know, I'd been on stage and backstage at Pittsburgh Civic Light Opera and the dressing rooms were huge. This was actually very small. I think it's always surprising to everybody because they think that Broadway is going to be the biggest but it's actually smaller than most theaters around the country in terms of road houses and performing arts centers.

———————————

Lenora Nemetz stood by for both Gwen Verdon and Chita Rivera in the original company of Chicago. *Once, she went on for Velma Kelly at the matinee and Roxie Hart in the evening! She later replaced Chita as Velma, and played opposite Ann Reinking as Roxie.*

———————————

———————————

[4] standby: an off stage understudy who covers a small number of lead roles

1968/1978: Working on *Working*

Craig Carnelia, Writer

The first Broadway stage I ever stood on was the 46th Street Theatre, which is now the Rodgers. It was an audition for a show called *A Mother's Kisses*, written by Richard Adler that closed out of town. The audition was on the stage of the 46th Street. *I Do! I Do!* was playing there at the time, so the stage was black marble, and it was *very* exciting to audition there. It was 1968, and I was in college, shortly before I got cast off-Broadway in *The Fantasticks.*

Exactly ten years later, in 1978, I made my Broadway debut as a writer in that theater. I hadn't made that connection until just now, that that was the first Broadway stage I ever actually stood on, but it was.

Back in those days, the 1970s, and even trailing on into the 1980s, some rehearsals took place on stage, and not just after tech began. We actually rehearsed the show *Working* on stage. Part of that was because two of our producers, Steve Friedman and Irwin Meyer then owned the 46th Street Theatre. We used it as rehearsal space. It was also the last show I did where there were auditions on stage in a Broadway theater.

Working was a great experience. Stephen Schwartz and I became good friends, and have remained so ever since. I just finished the first draft of a new show, and Stephen is the only person not connected with the project, other than my wife and daughter, who I've played it for.

Our first read-through of *Working* was in a circle of chairs on the stage, which was beautiful, and such a great way to do it. Stephen did a lot of talking those first couple of days, asking people about work they had done in their non-theater lives and what that was like.

We were in rehearsal, and then in previews, and my song "Just a Housewife" was not going well. We realized that we had miscast it. We had a wonderful performer, who had been great in other things, but she wasn't a good match for the song.

In any case, it was not working the way that Stephen and I imagined it could, and I asked him if I could work with the casting director to try to find someone else, and then to have her audition for Stephen. I found Susan Bigelow through the casting director, Scott Rudin. *Working* was his first solo casting job. He was a great casting director and a good friend at the time.

Susan and I worked on "Just a Housewife" and after a performance one night, when everyone else had left the theater, Susan sang on the bare stage as I played piano in the pit, and Stephen sat in the house. He said "yes" and the producers agreed to bear the cost of replacing a cast member. It was then my job to put Susan into the show, because part of the deal I had made with Stephen was that it wouldn't cost him any time as director.

The first night Susan did the song, it stopped the show. Stephen and I were standing in the back of the theater. I actually laid down on my back, in the standing room area, and screamed silently with the pleasure of having seen a song of mine work so well in a Broadway theater for the first time.

When you write something you think has a potential to be something special, and it's not coming to life the way you expected, something's wrong. Very often it's the writing. Very often the thing you felt for the song as a writer didn't make it into the writing. Sometimes though, it's another factor. Sometimes it's a bizarre factor like what happened three scenes earlier.

In this case, it simply was that the song had positives and negatives in it, and the actress needed to play the action of the song, and not the tone of the music. There's something in the music of "Just a Housewife" that causes people to think, "Oh, this is a sad song." It isn't. It's just a story and the person feels all sorts of things during it. I was right. There have been other times where I've thought I've known what was wrong with a piece of material, and I've ended up being wrong. In that case, I was right, and I just remember that crazy little celebration I had. *Working* was a great experience.

1982: As Simple As The Simplest Things Have Always Been

Maury Yeston, Writer

When we went into the 46th Street Theatre with *Nine*, I was a complete novice, but Tommy Tune, of course, was not. Tune said to me, "It's the 46th Street. It's the only one. It's the best one. It's the perfect theater for this show." In fact, he said, "It's the perfect theater for a musical," and he cited that *Guys and Dolls* had played there.

The reason is that the theater has this perfect sweep up. It's this perfect raked audience, and it allows the music to just blow off the stage and knock the audience through the back wall. It is *that* exciting. Before I even walked through the door, I knew it as a legendary theater.

I still get a wonderful feeling every time I walk into it. I'm the kind of author who gets to know everybody. By the time we were done with *Nine*, I knew not only all of the stagehands, but every single usher. Because we never got to go out of town, we had a fraught preview period. I remember hearing one of the usherettes saying, "I'm afraid for the little composer. I'm afraid he's going to have a nervous breakdown and starve to death." I got very thin. She was adorable; she was so kind.

When we were first starting on *Nine*, Tune said to me, "Look, I have an idea about the show. I want to do a workshop of it just to make sure that it can work. Yeston, I think all of the scenery is in the music and in the lyrics, so we don't need any scenery. It's all there. All of Europe is there. Italy is there." He was quite right. For the first line in the second act, Claudia says to Guido, "Guido, why did you bring me to this beach?" And you've now just saved $250,000 in sand. In any case, Tune said, "Because it's all in the music, I want to do our show on a white set, a white canvas. I think it should be a spa."

He unrolled a paper and he drew these 24 boxes, and a box in the front. I said, "Wow. If the women are all sitting there, they'll look like an orchestra, so I'll just make Guido the conductor. If he's the conductor of a 24 woman orchestra, why would we have the band play the overture? Why don't I write a vocal overture for the women?" That's how that happened.

When I walked into the 46th Street, the set was exactly what it was supposed to be, which was almost nothing. That's the kind of theatre that I've lived with ever since. I love nonliteral theatre where the score functions as if it's a radio play, as if you're listening to it and have to partially use your imagination to see what's happening. There's no need for the set to duplicate what you're hearing. That's what was so exciting about that particular set, that discovery.

Merrily was down the block from *Nine* and of course we kept hearing the stories of what they were going through. Their audiences weren't able to identify who was what, and Hal Prince had t-shirts made temporarily that had the names and functions of the characters. I remember being by our *Nine* stage door one day, and Sondheim came walking down the street. We said hello. Obviously, I'm a huge fan of his. I was a huge fan of that score. In fact, I was an assistant professor at Yale at that time and that particular year I had been teaching Music Theory to the freshmen. David Loud was one of the freshmen, and he actually left Yale that semester for a role in *Merrily We Roll Along*! I was very much connected to that show and a big fan of it.

That season, I was also a huge fan of *Dreamgirls*, so much so that I actually went to Boston to see it before it came to New York. That's how interested I was. When I came home I told everyone, "I just love that show!" I still do. I was a teacher *and* a writer *and* a fan that season. It's all part of it.

26

The 46th Street was a great theater to work in and I do have my one favorite story. One night, during a performance, I saw something that I had never seen before and that I have never seen again. The great Anita Morris sang "A Call From the Vatican". The choreography, by Thommie Walsh, was incredible. William Ivey Long's costume for her became legendary. She looked like a walking whorehouse, except innocent at the same time. Anita mixed sexuality and sensuality with innocence in a way that nobody had before or has since.

Every night, Anita would do "A Call From the Vatican" and stop the show. Then Liliane would come out and do "Folies Bergeres" and stop the show. Liliane always wanted to know how Anita did because if Anita did better, then Liliane would know that she would get a better reception, too.

One extraordinary night, Anita did "A Call From the Vatican" and the audience just went crazy. They screamed and screamed and they would not stop applauding. A man called from the back of the house, "Do it again!" Anita turned and looked over at her shoulder at Raul, who was playing Guido, and Raul looked at her and simply nodded his head yes. He gave the signal to Wally Harper, who was conducting, and Anita repeated the entire number. I've *never* seen that happen. That's what I always remember when I visit the 46th Street.

———————————

A simplistic portrayal of the beach scene during Nine *meant that the 46th Street Theatre was spared from sand blowing everywhere. They weren't as lucky during* Steel Pier (1997). Steel Pier *opened with the poetic image of cast members coming forward and letting sand slip through their fingers onto the stage. According to conductor David Loud, 16 years later, when he opens his* Steel Pier *score, sand still comes pouring out! The show even had special covers made for several instruments.*

The most infamous use of dirt on stage, however, was in 1972 during the musical Dude *at the Broadway Theatre. That stage was covered in dirt to simulate an earthy environment. It was quickly discovered that during that show, dirt was getting blown into the faces of audience members. So, water was added in order to turn the dirt into mud! That didn't work much better and the show closed after 16 performances.*

———————————

1982: The *Nine* Dress Parade

William Ivey Long, Costume Designer/Chair of the American Theatre Wing

In the Richard Rodgers Theatre, which was called the 46th Street Theatre during *Nine*, we had a dress parade[5].

The dress parade was traumatic for me. We did the show very quickly. We were rushing to get it up, because we only got our funding at the last second.

We'd done it so quickly that our director Tommy Tune hadn't seen a lot of the costumes yet. He had just seen the photo shoot. We covered the outside of the theater with photos of all the beautiful black costumes on the white background. It was stunning as you walked down the street. Stopped you in your tracks.

But I'd re-designed some of the costumes since then, because they weren't finished for the photo shoot. I made all of those black costumes basically in two weeks. Some of them, like the Anita Morris costume and Liliane Montevecchi's costume... they didn't work the first time. So we just showed headshots at first for them. When I finally finished them, it was done so quickly that there were sketches, but no one had seen the real costumes. It was all the women in all the black costumes on the white set.

———————————

[5] dress parade: when the costume designer presents the actors in their show apparel

And that dress parade... the women came out on stage, as they did in the real show, when they came out one by one, in order, and sat on their perch. I took off my glasses for all of them coming out. I thought: *I can't see this.* I took off my glasses. My assistant was with me. Everyone was oohing and aahing as the ladies came out.

Finally, Anita came out with her flame-red hair. No one else had red hair. There was no other color on stage, except for lipstick. And then here comes this flame-red hair and her black lace see-through costume. I'll never forget that moment when she came out.

There was dead silence. I said, "Oh my God, what happened?" And my assistant said, "Anita's come out." Silence. Not a word! Several beats. Pinter pauses[6]. And then, clapping. And then, the whole place broke into clapping. And then, they were clapping... and I started crying. I will never forget that.

Glasses off, eyes shut, mild happiness as they were all coming out, dead silence, and then applause. Clapping. Very theatrical clapping. And then I just burst into tears. Can't forget that!

––––––––––––

The first songs from the hit musical Nine *were actually heard in a different Broadway theater, years earlier, when Maury Yeston had been part of The BMI Lehman Engel Musical Theatre Workshop. Founded in 1961, this learning experience for musical theatre writers was a revolutionary class, the only one of its kind when it began. In its early years, writers including Alan Menken, Ed Kleban, Maury Yeston, Doug Katsaros, and many others, got to play songs from their musicals in early stages of development in a twice yearly showcase held at the Edison Theatre.*

The Edison Theatre on 47th Street is now an event space, but in the early 1950s, and from 1970-1990, it was a Broadway theater. The Edison housed the long-running naughty show, Oh! Calcutta! *for 13 years, and it's also the first Broadway theater where the BMI writers ever heard their songs played.*

Yeston remembers presenting "Guido's Song", "Unusual Way" and "The Germans at the Spa" on the stage of the Edison, years before Nine *came to fruition. "In fact," he says, "*Nine *literally was launched from that showcase."*

––––––––––––

1982: I Thought Each Theater Would Be Like Valhalla

Michael Berresse, Director/Choreographer/Actor

The first Broadway show I ever saw was *Nine* at what is now the Richard Rodgers, which I eventually played. That was my first show, and the next night I saw *Sunday in the Park with George*. It was the same weekend.

I didn't see my first Broadway show until I was 19. I was an accidental Broadway guy. I was never one of those kids who, at age five, said "I can't wait to see X." I didn't really know what was happening in the world of Broadway. I had this distorted illusion that everything was going to be glamorous and perfect and shiny.

I remember walking in the door. I got there and I thought: *Whoa. It's a big theater but I've actually already played bigger theaters in theme parks. It's a small world.*

The fact that all the theaters were so close together really surprised me. It never occurred to me! I thought each one would be like Valhalla. I thought they'd each have their own world, and I thought: *They're all smashed up against each other!* The marquees weren't particularly impressive, and the facades were all sort of sandwiched in between a pizza joint and...It was so strange. Until I walked in the door. And as soon as I walked in the door and sat down in the auditorium, the show started and everything changed.

––––––––––––

[6] Pinter pauses: a reference to the trademark moments of silence found within the work of Harold Pinter

Those were my first shows, and that weekend literally changed my life. I didn't really understand what Broadway was. I was kind of just floating along doing my thing, and then all of the sudden I saw community. I saw a realness and integrity which totally surprised me.

I thought Broadway was going to feel the most artificial of anything I had ever experienced as far as theatre went—and, in fact, it was the most real. The most intimate. There was just something about it. Partly because the technical components and the design had such integrity. Those were two pretty great shows to see in the same weekend, my first weekend.

I remember being really struck with the starkness of that physical production of *Nine*. How the silhouette of each of the ladies was so specific and so absorbing. I remember, suddenly seeing design for the first time, and thinking: *Wow, that boa, that collar, those shoes, those silhouettes of those ladies*.

And Anita Morris! Actually, I'm going to negate that, because I didn't see Anita Morris when I saw it live. By the time I saw it, it was Wanda Richert, but I've seen Anita do that number on tape.

That world was so stark. The silhouettes were powerful. I thought: *Oh. That's what storytelling is like, that's how design compliments character*. I thought Raul was fantastic, but it was mostly that I was completely infatuated with those women. The black and white of it, I remember. I remember the cubes. I remember the suggestion of a lot of things.

And I don't know if it's because it was my first show, but when I saw the revival, I felt like something had changed. I felt like something had shifted. Partly because I was inside the world then and not on the outside looking in, but also because I felt like it didn't trust itself the way the first production did. I'd never seen anything like that.

1982: I Wrote Away For My Tickets And Lied

Frank Vlastnik, Actor

The first Broadway show I ever saw was *Nine*. I came to New York for my high school graduation present and I got to see eight shows in five days. The first one was a Saturday matinee of *Nine*, where Sergio Franchi was playing Guido and Maureen McGovern was on for Liliane Montevecchi. They were great, but all I cared about was Anita Morris.

I was in seats F 5, 7, and 9 with my aunt and my sister. Back then, you wrote away for your tickets and I had done something terrible. I wrote a note that said, "I'm coming with my aunt, who's very hard of hearing and partially blind. Can we please have seats as close to the stage as possible?" It worked. And I had lied. My aunt is 87 now and she's in perfect health!

After Maureen McGovern sang "Be On Your Own", she came up the house right aisle and stomped off through the audience. I remember turning around and seeing her go up all of the steps of the raked theater. I thought: *Good grief! She's got to do that twice today and the steps are steep and it's dark!*

Anita Morris was just incredible. I loved her. Before that, I never understood the lure of getting autographs but my sister asked, "Are you going to get Anita Morris's autograph?" and I said, "Yeah. I should." So I waited by the stage door. At the 46th Street, it opened right up into the street. Anita came out and she said, "Oh, hi! How are you?" I said, "Ms. Morris, could I have an autograph?" She was flipping her hair like she always did and she said, "I don't have a pen." I found one, and she scribbled her name down. Then I looked over and I saw Grover Dale, her husband, standing there sort of rolling his eyes, and I thought to myself, *Oh. She wants to have dinner. She wants to leave.*

I was the only one waiting for her. That was 30 years ago and I've never asked for an autograph since then. Maybe it's because I'm an actor now too.

1988: Endgame

Chris Boneau, Press Agent

When I started as a press agent, I was answering the phones at the same time. It was incredibly glamorous and also not. Many meltdowns.

Checkmates was my first show. I was trying to learn it all as I went.

Denzel Washington and I have this pact that we always do Broadway shows together. He's done three Broadway shows to date and I've done all three with him. *Checkmates* was his Broadway debut.

It was wild because the producer was in jail. We found out later that he was a drug dealer.

Checkmates starred Ruby Dee, Paul Winfield, Denzel Washington, and Marsha Jackson. Denzel was coming off of the whole *St. Elsewhere* experience and had filmed *Glory*. He was about to become a huge star. Ruby Dee was one of the kindest people I've ever met. It was difficult because it was a show that just wasn't very good, but Denzel was becoming Denzel.

Checkmates taught me a couple of valuable lessons. It was at the Richard Rodgers but it wasn't called that.

———————

A couple weeks after Checkmates *opened, it was revealed that the 27-year-old co-producer was in prison, serving a sentence for attempted murder. He was indicted as part of an international cocaine ring. His company had financed half of* Checkmates.

All others working on the production were shocked, and claimed to have no knowledge of this criminal connection.

Many stories of productions financed in part by crime have cropped up on Broadway over the years.

One of the most famous is Adela Holzer, a strong-willed producer of revolutionary work like Hair, Lenny, *and* Dude. *She scammed several investors out of millions, masqueraded as a member of the Rockefeller family, and ran a business that created false residency papers for hundreds of immigrants. Adela was known for paying her actors in cash, and her last show,* Senator Joe, *closed during previews in 1989 after running out of funding.*

Of course, many thought it a crime when My Lady Friends *(the play on which* No, No Nanette *is based) was financed by the sale of Babe Ruth by Red Sox owner and Broadway producer Harry Frazee! Legend has it that* My Lady Friends *was responsible for The Curse of the Bambino, where the Red Sox didn't win a World Series for the next 86 years.*

More recently, the legendary entrepreneur and producer Garth Drabinsky was sent to prison for fraud and forgery. This happened shortly after his unprecedentedly expensive, extravagant, dazzling Broadway production of Ragtime.

———————

1988: I Was Just A Baby Back Then

Tim Pettolina, House Manager

I was working for the Nederlanders as a high school intern when they produced a play called *Checkmates* at the Rodgers. Denzel Washington was in it, and when he came to see *In the Heights,* 20 years later, I was the manager.

I brought him backstage and said, "You know, I saw *Checkmates* a couple times when I was in high school." He said, "I was just a baby back then!" And I said, "So was I."

1990: Renaming The 46th Street Theatre

Ted Chapin, President of The Rodgers & Hammerstein Organization/Past Chairman of the American Theatre Wing

The name change of the 46th Street Theatre to the Richard Rodgers started with a conversation between Alexander Cohen and Dorothy Rodgers, and, I assume, Jimmy Nederlander. Alex Cohen became determined, and Dorothy was very supportive. Alex went to the Nederlanders and said, "We've GOT to do this."

Dorothy Rodgers agreed to pay for the cost of changing all the signage. Therefore, it meant that changing the name of the theater was a cash-neutral transaction to the theater owners. In my files at the Rodgers & Hammerstein Organization, I have the drawings of the word "Rodgers" to go on the marquee on both ends and on the sign up on the roof of the building.

Once it was decided to make the change, the conversation got around to: how are we going to celebrate this?

We did it with lunch on stage. Who doesn't like the idea of having lunch on stage at a Broadway theater? It hardly ever happens, and it was just great. The Nederlanders were incredibly cooperative, and a Rupert Holmes show called *Accomplice* was about to go into the theater.

We pulled together an exhibit on Richard Rodgers' long career. We took over all the walls that were available—and there are a lot of corridors in that theater! Both ASCAP and the Lincoln Center Library helped enormously. When Disney came into the theater with *Tarzan,* they wanted to focus the exhibit and make it less sprawling, so they created some beautiful panels. Unfortunately, they all were hung in a gallery off the main lobby that people rarely go into. Someday, I'd love to rethink that a little bit, and now that the theater has been gorgeously renovated, we've started conversations with the Nederlanders.

How to Succeed was the first show I saw at that theater as a kid, and I loved it. It's a very interesting theater because of the strange way that the orchestra level slopes up. Standing room was tricky there because you cut off a lot of the top. But I didn't care!

Anyway, naming the theater was a great experience and the Nederlanders have been wonderful partners. I love the idea that whenever anyone sees a show at the Richard Rodgers Theatre, they get a little bit of branding. You can't help but think of who that man was and what he has left for us—what a legacy.

My goal is to get a Broadway theater named after Oscar Hammerstein II. He is arguably the single most important figure in the history of the musical, so I think he is more than deserving.

Before the Mark Hellinger Theatre was leased to the Times Square Church, there were plans to rename that theater the Richard Rodgers, and celebrate both Rodgers and the theater itself in an Alexander Cohen-helmed television special. These plans to revitalize the Hellinger fell apart, and shortly after, the 46th Street was renamed instead.

1969/1978/1990: Finally, People Will Spell It Right!

Bert Fink, Press Agent/Senior Vice President of the Rodgers & Hammerstein Organization

The first Broadway show I saw was *1776* at the 46th Street Theatre, and I remember it vividly. My parents took my brother, sister, and I to the China Bowl Restaurant, which is now Virgil's Barbecue, and we got to the theater very early. We stood by the stage door and we saw Virginia Vestoff and one or two other actors walking in.

I still remember my dad walking us into the 46th Street lobby, which was this long, shoebox-feeling room, and then going upstairs. We were in the balcony. I remember that the program had this postcard in it, which was very clever. You were invited to write on it about how much you enjoyed the show and then send it to your friends.

William Daniels was out that night, so we saw John Cullum as John Adams. I still remember that moment, watching him on the apron on the stage, in front of the curtain, doing his opening monologue before the music started and curtain flew up and the show began.

During high school, my friends and I were desperate to see *Working* at the 46th Street, but we didn't live in New York. We managed to come to the city from Rhode Island, but we weren't able to see the show. Still, we hung out by the stage door, and we met Rex Everheart, who was in the show, but was also in *1776*!

As a college kid, I went to the final preview of *Nine* there. It was one of those moments in the theatre where your hair stands up on the back of your neck. I was so dazzled by that musical, and I was sitting in the back of the mezzanine, and at one point a very tall figure sat on the aisle, directly next to me. It was Tommy Tune. I felt like I was sitting next to a deer; I didn't want to breathe and startle it! I was so amazed.

In my current job at the Rodgers and Hammerstein Organization, one of my biggest projects was the renaming of the 46th Street Theatre as the Richard Rodgers Theatre. I worked with Ted Chapin, his mother, Betty Steinway Chapin, Dorothy Rodgers, Alexander Cohen, and the Nederlanders to create the event and an exhibition about Richard Rodgers for the theater.

On March 27, 1990, the theater officially became the Richard Rodgers, and we revealed exhibits made up of sheet music covers, window cards, and other memorabilia from every show Rodgers wrote. There was a connection because *Do I Hear A Waltz?* and a revival of *On Your Toes* had both played the theater.

It was a beautiful event, and one of my favorite moments was when Mary Rodgers was interviewed out on 46th Street by Stewart Klein from Channel Five News. He said, "Mary, there's your father's name in lights, 15 feet high! What do you think?" And in typical Mary Rodgers fashion, she quipped, "Finally, people will spell it right!"

We've been through several incarnations of the Richard Rodgers exhibit in the theater. There was the big launch exhibit in 1990. Then we replaced it around the Richard Rodgers centennial in 2002. When Disney brought in *Tarzan*, we did a further revision at their request. We're so grateful to the Nederlanders, not only for naming their theaters after Broadway figures, but for allowing these exhibitions that honor theatrical history. When you're in the Richard Rodgers Theatre, you're learning something about Richard Rodgers.

Although, I was at a performance of *Lost in Yonkers* there once and a woman looking at the display said to her husband, "Honey, I didn't know that Neil Simon wrote *South Pacific*!" We still have to work on that.

The crown jewel of the exhibit is the beautiful portrait of Richard Rodgers that we commissioned for his centennial. It still occupies a private place in the lobby. It was created by the wonderful portrait artist Kim Beaty, who has drawn many distinguished Washington and New York political figures, and who also happens to be the granddaughter of Richard Rodgers. I'm very proud of that painting which occupies a special place at the Richard Rodgers Theatre.

I have a lot of great memories of that theater. I saw the original production of *Chicago* there, of course *In the Heights*, the beautiful production of *Cyrano de Bergerac* with Kevin Kline, that great production of *Merchant of Venice* with Dustin Hoffman, the list goes on. I'm sure I'm forgetting many. The 46th Street Theatre. You never forget your first.

1990: After Four Episodes of *Seinfeld*

Jason Alexander, Actor

Seinfeld had done its first season which was a whopping four episodes. We had shot our second season, which was only thirteen episodes, and they hadn't aired yet.

While I was doing *Accomplice*, I was being courted for another TV show. Both *Accomplice* and the other TV show needed an answer as to whether or not *Seinfeld* was going to be picked up again for a third season. It was certainly not a hit in any way, shape, or form.

Accomplice was different because it was the first show I did after winning a Tony for *Jerome Robbins' Broadway*, so I guess it had that little buzz to it. Other than that, no, there was no stink of celebrity on me yet.

I think the Tony thing was what I brought to it. I kept thinking: *Okay, I got away with it, but they may really find out—they might take my Tony back!* But it ended up that it wasn't there long enough for me to get noticed one way or the other.

1991: *Lost In Yonkers* Would Play Anywhere

James Woolley, Stage Manager/Usher

We opened *Lost In Yonkers* in North Carolina, and then we went to Washington. We knew we had something good from the very beginning. The original cast was spectacular. We came into the Rodgers, but I really think *Lost in Yonkers* would play anywhere. It's such a good show!

One interesting thing about the Rodgers is that in the old days, if you didn't know what theater you were going into yet with a show, you designed it for the 46th Street. It's very shallow, and if you could fit your show in the Rodgers, you could fit in any Broadway house. That's interesting when you think of all the hit musicals that have played there, from *Guys and Dolls* to *Chicago*.

In addition to having been the home of more Tony Award-winning Best Musicals than any other theater, the Richard Rodgers was the home of two Tony Award-winning Best Plays: Lost in Yonkers *and* Fences. Lost in Yonkers *actually received bad reviews out of town. But while The Washington Post panned the show, it went on to win not only the Tony Award but also the Pulitzer Prize.*

———————

1991: A Play About Family

Deborah Abramson, Musical Director/Conductor

The first Broadway show I saw was *Lost in Yonkers*. I was with my family. We went to TKTS, and we got box seats. We thought that was super, super special.

We had just had a crazy, weird fight in the hotel room right before we went. To go to the theater and be enclosed in a box seat situation was uncomfortable at first. But then there was something about the Neil Simon magic of a play about family. I remember sitting there and thinking it was healing.

1991: Trap Doors And The Muppet Room

Penny Davis, Wardrobe Supervisor/Dresser

The wardrobe room in the Richard Rodgers is extremely tiny. And there's a little room within the wardrobe room that we used to use as a closet. With *Lost In Yonkers*, I was always looking for space.

At one point, I was stacking things in there when I noticed that there was a trap door in the ceiling! I thought: *What's that for?* I got Jan Marasek, our prop man. He got a chair, and climbed up, and lifted the lid. And there were all these old liquor bottles! Probably from the 1930s and 1940s. All these old whiskey bottles.

We took them all down. We had no idea who they were from or what that was about! But Jan kept them with his little props. He said, "Well, you found them." I said, "Yeah, but, really, they're props. So you should keep them."

He said it because I was legendary with my stuff, in terms of what I would troupe around with me. I always had something that would do for your costume until the real thing came along. I had enormous amounts of things, because I never threw anything away and I saved everything from shows, rather than see it get dumped. Most Prop Men started cringing whenever they saw me coming! But I let Jan keep those whiskey bottles.

I also found the Muppet room at NBC, and nobody ever gave me credit for that. In 1969, Ann Miller was making an appearance on *The Johnny Carson Show*. The two of us were sitting in the dressing room, waiting. Ann had a toothpick thing from the dentist, a proper, professional one. She was picking her teeth, and I was just sitting there. And in the dressing room, there were about five doors. So, I just started opening them.

Behind one door was a closet, and then one was a bathroom... and then I opened this one door. It had all these pipes in it, plumbing pipes of various widths and heights and curves. Jim Henson and his gang must have been in that dressing room at some point, because they had drawn all these Muppet faces there. When you opened it up, it was like a closet full of Muppets. It was thrilling. I said, "Ann, look at this!" She turned and went, "Oh yeah," and went back to picking her teeth.

I went out into the hallway, because I had to find somebody! And the person that I found in the hallway was Shirley Wood, the talent coordinator for the Carson show at the time. I said, "Shirley, come here. Come look at this!" She was like, "Oh my God." And the next thing I know, everybody was piling into this dressing room to see this Muppet closet. I've heard about it since then. Nobody ever said, "... And it was discovered by Ann Miller's dresser." But to the best of my knowledge, I'm the one who found it. That was very thrilling. It's still there, I think.

———————

In 1978, the 46th Street Theatre garnered special attention when the marquee atop the theater was made to read: "WHOREHOUSE". Indeed, The Best Little Whorehouse In Texas *had moved in, and would stay for 1584 performances. At the time, porn theaters dotted the streets, so the sign was not out of place!*

———————

1993: Everyone Should Have Something To Point To

Joe Traina, House Manager

Every Broadway theater is beautiful in its own way. When I was working for the Nederlander Organization, I had an opportunity to spruce their theaters up and do a little painting. It was smiled upon because I took the initiative to do so. I was highly motivated to improve their cleanliness and décor.

The most conspicuous evidence of what I was able to do was in the Richard Rodgers Theatre. I was there for four years as a house manager and left a discernible difference during my tenure. I was happy to do it. It was essentially a labor of love.

We painted some of the bas relief[7] that had been painted a solid for a show. This project continued until every area except the ceiling was accented in some way. Murals were cleaned in what was then known as the smoking promenade. This area has a terrazzo floor and murals of shows that had played that theater. They were drawn by scenic artists of the day.

The Rodgers & Hammerstein Organization graciously provided slides of backdrops from Richard Rodgers shows. I remember one was the beautiful Lemuel Ayers design from *Oklahoma!* We had them enlarged, laminated and mounted in the lobby. They really added a sense of history and beauty to the theater.

During the 1989 revival of *Born Yesterday*, a man had a seizure in the mezzanine at the Rodgers. They had to stop the show and I ran upstairs. Of course, I twisted my ankle as I ran to the mezzanine. I'm the only one who got hurt! The man had not taken his medication. When I got there, it was kind of a bizarre scene because someone had loosened the belt on his pants, so he was walking around with his pants around his ankles.

The policeman on the beat came and calmed the fellow down. They took him out of the theater and the ambulance driver said, "Oh, this guy again? He had a similar episode in Grand Central the other day, and he wouldn't accept medical attention so he just walked away." I made a curtain speech, which is rare for the house manager, and the show went on.

1993: Laughter On 46th Street

Randy Graff, Actor

Doing a play is a lot easier than doing a musical. You don't have to worry about your voice all the time. When you wake up in the middle of the night to go to the bathroom you're not constantly clearing your throat.

———————

[7] bas relief: wall sculpture

I had a blast doing the play *Laughter on the 23rd Floor*, because I was working with the funniest, sexiest men in New York. I loved every second of it.

When we were out of town at Duke University, one night we were getting notes, and I was sitting between Jerry Zaks and Neil Simon. I just couldn't believe where I was.

We laughed a lot during that show. We laughed so much. Talk about audience reaction! The reaction to that play... Neil Simon said that he'd never heard laughs like that at any of his plays. And that's saying a lot! People were laughing hysterically all through the preview period—and then when the *Times* said that it wasn't funny, they stopped laughing. It took us about a month to get them back. That's the power of the printed word.

Some of the other reviews were good. And no one said anything about closing because of the *Times* review. We did get our audiences back. And we ran for ten months—which is pretty good for a straight play without any big names at that time. I mean, now, look at Nathan Lane and John Slattery and J.K. Simmons! We were all in that show.

1996: He's Looking At Us And I'm A Part Of This!

Eric William Morris, Actor

The first Broadway show I ever saw was *How to Succeed in Business Without Really Trying*. It was the Matthew Broderick revival, but by the time I got to it, it starred John Stamos. I was in seventh grade and my school went to see *How To Succeed* on a field trip. I wanted to go because I'd started to get interested in music, but I couldn't make it that day. Then my mom took me two days later anyway! She thought I should see Broadway, because she grew up listening to cast albums and going to shows. She grew up in New Jersey, like I did.

I remember in that production of *How To Succeed*, when opportunities would come up for the character of Finch, they did a little "Ding!" I know it's in the score, but I loved the way they let John Stamos have whatever time he wanted to look at the audience and clue them in. Every time there was a "Ding!" I knew: *Ooh, something's about to happen here.*

I remember feeling like such an adult, because I understood what was happening. I thought: *Oh my God, all the people in this theater are now along for this guy's ride.* It felt exciting to me. Now I know to call it 'breaking down the fourth wall,' but at that time it was just like: *Oh my God, he's looking at us and I'm a part of this!* That's what I remember. I also remember "Brotherhood of Man", and the woman who sang the solo in it. That brought down the house!

1996: Sarah Jessica Parker And The Stage Door

Caissie Levy, Actor

The first Broadway show I ever saw was *How To Succeed* with Sarah Jessica Parker in it. I was 13 and with my parents. We stayed at the Marriott Marquis Hotel and walked next door to see the show. I had seen *Les Mis* and *Cats* in Toronto, where I grew up, but I had never seen a show in New York.

I was in love with *How To Succeed*. We got front row seats at the last minute! I watched the show and was obsessed with Sarah Jessica Parker. I didn't know her from anything else. She was a pretty big star then, but I was only 13 so I had no clue. I kept turning to my mom during the show and saying, "She's looking at me!" I felt like she was doing the whole show for me. At the curtain call, she bowed and winked at me and I felt so special.

When *How To Succeed* ended, it was pouring rain outside. I had never wanted to go to the stage door for any of the shows I'd seen before, but I asked my parents if we could go to the stage door and meet her. We waited and waited and waited in the rain, and finally she came out. She said, "You were that girl in the front row!" And I said, "I just want to do what you do, you're amazing! She gave me a big hug, and was so kind to me, and I never ever forgot it. She inspired me to always, always *do* the stage door as an actor.

Years later, I was playing Elphaba in *Wicked* in L.A. and her brother, Timothy Britten Parker, was playing Dr. Dillamond. I told him that story. I said, "Your sister really impacted my life and how I connect with kids who come to see our show."

I've had so many heartfelt experiences and exchanges at the stage door with people who've come to see shows I've gotten to do. I don't take them for granted. That was me.

—————————

When Sarah Jessica Parker co-starred with Matthew Broderick in How To Succeed, *it was her first role in a Broadway musical since starring in* Annie *as a child. She was 31 and he was 34 and they had been dating for just a couple of years.*

A 1996 New York Times *profile[8] on the couple by Bruce Weber noted how adorably Finch and Rosemary-like they were in real life. To ask Sarah Jessica out on a first date, Matthew had left a nervous message on her machine, starting with "Hi. This is Matthew Broderick." Sitting in her own cluttered apartment, which she reported to only use as an office, Sarah Jessica stated, "I can't imagine fighting with any actor about anything, and certainly not Matthew. I'd rather have him as a boyfriend than fight about whether I upstage him or not. I'll be happy to be upstaged."*

At the time of How To Succeed, *Matthew was best known for films like* Ferris Bueller's Day Off, Glory, *and* Torch Song Trilogy, *as well as stage work in the Neil Simon plays* Brighton Beach Memoirs *and* Biloxi Blues.

While both actors were genuinely enthusiastic about balancing their stage and film careers, Sarah Jessica said, "A woman's movie career is much shorter than a man's, and it's awfully nice to have a career in theatre, where a woman can work longer. So I do this out of love, but not without a certain degree of calculation. I want a career in theater because in a couple of years my opportunities in film will change drastically." They certainly did.

—————————

1961/1996: Fosse and Rodgers and Bobbie

Walter Bobbie, Director/Actor

The first show I ever saw on Broadway was the original production of *How to Succeed in Business Without Really Trying* at the 46th Street Theatre, which is now the Richard Rodgers. It had dances by Bob Fosse and, interestingly, the first Broadway show I opened as a director was *Chicago*—a Fosse show at that same theater.

We opened *Chicago* at the Rodgers, then moved to the Shubert, and now we're at the Ambassador. The show was originally designed for City Center Encores, and no one was expecting it to transfer anywhere. When Barry and Fran Weissler optioned it for Broadway, the only theater we could get was the Richard Rodgers, which was only available for two months. We were opening in November, and *Steel Pier*—another show by Kander and Ebb—was coming in January.

---

[8] Weber, B. (1996, April 25). At Home With: Sarah Jessica Parker and Matthew Broderick; Too Cute for Words? *New York Times*. Retrieved from http://www.nytimes.com

I said to Barry and Fran, "Take it! If the show doesn't work, we'll be closed in two months anyway. Only a real success can make it through the winter season. And if we are a hit, nobody closes a hit. A new theater will emerge."

We got the Rodgers for two months, as an interim booking. We were such a big hit that we were moved to the flagship theater of Broadway, the Shubert.

We were at the Shubert for six years, and then the theater owners wanted the house for Bernadette Peters in *Gypsy*. At the same time, we were ready to downsize. It was smart to reduce expenses and keep running. We moved to the Ambassador, which was not a coveted venue—but it was perfect for us. *Chicago* has been very comfortable there ever since. We sell out without needing to fill a second balcony, as we did at the Shubert. Our *third* move extended the longevity of the show without the overhead of a larger theater like the Shubert. These moves from theater to theater have been fantastic and have protected the show.

As a director, there's no particular Broadway theater I want to work in more than any other. When I have the right show, the right theater shows up and I'm grateful to be there. The Winter Garden is a great theater, but I didn't need the Winter Garden for *Venus in Fur*. I needed the Lyceum. Ideally, the search for a theater is driven by the material. If you don't have a good show, no theater will save you. If you have a good show, the theater will seem perfect. *Chicago* has proven that. We had no theater until we were a hit, and now we've had three.

————————

While Chicago *was the first large-scale musical Walter Bobbie directed on Broadway, he did technically make his Broadway debut as a director on the Rodgers and Hammerstein revue* A Grand Night For Singing *at the Criterion Center Stage Right.*

The Criterion Center was one of the shortest-lived Broadway theaters of all time. Only in use as a legit space from 1988 to 1999, the first show in the theater was the musical Starmites. *The Criterion Center was leased by Roundabout from 1991 on. In 1992, the production of* Anna Christie *that introduced Liam Neeson to Natasha Richardson took the stage. Revivals of* She Loves Me *and* Company *both starred Boyd Gaines, and* Little Me *won a Tony Award for Best Actor for Martin Short. The last production in the theater was* The Lion in Winter, *starring Stockard Channing and Laurence Fishburne. Then, the theater was demolished to make way for the Times Square Toys"R"Us.*

Those who worked in the Criterion tend to describe it as a relative of the Marriott Marquis—a theater that felt modern, plush, and a little bit cruise ship-like. A grand staircase at the entrance led audience members to a second floor lobby. With its space on the corner of the block, the auditorium of the Criterion had a unique triangle shape that hugged the stage. A neon ferris wheel and giant Tyrannosaurus Rex stand where the stage once was.

From 1935 to 1988, the space had been a movie theater called the Criterion. Prior to that, the Olympia Theatre had been built on the same property. Opened in 1895 by Oscar Hammerstein, the Olympia was like no other theater. 50 cents would gain you admission to two Broadway theaters, a concert hall, a roof garden, a dining room, a bowling alley, and a pool hall!

————————

1996: The Spirit Of Fosse

William Ivey Long, Costume Designer/Chair of the American Theatre Wing

Chicago is my unique experience of a show running 17 years, as we speak, and counting.

I remember when I designed the first national tour of *Chicago,* after the Broadway revival. Charlotte d'Amboise took it out and was Roxie. Walter Bobbie, the director, encouraged me to think up new looks. Immediately, we realized the error of our way out of town. We called up New York and said, "Can you send us some of the old stuff... this one and this one and this one?" We realized that we had created classic *Chicago* looks.

We underestimated it. We just thought: *Oh, let's make up more stretch clothes, let's make up new things, I'll keep going.* Then Walter said, "Oh I miss the such-and-such dress." Named after the person who'd worn it. Jim Borstelman. "Where's 'The Borstelman'? I want to see that on stage." We worked like crazy to make the tour costumes. We still make everything in *Chicago*, even the men's dance shoes.

When we did *Chicago* in Australia, there was a guy in the ensemble we nicknamed Spikey Chris. His name was Chris, and he had streaked, blonde, spiked up hair. Ann Reinking said, "Do you see what Spikey Chris rehearses in? He rehearses in leather pants! Rehearsal! Do you think we could do something like that for his character on stage?" And I did. We had leather pants made, and gave him a different top, that fit in with *Chicago*. Thus we added the 'Spikey Chris' look.

Previously, we were in London, and there was one performer who was really capturing the Fosse spirit. Ann Reinking said, "This character is truly the spirit of Fosse. Will you do something special for him?" So I did.

That costume, the 'Spirit of Fosse', is not in every production. It has to be awarded by the choreographer or associate choreographer. A person has to be correct. Some companies don't even get a 'Spirit of Fosse'. And it just happens. It's one of those things. In other words, it's not one of our classic looks. We reward it. Someone is in rehearsal, and I get the call: "You know, we gave so and so 'The Sergio' look, but I really think he's the 'Spirit of Fosse'. I think we need to do that for this one." That's how it happens.

It's one of our theatre traditions. You have to earn that costume.

1996: An Actual Encore

Ken Billington, Lighting Designer

When we first opened *Chicago*, some nights, Bebe Neuwirth would do "I Can't Do It Alone", and the audience just would not stop applauding. So, Ann Reinking would turn to her and say, "Could you show that to me again?" and they would go back to the middle of the number!

Bebe and Ann did an actual encore, because the audience just wouldn't stop. And that was a New York audience. That was New Yorkers going to the theater. When you see something that great happen, it's rare. I've only seen it a couple of times in my life and I go to the theater all the time.

1997: All The Props Flew Into The Pit

David Loud, Musical Director and Supervisor/Conductor/Actor

Things go into the pit all the time.

Steel Pier was a thrilling show to conduct, because it was a dance musical and you were inside those dances. The acting of the dances in that show was phenomenal, and as the conductor, you were sort of inside the thing.

Steel Pier also had many props and they all came into the pit at some point. You would go, "Incoming!" and people would cover their precious instruments and catch them.

The other thing that I remember from that show was the top of act two. It was this beautiful number that Susan Stroman choreographed. The number took place on an airplane in the sky, covered with beautiful girls dancing, and Karen Ziemba dancing on the wings. It was terrifying to tech. Some of the girls were crying because they were so scared, but they mastered it. It was a beautiful number.

The stage was covered in fog and all the fog would go straight into the pit. You couldn't see the music. The men sang that number from off stage so they had to watch me on camera. I hoped that I could be seen through the fog on the camera. I would give the cues to where I remembered the camera was, because I couldn't actually see it during that song with all the fog in the pit.

On opening night, one of them took a movie of what they were actually looking at when they looked up at the TV monitor. It was the funniest thing I'd ever seen because it was completely white. They could not see the conductor at *all*! And they were always fine, which I chose to interpret as affirmation that I had taught them well, and not as affirmation that they did not, in fact, need the conductor! But the fog was amazing.

There was also a terrifying moment at the end of that show, when the dancers were exhausted and they had to do a semicircle in couples. Spot turns, very fast. They came down right towards the conductor, and then would spin back up in this big large semicircle. They would get terrifyingly close to the edge of the pit, zipping around really fast. And I would yell, "Oh! Oh!" if they were getting too close, like I was the lighthouse. I remember Greg Mitchell and JoAnn M. Hunter almost stepping off the stage... but of course the two of them were so magical, they could probably have flown back up if they needed to.

There was a night that a huge set piece made of light bulbs that flew up over the stage smashed into another piece of scenery. Glass rained down on the stage. We were in the second act when this happened—and coming up was the number "Running in Place" where Karen Ziemba danced barefoot and threw herself on the floor—and there was glass everywhere!

I picked up the phone to call Beverley Randolph, our stage manager, and said, "Uh, there's glass on the stage." She was way ahead of me. As soon as I picked up the phone, she said, "I'm sending out Brad Bradley and Casey Nicholaw with brooms—they're gonna be janitors in the next scene and clean up all the glass. You tell me when it's all up." I said, "Okay!" So they came—there was Brad Bradley and Casey Nicholaw in, like, two seconds!—with big mops and they were mopping up all the glass.

Beverley checked in with me, "Is the glass gone?" "Yes, there's no more glass on stage." And Karen didn't hurt herself that night. That was something. Beverley had been my stage manager on *Merrily* and then I got the incredible opportunity to work with her again as music director on *Steel Pier* and then on *Curtains*. And she never treated me like a kid. She always treated me like a music director.

1997: No Space!

Casey Nicholaw, Director/Choreographer/Actor

The Richard Rodgers is a beautiful theater to be in, but when you're backstage, it is crazy! There's no space.

I always remember walking by and going, "God, everyone just loves sitting outside in the sun at this theater! Why is everyone always sitting outside?"

It's because there's nowhere to go.

1998: Puzzles From The Pit

Doug Katsaros, Orchestrator/Writer

I was conducting *Footloose*, and Dee Hoty, who I love, was in the cast. There was this moment in the second act where the young men were on stage left singing, and the rest of the cast was stage right, in church pews.

There was a 20 second window where nobody would pay any attention at all to stage right. So Dee and I had a little game. I would draw something on a little sign and hold it up, and she'd have to guess what it meant. I did that every single show, and I kept every one of them. There were over 200! Little 20 second puzzles.

2000: I Know You Just Got Here, But We're Closing

Christian Borle, Actor

I did *Footloose* on tour, and I really thought that I had had my fill after being on the road for a year with it. I didn't think I would ever do it again.

But it was a very exciting thing to be asked to go back in as a replacement in the role of Willard on Broadway. It was fun to do it with a whole new group of people.

I had just made my Broadway debut in the 2000 revival of *Jesus Christ Superstar* a couple months earlier. I left *Jesus Christ Superstar* to go back and do *Footloose*.

I was at the end of my first week at *Footloose*, sitting in my dressing room, and the stage manager came in and said "Well, we're closing in two weeks." So *Footloose* ended up being a three-week run for me.

2000: A Secret Clubhouse

Lynn Ahrens, Writer

I love stage doors. It's like being able to go into a magical secret clubhouse that you're let into and no one else is. And they know you there. You get to know the guys at the stage door so well.

When we first moved into the Richard Rodgers with *Seussical*, I had an experience. We were in tech, and I walked in the stage door by myself for the first time. Before, I had always been with other people. There was a guard at the door who didn't recognize, so I said, "Oh, hi. I wanted to introduce myself. I'm Lynn Ahrens, one of the authors." And he said, "Oh, nice to meet you."

And in I went. I looked around and thought: *Oh, they've made this place so homey already. There are photos up, and posters, and all sorts of personal things.* Then, I saw a rack of costumes. I looked at them and thought: *Wait, what did they do to our costumes? They look filthy and ragged! Was there a flood or something?*

I got so freaked out, for just a moment, and then I realized… they had let me into the *Les Mis* stage door! They were the *Les Mis* costumes! It was the funniest moment.

The stage doors are right next to each other, and I just walked straight into the wrong one and made myself at home.

2000: They Bought Me A Little Blue Ice Skating Dress, And Glued Some Feathers On It

Ann Harada, Actor

I went on as an understudy all the time in *Seussical*. I covered Alice Playten as Mrs. Mayor. I loved her.

Early in the run, each role only had one cover. Janine LaManna, who played Gertrude McFuzz, was sick, and her cover was also sick. They were both there, but there was that moment when you could tell that somebody was going down.

I went to talk to the stage manager on a Thursday night after the show and I said, "Look, in an emergency I think I could go on. If it gets there." The next day she called me and said, "Well, you're on! Nobody else can do it."

I'd never done it. I did not know the track. I had no clothes, and I did not fit anything that those girls wore. So I showed up at noon, and they ran to Capezio, and bought me a little blue ice skating dress. They glued some feathers on it, and they painted lots of shoes for me. The musical director went over the songs, and at 5pm, the dance captain showed up. We were going over the dances and I was thinking: *Okay. Whatever happens, happens.*

I went on and right away, I turned the wrong way. I went to myself: *Okay that's your mistake! Now, just go on with the show.*

I sort of trusted that people would move me around in a group, and they did. At that point, you're like on crazy emergency auto-pilot and you're just like, "I'm going to do it! I know the songs, I know the words!" And I did!

I ended up going on a couple of times that weekend, and then afterwards they officially made me the third cover. It was like being shot out of a cannon.

In *Seussical*, I would go to one of the boxes on house right of the Rodgers. That was my own place to collect my thoughts and be by myself. For some reason I think 13 years ago, it was easier to hang out in the house. Now I just feel like somebody would come and catch me and make me go away.

———————————

Ann and I agreed that her understudy story was "right out of Smash." *In fact, every time I spoke to a* Smash *cast member about their experiences on Broadway, at least one story came up that they described this way.*

Ann played stage manager Linda on Smash, *and she confided that fiction was mixing with reality because she had become an unofficial stage manager at her current show,* Cinderella. *The stage manager role had become ingrained in her during* Smash, *and she'd now find herself saying things like, "You know, this is a 15-second change. So plan accordingly."*

"The thing about Smash *is that there are ludicrous situations," Ann said. "But the sense of chaos is really true to life. I think of Eileen saying, 'Ivy! We've got to control the damage at* Bombshell!' *That all feels very real to me."*

During one episode, Christian Borle's character, Tom, restages a Bombshell *number in the house. Ann noted, "Christian and I were sitting there looking at each other like:* This would never happen. *And the* Smash *folks knew that too, but it was part of the story."*

About Smash *vs. real life on Broadway, Christian weighed in, "I think one part of* Smash *that is quite accurate is how people's emotions run high in theatre, because we care so much about it. I think it takes all of us a little while to get over the competitive part of the business. So much of what theatre is, is putting your soul on the line, and that makes all of us take everything very personally. So, if you're not careful, you can make enemies out of people.*

"The gestation of shows is accelerated on Smash, *but how difficult it is, and how expensive it is, and how tenuous it is—all of that feels real. You just never know if people are going to come, whether or not you're going to make money, but we gamble every single time."*

Ann also told me that stage managers come up to her in the Equity building now and thank her for representing them on screen.

———————

2000: One True Friend In The Universe

Andrew Keenan-Bolger, Actor

I was 15 when I did *Seussical*. I was going through puberty during it, becoming a teenager. Anyone who worked on *Seussical* will tell you that it was a beautiful idea for a show, and a gorgeous score, and an incredible concept, and was just plagued with trouble right from the beginning.

It was right at the beginning of when the Internet theatre people started emerging. People were just talking in a different way; there was a lot of gossip surrounding the show. It was one of the first shows that I feel got killed by the All That Chat message boards, and things like that. We lost our director, and there were people replaced on the creative team. So, it was a real challenge. The show ended up losing sight of the kind of message and heart that was there. What I do love now is that it's one of the most-performed shows in the country as far as regional theaters and high schools—it's done everywhere. It's been given a second chance.

To this day, one of my all-time favorite musical theatre moments is in the first act, when Horton and Jojo sing "Alone in the Universe". I think it's one of my all-time favorite songs in musical theatre. It's a really beautiful, really simple moment, that I think was directed really well. And getting to do that with Kevin Chamberlin, who was Horton... he's a magnetic, beautiful performer, and that's definitely a highlight I remember. Even as a kid, I was thinking: *I feel kinda lucky to be doing this song. This feels like something sort of important.*

———————

On my first visit to New York ever, my family stayed at the Broadway Inn. The Broadway Inn was a small, family-owned hotel on 46th Street, almost at the corner of 8th Avenue on the southern side. The hotel had only a dozen or so floors, and the lobby was on the second level. With brick walls, a fireplace, and bookshelves filled with dusty theatre books, the lobby was the most romantic place I'd ever seen. Lobbies of Florida hotels had palm trees and linoleum, but this lobby had a true New York ambiance, complete with an array of Broadway pamphlets, an always-fresh tray of pastries and a concierge who would talk to you about all of the shows on the block.

I was 14 and I could see the marquee on top of the Booth Theatre from my window at the Broadway Inn. The night we checked in, I stared at it and wondered who else had gazed at the bright lights on 45th Street from that very window. The next day, my sister and I went exploring—by which I mean we walked a couple steps toward Times Square. Right outside our hotel door, to the right, was the back of the Les Mis *theater! Cool! We were seeing that the next night. Next door to that was another theater, but this one had small white signs taped up on all the doors. We read them:*

*"*Seussical *played its last performance on May 20, 2001. For refunds, please call Telecharge at..."*

I stared at the signs, at the locked doors, at the dark theater. I had understood what it meant for a show to close on Broadway, but I had never before seen it in front of me. It sunk in. People were going to walk by the Richard

Rodgers Theatre, and want to see the show they had had tickets to, the one on the marquee with the fun-looking costumes and famous characters, and they never could. It was gone forever.

We went back to the hotel and I saw that a magazine in the lobby advertised Seussical *among its Broadway listings. I crossed it out so that nobody would be misled and then disappointed. Things in New York moved fast.*

The Broadway Inn was demolished around 2006 to make way for a new hotel by a corporate chain. The imminent installation stalled after the real estate market crashed, leaving an empty lot that is currently being used for a small summer flea market. The 1983 film sequel to Saturday Night Fever, Stayin Alive, *shows John Travolta running into the old place. It was called the Fulton Hotel then. You can also see McHale's bar across the street.*

––––––––––––––

2000: A Battlefield

Stephen Flaherty, Writer

On *Seussical*, I felt like I was watching our little show walk across a battlefield. "Whoops, there goes an arm! Oh no! You lost the leg." At that point, you're just trying to get across that line to some sort of dignity.

By the closing, I felt slightly unhinged. I remember we took the stage at the Richard Rodgers after the final performance and Cathy Rigby, gymnast that she is, encouraged me to do a handstand. I did a handstand on stage, came down, and thought: *This is how this experience has felt. Like I've been upside down. I've done this weird thing on stage to mark the ending, and now I can walk out the door.*

We had a famously rough out of town experience. We were really the first "Internet show." Oddly, we had done so many more rewrites and changes out of town with *Ragtime*, but that wasn't documented in the same way. This was only two years later, but the Internet changed everything. Everything we did at *Seussical* was written about online.

It actually felt a little scary! It felt like an espionage flick. I'd go online and read a post that said: "This was overheard at *Seussical* tonight." And I'd think: *Who's writing this?!* I started to look under the stalls first to check for feet, if I was having a conversation in the bathroom.

It started out rough, with many firings in Boston. We opened in Boston with the Bird Girls wearing their own black brassieres as costumes. We cut 400 costumes. Favorite sections of ours that we loved were deemed not to be working, and cut. All of a sudden, you'd see the land where the Lorax lived, and it would be in the alleyway behind the stage door. These cute little truffula trees by the trash.

People were always coming and going. You'd be in the hotel going, "Oh hello, Walter Bobbie. What brings *you* to Boston?" "Hi, Scott Ellis." "Hi, Hal Prince." We saw every director. And I remember one day, I looked at Lynn and said, "You know who's coming next? Kander and Ebb."

At every run, it felt like we were under siege, and that continued into New York. It was wobbly and so much was changed right up until the last night before we opened at the Rodgers.

It's a tradition of mine that for opening night of every show, I find all of the songs that never made it in, that were lost along the way or altered, and I put them in a book. I put them in a little historical tome, that I present to my collaborator, my dear Lynn Ahrens. It's our history of "songs that never left the living room," "songs that never made it into the workshop," "songs that never made it past the first preview." You can really see the creative process, in book form.

On *Seussical*, we just kind of ran out of time to work, and suddenly we were opening on Broadway. I knew in my gut that there was unfinished business with the show on so many levels. So I did not give Lynn that book. I said, "We're just opening; we're not done with the show."

And we did go back to it. We had a really successful national tour. We worked on a new version that was brought back to the Lucille Lortel Theatre in New York, and got a great review in the *New York Times*.

Now, it's the most performed show in America. It's so exciting. I've gotten to see so many different productions: amateur, school, professional. And I love it because I always knew it was a good show, and we just had to reclaim it.

I call the Broadway production: The World's Most Expensive Workshop. I take it at that. And then later Lynn got the book.

2000: Anything's Possible

Eddie Korbich, Actor

Years after I saw my first Broadway show, *No No Nanette* at the Richard Rodgers, I did *Seussical* at the same theater. I'm still sad about how the show worked out, because I loved that score so much.

I started out with a song called "The Lorax" in *Seussical*. It was the first time in my entire career that I didn't audition. Lynn Ahrens and Stephen Flaherty told me, "We have a wonderful song. We want you to do it." It was fantastic.

First, "The Lorax" got cut down in length. Then I got this phone call from the writers: "The entire thing is being cut, but we're writing you a new song." That didn't happen. And when it didn't, Lynn and Steve said to me, "You know what? We understand. You can go. You can just leave if you want."

I said, "I've been with this for a year and a half! I don't want to leave. I want to make the album, I want to go to opening night! I will eventually leave, because I'm just Grandpa Who now, and that's fine! But I will go to the first of the New Year." Why not? New beginnings, New Year. Great!

Then, in mid-December, word came out that Rosie O'Donnell was joining our cast in January. Our stage manager came to me and said, "When are you leaving?" I reminded her: the first of the year. She told me that things had just been so crazy with Rosie rehearsals, that they hadn't even had time to audition for my replacement yet. She asked if I could stay an extra week in January, and I said sure.

It was one of the worst moments of my professional career, to tell you the truth, because I took it all on myself. *If I were only better, this would not have happened. If I could've held an audience with the number, it wouldn't have happened.* We do this to ourselves. But I stayed in the show.

The first time I met Rosie, I said to her, "I'm so happy to meet you, and I love what you do for kids, because I'm adopted!" And she said, "Good for you." Okay, so that's it.

One night, we were all in the wings getting ready to go on for "The Butter Battle" scene. Mary Ann Lamb was saying to me, "Why are you going to leave? Do you hear that audience out there? Where are you going? Stay for the rest of Rosie's run and leave on a high." Ann Harada looked at me very sweetly and said, "It's just because we love you, Eddie. We don't want you to go! You're one of the originals and we don't want you to go." I went home to my partner Andy and I said, "Okay, what should I do?" He said, "Stay! Might as well get three more weeks of paychecks!"

A week later, I went out into the stairwell after a number to cool off, and Rosie was sitting there. She looked at me and said, "Hey doll, how you doing?" I said, "I'm okay. Look, can I ask you a question?" She said okay, and I told her, "My partner and I have been trying to adopt for a year and a half and nothing is happening."

Rosie looked at me and said, "What do you want? You want a girl? You want a boy? I can get you a mother in two days." I was stunned. She continued, "Look, my lawyer's going to come. You're going to meet him tomorrow. We'll get everything set. You'll give us your home study. Everything will be fine."

She was so warm and so wonderful. What I realized is that Rosie has to deal with celebrity so much that she's protecting herself, and that's why she's on her guard a little bit. But when there's something that's true to her heart, she becomes your biggest champion.

A year later, through Rosie, our daughter, Alexandra, was born. The worst experience of my professional career became the best experience of my personal life.

2008: The Latino Community

Brig Berney, Company Manager

The first preview of *In the Heights* was absolutely crazy. Lin came out at the very beginning of the show to sing "Lights up on Washington Heights", and the audience just started cheering and never stopped.

Lin had family there, and he's very connected and adored in the Latino community. The audience applauded for about a minute right when he entered. There was just this excitement amongst the whole community that this show had made it to Broadway.

2008: Home

Lin-Manuel Miranda, Writer/Actor

Kevin McCollum and Jeffrey Seller always wanted the Rodgers for *In the Heights*. They were like, "We're waiting for the Rodgers. We're waiting for the Rodgers." *Pal Joey* was supposed to go into the Rodgers, so we announced we were going to Broadway, like many do, without a theater. And about a month after we announced, *Pal Joey* was cancelled.

Then Kevin, Jeffrey, and Jill Furman did whatever it is producers do to get a theater. They took a chance on us.

There were other theaters that we looked at when it looked like *Pal Joey* was going to happen. We looked at the St. James, and we were terrified by that third balcony because the sight-lines are just tough. I saw *The Producers* from there and I still don't think I saw *The Producers*. I think I saw *The Producers* from space! When we did *Bring It On* there, we just didn't sell the balcony because it didn't make sense. So the St. James scared us, because it was a little too big. That was the only one we could really also consider, and we were sort of like, "Rodgers or bust!" We were really happy about the way it played out.

I remember the first day they let us into the Rodgers. I met Tim Pettolina, who was the house manager, and he was like, "You're going to have a great time here." He is such a Broadway griot, one of those people who collects the history of these shows. He knows everything that's been through that place and just loves theatre.

That's the fun thing about when you move into the house: everyone who's there loves theatre. I remember meeting Jimmy the door man for the first time. He's a legend at the Rodgers. I've always told him that I want to write a show called *Jimmy With the Fix*. The problem is that it overlaps with *Bullets Over Broadway* too much. Jimmy's seen so many shows come and go that he could probably fix shows in previews faster than a lot of the creative team. He'd be like, "The thing with *Tarzan* was that they flew right away and there was nowhere left to go." And I'd be like, "Jimmy. You're my new show doctor."

Jimmy fascinates me because he took over the job when he was a kid. He's been in that theater since before it was the Rodgers! And all those characters: Jimmy and Angelo, our other door man, were both great. There's an usher there named Frances who was always like, "You remind me so much of my son." Still, every time I go see a show, I see her and hug her. Eight shows a week you live at the theater. You're at the theater more than your home, or at least it feels like that between understudy rehearsals and meetings.

The stage door guys and theater staff are in this funny world because they live there, and we're visiting. We all think about getting a show on Broadway and there they are, living in a theater on Broadway and waiting for a show to be good and run a long time.

I remember walking in the first day the set started to be put up. That was surreal. Here was a slice of my neighborhood, on Broadway! That's a tribute to Anna Louizos' set.

Off-Broadway, our entire cast was sharing two bathrooms, and we had to block the whole show so that it only used one entrance, stage left. There was no exit to the dressing rooms on the right side! So yeah, the Rodgers might not have that much wing space, but we had this downstairs. We could exit stage right! There were dressing rooms and bathrooms!

I had the first dressing room on stage right. James Naughton had my dressing room during the *Chicago* revival, and I know we both used the bunk bed. Audra used it after me, during *Porgy and Bess,* and we talked about how we both loved the steam heater in the bathroom. Because the theater's so old, there was a steam heater! It was like Bikram yoga in that bathroom, great for warming up. Joel Grey was once in that dressing room.

My pre-show tradition was to get dressed as fast as I could, and then go visit everyone else's dressing room one at a time. I'd go up and see Priscilla Lopez and Olga Merediz who were one up from me. When Jennifer Garner was there for *Cyrano* right before us, those rooms were her room and baby nursery. I talked to her about it when we did the *Timothy Green* movie. Downstairs from me was Carlos Gomez's room, so I'd go there next, and then I'd go under and up and visit everyone one floor at a time.

It went, first floor: Benny, Nina, Vanessa. One above that were the salon ladies, Janet Dacal and Andréa Burns' room was THE Salon, for real. They painted it pink, and they put a bunch of pillows out so people would come in and sit in this beanbag-ery thing and gossip. They were sort of the earth-mothers/healers of the cast. People would go in there, and they were sort of at the midway point of the big climb. One flight above the salon ladies were Graffiti Pete and Sonny, then one above that was girls ensemble, and then one above that was mens ensemble. So it was like you visited these little different worlds every time you went up. That was one of my favorite parts.

We had picnics on the Rodgers fire escapes, out on the front of the theater. I would skateboard in the Rodgers museum, in the outer lobby that has all the pictures. That was great, because I'm not a very good skateboarder, but it was a very nice, mind-clearing thing. It's a perfect little slope, almost like a half-pipe for a two-year-old. So I would skateboard back and forth between shows. I befriended a lot of the ushers that way, because they'd be like, "Hey, man. The guy who wrote the show is skateboarding outside!"

The nights when someone you love is in the audience, or the nights when it's packed with kids from Washington Heights and this is their first show… those are the easiest to do, because they're giving you all the energy you need. You just ride the wave of love that is coming at you, and it gets you where you need to go. It's the Saturday matinee when three dudes are asleep, that's hard!

The Rodgers is intimate, and since I had license to talk to the audience, I could really see the faces. I would keep tabs on the couple over there, or the dude with the crazy laugh, or the person in the fifth row who started taking pictures and the usher caught it but I'm keeping an eye on it anyway. If we had a student matinee, you'd add measures in "Sunrise", because they'd lose their MINDS when Nina came out on the fire escape. "Oh my God, it's sex!"

I always thought it was cool when audience members would tell me how they felt in the scene near the end with Sonny and Graffiti Pete. There's that part where you don't know what they're doing, and they say, "No one knows about this but you and me." Audience members would tell me that they had thought it was a drug deal and it made them confront some stuff after they saw what it really was. I thought it was brave to tell me that, and it was interesting to me.

Our company manager, the beloved Brig Berney, knew no pop culture references outside of the theatre. He would tell you everyone who won the Best Score Tony Award for the last 50 years, but then he'd be like, "Usher Raymond is here tonight?" My favorite part was him telling me who was in the audience each night.

I loved knowing who was in the audience. Maybe that's old-school; I just really like show-and-tell. If I know Antonio Banderas is in the audience, I want to work an Antonio Banderas accent into a moment. It keeps it fresh and exciting for me. Other people don't like to know. Mandy Gonzales never liked to know, so we'd always be standing backstage together before bows and that's when I'd tell her.

One night, Leonardo DiCaprio came to see *In the Heights* with his mom and a couple friends, and when Mandy asked, "Who was here tonight?" I told her, "DiCaprio's here." She went, "No." I said, "Yeah." And she went, "... No! No. No. No." As if I told her family had been killed. Then she ran out to bow. She had a poster of Leo on her wall when she was 15 years old. She had a *Titanic* poster over her bed. He was her guy.

The hardest one for me was when a songwriter named Juan Luis Guerra came; he's one of my favorite songwriters. With that, I was thinking so much as a songwriter, about how everything sounded. I remember the horn boned this one note, and Robin De Jesus turned to me and joked, as he always did when anyone messed up, "They think you wrote that." We had a lot of time together just in the bodega on stage being quiet, so that was a really fun time. It would be: who's cute in the front row, who's here tonight, what are we doing after? Some of the most fun things that ever happened on stage were during moments when Robin and I were supposed to be being quiet in the bodega.

Priscilla Lopez had done *Nine* at the 46th Street Theatre in 1982. She understudied Liliane Montevecchi. On our opening night, Priscilla gave me a picture of her in her 20s, in our theater, wearing nothing but a treble clef. Amazing.

She had that whole *Nine* experience and then was back there for *Heights*. I remember Priscilla telling me when we were in previews, "This thing has ripples you don't even know about yet. You just don't know yet." Then, in the prayer circle that night, one of the understudies in the show, was like, "I do this for a living because of Priscilla Lopez," and she made a tearful speech. That's when Priscilla said to me, "This is going to happen to you too. Get ready. You don't even know." She just kept being like, "You don't even know, Lin-Manuel."

And she was right. It's crazy. I've felt that now as the stock and amateur rights have gone out. There are 70 productions of *Heights* happening this year in high schools and middle schools and regional theaters.

I went and spoke to a group that was doing *In the Heights* in the Bronx and these girls came up to me during the break and said, "Our school did the show two weeks ago, and it's an all-girls school." This one girl was like, "I was Usnavi!" I think the Benny and the Kevin, they borrowed from the boys' school but Graffiti Pete was a girl, Usnavi was a girl.

"We had to hug at 'Champagne' but everything else was the same!" She showed me all these pictures on her phone of her as Usnavi, and it looked so, so great.

It's just this gift that keeps giving and it's really crazy. Anyone who writes a show that has any kind of life has that experience. That's why we keep doing it.

———————————

The opening night party for In the Heights *was unlike any Broadway opening night I've ever attended.*

Of course, the performance itself was electric. I sat in the mezzanine with the [title of show] *gang. The two shows had Kevin McCollum and other producers in common, so we were invited—although we did miss the bus to the party at Chelsea Piers when someone in our group lost their glove. I remember standing in the cold March air on 46th Street and exclaiming, "Now I'll never get to ride on a party bus with Sherie Rene Scott and Brian D'Arcy James!"*

The party was huge and the room was a panorama of the who's who of Broadway. I walked around starstruck, and had a great time being part of the celebration. But the thing that made it unlike any other opening was the moment when the reviews came out.

When a brand new, original, homegrown musical like In the Heights *gets a rave in the* New York Times, *it really is like every Hollywood movie you've ever seen about Broadway. The room exploded in champagne. Lin danced with his mom, Kevin danced with Jeffrey, the entire company danced together in a group of childlike joy.*

———————————

2008: Lights Up On Washington Heights

Anna Louizos, Scenic Designer

I have the Rosario Car Service sign from *In the Heights*. It's lightweight, and came down, and it was going to end up in the trash. So I laid claim to it. It's in my studio. Some of the pieces from the set, they saved. Because they had the tour, they saved like the Piragua cart, and the counters and those kinds of things.

There are always pieces that you have to assemble on stage, and combine with the lighting. I do my best to figure out how these things will work in combination with each other, but ultimately, I don't know until it's lit. That's because lighting changes sometimes, based on what you want to focus the audience to, as the show develops. It's a way of controlling the story on stage. That's where working with the lighting designer is very important. The discoveries happen when you're in tech, and you can finally actually look at the scenery and the lighting at the same time.

The orchestra seats at the Rodgers have a wonderful rake to them, so the shows just look better and better, the farther back you go. I loved the Richard Rodgers for *In the Heights*.

2008: Our Load-In Dock

Robin De Jesus, Actor

During *In the Heights*, we spent a lot of time hanging out on the load-in dock. That was actually one of my favorite things to do at the Richard Rodgers. I didn't like being behind walls all the time, so I always tried to go outside as much as possible. That was the best, during two show days, going and chilling outside of your theater on the dock. Every time, four more people would come around, and we'd just people watch on 46th Street. We'd enjoy whatever was going on at the Lunt-Fontanne or the Scientology protests across the street.

When *Little Mermaid* was running, we would see each other all the time. When your show lets out, you tend to cross the street when you leave, because all the audience members are on the sidewalk. So I'd always see the cast of *Little Mermaid* cross over to our side, as we crossed over to theirs.

And the *Heights* cast members just never got out of the street. We always loved taking pictures with the Richard Rodgers sign in the background. There are so many photos of us doing that. We'd be out there, hanging out with Jimmy, our door man, shooting the shit.

I went to the Richard Rodgers a couple weeks ago. I wasn't expecting to go in but they gave me a hard hat, and sent me in to where they're renovating. They had ripped out the carpet, the seats. I saw bare wood and scaffolding. It looked like Michelangelo was painting the ceiling or something. The door man was telling me about all the things they found that they didn't even know were there! There's so much in these theaters that's under the walls! Let's be real. There's probably a body somewhere.

———————————

If you're looking at the Rodgers, the load-in dock is to the right of the entrance to the theater. It's a nook in the wall, where the cast of every show at the Rodgers tends to hang out. Right across the street is the "Lunt-Fontanne stoop" where everyone in that theater's show likes to hang out!

There's also a door at the top of the orchestra section of the Rodgers on house right. It leads to a hidden outdoor staircase. You can hang out on the staircase in view of the beautiful Rodgers marquee and the other lights of Times Square, or you can take it down to street level, where it opens just next to the load-in dock.

———————————

2008: Define A Community

Krysta Rodriguez, Actor

On *In the Heights*, we had a circle before every show. Chris Jackson would lead us and he would do a prayer and everyone would get to announce things. If someone was going into the show for the first time, we would put them in the center of the circle and we would lay our hands on them. It may sound weird when I say it, but as a cast, it was really a special thing. The show is so about a community that you couldn't fake that. Anybody that came in needed to be part of our family immediately, so you had to rally around them.

It was such a different experience than *A Chorus Line*, which I had done right before. We were deliberately separated and didn't see each other until the lights came up. You'd be like, "Oh! Grant's on! I didn't even realize that." And it's sort of supposed to be like that because you're not really supposed to know the other characters, and you're not supposed to have interacted with them. The different things before a performance that help you define a character and a community of people are really helpful.

2010: Bleusnavi

Corbin Bleu, Actor

I had actually seen *In the Heights* about a year and a half before I was in the show. I sat in the fourth row, right on the edge, and when the show finished, I leaned over to my dad and said, "If I'm ever going to do a Broadway show, it has to be something like this."

It was so new and different and so of-its-age—and I *loved* the incorporation of hip-hop and rap. It was also such an uplifting show. It really, really touched me. I went and I bought the album.

And what do you know? About a year later, I ended up auditioning for the role of Benny. I went in, and I ended up telling them how much of a fan I was of the show. I was listing a lot of the names of the songs. A lot of them are Spanish names, and I said them with the proper accent—because I grew up in New York, and all of my mom's friends were Dominican and Puerto Rican. I don't fully know how to speak Spanish, but I grew up around it, and I understand it well.

I was saying all these things, and I found out that's when they decided to consider me for Usnavi. Usnavi is such a wonderful character in the show, but it wasn't an obvious choice. I'm a black actor, so, of course, I'd be more likely to be considered for Benny.

When it was announced that I'd be playing Usnavi, there was a bit of an uproar in the Latino community because I had no Latino blood in me. This outcry was leading up to my debut in the show.

I just blocked all of that out, and did my show. I remember people saying, "You can do it," and being so welcomed by the company and the fans, after this whole initial announcement and horrible backlash. Being welcomed by the show had started before I even got to the theater, but I really, really felt it walking on that stage for the first time.

After a week of rehearsal, I had a major run-through on the stage. And I wasn't afraid. It felt so right. I had no nerves! Of course, when the day came, when there was an hour to curtain, that's when I got really nervous. I went over every single line in my head.

And then the second I walked out on that stage, the nerves all disappeared. It was a blur. And then I was doing my bow! I don't really remember a whole lot of my first show, it was just so adrenaline-fueled. But I remember the bow. I remember finishing the show, and thinking: *I want to remember this part of it.* I came out, looked into the audience and I took my first bow on a Broadway stage.

One wonderful thing about *In the Heights* is that we did a full cast circle before every show. We would stand below the stage, and we would all gather around. It wasn't just to say a prayer for the show that night, it was also a time that any cast member could share something that was troubling them, or something on their minds, someone that needed praying for them. Anything that people needed to put out there so that they could do their show, they did. And everybody else was there for them. It was uplifting.

I remember my very first night, because they wanted to say a prayer over me since I was joining the cast. I remember standing in the middle of this circle, having the entire cast put their hands on me. Every single one of them, they came and laid a hand on me, and they were all praying. The surge that went through my body, from all of that energy focused on me, and all that heat, I knew… you could feel the electricity. It was crazy. You could feel the wonderful aura of everyone at the same time.

We also had show rituals throughout the show. Everyone had their own track, of course. But there were shows going on behind the show itself. There were certain lyrics to songs that we'd lip synch backstage. There were traditions I learned.

Every week, we'd do "Saturday Night On Broadway." Before the Saturday night show, whoever was playing Usnavi would go over the loudspeaker and do some sort of a rap to commemorate that we got to spend our Saturday nights doing a Broadway show together. It was such a grateful cast.

"Saturday Night on Broadway" started with Lin. Of course, he's a ridiculously phenomenal rapper and freestyler, so he would just think about whatever was going on that week— whether it was something political, something that was going on in New York, something funny that had happened during the show that week, or something going on backstage. He would do a freestyle rap over the loud speaker and at the end everyone would sing, "Saturday Night on Broadway!"

When Javier Muñoz took over, he would write them out, and then I took over after that. Every single week, I would come up with a rap, or I would write songs. Sometimes I would rap and other cast members would do harmonies.

There was one rap I did about when a roach had crawled up on our stage mid-performance! I did a whole rap to the melody of "La Cucaracha". There were always lots of fun things on "Saturday Night On Broadway." It was our tradition.

2012: We Banded Together

Irene Gandy, Press Agent

Porgy and Bess almost didn't come in. And then the triumph was so great. Michael Riedel wrote awful things about it out of town, but we banded together and got it in anyway.

One thing I love about Diane Paulus is that her children are always around. And several of our cast members also had kids. So, during *Porgy and Bess*, there were always kids.

And out of town, in Boston, there was a live baby! The actress who played Mariah had just had twins, so one of the twins was the real baby in the first half.

2012: People Leaned Forward In Their Seats

Diane Paulus, Director

My main memory of the audience at *Porgy and Bess* was seeing people sit forward. People leaned forward in their seats to hear that score. The audience was completely wrapped in the performance on stage, and so excited by the orchestral sound coming from the pit. *Porgy and Bess* was one of those shows where people would peer into the orchestra pit. You'd see people conducting during the show with their hands, because they knew the score so well.

The Richard Rodgers is an incredible theater. The orchestra feels so intimate. We created the show at the American Repertory Theater with under 600 seats, and there are around 1400 seats at the Rodgers. And the orchestra on Broadway felt even more intimate than our little theater in Cambridge, even though it had more seats! There's just something about the rake in that theater; it takes you right onto the stage. It makes you feel like you're right in the action. You feel like you're being lifted so you can see everything. We also had a set that jutted out over the orchestra, so you really felt like the stage was directly in front of you.

2013: Backstage Looks Like A Ship

Neil Mazzella, Technical Supervisor

All the time I look back at things I learned in the beginning of my career. Union rules, rigging situations...

52

We just did *The Rascals* at the Rodgers and the production was all LED walls. The LED walls were heavier than the forklifts, so there was the danger of a forklift turning over. I just said, "Stop," and we did it by hand. We loaded it down the ramp: ropes went down, and ropes pulled it back up the ramp. It was very fast and very efficient. It was very old-school!

So there are constantly little things at the theater, where you say, "Oh yeah. Let's do it this way. It worked 20 years ago." That always happens. Now, with technology being the way it is, all the scenery is controlled by computers, the sound is controlled by computers, the lights are controlled by computers—everything is controlled by computers! You sometimes get away from how theaters were originally designed to be used.

Our theaters are designed based on the theaters in England. The original stagehands were all seamen. That's why all of the rigging and rope backstage looks like what you'd see on a ship—because when the seamen were not at sea, they'd work as stagehands. All of that was passed on to the theaters. Many New York theaters are hemp houses[9], and all of the rigging is still based on nautical rigging, to this day.

That's forgotten. Now we go into a hemp house, and the first thing we do is bring in counter-weights and motors, because we don't want to operate a hemp suspend. You have to operate it all religiously. And we have to automate a whole show. So operating the rigging that way has become one of the lost arts.

2013: My Favorite Theater

Frank Wildhorn, Writer

I love the Richard Rodgers. It's my favorite theater. The recent *Jekyll & Hyde* revival was supposed to go in there, and for circumstances beyond my control, it did not. I missed it very much. I think the theater would have helped the show in every way because of the intimacy and the closeness to the performers and the way the music comes over the audience at the Rodgers. They get to feel part of the evening there.

I hope one day I'll get to play the Rodgers. Also, of course, it's named for the greatest composer in the theater. Playing there is a dream of mine. One day.

———————————

On a Saturday afternoon, I went to see Romeo and Juliet *at the Richard Rodgers Theatre. I was so excited to see Tim Pettolina house managing up a storm as I walked into the newly renovated house. It looked beautiful!*

As I entered the left side of the orchestra section, I noticed several emergency exits I had not paid attention to before. At intermission, I ran to ask Tim: "Where do those lead to?"

He opened one of the doors, and we went outside into a narrow alleyway. Tim explained that the alley led to the an outdoor entrance for the star dressing rooms on stage left, and that was how Orlando Bloom made some of his entrances in the show. The alley also led to the basement of the Imperial, and a back door of the Music Box.

———————————

———————————

[9] hemp house: a Broadway theater that uses hemp rigging—ropes, pulleys and sandbags—in order to operate the scenery; one of the two major types of houses (the other is a counterweight house)

2014: The Future

David Stone, Producer

If/Then will be opening at the Richard Rodgers Theatre in Spring 2014.

The Nederlanders are my primary theatre-owner relationship. They have made more money on *Wicked* than anything in the history of the organization. Jimmy Jr. co-produced *Spelling Bee* and *Next To Normal*, and is going to be similarly involved in *If/Then*. Since the organization is investing in the show, it is going to go into one of their theaters.

I always knew that the ideal theater for the show was the Rodgers. Nick Scandalios and I began planning the show for the theater in Fall 2011. That's why he put two plays in it— because he knew when I needed the theater, and the only way to guarantee that was to not put a musical in, since that might run. They had an engagement of *Cat On A Hot Tin Roof*, and right now they're doing a renovation, before *Romeo and Juliet* comes in. Those are play revivals with stars—with set limited runs. The plan was very clean, very easy.

The renovation they're doing is thorough. The theater is going to look great. Apparently, it's been more work than they thought, but in a good way. They've found things! They told me, "Oh God, we've got to restore that beautiful original proscenium arch."

———————

At the Rodgers, I saw Bengal Tiger at the Baghdad Zoo, *written by one of my college professors, Rajiv Joseph. At the Rodgers, I saw the first preview of* Tarzan. *At the Rodgers, I saw* Movin' Out *on the day I moved into the city. At the Rodgers, one snowy Wednesday afternoon, I waited in line for two hours to get tickets to* Cyrano de Bergerac, *starring Kevin Kline.*

The Rodgers is cozy and big and feels welcoming. The Rodgers has the infamous great rake in its orchestra section, and a special load-in dock, and messages from the 1940s in the walls. Maybe because of its proximity to the Marriott Marquis, the Rodgers feels like a survivor on a block with lots of ghosts. In fact, nearly everything on the south side of 46th Street, between Broadway and 8th Avenue, is new since the 1980s. Dinty Moore's is gone. The old Helen Hayes Theatre, which was demolished to build the Marquis, is gone. The Broadway Inn is gone.

The Richard Rodgers Theatre, built in 1925, stands.

The Winter Garden Theatre

Built: 1911
Location: 1634 Broadway
Owner: The Shubert Organization
Formerly Named: Winter Garden Theatre (1911-2002), Cadillac Winter Garden Theatre (2002-2007)
Longest-Running Show: *Cats* (1982-2000)
Shortest-Running Show: *Georgy* (closed after four performances in 1970), *The Roast* (closed after four performances in 1980)
Number of Productions: 150

I saw my first Broadway show at the Winter Garden, and I made my Broadway debut in *Cats* at the Winter Garden. One time, during the show, I thought I saw a young boy and his mother and grandmother in the box seat that I had sat in many years prior. I really thought I saw that. I don't think I've ever seen a real ghost, but when you play a theater like the Winter Garden, you think about how Barbra Streisand was *Funny Girl* there, how Angela Lansbury was *Mame* there, how *West Side Story* with Chita Rivera was on that stage. You're always thinking about how you're on that same stage where all these legends have played.

-**Bryan Batt**, Actor

Introduction: My First *West Side Story* And Barbra's Final *Funny Girl*

Larry Fuller, Choreographer/Actor

The first Broadway show I did was at the Winter Garden. In the fall of 1957, *West Side Story* opened on a Thursday in October. They had not had a Jet swing[10] the entire time they were rehearsing and out of town. It was not required by Equity at the time. So the next morning after opening night, they had an audition for a Jet swing. I went in and danced for Jerry Robbins and Peter Gennaro. There were hundreds of guys there, most of them too old because the original cast was between 16 and 25.

I got called back, and I got cast. I was in *West Side* for seven months. That was my original theater on Broadway to work in, in the cast.

I remember the first time I saw *West Side Story*, after I'd been hired and signed the contract already. I saw it that night, standing in the back of the Winter Garden orchestra. And I was scared to death. I thought: *My God. I have to go in and dance for all those different Jets? If I don't kill someone, they'll kill me. Just by accident.* There were bodies flying everywhere, and there was not a straight line in the show anywhere, as far as dance formation. And I thought: *I'll never learn this!*

But in two weeks, I did learn it. And I started getting put on—every matinee I'd go on for a different Jet. It was a great way to get experience and prepare to be able to go on at a moment's notice, because since I knew which person I'd be on for each week, I had a couple days to follow them backstage and study them on stage. I'd make tons of notes. But it was very frightening at the beginning.

---

[10] swing: an off stage understudy who covers multiple roles

Fade out, fade in, and in the spring of 1965, I opened in the original *Funny Girl*, with Barbra Streisand, back at the Winter Garden! I was the assistant choreographer and dance captain for Carol Haney, who was the choreographer. Unfortunately, Carol passed away about three months after the show opened. So I inherited the show, and I got to choreograph her work, and maybe a little extra stuff. That was my entrée into choreographing, officially. I did the national tour and I did the show in London.

I remember the night that Barbra left the show on Broadway. We were told that she was going to sing "My Man" at the end of the bows at her final performance. I had made myself the swing by that time, so I wasn't in the show that night.

Michael Bennett and I were roommates at the time. I told Michael, "You've GOT to see this, 'cause Barbra's gonna sing the quintessential Fanny Brice song "My Man" at the end of the bows!" I met him at the stage door, and walked him in before the show was over. We stood in the back of the orchestra. When the bows finished, and everybody was off stage but Barbra, she quieted the audience and said, "I'm sure you know that tonight is my last performance in the show. This is the same stage on which Fanny Brice, who I play in the show, did her last performance on Broadway. And so, as a tribute to her, I would like to sing..."

Then they started "My Man", and she sang the hell out of it. God! It was one of those moments that you remember for your entire career. A stunning moment.

In between *West Side Story* and *Funny Girl*, in 1959, I had been at the Winter Garden to see the gypsy run[11] of the original production of *Gypsy*, before they went out of town for their pre-Broadway tryout. They did the show in public for the very first time ever on the bare stage of the Winter Garden, and you knew that it was going to be a sensational hit. It was theatre history. My favorite Broadway theater is the Winter Garden.

The TV show Smash *is loosely based on the novel* Smash, *which is loosely based on Garson Kanin's experience directing* Funny Girl. *At different points in the development of this new musical about the life of Fanny Brice, stars attached included Mary Martin, Anne Bancroft, Carol Burnett, and Eydie Gorme. Writers attached included Jule Styne, Stephen Sondheim, Dorothy Fields, and Bob Merrill.*

Finally, Styne took producer Ray Stark down to the club Bon Soir in the Village, to see Barbra Streisand perform. She was frumpy and "downtown" and they hired her on the spot.

Jerome Robbins and Bob Fosse had both been attached to the project as directors, but by the time the show headed to Broadway, Garson Kanin was at the helm. David Merrick had suggested him to direct Funny Girl *shortly before leaving the production himself. The show was very long. 30 minutes were cut in Boston, and 30 minutes were cut on the way to Philadelphia, and the opening in New York was postponed five times. When Garson Kanin tried to cut "People", there was an uproar and soon after, Jerome Robbins came back to replace him as director.*

In the novel Smash, *a slimy producer, neurotic writers, womanizing director, demanding star and others set out to create a new musical based on the life of vaudeville star Nora Bayes. For the TV show of the same name, Nora Bayes became Marilyn Monroe.*

----

[11] gypsy run: an invited dress rehearsal prior to the first preview, often for other members of the Broadway community

56

1954: Seeing All The Wires

André Bishop, Artistic Director of Lincoln Center Theatre

The first Broadway show I ever saw—this will date me— was Mary Martin's *Peter Pan* at the Winter Garden Theatre. I was five or six.

I was a New York City kid. I grew up here and I had a very theatrical aunt who always took me to shows. She loved to sit in the first row.

I remember thinking the show was wonderful; I remember thinking Mary Martin was wonderful. But the memory of it that stuck with me most was that at one point, because we were in the front row, I saw the wire for the flying mechanism! The light happened to hit the wire at one particular point, and I saw it!

What that did for me—although I didn't know it because I was five or six—was that I was completely taken in by the magic of the flying and the illusion of it. But I was also so aware of how it happened.

I'm convinced, in some completely crazy, psychological, ridiculous way, that that is what ultimately led me to become a producer, rather than an actor, which is what I had wanted to be. It was a seminal moment for me, and I only realized it a few years ago.

So one might say that sitting in the front row and seeing the wire as the light hit it ruined my life. Or one might say that it saved my life. But that's what I remember about *Peter Pan*.

1954: Seeing Into The Wings

John Weidman, Writer

The first Broadway show I remember seeing was *Peter Pan*. I was eight or nine. My most vivid memory of the experience was the fact that we were sitting in a theater box. At the time I thought we had the absolute best seats in the house. I thought: *If the King or Queen were here, this is where they would sit!*

I thought the show was cool because I could see into the wings. I could see people pulling stuff. It was only later on when I realized that that was not the ideal way to see a show.

1954: My Home Where Dreams Are Born

Jack Viertel, Creative Director of Jujamcyn Theaters

My first Broadway show was *Peter Pan*. It was at the Winter Garden, and I was in the very front row on the side aisle. I remember it absolutely vividly.

There were four of us, and there were two pairs of tickets. Two were farther back, and two were in the front row. So they plunked me down in the front row. I was not quite yet six years old, so my family members each took a turn sitting with me.

I remember Mary Martin flying. I remember being told beforehand that there were going to be wires, and I would be able to see the wires, and I shouldn't be disappointed—but the wires actually just made it better.

I remember looking down at the pit and seeing a lot of brass instruments during intermission. I remember the story and how excited I was. To this day, I can't watch that version of *Peter Pan* without coming to tears.

It really did ruin my life. I wasn't interested in anything else after that. Those were probably the most powerful two and a half hours I've ever had. It was just where I wanted to be from then on.

It was great fun to hear about how, unbeknownst to each other, three separate greats of the theatre who are around the same age—John Weidman, Jack Viertel, and André Bishop—all saw Peter Pan *at the Winter Garden as their first Broadway show! And what they all seemed to love most was not the seamless magic of the show, but seeing how the pieces all came together.*

In conducting interviews for this book, several productions cropped up that were influential specifically because they were so many people's first Broadway show! Pippin, Sweeney Todd, *and* A Chorus Line *were often claimed as the first Broadway show of those who started their theatergoing career in the 1970s. And I imagine that if this book were written 30 years from today, we'd find that* Rent *and* Beauty and the Beast *were influential in the same way to the generation of young artists in the 1990s.*

But what I loved about the Peter Pan *discovery was that this production only played for four short months in the winter of 1954! Unlike the juggernauts above, if you blinked, you missed this one.*

But if you were there, you may have been sharing the performance with future giants of the New York theatre scene.

1957: A Jet Girl

Marilyn D'Honau, Actor

I was an original cast member of *West Side Story* on Broadway. And that was at the Winter Garden.

I went to the Equity audition, and all I remember is that all of a sudden, it went down from this big group of dancers, to very few people left. There was Carol D'Andrea and I. We became part of the Jet Girls!

You'd think I'd remember more, but it was at the same time as my last year of high school. I was thinking about the prom! I didn't know a lot about working with Jerry Robbins. I didn't realize! I didn't know until later in life how wonderful it was to be picked by him and to do that show.

Whenever I came up into the dressing room, if the older girls were saying something they didn't want me to hear, they would change the subject. And I knew that! I was the young one. I remember that once I almost missed a cue because I was all the way up in our dressing room. We wore these little Mary Janes in the ballet, and I ran down the stairs so quickly that the shoes broke. I had to go out there and dance shoeless.

The out-of-town audience was shocked on opening night of *West Side*. Both acts ended with a death! It was the first time a musical really ended with something like that.

We got much better reviews when we opened in New York than when we were out of town, but they still weren't like what they should have been. *West Side* became the classic it is now only after it opened.

Jerry was so wonderful. The way that he choreographed, you didn't even have to speak. You could dance, and the audience would know what was going on. That was what was so wonderful. It wasn't just a dance number for the sake of being a dance number. Sometimes Broadway is great when it's that way, but with Jerry, dancing was part of the action, or the talking led to the dancing. It was brilliant.

Jerry was a genius in many ways. He could do Broadway; he could do ballet. He saw things that I don't think many choreographers see. With Jerry, no matter what stage it was—Broadway or ballet—he was telling a story.

Recently, I went back to the Winter Garden and saw three of my students, Gerard, Sydni and Jacob all in *Mamma Mia!* That was exciting, to see all three of them dancing on that stage.

————————

There used to be Winter Garden dressing rooms on top of the theater. Marilyn D'Honau and the ladies of West Side Story *were up there. Years later, the original* Follies *ensemble was on the top floor. At some point, during the expansion of the restaurant next door, that room was taken away from the theater. The old Winter Garden ensemble dressing room is now occupied by Applebee's. Go to the Times Square Applebee's and you might be eating your spinach and artichoke dip where chorus girls of an era gone by once dressed!*

The Winter Garden is entrenched on an island of real estate that occupies the space between 50th and 51st Streets, between Broadway and 7th Avenue. It has had many showbiz neighbors over the years, from Nappy's, a record store with the same owner as Colony, to Ellen's Stardust Diner, where future Broadway performers sing for their supper. A Capezio dance store is nestled above Ellen's Stardust.

Perhaps the most famous showbiz neighbor of the Winter Garden is the real estate directly to the right, as you walk into the lobby. What is now a New York souvenir shop, an Asian restaurant, and the Times Square Applebee's were all at one point part of the same structure: a dance hall/club on top of the Winter Garden!

Between 1911 and 2003, the space was a ballroom dance venue called Palais de Danse, a French nightclub, a Spanish nightclub, and a Hawaiian nightclub.

In 1930, it was Les Ambassadeurs, where 22-year-old Ethel Merman got a big break and started a friendship with headliner Jimmy Durante. In 1943, the Café Zanzibar opened on the spot, with a bill that featured Ella Fitzgerald. In the next couple of years, legendary African American singers and musicians—from Louis Armstrong to Billie Holliday to Duke Ellington—graced its stages. The club was known for its integrated policies: black and white patrons were all welcome, and everyone danced together.

For years, advertisements billed the address of whichever club was next door as "Above The Winter Garden." The reputation of the venue was truly attached to the Broadway house downstairs.

————————

1959/1962: Queen Anne's Diamond

Charles Strouse, Writer

I was a rehearsal pianist when I started out. The only Broadway show I remember playing in the pit for was *Saratoga* at the Winter Garden in 1959. Usually, I played rehearsals or was an audition pianist for singers. I thought playing in the pit was boring.

Three years later, my show *All American*, with lyrics by Lee Adams and a book by Mel Brooks, opened at the Winter Garden.

At that point in my life, I wasn't as knowledgeable. It was a theater. I didn't realize it was *the* Winter Garden. I suppose it's like a diamond merchant. It's always a diamond, but only if you're knowledgeable are you aware that it's Queen Anne's Diamond.

Today, I'd be aware that the Winter Garden is Queen Anne's Diamond. Today, I know that it has a certain location and prestige and I know about the power of the Shubert Organization. But then, I was not that knowledgeable; I was more into the notes. I'm still that way, but today I'm also very excited, like: "Gee, could we get such and such a theater?"

Mel Brooks is one of my oldest friends. Mel and Lee and I had a lot of fun writing *All American*. The director at the time was Josh Logan, a man I grew to love, and still do, in memory... His choices were very different from Mel's and Lee's and mine. I really feel that we would've written a different show without Josh. I say that with such great affection for him. He was a man who was very dear to me. He was a friend. He's the first person who said, "Marry this girl!" back before my now-wife of 51 years and I got married.

He was also a great director, but his concept for *All American* was old-fashioned. When *All American* had just started, I brought him Barbra Streisand. I had played piano for her and thought she was terrific. Josh said, "She has a very good voice, but where am I going to hide her?" I never forgot that. Those were the days before feminism.

––––––––––––

The Winter Garden became a Broadway theater in 1911. It has the distinction of being one of only two currently operating Broadway theaters that began life as something else entirely! In 1880, the building we now know as the Winter Garden opened as the American Horse Exchange. Before that, the land was occupied by a farm.

The American Horse Exchange was a beloved landmark for those in the horse and buggy trade for about 30 years. Not all New Yorkers were thrilled that it was being demolished for a new "music hall." The Winter Garden has a unique shape: it's the widest theater on Broadway—and its mezzanine is only seven rows! That's because it was once a giant stable for horses and buggies.

––––––––––––

1960: Unsinkable

Jack Viertel, Creative Director of Jujamcyn Theaters

At *The Unsinkable Molly Brown*, I remember thinking for the first time: *You know, it's possible to not have that good of a time at the theater*. And you carry those prejudices with you forever. People keep asking me why Encores! hasn't done *The Unsinkable Molly Brown*—and it's because I didn't like it when I was 11! What do I know?

I wanted to be very careful at Encores!, not to make it my nostalgic trip down memory lane. I probably would've been kicked out if I tried! I will say though, that I always wanted to do *Anyone Can Whistle*. I saw the last performance of the original production right across the street from my office, at the Majestic. I knew it would take a while to get there, but I wanted to do it.

I don't know that there have been many others that I've done because I saw and loved them as a kid. The one thing we did do recently, that was silly beyond belief, had to do with the show *Nowhere To Go But Up*.

Nowhere To Go But Up has always been an obsession of mine, largely because it has never become a cult anything. It is a show that no one gives a damn about at all! Michael Bennett was associate choreographer and he danced in the chorus. Dorothy Loudon made her Broadway debut in it. Neither of these things made it a good show. It wasn't a good show, in fact.

60

I saw the second-to-last performance of it in 1962. It ran a week, and I saw the Saturday matinee before it closed on Saturday night. But I always, always have suspected that there was a much better show in there than the show they ended up with. The only things I really remember about it vividly were this dance number called "Yes, Mr. Baiello", which Ron Field choreographed, and the overture.

It was a prohibition era, bathtub gin, Tommy gun musical. It was like a comedy version of *Boardwalk Empire*. It was orchestrated by Red Ginzler, who died right after he orchestrated it. Jonathan Tunick was a mentee of Red Ginzler, and he followed him around.

At an Encores! orchestra rehearsal, I said to Jonathan, "Do you know where the overture to *Nowhere to Go But Up* is?" He actually *had* it, because he had inherited Ginzler's materials when he died.

That's how we ended up playing the *Nowhere To Go But Up* overture at the City Center Gala last year, for the 20th anniversary of Encores! I must say, it's one of the few times where I thought: *I have actually gotten the power to say we're going to do this, and no matter how stupid an idea it may be, we're going to do it.*

It's not that good, but it's relevant in the way that I remember. The overture starts out with four gunshots, and it ends up with a man being machine gunned to death, musically. It's got a lot of little ricky-ticky tunes in it. I just wanted to hear it one more time before I died.

Afterwards, at the dinner after the gala, one of our board members came up to me and said, "I was sitting next to James Lipton during the gala, and he nearly fell out of the mezzanine when he heard you were going to do this. He wrote the book and lyrics to *Nowhere To Go But Up*, and had not heard the overture in 50 years, since closing night." I went and introduced myself to James Lipton, who was very sweet and now runs *Inside the Actor's Studio*.

The show was important to me, because it was just a show that didn't work for anybody. It didn't work at all. I felt sorry for it. But something about it was special.

———————

One of my theatrical heroes, Ted Chapin, likes to ask people the telling question: "What was the first musical that you saw that you knew wasn't a good musical?"

The question is based on the idea that there's a turning point in each dedicated theatergoers' life, where they discover that Broadway isn't all Fiddler on the Roof *and* Hello Dolly! *There are also shows that don't quite come together—sometimes you wrinkle your nose up at them, and sometimes, you love them despite their flaws.*

I grew up in Florida, far from the bright lights of Broadway, so my discovery of "good" and "bad" musicals was quite different. I learned every show first from a cast recording. I had the chance to listen to a lot of shows that I knew weren't as acclaimed as a Fiddler *or a* Dolly, *and make up my own mind about them. Some of my recordings were from shows that ran a long while and some ran only for a moment—but they all got a fair shake as I read liner notes and made up my own mind.*

The original Broadway cast recording of Merrily We Roll Along *was one of the first that truly shaped my sensibilities as a theatre artist, not only because of the show itself, but because I thought:* Wow! How could this have been anything but a huge hit? I have to get to the bottom of this.

However, my own Nowhere To Go But Up *didn't come until years later. My first show-I-actually-saw-on-Broadway-that-I-knew-wasn't-a-good-show-but-loved-anyway was* Good Vibrations. *During my freshman year of college, this cheesy, teen-movie-style jukebox musical featuring the songs of the Beach Boys opened at the Eugene*

O'Neill Theatre on 49th Street. It featured a group of intensely talented young people making their Broadway debuts and singing and dancing their guts out, despite some elements of the show that didn't quite work.

It was my first year living in New York, and for the first time ever, I could just hop on a subway at NYU and go to "Broadway!" Having grown up light-years away from the Great White Way, the N/R train from 8th Street to 49th Street was a dreamland. I'd see the marquee for the Eugene O'Neill Theatre looming ahead closer and closer, as I ascended the subway steps. And every other weekend, I'd buy a student ticket to Good Vibrations.

Like Jack Viertel and Nowhere To Go But Up, *my inexplicable love for the show was swirled up with feeling a little bit sorry for it. The theater was often empty, despite great music and magnificent performers who were just starting out like David Larsen, Tituss Burgess, Chad Kimball, and Krysta Rodriguez. I rooted for the show, and found a special joy in it.*

At the final performance, I sat in the front row. As David Larsen sang the title number for the last time, tears flung off his face and hit the edge of the stage. I reached out and touched them.

I have a Good Vibrations *beach ball signed by the full cast of future stars. And I have a lot of memories of my first winter in New York, spent inside the sunny atmosphere of Beach Boys-land on 49th Street. Maybe it reminded me of sunny Florida and kept me from being homesick.*

I think I may have been the only person who repeatedly got a student rush ticket by herself to Good Vibrations, *and because of that, the box office treasurer remembered me. Six years after* Good Vibrations, *the Eugene O'Neill became home to* The Book of Mormon, *while I was working in a theatre office right next door. I passed the box office treasurer every day and we sometimes smiled at each other, remembering different times on the same street.*

I saw every new musical that came out that year, my first year in New York City. I loved a lot of them. But Good Vibrations *was special. It belonged to me.*

———————

1961: Caught In Chiffon

Eileen Casey, Actor/Wardrobe

I first moved to New York in the early 1960s. My parents drove me here. I stayed at a girls' residence on 85th Street called The Brandon House. You got two meals a day and your own room for $15 a week. I studied at the Metropolitan Opera Ballet School.

The first job I got was a television commercial for Welch's Juice. Donna McKechnie and I both danced in it. Then I did summer stock, and shortly after, I got my first Broadway show, *The Unsinkable Molly Brown* with Tammy Grimes.

It was at the Winter Garden, *Unsinkable Molly Brown.* It was like paradise. Oh my God, it was great. There was a definite feel in the air, there was a smell to the theater. It was just amazing; it was so exciting.

I was a replacement in the show, and my mother and father came to see my first performance. Gene Foote was my partner in the show; we did every dance together. Everything was going fine until the second act. In one scene, I had a chiffon dress with all this draping fabric on it, and a huge hat. Gene and I were doing this very fast dance and all of a sudden, my heel got caught in the chiffon. All of the material started trailing behind me, and every time I went to pick it up, Gene would yank me forward to keep dancing.

When the number was finished, I was in tears. It was my first night on Broadway! And my parents saw that! What a disaster. The next day, they fixed the costume, but I thought: *Oh, my career is over.* Every time I see Gene Foote on the street, we still laugh about that.

One night during *Molly Brown*, there was a fire in the kitchen of an adjoining coffee shop. Smoke started coming on stage! Tammy Grimes stopped the show and said, "I think something's on fire." We all ran out onto 7th Avenue, and it was the cast of the show, the audience, and all these coffee shop ladies with aprons. I remember it was pay night, because I asked my dresser, "Did you grab my money?" They paid us in cash in those days, and I used to pin it to my bra or give it to my dresser to hold.

The Winter Garden is my favorite Broadway theater. I did *Mame* there, too.

1964: Starting Now

David Shire, Writer

I played in the pit of *Funny Girl* for a couple years. I was the second pianist. The first pianist, Peter Daniels, was Barbra Streisand's first accompanist and arranger, who used to do her nightclub shows. He left after the first year and turned it over to me. I became the assistant conductor too, which was great because eventually when the conductor went on vacation or had to miss a matinee or something, I got to conduct in the pit. Conducting Barbra was—well, what could be more exciting?

After you play a show for a long time, you get so that you can almost play automatically. You know exactly when you need to get ready to play again, so in the meantime, you'd see a lot of magazines, newspapers, and paperbacks in the pit. And one day, one of the trombone players was reading *Playboy*. He was going through it, during a good part of "People". Barbra looked down and saw a centerfold unfolded in the pit. Immediately, we got a message that if Barbra ever saw anything like that distracting her from the stage, there would be no more reading in the pit. After that, everybody was a little more discreet.

Usually, I knew when I was going to be conducting in advance. But one night, I got to the theater very late. It was actually because I'd had a health scare and had to go to an emergency room. I was a little bit shot up with a narcotic. I got to the theater about 8:25 because then, shows started at 8:30. I thought: *Gee, how am I going to get through the show? I'd better be careful, because I'm a little woozy*. When I walked in, the stage manager said: "Oh there you are! Thank God! The conductor has phoned in sick tonight, you're on!" So I thought: *Oh my God. I'm going to be conducting* Funny Girl *on Broadway, high*! But I managed to get through it. I don't know how! It was pretty harrowing for a while.

Barbra recorded a song of mine and Richard Maltby Jr.'s before I was even at that job. Because all the young composers at the time were so excited about the emergence of Barbra, we all started writing songs for her. She picked a song that was in mine and Richard's first college musical, which was an adaptation of *Cyrano de Bergerac*. The ballad at the end, that Roxanne sings after Christian is killed, is a song called "Autumn", which was really the first decent song that Richard and I ever wrote. That was the first one she recorded of ours. It's on her fourth album. Peter Daniels, her pianist, recommended me for *Funny Girl* because he knew who I was from that. That's how I got the job.

Then, while I had closer access to Barbra for the next couple years, I would occasionally go up to her dressing room and play her songs. I took up a pile one matinee day and I remember playing her a song called "What About Today?" I wrote it as a folk song, for Peter, Paul and Mary. She said, "Well, let's play around with it." And of course, it was her idea to have that huge belt in the middle. We worked out the arrangement in the dressing room and it completely transformed the song. Thank God for Barbra, because Peter Paul and Mary thought it was "too Broadway" and never recorded it!

Another time I was up there, playing her songs, and... well, everybody would take her "Streisand songs," songs that sounded like all the songs that she was already famous for singing. But those were the songs that she'd already done, and she was always working for the *next* thing she was going to do. She didn't want to do pale imitations of things she'd already done.

I played her a few of those pale imitations, and she said, "What else you got?" Then I skipped a song that was in my folder, and she said, "What's that one?!" I said, "Oh, that's nothing, it's just a bossa nova I wrote, and it's a man's song anyway. I'm giving it to Robert Goulet." She said, "Play it for me!" And that was "Starting Here, Starting Now". I said, "It's a man's song." And she said, "No it's not." We transformed that one, just like "What About Today?" And that became one of the better known songs that I ever wrote.

I remember meeting Jule Styne a couple of months later. I said to him, "You know, Barbra recorded a song of mine. It was a man's song, but she wanted to do it." And he looked at me, and said, "Well, don't you know that's what Barbra always does? She likes the strong male songs. In fact, "People" was originally a man's song, but writing for Barbra, was... well, let's just put it this way: I used to think it was a song for a man." He wasn't surprised at all.

———————

David Shire got his start as a substitute pianist for Funny Girl, *and Barbra Streisand eventually recorded five of his songs, written with Richard Maltby Jr. These recordings launched the collaborators into the public eye.*

Two decades later, Maltby and Shire made their Broadway debut as a writing team with Baby. *The two became one of the most influential musical theatre writing teams of recent years, with other collaborations including* Big, Starting Here Starting Now, *and* Closer Than Ever.

For their Broadway debut with Baby *in 1984, Maltby and Shire wrote a much heralded score, with the jewel in the crown being "The Story Goes On". The song, premiered by Liz Callaway, is often pointed to as a landmark in modern musical theatre, a song that chronicles a moment no other song ever had (the first time a woman feels her baby kick) and a song that sounds like no other song ever had (Liz Callaway's voice inspired a generation of theatre singers).*

When I interviewed Liz Callaway, she told me about the time, a decade after Baby, *when she got to go into* Cats *at the Winter Garden, as Grizabella:*

"I went into Cats *and thought... I have part of Barbra Streisand's dressing room! Ken Prymus and I both had part of it, and a door between. It was a big thing to have a bathtub!*

"It wasn't a large dressing room. It was nice though, because you could look out the window on New Year's Eve, and you could see the crowds getting bigger and bigger on 7th Avenue. That was always incredible.

I know everything at the Winter Garden is all renovated now and looks great. But knowing that I had a part of Barbra's dressing room, that was really neat. Feeling like you were living inside the history of the theater."

David Shire had once shared the room with Barbra when they were both just starting out, and years later, Liz, who starred in David's first Broadway show, occupied the same space!

The story goes on.

———————

1964/1980: From Point A To Point B

Gene O'Donovan, Technical Supervisor

The first Broadway show I saw was *Funny Girl*.

I grew up in Brooklyn, and I couldn't remember ever having been that far north in Manhattan before. My family thought Manhattan was another country. I went with a woman I was dating.

Theatre was out of my periphery, totally. I wasn't particularly interested in it, although I remember having a great time at the show.

Years later, well into my career, I was there for *42nd Street*. It was the most complicated show I had done to date. When I look back now, the shows don't seem like they were technically challenging. But, at the time, *42nd Street* had this unprecedented volume of sets. How to make them move around was complicated, because at the time, we didn't automate things the way that we automate them now. We needed manpower to coordinate every single problem of: "How do we get this piece from Point A to Point B?" We couldn't have 12 people push it.

Honestly, you're always at the mercy of the theater, and every theater is different. You can look at the ground plan, but a lot of the time, you don't know what problems you'll really have until you're there.

1966: Everyone Was Laughing And I Laughed Too

Ira Weitzman, Musical Theatre Associate Producer at Lincoln Center

The first Broadway show that I remember seeing was *Mame*. My father took me to *Mame*, with Angela Lansbury.

I was just a kid, and the dazzle of it got to me. I remember thinking: *Oh, "Bosom Buddies" is so funny*, and of course I didn't understand the nuance of all the sarcasm like what "somewhere between 40 and death" meant, but everyone was laughing and I laughed too. It stuck with me.

1966: Coaxing The Blues Right Out Of The Horn

Red Press, Musical Coordinator

When you're a musician in the pit, you really can't tell if what's on stage is any good sometimes, until there's an audience. In 1966, I had just done five flops in a row. I was hired to do *Mame*, and I was really hoping it was good.

During tech rehearsals in the theater, I called my wife up and told her I didn't think the show was much of anything. Then, the first preview, the audience practically came in laughing hysterically! I looked up from the pit, and they were laughing, they had tears in their eyes at the young boy, they loved it!

One person alone sometimes can't really know what a group of people will laugh at. And another thing I realized: their laughing made me understand the show better, and *I* laughed. And it's not to be part of the mob. It's just that it's infectious. No matter what a show is, if you don't have much of an audience, they don't laugh much. Also, if you go to the theater alone, *you* don't laugh much! But when you go with your friends, it's contagious. That's a dramatic change.

Later on, I did a show called *Annie 2*. At the backer's audition[12], I thought it was hilarious. I called my wife and said, "This is going to be a smash!" We took the show to Washington, did the first preview, and watched people walk out. I understand why. They thought that Miss Hannigan really wanted to kill Annie, and they didn't understand the other side. To me, the show was funny. I liked its kind of humor. But the audience didn't! So you just never know.

1969/1970: Florida To Broadway

Penny Davis, Wardrobe Supervisor/Dresser

I grew up in Miami. When I was around 13, I had a lot of friends who went to the University of Miami, so I'd spend time there. A recruiter came over from the Coconut Grove Playhouse one day, asking if anybody wanted to come over and be a dresser. It was a paid position. I raised my hand, and they said, "Fine, come on over and meet our manager." I did, and he asked, "How old are you?" I said 18. I just kept being 18 for several years. And I started working as a dresser there.

Ann Miller did the last show of the season at the Coconut Grove Playhouse in 1969, which was *Mame*. I was the wardrobe supervisor and the star dresser for Ann. When she was hired to come up to New York to take over on the Broadway company, she asked me if I would come with her. Since we didn't do summer stock in Miami— we did winter stock—that suited me fine, because I never worked during the summer. So I went, "Sure," and came up to New York for six months. That was 40-some years ago. I kept getting work, so I stayed.

On Broadway, at one point, during "Open a New Window" the stagehand didn't lower Ann far enough down, so she had to jump off the swing—and she sprained her ankle. She filled out the accident report, and I handed it to the stage manager. He said to me, "Penny, I can't turn this in. You fill it out for her." Because where it said "Occupation," she had written: "STAR."

We were at the Winter Garden Theatre, and in those days the star dressing room, which was on the fourth floor, was actually three rooms. It was a little suite. The bathroom had been decorated by Barbra Streisand during *Funny Girl*. There was red paisley wallpaper that was quite fabulous and a full bathtub! The whole bathroom was very ornate and lavish.

Then there was the main room that Angela Lansbury had decorated when *Mame* started. She had done a commercial for the department store Korvette's and in exchange they furnished the dressing room for her. It was this very English style décor: green bamboo, with white crowns. There was an elaborate sitting room with a wet bar!

A year after *Mame* was gone, I went to see *Follies* at the Winter Garden with Ann and we went backstage afterward to say hello to Gene Nelson and Alexis Smith. At that point, I saw that the dressing room had been broken up into two or three smaller rooms.

There were a lot of funny things that Ann did. I never saw anybody work so hard. And she didn't know how to mark[13], so she just did well.

She was blind as a bat, so when she was on stage, it was difficult for her to see with those bright lights in her face. During the cakewalk of the "Mame" number, girls' hairpins would always fall out of their hair. Ann was always worried that somebody would slip on a hairpin, so one night, during the number, she kept bending over

---

[12] backer's audition: a presentation of the material in a show for potential investors
[13] mark: to perform with only partial commitment and energy

to pick the hairpins up. As Kathy Robey was going around in front of her, Ann dropped the pins down Kathy's bodice. When the intermission came, Kathy screamed Ann out. Ann was so bewildered, because she meant well. She just didn't think that it was going to be distracting in any way to drop hairpins down somebody's bodice while they were dancing!

I only did two shows as a dresser before I became a wardrobe supervisor on Broadway. *Mame* and then *Georgy*. We're up on Joe Allen's wall[14] for that one. It was a short run.

I can still remember a couple of the songs from it, but it was never recorded. It was a charming show. Not without its problems, but it really was sweet. That was at the Winter Garden, too.

On *Georgy*, we went to New Haven, and there was a two-thousand-pound jungle gym set that opened the show. The jungle gym was huge, and flew in, and ran the whole proscenium. The show originally started with Georgy and all these kids playing on this jungle gym.

They decided the jungle gym scene wasn't the best way to open the show so they scrapped the whole thing. When we loaded in to our next pre-Broadway stop, the Colonial Theatre in Boston, there was a gigantic pile of steel outside the stage door. It was sold for scrap metal for $27! That was the big surprise to me in my first experiences with Broadway. That there was so much waste.

Georgy was my first show in New York in production. And in Florida, we did huge productions, but we were very efficient. For example, in Miami, we did the same-size *Mame* with five dressers, that in New York we did with 19! I would sometimes say, "In Florida, we did…" and the wardrobe supervisor would say, "This is Broadway, dear. This is how we do things here."

———————

Georgy *was a musical very closely based on the movie* Georgy Girl, *which starred Lynn Redgrave and had come out only four years earlier. This was a rare occurrence on Broadway in 1970, to base a new musical on a recent movie. And even when it did happen, the writers would have to distinguish the properties from each other to discourage constant comparisons. They certainly didn't capitalize much on the movie's brand.* Promises, Promises, *which was based on the movie* The Apartment, *wasn't called* The Apartment: The Musical.

Part of what critics didn't like about Georgy *was that it seemed like a movie that they had just seen—but slowed down. This kind of adaptation wasn't the norm, and critics were sour on it. But the show, about an unlikely young heroine in an unconventional storyline about unexpected pregnancy and the compromises of modern American life, had a lot going for it that critics didn't see.*

The lyrics were by a 22-year-old Carole Bayer. (She would add the married name "Sager" later, and also write hit tunes like "That's What Friends Are For" and "Don't Cry Out Loud", among others.) The book was by Tom Mankiewicz, who, after an executive from United Artists saw one of Georgy's *four performances, was whisked off to Hollywood and wrote many of the James Bond films. The score, by George Fischoff, had a really brassy, bouncy, young pop sound, that was new to Broadway at the time. It would be done to more acclaim later in the decade, such as in Sager's 1979 musical with Marvin Hamlisch,* They're Playing Our Song.

———————

---

[14] Joe Allen's wall: Joe Allen, an iconic theatre district restaurant on 46th Street, has its walls covered in posters from short-lived Broadway shows

1971: You Could Hear The Drums

Jason Kantrowitz, Lighting Designer

I remember on my junior high school trip to New York, we ate at Hawaii Kai before going to see *Purlie* at the Winter Garden. It was multi-level, and they used to have a Hawaiian show. You would be in the Winter Garden, and you could hear the drums!

————————

Just like having an apartment in New York, being in a theater in New York is a guarantee that you'll get to know the neighbors.

In 1962—after a string of short-lived dance-halls and nightclubs—a more successful tenant moved in next door and on top of the Winter Garden. Hawaii Kai was a Polynesian-themed restaurant that luau'd next door for three decades. At Hawaii Kai, you could sip a rum punch while gazing at a waterfall and a bevy of hula dancers. As Jason remembers so vividly, the luau could often be heard backstage at the Winter Garden! In 1990, when Times Square began to be cleaned up and rents skyrocketed, Hawaii Kai had to close up shop. Shortly after, Applebee's moved in.

Since the Winter Garden is indeed so anchored in a block filled with other businesses, there were many accounts of the neighbors in my interviews. The coffee shop fire during The Unsinkable Molly Brown *took place on 50th Street and 7th Avenue, where a New York souvenir shop called Toast of Broadway now stands. During* Follies, *cast members would complain that the stage left wing smelled like Chinese food, because air from the restaurant downstairs came up through the vents. Several actors who started out as singing waiters at Ellen's Stardust next door, have become Broadway performers themselves. The Winter Garden island is always changing around it.*

————————

1971: Stages Like That

Ted Chapin, President of The Rodgers & Hammerstein Organization/Past Chairman of the American Theatre Wing

The Winter Garden. First of all, anybody who did not see the original production of *Follies* has to put the Winter Garden and *Follies* in proper perspective. The genius—the *overlooked* genius—in every subsequent production of *Follies* has been what designer Boris Aronson did.

Boris designed the set of *Follies* specifically for the Winter Garden, which has a proscenium opening wider than most Broadway theaters. There were two downstage towers that were obscured behind the proscenium arch at the Colonial Theatre in Boston when the show tried out there. Some of the staging got lost in Boston, but everyone knew it would be different when we got to New York.

When we all saw the set for the first time in the Winter Garden, it was like: *Oh! That's what he had in mind!* The scenic design of *Follies* is so anchored to what the house is like. The proscenium is one continuous frame at the Winter Garden, so Boris had designed columns on either side with tops that made it look more like a traditional proscenium opening. Of course this being *Follies*, they were crumbling. It gave a definition to the proscenium that was subtle but really, really smart. Also, it looked great from the balcony.

I do remember that backstage, if you kept walking up, there were one or two big chorus rooms, and also a wardrobe room. There were two overcoats up there that were to be worn by Young Buddy and Young Ben. They were black and white because all the ghosts were in black and white—and they cut them. I loved those coats, but I didn't have the guts to say to someone, "Can I have one of those?" Probably a naive thought that I could have been given one...

68

That must have been the wardrobe room, with windows overlooking 50th Street. I think that space has probably been taken by the Applebee's now. I also have a very cool photograph of Gene Nelson standing on the marquee that I think Van Williams took for some article.

I didn't hang around the theater in New York the way I did in Boston so I don't know too many of the antics, but I do know that you could go up, on stage right, a couple of floors up to where there was a little balcony. You could look down on the stage which was kind of cool.

I was not at the closing performance. I was working in California. I kind of went on to the next thing. I would touch base every now and when I was in New York and the company was cordial to me. It didn't feel like a cult show, but there were also rabid fans who made it known they were coming back to see the show again and again.

Even though I moved on, I had kept notes from my experience, which was very lucky. I had never kept any kind of journal before, nor have I kept one since.

One of the things I'm very proud of in my book is that it shows how in those pre-computer days, you could actually change technical things quickly, like where the first act ended. It was a matter of manpower and instructions written on paper, so the stagehands could try something new each night. The end of the first act was indeed changed in four subsequent preview performances, and then eventually it was decided to do the show without an intermission. It would take a week to program the computers for even one change these days! The workshop process is where that kind of structural work is supposed to happen these days, so that the show is pretty set when you go into the theater. You've got a lot of computers to deal with now.

There was a gathering of some of the *Follies* cast members the other day, and I was looking through Martin Gottfried's big *Broadway Musicals* book, because I wanted to point out to someone the photograph of Harvey Evans in *New Girl In Town*. I was flipping through it, and I saw a shot of a guy backstage during *Annie*, which was a few years after *Follies*, and there are the old-style lighting dimmers. *Wow. That's a thing of the past.*

For my thesis at NYU, I adapted the book Everything Was Possible, *by Ted Chapin, into a screenplay.*

Ted was the production assistant on the original Broadway production of Follies *when he was in college in 1971 and he kept notebooks about his experience. In 2005, he turned these notebooks into a book.*

When I was the director's assistant on the original Broadway production of [title of show] *as a senior in college in 2008, I kept notebooks about my experience at the same time as I adapted Ted's. So,* Follies *and* [title of show] *will always be tied together in my mind. That year, as we were getting ready to move into the Lyceum, I could rattle off five thousand details about* Follies, *but I often just looked around and said one: "Everything was possible." So many of Ted's experiences seemed to mirror mine, and this was a Broadway almost four decades later!*

I was constantly inspired by Ted's enthusiastic tales of being a sponge in the midst of a new Broadway musical being created. If you haven't read Everything Was Possible, *you're missing out, and you should take a quick break from this book and go buy a copy of that one.*

1971: Pinwheels And Maroon Shoes

John McMartin, Actor

Follies tried out at the Colonial, and then we came to New York. I just knew that we were in something unusual because everything about the process itself was unusual. We rehearsed in the Bronx, on the set, which was exciting and rare. We had these major movie stars doing a show, which was rare. We had two directors, Hal Prince and Michael Bennett, which was rare. And they worked beautifully together. It was a marvelous time.

We worked a lot on the intermission. Eventually we didn't have one, but we tried putting it in lots of places. It was always hard for the audience to get back on track. With *Follies*, you really needed the audience to stay there. "You will stay here and watch this or the mood will be ruined!"

At the start of *Follies*, the stage was pitch black. An oboe came in, and then there was a lightning flash on stage, where you thought you saw something there. Then, these Vegas showgirls who were about 6'7'' entered. When we took the show to Los Angeles after it closed on Broadway, we stopped at the MUNY in St. Louis, which is outdoors. I remember starting *Follies* with the sun still up. The whole thing didn't work at all!

There's nothing like being in a theater. The Winter Garden was perfect for *Follies*. I do remember one thing with my dressing room. I had a nice little room, with a cot for relaxing. Sometimes, I'd lay down on it and think, "My God, there's a leak there." Later on, I found out it was coming from the chorus bathroom. There were pipes above me, and every time they'd flush, water would come into my room! So, it's not all glamour.

Whenever I go by the Winter Garden, I think: *I played here.* I think that about the Palace where I also played, but even more so the Winter Garden, because it's always fresh in my mind since *Follies* is still such a talked-about musical. Some people hated it and other people came to see it many times.

People used to come up to me and tell me that they thought the breakdown I had during "Live Laugh Love" was for real. They really believed I had forgotten the lyrics. I never looked forward to doing that part because it hit too close to the bone. Fellow actors tend to remember that moment, because we've all been there. That's our nightmare: that we'll go out on stage and be totally on, and then experience that sensation where our eyes become pinwheels.

Once the curtain comes down on a show I'm in, I'm usually the first one out. However, I'm always the first one there, too. I always get to the theater an entire hour before half-hour[15]. Don't ask why, I have not a clue! Then, once the show is over, I want out, and fast. One time, during *Follies*, I was at a bar afterward, and realized that I still had my maroon shoes on from the show. I had to go back to the Winter Garden. Another odd thing was that since I'd get to the bar so quickly, sometimes people would think: *That couldn't be him.* And they'd start talking loudly about how much they loved the show, or hated it!

The closing performance of *Follies* was devastating for me. I don't know why. I suddenly found myself in tears. It's hard to sing that way, and I surprised myself by being so moved. I didn't always have that when I closed shows, but now I find that it's there all the time. It happens especially when the show's had a long run. Because it's your life.

———————————

As a young person who had just moved to New York, spotting John McMartin at Sardi's was the most "New York" thing I did. I couldn't believe that I could actually see the original Benjamin Stone having a drink at the most theatrical spot in town.

---

[15] half-hour: 30 minutes before the performance is scheduled to begin; when most performers are expected to be in the building

As my years in New York continued, I became even more in awe of John McMartin, getting to see him in many shows. I even got to watch his performance of "The Road You Didn't Take" from the wings of Avery Fisher Hall during the Sondheim 80th Birthday celebration.

For my interview with him, like so many other Broadway luminaries in this book, John actually invited me into his home. It was a great privilege to see so many parts of New York via the location that each interviewee chose for our chat. In Riverside Park, Danny Burstein and I chatted amongst playing children and summer winds. In William Ivey Long's studio, I got to see costumes for his upcoming season of new shows. I interviewed Brynn O'Malley in her dressing room at the Palace and Jose Llana in front of the Public Theater, both in the middle of two-show days. I met people's wives, husbands, kids, and dogs.

I saw more of New York when gathering interviews for this book than I had seen since I moved here. I conducted 200 interviews all over Manhattan, Brooklyn and Queens. And not only did so many of the locations tell me more about the subjects, they taught me more about New York. I met producers in their offices, actors in their dressing rooms, and set designers at diners. I know who has a regular table at which restaurant. I know who likes coffee and who likes tea. I know all these big things, and all these little things too.

———————

1971: One Or Two Acts?

Harold Prince, Producer/Director

Follies. I just loved *Follies.* Everything about *Follies.* It ranks among my favorite shows that I've done.

The most important thing about *Follies* is that I dug deeper into myself and, because of that, it was one of those shows that was inspired. You cannot make a career of that as a director or as an artist, and wait to be inspired every time you work. It won't happen. But this was one of the rare occasions when I felt: *I'm inspired. Something is working inside of me, and I'm coming up with ideas and solutions that I haven't thought through— they're just there.* That was *Follies.* I'm very very proud of what I did with it. And I will never see a revival of it.

The thing with *Follies* was: *Should it be one or two acts? One or two acts?!* And I don't know what it ended up as, actually. I can't remember.

———————

From 1912 to 1924, the Shuberts produced an annual edition of The Passing Show *at the Winter Garden. A large scale revue in the style of the* Ziegfeld Follies, *the productions often spoofed the theatrical events of the previous year. A* Forbidden Broadway *of the early 20th century!*

The 1922 edition marked the Broadway debut of Ethel Shutta. Ethel was a star of vaudeville, Broadway, and radio. In 1971, at the age of 74, she returned to the Winter Garden Theatre to sing "Broadway Baby" in Follies *and look back on her days "pounding 42nd Street to be in a show."*

The Ziegfeld Follies *and* Follies *were both held at the Winter Garden, decades apart. This eerie detail added another layer to the latter show's time warp element.*

The 1936 edition of the Ziegfeld Follies *at the Winter Garden starred Fanny Brice and Gypsy Rose Lee, and two decades later, both women would be posthumously immortalized in shows about them,* Funny Girl *and* Gypsy, *on the very same stage.*

———————

1971: Echoing Their Old Steps

Christopher Durang, Writer

I have a vivid memory of seeing *Follies* from a partial view, $10 seat when I was in college. I saw it twice, and it's one of my favorite productions of all time. The brilliant work of Stephen Sondheim and James Goldman, Hal Prince's direction. I was so impressed with all of it, even though there were parts that I couldn't see.

And the "Who's That Woman" number was one of the best things I've ever, ever seen in my life. The older women who were in the "Follies" years ago were suddenly dancing with their younger selves and echoing their old steps. It was just so intricate and emotionally complicated—the conception of the song and the choreography by Michael Bennett was just thrilling.

1970/1971: Breathtaking

Michon Peacock, Actor

One show that hugely impacted me was *Follies*. *Follies* is probably my favorite musical.

Being an erratically employed dancer, I didn't go to the theatre much. We were just too poor, but somehow I managed to see it. That original production of *Follies* was just breathtaking! During the overture, I sobbed. I was amazed at the theatricality but also the storytelling through the book, music, songs and dance. First of all, I couldn't believe that Hal Prince and Michael Bennett were working together on this. Their vision was just fascinating. I thought it was stunning, and it showed a lot of heart as well. I really felt the characters' struggles.

Obviously, it must have been a great partnership—Stephen Sondheim and Hal Prince and Michael Bennett—because each one of them had such an impact on the show as a whole.

When I did *Seesaw* with Michael, he created this commercial, slick, New York show that was maybe two-dimensional. But *Follies* had a huge amount of depth. It didn't feel like a commercial product. I was in awe of it.

I don't even remember much about being at the Winter Garden performing in *Georgy*, but I remember vividly being there seeing *Follies*.

About *Georgy*, what I do remember is that we had a large cast, and an enormous number of costume, make-up and wig changes. It seemed like we were always running around, trying to find our way back to the stage. It was an amazing theater, but we had this feeling the whole time that we would be doing a short run. We were in previews, saying to ourselves: "Just breathe it in, breathe it in, and get ready to move on!"

I ended up with a lot of friends from that company that I stayed connected with for a long time. But our time at the Winter Garden went by in a blur.

───────────

Because the Winter Garden is where Follies *opened, it has become a touchstone for me, in the heart of Times Square. I can sit for hours between 50th and 51st Street, across from the Winter Garden Theatre.*

It's become my personal tradition to check in at that spot each year on the night before the Tony nominations and take stock of what the season has brought. I think about our great business of show, and all of the dreams coming true and all of the hearts being broken. The spirit of those things combining feels very Follies. *Good times and bum times...*

72

The Winter Garden represents the grandness and timelessness of Broadway to me. Its wide amount of real estate on Broadway itself has stood unchanged for a century. In photos from the 1920s, everything else on the block looks completely different, but the Winter Garden still stands the same, with its long marquee and gleaming billboard above the theater.

1972: Much Ado About The Winter Garden

Peter Link, Writer/Actor

One day, I got a call from Joe Papp. He said, "I've been watching you. You write really good music but you don't understand theatre." And I said, "Yeah, you're right. I can't figure this out." So he said, "Why don't you come work for me? I want you to be the composer-in-residence." So that's why I went to the Shakespeare Festival and did 40 shows there in five years.

It was fabulous. It was 'where it was at' the time! One of the productions we did was *Much Ado About Nothing*, which we did in the park and then moved to the Winter Garden. The production had a great concept by our director A.J. Antoon. It took place during the 1904 St. Louis World's Fair and I'm from St. Louis so I had a sense for the music. I understood the old songs from that period and the feel of what the score should be.

We had a perfect cast and a beautiful set, and when Joe moved the show to the Winter Garden, it got even better. We said, "How can we ever match what was in the park?" But we did. There was a beautiful little gazebo built on the Winter Garden stage, and we did a 20-minute concert before the show started, just like we did in the park. The oom-pah ragtime band played about ten songs that I had written, and in Central Park, people would come early and sit with the band. It was a beautiful preface to the show. And we did it on Broadway too.

The Winter Garden is my favorite theater by far. I mean, it's *on* Broadway! There's something about the way the Winter Garden feels and sounds. They built it right. There's something about it.

1974: She Has A Man Dressing Her!

Randy Graff, Actor

I grew up in Brooklyn. *Fiddler on the Roof* was my first Broadway musical, but another show that really struck me was *Gypsy*.

Gypsy was a big one. I was in college, and my father brought me to see Angela Lansbury. We went to a matinee, and we sat up in box seats. Because of where I was sitting, I was able to see the actress playing Gypsy Rose Lee make all of her quick changes in the wings.

I remember what her dresser looked like. He was this short, stout man. And I remember thinking: *Oh my God, she has a man dressing her!* I could see her make every single quick change. It was enthralling, just to watch the backstage business. That was pretty magical for me.

1974: Sing Out, Louise

Kathleen Marshall, Director/Choreographer

My first Broadway show was a revival of *Gypsy* with Angela Lansbury at the Winter Garden Theatre. I grew up in Pittsburgh, and my grandparents were in Boston, so every year at Christmas we would drive back and forth.

One of our Christmas presents in 1974 was that on the way back to Pittsburgh we would stop in New York and see a show.

We didn't know what it would be, and we didn't have tickets; we were just gonna pull up and try to see something. So, we came in with our station wagon and we wanted to see *Gypsy* because of course, we knew the show. We had the cast album and we knew who Angela Lansbury was from cast albums and movies like *Bedknobs and Broomsticks*.

We pulled up to the Winter Garden, my parents went in, and I remember they said "Oh, we don't have any tickets to the matinee but we do have five tickets for tonight." Now, I realize those were house seats[16]. I remember my parents had to have a little conference in the lobby of the Winter Garden because I think the tickets were something like $17.50!

Of course, we begged to see it. It meant staying overnight in a hotel in New York City—which was a very big deal. They bought the tickets. We were in the tenth row center. So there we were, our first Broadway show, and there comes Angela Lansbury with her entrance down the aisle saying, "Sing out, Louise!" That was pretty magical.

1976: Respect For Each Other

Lonny Price, Actor/Director/Writer

My only tradition that I always do on shows is that on the first day of rehearsal, I remind people how lucky we are to be doing this, and that there's a long line of people who would love to be here, and that we must have respect for what we're doing because people don't get to do it. I think it's a privilege to be here, and I expect everyone to treat this show with that kind of respect. Just that. That's the speech all the time.

It's not just "don't be late" but "have respect for each other" and "have respect that there are a lot of people who are waiting tables who wish they were here so let's honor them by being truly grateful." That's something that I do on every show.

I just know that everyone is so important. What I learned from Hal Prince and Steve Sondheim, when I was working on *Pacific Overtures* as the gofer, is that everybody is needed. The stage door man is to be respected as is the woman who beads the clothes in the afternoon as is the star. Everybody gets treated the same, with the same kind of respect. They exhibited that every moment I was around them. They still do. That was something that impressed me greatly.

The thing about Hal is that when I first started directing, he was doing *Phantom* and I was doing a show in the basement of a supermarket on 28th Street, and he'd say, "Lonny! How's your show going?" as though we were both doing the same thing. He always made me feel like we were both directors and we both had the same problems. It didn't matter that his show cost ten million dollars and I paid $4.50 for my set. Those men taught me to respect everybody and that stuck.

During *Pacific Overtures*, I was at the Performing Arts High School, and I worked for Hal as a gofer after school. He gave me the run of the theater, so I had a great time just watching. The Winter Garden was a beautiful theater to be in. You don't get in it much because there are always hits there. You'll be in it once, and then not again for ten years.

---

[16] house seats: tickets in prime locations for each performance, reserved for actors and members of the creative team; the most powerful people involved with each productions usually have a certain number of house seats in their contract and can choose to pay for them or release them for each performance

I watched *Pacific Overtures* a lot, I also mimeographed the new pages and kept Hal's script up to date. I stuffed envelopes. I did whatever they told me to do, just so I could be around. They were my heroes. I loved it. And *Pacific Overtures* was an amazing piece of work. The idea that Hal produced that on Broadway still blows me away. It was a hard sell. No stars and this Japanese kabuki concept!

That's part of why I thought *Merrily* would run. I thought: *Well, they ran* Pacific Overtures *for six months, and that was a really hard show to get people to want to see. We've got snappy music! He'll at least run it six months.* So when our closing notice went up, I was shocked. He had never closed a show that quickly.

Pacific Overtures was the first time I was really allowed backstage, and I was 15 years old. I was over the moon. I was the boy who had taken his Bar Mitzvah money and invested it in the show!

The day of the opening, Ruth Mitchell, Hal's associate, called me. She said, "Someone has stolen the rickshaw! You need to go to the theater and wait for the Pinkerton men."

Pinkerton was a detective agency. There I was, 15 years old, and I got out of bed and went to the Winter Garden Theatre. I sat on the hanamichi in a darkened theater. If somebody were to come, what was I going to do? If they said, "Give me the other rickshaw!" I would have screamed, "No! You can't have it!" I mean, I was protecting the set from robbers and I was 15. I sat there waiting, like: *Someone's stolen the rickshaw! I need to sit on this stage and protect the rest of the set!* And I did. I remember sitting there all morning.

I don't know who has that rickshaw though. I don't know where that is!

———————

After I interviewed Lonny, I took the 1 train downtown to go meet some friends. Wrapped up in the moment of having just gotten to interview one of my favorite people, who embodies what I love about theatre, and who also happens to be an original Merrily *cast member, I barely noticed until it was right in front of my nose. I was walking up the subway stairs at Broadway and 50th Street to the view of the Winter Garden Theatre, sparkling right in front of me. I couldn't help thinking:* I should really look for that rickshaw.

———————

1976: I Was Younger Then

Amanda Green, Writer

I loved musicals growing up. I don't think I ever thought I would write one myself, but I do remember vividly seeing *Pacific Overtures*, hearing "Chrysanthemum Tea" and going "Oh my God, if I could just do *that*!"

The rhymes were so ingenious. It was the weirdest subject in the world, but it really appealed to me as a kid because of the genius, fun, witty rhymes. So I think that spurred my passion.

1976: A Post-Law School Education

John Weidman, Writer

While I was in law school, I decided that I was going to write something for the theatre, and all of a sudden *Pacific Overtures* was being optioned by Hal Prince and going into production.

I had never had the experience of working on shows at another level, off-Broadway or even in college. I had *gone* to shows my whole life, but I had never been part of the process of getting something from the page to the stage. Everything was new to me. Tech rehearsals in Boston, getting a really bad review from Kevin Kelly in the Boston Globe ... everything was surprising. Everything had kind of an incandescent quality to it: the good stuff, and the other stuff as well.

I do remember coming back from Boston and arriving at the Winter Garden Theatre for the first time, and seeing the front of house. I remember seeing the name of the show, and seeing the cards that were up, and thinking: *WOW. This is my show, and here it is.* I'd seen a number of shows in the Winter Garden, which was, and still is, an amazing theater. But to see my own there was astonishing. It was a little scary and very thrilling.

There was one preview where we had a bomb scare. We were approaching the end of a matinee performance, and they had to empty the whole theater out. Everyone hung around and then came back and we actually finished the show.

I also remember that when the show opened at the Winter Garden, there was a scene in the second act that involved a rickshaw. Later on, we would cut it. But during the load-in, the rickshaw, along with a lot of other stuff, had been left on the sidewalk in the back of the theater. Because the rickshaw had wheels, somebody stole it.

Apparently, there was an understudy rickshaw ready to go on that night. But I remember that in the middle of everything else that was going on, someone ran up to Hal Prince and yelled, "Somebody's stolen the rickshaw!" Hal was sorting out a lot of problems, and that was one that he certainly didn't need to deal with.

One of the things that is remarkable about the Winter Garden is how big the orchestra section is, and how shallow the balcony is. You can stand at the back of the house and see almost the entire audience, along with the show in front of them. Which means you can get a great sense—not just from the noises they are or aren't making, but visually—of how things are playing.

I've always loved houses that accommodate authors at the back of the orchestra, in a way that allows them to watch the show, and pace, and go outside and come back in. Theaters that don't architecturally permit that really piss me off. Theaters with seats all the way to the back wall just seem genuinely cruel. So I love that spot in the back of the orchestra at the Winter Garden.

––––––––––––––

You can't imagine my delight at having heard the same story, from different perspectives, about a rickshaw from Pacific Overtures *that hadn't been seen since 1976. Everyone has "a fragment of the day."*

In writing this book, many times I heard the same memory, but from two or three different perspectives. Every theatre experience is made up of big moments shared by many. Opening nights and standing ovations and waiting at the stage door in a crowd... we all share those. But a magical thing about theatre is that even the little moments are shared, and we might not know about it.

When you turn the corner and get your first excited glimpse at the marquee of the Broadway show you're about to see, there's an actor, who's about to perform for you, looking at that same marquee out their dressing room window.

When you're in the wings on stage right perfecting that dance move, there's a treasurer in the box office who just sold a ticket because of how exciting the dancing looks.

When you're in the basement, putting a final touch on a costume that will later win a Tony Award, there's someone changing the lyric to a song that will be sung months later on the broadcast.

There are people on opposite sides of New York City who think about a show that they did 37 years ago, and both conjure the same memory of a small wooden rickshaw.

1976/1982: My Second Family

James Maloney, Stagehand

Because my dad was a stagehand, I got to be around a lot of theaters when I was growing up. On *Pacific Overtures*, I learned how to operate piano boards, which don't exist anymore on Broadway. It was the first time I'd really gotten to run around and explore a theater. Later on, I did that with my kids.

During *Pacific Overtures*, I was 16. I ran the piano boards and I fell in love with the business then and there. At one point, I tried working electrical construction, but it didn't feel the same as working in the theatre. To this day, the theatre is my second family. I've gotten close to people on every show I've ever done. I've worked in many, many theaters and now I'm the production house electrician at the New Amsterdam. I've spent a lot of time there, but I still go and work outside that theater on new shows. I like to continue working in all of the houses.

Years after *Pacific Overtures*, I got to go back to the Winter Garden to do *Cats*. My dad was the production electrician, and I was his assistant, the board operator. We worked together there and everybody at the theater was great to work with.

Cats was early on in the new trend of megamusicals that started coming to Broadway. We had to cut a hole in the roof so that the staircase in the set could ascend to the heavens. It was a huge production and a big undertaking.

I worked on *Cats* for 14 months, and then I left to do other productions. For me, it's hard to sit on one show for a long period of time. I always love to keep moving. The industry does not sit still for a second. If you sit on a long-running show, the business is going to move past you, especially the technology. Today, everyone's using LED lighting fixtures, which we never had back then.

McHale's on 46th Street and 8th Avenue was a famous place to me, growing up. My dad would take us there for dinner on a Sunday. He knew everybody. All the stagehands would stop by after their matinee. Musicians would hang out there, too. You could go to McHale's to get a job. Someone there would always know work that was coming up at a theater. When there were jobs on a new show, the house carpenter or house prop man from that theater would go to McHale's and everyone would meet and find out what was going on next. It was more than just a watering hole.

Now, I have a daughter, Ashley, and three sons who are in the business: Jimmy, Brendan and Matthew. They work side by side with me on projects. Matthew is one of the flight operators on *Newsies* right now. Brendan travels around the country working on systems in theaters. Jimmy is a prop man and also works as a carpenter in automation. All three of them love the business. It's a great tradition to pass on.

McHale's on 46th Street and 8th Avenue was THE Broadway stagehand bar. Many lament its demolition, in January 2006, to make way for Platinum NYC, a tower of condominiums.

McHale's was one of those bars that made Broadway feel just like a small town, where everyone knew everyone and you could get a casual bite to eat and see half your friends. When asked about lost Broadway haunts, producer David Stone said, "Everyone's going to tell you about McHale's. McHale's was a stagehand bar, mostly. They had good burgers, and you didn't go there after the show to see and be seen, the way that Bar Centrale is now. You went to McHale's to say hi to your crew and get drunk. It is very missed. People will talk about it for years."

When McHale's went out of business, the theatre community thought the bar might open in a new location. The place was too popular, too beloved, to just disappear completely. The stagehand community had flocked to the place every day and night for decades. And as the legend goes, on St. Patrick's Day all stagehands drank for free at McHale's!

But like so many other theatre joints over the years, McHale's did just vanish. There's no sign on the corner of 46th and 8th of the thousands of stagehands and theatre professionals who, during the 62 years McHale's was in business, raised a glass together there..

When McHale's closed, several pieces of the bar were sold or scattered. In fact, if you find yourself in the back room of Emmet O'Lunney's bar on 50th Street—within view of the Winter Garden Theatre—you can sit next to a big neon sign that was saved from McHale's.

1976: Cancel The Auditions!

Joanna Merlin, Casting Director

I was an actor in *Fiddler on the Roof* and then Hal Prince asked me to start casting for him. The first show I worked on was *Company* in 1970. He asked me to be his casting director because he knew I liked actors and we had a good relationship from when he produced *Fiddler*.

I came in halfway through the casting process of *Company*, and then for *Follies*, in 1972, I cast the whole original company. I cast *A Little Night Music*, and meanwhile, I was on Broadway, performing in the musical *Shelter* at the same time.

Then Hal told me he was going to do a straight play called *Pacific Overtures*, about the opening of Japan. It seemed very adventurous. There were many Asian roles in it, and it was very difficult to find actors of Asian descent at the time. Because the only two shows that really cast Asian or Asian American actors up to that point were *The King and I* and *Flower Drum Song*, shows frequently used Caucasian actors to play Asian parts.

We sent out an audition call and no actors of Asian descent arrived. None! I began a search. I contacted little community theatre groups, I put ads in newspapers in Chinatown. It was very difficult! There were a few actors in Los Angeles who had worked on television. Slowly but surely, I started gathering appropriate actors. There were also some Caucasian roles in the play, that would be played by Caucasians.

On the day of the final auditions, Hal called me and said, "Cancel the auditions! *Pacific Overtures* is going to be a musical." I asked, "A musical? About the opening of Japan?" He said, "Yup. Steve Sondheim is going to write it." And then he decided that every single role would be played by an actor of Asian descent.

I began a huge search. I needed Asian or Asian American actors, and they had to act, sing and dance. I went to San Francisco and found Gedde Wantanabe, who was a Japanese American street singer, and he ended up in the show.

I would have these crazy open calls. At open calls, you don't ask anyone to make appointments, you just say, "Anyone can show up!" At one of the final open calls, a Japanese man walked onto the stage, and sang. He was amazing. We had him read a scene, and he was amazing. I said, "Who are you? Where did you come from?" He replied, "My name is Isao Sato and I am from Japan. I heard about this show and I came from Japan to be here."

He hadn't even contacted me! He just came over from Japan in 1975! He ended up playing one of the lead roles in the show.

We saw guys who were nightclub singers, people who had only done community theater and school productions, street performers. What was so amazing was that these performers were given the opportunity to work in a beautiful production with people who were at the top of their game and the top of the industry. They were given very rich things to do. It was a show with great substance and beauty. There was such a wonderful uplifting spirit about the production because it was as though things had changed and Asians and Asian Americans were now on Broadway, being seen in a different way. There was the expectation that all of their careers had kind of begun.

Of course, the world had not changed, and what was so disappointing was that afterwards, most of them didn't work. They booked some commercials. And anyone who needed an occasional actor of Asian descent called me for advice.

Toward the end of casting, we had only one role left to cast. An actor came in who looked Caucasian. He said, "My grandmother is Japanese. I am one fourth Japanese!" Well, at that point, I didn't have anybody else. He was great, and we cast him. We made up a fake middle name for him: Omi. So, he was James Omi Dybas. We chose to believe him.

The other unfortunate thing about the show that I always think about is that shortly after it closed, one of the younger performers died of AIDS, and another young performer died in a car accident. Isao Sato was going back to Japan, flying his own plane, and he was killed. It was really tragic because they were all really young. I had developed a different feeling for that cast.

The Broadway audience was not really ready for the show and its level of sophistication. I'm not sure that they were really interested in the subject of what the show was about. In 1976, they were used to more commercial shows. Broadway was different then. There were a couple Sondheim shows, but this was still early in the game. Overall, Broadway was more commercial then.

Everyone rose to the occasion in different ways. Hal and Steve went to Japan. All of the fabric and costumes were actually from Japan. Boris Aronson's set was one of the most beautiful I'd ever seen. There was a great camaraderie between the creative team and the company. It was very exciting.

Subsequently, there have been many revivals. It's an extraordinary show. I remember how exciting it was to see the score develop. Steve used to have this sunny room, like a solarium, and many of us on the production went to listen to the score at his place at a certain point. I listened to it many times when it wasn't totally finished. The first time I heard his songs for *Pacific Overtures*, I thought: *This man is a genius.* I had known it before, but what was born out of this story was so creative and so connected with history and culture—and also so entertaining! I'll never forget those days, first listening to the songs.

1976: Faux Japanese

James Dybas, Actor

I told a fib to get into *Pacific Overtures*.

I had just worked with Pat Birch on *Truckload*, and one afternoon, I got a telephone call from her. I knew she was going to be doing the choreography for *Pacific Overtures*. In fact, I had already gotten her an opening night present, a copy of the book *Shogun*.

Pat said, "I have recommended that Joanna Merlin, Hal Prince's casting director, call you about auditioning for *Pacific Overtures*. You're part Asian, right?" I said, "Absolutely."

Hal Prince wanted the show to have an all-Asian cast, since it was being done in the kabuki style. They'd cast a ton of actors of Asian descent already and some of them even had real experience in kabuki. When we were chatting, Pat told me I might want to use my Asian family name for the audition.

I told Pat there was someone at the door, and I ran to the copy of *Shogun* on my table. I flipped through the pages, and I kept seeing the name "Omi." So, I ran back to the telephone and said, "Sorry to keep you waiting. As a matter of fact, my mother's grandmother's last name was Omi." We decided that my name would be James Omi-Dybas.

On our first day of rehearsal, several actors wore kimonos and special shoes. So during lunch break, I jumped in a cab and went down to Chinatown to buy some.

One day, Hal came up to me and said, "How much of you is actually Asian?" I thought: *Here we go. I'm out.* I made a joke, and he laughed. I think he knew. However, I had been doing the work, and they liked what I was doing.

"Someone In A Tree" was my favorite part of the show to perform. How could you top that? "Someone In A Tree" wasn't my song originally. At one point in Boston, the song wasn't working, and Hal came up to me and told me that he and Steve both wanted me to try it instead of the other actor who had been doing it. The song is about eight minutes long, and I learned my part over a weekend. I spent a lot of time in Steve's hotel room behind the theater, with the ashtrays filled with cigarette butts and cups of coffee on the piano. Then, I performed it for him, Hal, Pat, and Ruth Mitchell. When I got to the theater later that day, they told me the song was mine. I thought: *Now the work really begins!* What an honor and a privilege it was to perform that song.

I got the Gypsy Robe during *Pacific Overtures*. It was opening night and we were in our dressing rooms. All of a sudden, I heard a woman calling my name. It was Donna McKechnie in our theater, with a big Hefty garbage bag! Donna comes over and says to me, "Happy Opening!" She had the Gypsy Robe for me, that she had just gotten for *A Chorus Line*. We had a ceremony on the stage.

I had help making a fan with everyone's name on it, to go on the robe. Then, a little while later, I gave the Gypsy Robe to an actor in the next show that opened, *Rockabye Hamlet*! It just so happened that the recipient was Louann Ogawa, the only Asian American actor in *Rockabye Hamlet*! I guess turnabout is fair play.

After that show closed quickly, Louann called me up and said, "Are you going to take the Robe back?" I told her of course not, and that we had to give it to the next show. "But it's full!" she said. So I made a new Gypsy Robe out of cheese cloth backstage at the Winter Garden and we gave it to Barry Preston, who was in *Sophisticated Ladies*.

Now, people make really elaborate patches, so only about six or seven shows are on each robe. But back then, there were about 20 shows on a Gypsy Robe! The Gypsy Robe that ended with *A Chorus Line*, *Pacific Overtures* and *Rockabye Hamlet* had a patch from *Gypsy*, and a long yellow brick road from *The Wiz*.

I will never, ever forget closing night of *Pacific Overtures* on Broadway at the Winter Garden. We sang "Someone In A Tree", and my last lines are "cups of tea and history and someone in a tree." My hands go up to the skies and I lift my head and look at it and then I fold my arms and then I walk off. My dressing room was on the second or third floor, so after the song, I would schlep up all those stairs at the Winter Garden. That night, the applause was still going on as I was walking up the stairs. I mean, what a thrill!

————————

The tradition of the Gypsy Robe began in 1950, when Bill Bradley, a chorus member in Gentlemen Prefer Blondes, *sent a dressing robe from the show to his friend in* Call Me Madam, *to bring him good luck. The chorus boy from* Call Me Madam *fastened a rose from Ethel Merman's costume onto the robe, and sent it onto a friend in the next show. Because a musical's chorus members are often referred to as "gypsies," this tradition was born as "The Gypsy Robe."*

On opening night of a new show, the Robe is bestowed on the chorus member with the most credits. The entire company forms a circle on stage, as the newly crowned king or queen of the gypsies goes around the circle three times, counter-clockwise, letting everyone touch the robe for good luck. There are now dozens and dozens of retired robes, filled with patches from every new musical production.

1964/1976: The Greatest Show Of All Time

Jack Gale, Musician

I can't help but feel like *Fiddler on the Roof* is the greatest show of all time. I was lucky to play it in 1976, when Zero Mostel returned to the role at the Winter Garden.

It was transcendental! There are parts of the show that bring tears to your eyes and other parts that make you laugh, and they are seconds apart. Later, my daughter did *Fiddler on the Roof* in grade school and it was just as brilliant of a show. That's a mark of a great musical: no matter who does it, it turns out great.

Earlier, at the same theater, I played in the pit for *Funny Girl*. One night, a dancing girl on stage was being spun around, and she flew right into the pit—it looked like a missile was coming, because she was spinning into the pit! She landed right on top of one of the musicians, and we were terrified that she was dead. But the orchestra kept playing, and the people on stage kept dancing, and she bounced out of the pit and finished the number.

1977: The Beatles' Broadway Debut

Abe Jacob, Sound Designer

Back when we did *Beatlemania* in 1977, it was very difficult to try to recreate the sound of the Beatles' recordings! We almost had to try to do it on the fly eight times a week. George Martin and the Beatles only had to make it right once in the studio, but the live show was over and over again.

I think we were relatively successful with *Beatlemania* at the Winter Garden. We made sure we had the right loudspeakers and right amplifiers for that sound and the mixing console was adequate. Everything else was done analog, as opposed to how we'd do it today: digitally.

Beatlemania was a look at the 1960s as seen through the music of the Beatles. It wasn't so much a tribute to them. *Rain* was different, because that was really a homage to the Beatles themselves. *Sergeant Pepper* was another Beatles music show that Tom O'Horgan put together, which was really one of the first jukebox musicals. It used the music of the Beatles to tell the story of Billy Shears.

For *Beatlemania*, we were able to take seats out of the middle of the Winter Garden floor, and make the place look like a concert hall. We had sound and lighting set up right in the middle of the theater. Sound designers always have to bear in mind the economic factor of taking away seats. Now, when you're talking about $125 per seat, eight times a week, over a long run, it makes a big difference how many seats you take out for the sound console.

The songs of the Beatles have been used in many Broadway shows over the years. The first was Beatlemania *in 1977, followed by* Rain *at the Atkinson in 2010 and* Let It Be *at the St. James in 2013. Songs by members of the Beatles were also used in the Broadway shows* Rock 'N Roll! The First 5000 Years, *a revue that played the St. James in 1982, and* Lennon, *which told the story of John Lennon's life and played the Broadhurst in 2005.*

1977: Projector Problems

Randy Morrison, Stagehand

Beatlemania was an enormous amount of fun. Everybody enjoyed it. It was the last show on Broadway that used what's called piano boards, which are the old-fashioned resistance lighting boards. And we had slide projectors, as well as two 16mm movie projectors.

There were two Beatles bands who performed *Beatlemania*, and we used to call them Bunk One and Bunk Two, like we were at camp. Before the show began, they studied movies of the Beatles and watched the way they moved. They sat in a studio and mimicked it over and over and over until they got it right.

We went to Boston to try out the show and the projection area had a huge amount of technical difficulties. The slide projector had over a thousand cues in the show! It was very difficult to get through the show without a disaster. Something always went wrong. It took us at least three or four months to call a totally clean show.

We were always behind, and when we got near the end of the show each night, we'd say, "We're never going to catch up the slides, so we might as well just pick an image to end with." We put up a picture of all the people at Woodstock and that was on the curtain when it came in.

During *Beatlemania*, we would go to Barrymore's all the time. *Beatlemania* had an early curtain, so we could get to the round table in the back before anybody else got there. All the Broadway sound people used to go to Manhattan Chili Company on 43rd Street, which is no longer there. Now, everybody goes to Glass House Tavern on 47th Street.

1979: Hysterically Filthy

Bryan Batt, Actor

My first Broadway show was *Gilda Radner Live from the Winter Garden*. It was a limited run one summer. *Saturday Night Live* had just hit like crazy and I was mad for Gilda Radner. It was one of my first trips to New York and my mother and my grandmother took me. It was at the Winter Garden Theatre where I would later play for a year and a half in *Cats*.

I remember everything about Gilda's show. And I have a memory of my grandmother—a very proper Southern lady, who came to the theatre wearing gloves. We were sitting in one of the box seats and Gilda Radner came out in these cute little pink overalls and a little headband and started to sing this hysterically filthy song called "Let's Talk Dirty to the Animals" in which she just uses every four letter word possible. I really thought my grandma was going to grab me by the scruff of my neck and drag me into a cab and send me home, never to see another Broadway show. Instead, I looked over, and my mother and my grandmother were in tears of laughter, hysterically enthralled with Gilda.

The Winter Garden has a long history of great comedians, starting with Al Jolson and Fanny Brice in the 1910s and including everyone from Rob Reiner, who appeared there in his only Broadway credit, a play called The Roast, *to Gilda Radner, whose* Live From New York *was the hit of the summer of 1979.*

Al Jolson's reign at the theater at the beginning of the 20th century was extraordinary. Jolson had his first big Broadway hit there, with La Belle Paree *in 1911. He opened several musical extravaganzas at the Winter Garden in the 1910s. The Playbill of the wartime 1918 Al Jolson musical* Sinbad *had the interesting program note: "The young men of the chorus are not eligible for military duty." From 1928 to 1932, the theater fell out of theatrical hands and was turned over to Warner Brothers, who showed movies. The first attraction was Al Jolson's movie,* The Singing Fool. *Jolson would find a way to get to the Winter Garden, no matter what!*

––––––––––––––

1980: How Lucky I Was

Don Stitt, Actor

This friend of mine, Raymond, convinced me to come to New York from San Francisco. I took the chance, and decided to give Broadway a shot. Raymond had a job tending bar, so if I needed something to eat or if I needed a beer, I could just show up.

One night he said, "Come on, Stitt, we're going to a show tonight." I said, "What are we seeing?" He said, "*42nd Street*." "You mean, like, the Warner Brothers movie? I saw the movie for free! It's going to be 20 bucks for standing room!" "Trust me, you want to see this."

This was the Monday after it had opened. I had heard that the director Gower Champion had died and like everybody, I was sad because I had so much admiration for the man. But I'd recently seen his short-lived *A Broadway Musical*, a long way from his *Hello, Dolly!* and *Bye Bye Birdie*. So, I wasn't expecting *42nd Street* to live up to the hype. I thought: *Oh, they just feel bad because he died on opening night.*

We got standing room tickets and when we walked into the theater, we saw Adolph Green with Phyllis Newman. I said hello to him, because we'd worked on the movie *Simon* together. They were there with Betty Comden and her husband, and Stephen Sondheim was also there with Tony Perkins. Everyone was talking about how *42nd Street* had recorded their cast album the day before. I was seeing the sixth performance of *42nd Street*.

All of a sudden, I just couldn't believe how lucky I was to be in the world of the Broadway theatre. I mean, I wasn't actually in it yet, but I was hanging around with people who actually knew people from Broadway and I was seeing Broadway shows. And the show was *fantastic*.

1981: Assistant's Assistant Assistant

Fritz Frizsell, Stagehand

42nd Street at the Winter Garden Theatre was my first Broadway show—I was an assistant's assistant sound designer, essentially little more than an intern, a note-taker and a place keeper.

I had heard a lot of stories about David Merrick, the abominable showman, and I didn't know what to expect. He cancelled a preview at the last minute. "There was a snake loose in the theater", he said.

Opening night was crazy. It was clear at the curtain call that the show was a huge hit. The cast and audience were jubilant, and the crowd went wild when Merrick himself took the stage. "I have very sad news" he said.

The audience burst into laughter. "No, no" he went on, "Gower Champion died today." The mood instantly shifted from ecstatic to a shocked chaos. Everyone was stunned, some of those on stage near break down. Jerry Orbach ended the uncomfortable situation by shouting into the wings "Bring in the curtain!" The curtain was rung in, and the baffled audience filed out, murmuring, wondering what the hell it was that they had just witnessed.

The opening night party at the Waldorf was surreal, a bizarre amalgam of funeral and celebration.

That was David Merrick - he would do or say anything, no matter what the cost, be it financial or emotional, to get the results that he wanted.

———————

One preview of 42nd Street *was famously cancelled when David Merrick told the press there was a snake in the theater—oh, he didn't mean it literally: an unwanted reporter had shown up. Merrick wanted his show protected until the very last moment. Newspapers reported that the show was in trouble and that Merrick's stunts were failing him. But just like Peggy Sawyer, the show went out there a youngster and became one of the biggest hits of the decade.*

Merrick's bio in the 1964 Playbill for his hit Hello, Dolly! *read, in part:*

Mr. Merrick is the greatest producer, living or dead, the latter condition being wished upon him by most of his competitors. In the past ten years, Mr. Merrick has presented 38 shows, most of which have been smash hits…. A man of unlimited virtues, not the least of which is becoming modesty, Mr. Merrick is handsome, affable, affluent, and influential.

Merrick's 1980 bio in the 42nd Street *Playbill read:*

DAVID MERRICK (Producer) puts on plays, puts on movies, puts on musicals, puts on comedies, puts on everyone and everything. He has been doing these things since November 1954, when his first musical, Fanny, *opened. The end is not in sight.*

42nd Street *was David Merrick's last Broadway hit.*

———————

1981/1994: I Actually Packed Up My U-Haul

Heidi Blickenstaff, Actor

The first Broadway show I ever saw was the original David Merrick production of *42nd Street* when I was around nine years old. That was at the Winter Garden.

My family didn't know what TKTS[17] really was, but we got in line and felt so insider-y. We got tickets that were in the balcony. I remember the curtain coming up, and seeing all those tap shoes doing time steps and just thinking: *This is it. This is totally it.*

It struck me hard. Even though I had known since forever that I wanted to be on stage, I was having that synergistic moment of being in my first Broadway theater and seeing a show like *42nd Street*, so classic and so satisfying. It certainly crystallized my dream for me. I remember literally sitting at the edge of my seat and my mom smiling at me because she could see that I was totally hypnotized.

---

[17] TKTS: discount ticket booths in the middle of Times Square operated by the Theatre Development Fund

I moved to New York in 1994, when I graduated from Duke University. I actually packed up my U-Haul, just like the song says, and drove with a couple of my good friends who were also graduating, from Duke up to New York, New York. I moved into a place in Murray Hill with a friend of mine from high school who had not gone to college and was working as a model. And I got a job almost immediately waiting tables at Ellen's Stardust Diner, next to the Winter Garden.

I actually opened Ellen's Stardust Diner. I trained at the old Ellen's, which was on 6th Avenue near Carnegie Hall. Then we opened Ellen's Stardust where it is today, on 51st and Broadway. We were hired as singing waiters. I waited on JFK Jr. twice, and he ordered the corned beef sandwich.

Most of my customers were wide-eyed tourists, so excited to be going to see *Cats*. That was always fun, because I was there pursuing my dream, and they were there, excited to go to Broadway shows, so it was all part of the same stew. It certainly wasn't my favorite job, but it was the only time I waited tables. Five months later, I booked the national tour of *Tommy* and left the restaurant. That's when I started working as an actor.

1982: The *Cats* Theater

Nancy Coyne, Advertising and Marketing Executive

When *Cats* moved into the Winter Garden, that was a moment in time. My daughter was six years old, and I took her to opening night. Nineteen years later, when *Cats* closed, she said, "Mommy, I didn't know it was the Winter Garden Theatre, I thought it was the Cats Theatre!"

It said *"Cats"* up there for so long, how could *Cats* be leaving the Winter Garden? But now *Mamma Mia!* has re-branded it the Mamma Mia! Theatre. The Winter Garden is a great theater to have landmark status. It's right there, front and center, as is Broadway.

———————————

In the last 30 years, only two shows have played the Winter Garden: Cats *(1982-2000) and* Mamma Mia! *(2001-present).*

There was nearly a year between Cats *and* Mamma Mia! *where the Winter Garden sat empty, being un-felined, as it were. The entire theater had to be revamped and all the cat fur had to be dug out of the walls.*

But before Cats *and* Mamma Mia! *took over for their three decade reign, the Winter Garden was filled with new shows all the time. In the 1950s, the original production of* Wonderful Town, *starring Rosalind Russell, opened at the Winter Garden. The show had hits like* Funny Girl, West Side Story, Purlie, *and* Mame, *and short-runners like* Doctor Jazz, Georgy *and* Jimmy. *From 1950 to 1980, over 65 productions played the Winter Garden.*

As of this printing, Mamma Mia! *has just left the Winter Garden and the new musical* Rocky *will open at the Winter Garden in spring of 2014.*

Rocky *will be the first new American musical to open at the Winter Garden since* 42nd Street *in 1980.*

———————————

1982: 43 Years at the Shubert Organization

Robert E. Wankel, Co-CEO and President of The Shubert Organization

I've been at the Shubert Organization since 1970. That's a long time, so I've seen a lot of shows. I've developed many favorites over the past 43 years.

I'm an accountant by profession and I was part of the outside auditing firm that audited the Shuberts. I came here in 1970 as an auditor. I was offered a job within the organization in 1975 as Manager of Financial Planning. I was in a more corporate position at first and didn't have direct involvement with shows. I would say the first shows I worked on with more involvement were the larger musicals in the 1980s, such as *Cats* and *Jerome Robbins' Broadway*.

We like to think that all of our Shubert Organization theaters have a fantastic history. There's a lot of history in the theatre in general, lots of excitement.

The theatre is a community and we're very involved. We're a theater owner, we are producers, we are a ticketing company with Shubert Ticketing/Teleharge, we have road theaters so we're presenters. We wear a lot of hats and are very involved in every element of the business.

The entire theatre industry is very involved with each other through our trade association, The Broadway League. The League pulls together lots of different committees and everyone there is a family.

Even though we have "competitors," we're not really competitors. We all believe that the more theatre, the better. Sometimes you're very competitive with each other temporarily, in chasing after a show. But in the end, the more hits on Broadway, the better the community is as a whole.

Cats started in London, and was very successful there. We became the United States producers, with our partners. It was exciting. We had just renovated the Winter Garden Theatre, and then Andrew Lloyd Webber wanted us to paint it black! And of course, we had to build that heaven scene. We actually created a 60 foot structure above the theater, for the "heaviside layer." It was a pretty big construction job, and at one point the show ran two million dollars over budget.

Cats opened to less-than-wonderful notices, but it was a big mega-hit. It played for 18 years and made the Shubert Organization a great deal of money. At one point, we had five companies around the country!

1982: Don't Let The Cat Out Of The Bag

Bert Fink, Press Agent/Senior Vice President of the Rodgers & Hammerstein Organization

There's a reason why the longest-running show on Broadway in history is *Phantom* and the second-longest-running is *Cats*. Those musicals have global appeal. At the St. Louis MUNY, this week they're doing *South Pacific* and next week they're doing *Les Mis*. Some people may say negative things about "the British invasion," but I think it's great.

Now, these shows seem like they've been around forever, but when *Phantom* opened, it was an event. When *Les Mis* opened, it was an event. When *Cats* opened? It was utterly audacious! A song and dance cycle, set to the poetry of T.S. Eliot? It was a bizarre, unique theatre piece.

And the Fred Nathan Company and Serino, Coyne & Nappi came together and used some ingenious marketing and press ideas. *Cats* ran for 18 years and there was never a photo of the show in front of the theater! For two decades, you walked past the Winter Garden and all you saw were black posters with yellow eyes.

During its first year, *Cats* turned down a chance to be on the Macy's Thanksgiving Day Parade. Nobody does that! But they didn't want to give it away; they didn't want to show on television what was happening in the theater. They kept it mysterious. You didn't get to see an image of what happened inside unless you bought a ticket! For the first year of the run, every night when the first actor dressed as a cat came on stage, there would be a gasp. Nobody knew what to expect.

1982: Nine Years Of *Cats*

Sally J. Jacobs, Stage Manager

Because my father, Bernie Jacobs, worked for the Shubert Organization, I went to the theatre all the time when I was little. He used to hoist me up on balconies to watch shows like *The Music Man* and *My Fair Lady*. I saw a lot.

He was the Shuberts' lawyer at first, and then in the 1970s, around the time that I was graduating college, he became President of the Shubert Organization. That was good for me, because I needed a job. So, I got started. I had no idea what I wanted to do in the theatre, but I was in the fine arts, so I started with props.

My first professional theatre job was at the Public Theater, during the time that *A Chorus Line* was happening. I was 23. I worked there for several years.

Then I started to stage manage on Broadway. I did *Cats* for about nine years. It was a very exciting production. *Cats* took every trick in the book, from any actor.

At some point during a long run like that, you start having to spend time trying to keep the understudies engaged, so they don't dress up in drag backstage because they're bored.

Bonnie Simmons, who was in the show, used to put a cough drop on the emergency light before each performance. By the end of a few years, there was a stack of cough drops that was so high.

I remember one night, Laurie Beechman stopped the show completely in the middle of a song, and made the orchestra stop playing because she heard a man in the audience who was having a heart attack. She helped to save his life, and he came back to see the show.

1982: Crashing Through The Heaviside Layer

Harry Groener, Actor

Everybody knew from the minute that *Cats* was announced. Everybody knew that if you got into that show, you'd have it forever, for as long as you wanted it. It was a given that whoever played Grizabella was going to win the Tony. There was this formula set forth by *Jesus Christ Superstar*. *And* the show had been such a hit in London. *And* they had built up such audience anticipation in New York! A year before the show came in, there were posters all over the place. *Cats* everywhere.

Getting a Tony nomination for *Cats* was unbelievable. I couldn't believe it was happening. I stayed in the show for 14 months. It was an incredible experience! We were in the hit of the season. I had never heard a response from an audience like the one on *Cats'* opening night.

Of course, in *Cats*, we were supposed to crawl all over the audience and interact with people. The kids went nuts, but adults did too. They got the fantasy of it and had a grand time. One night, I was downstage center on the lip of the stage and I saw, in the second row, Robert Redford and his kids. Diana Ross and Michael Jackson came. Gregory Peck led a standing ovation one night.

During the Rum Tum Tugger number, Terry Mann would go out into the house and get someone to come on stage and dance with him. One night, he saw my wife, Dawn, in the audience, so he got her! After they danced, he brought her back into the audience, and her earring was still on stage. It was a gold bauble earring, and he picked it up and threw it to her. She was at least ten rows back in the audience, and she raised her left arm up and caught it! The audience went nuts; they thought it had been staged. Terry was stunned. I said, "That's my baby!"

At the end of the show, a hole in the ceiling opened and this magical staircase lowered down so that Grizabella and Deuteronomy could get onto it and go up to the heaviside layer. There was one crazy night when the scenery making up the heaviside layer crashed. The hole opening was controlled by a stagehand pulling a rope, and the staircase was controlled by a button being pushed. This night, it seemed to us on stage like the stagehand had pulled the rope too hard. The hole opened, and then it snapped shut. But someone had already pushed the button for the staircase to go. There was a huge crash. And the staircase started crashing through the plywood that was supposed to move aside!

A couple things fell onto the stage! We scattered out of the way but the show kept going. There was a crazy amount of noise, and we scattered, but the show kept going. When the staircase finally got there, Betty Buckley just shook her head. Grizabella changed her mind. She wasn't going to the heaviside layer. The staircase left without her. We tried not to laugh!

1983: The First One

Charlotte D'Amboise, Actor

My most memorable audition in a Broadway theater was at the Winter Garden, where I auditioned for *Cats*. It was Easter Sunday, it was 11 o'clock in the morning, and I was about 16 years old. They never do auditions at the theater anymore and they never do auditions on Easter Sunday now either.

In those days, you'd have just a light on the stage and you'd walk in the stage door. It was really cool. That day, there were five of us called back for three roles. I remember my mom and dad said, "See ya later!" and left me at the theater. It always amazes me that they did that, because I wouldn't do that with my kid!

Cynthia Onrubia walked into the room and I thought: *Ah. I lost the job. I'm not gonna get it now*. She was already well-known. She got one of the roles, deservingly. And I'll never forget that day of auditioning. It was an incredible experience. I didn't get it, but I wasn't ready for it. I was 16. Eventually, I got the first national tour, and then I got moved to Broadway and I met Terry Mann, my husband. Another thing I remember about the Winter Garden is a lot of making out with him in the *Cats* tunnel pipe that's part of the set. We'd come out afterward and I'd have smeared make-up all over my face. "Nothing was going on in there!"

I also remember lots of times sleeping in a dressing room between shows and hearing Scott Wise tapping up and down the hallway. He would just tap and tap and you could hear it all over the place, because he had so much energy. A lot of my favorite memories are of that theater because it was the first one. The first is always the most memorable.

————————

30 years later, Charlotte is currently co-starring with her husband, Terrence Mann, in Pippin *at the Music Box Theatre.*

————————

1983: L.A. to Broadway

Steve C. Kennedy, Sound Designer

The first Broadway show I ever worked on was *Cats*. I was working on *Evita* in L.A. for Abe Jacob. He asked if I would come to New York and open *Cats*.

When I first got to the Winter Garden, it was completely torn apart. I've never seen the inside of the Winter Garden as a theater! I've only seen it gutted, and then how it looked for *Cats*.

Working on the show was great. I was new in New York and I didn't know anybody. The crew was friendly and we all got along wonderfully. *Cats* did a lot of things that were innovative. The band was off stage. They had pieces flying in the air. They restructured the building for the weights needed for the set.

Andrew Lloyd Webber used to come up to me while I was mixing *Cats* and tell me, "Loni said to say hello!" because he'd just been over at *Evita*. Loni Ackerman, my wife, was playing Eva Perón across the street at the time.

I'll never forget opening night of *Cats*, because Abe Jacob, the sound designer, had been fired from the show. So instead of going to the party, we all took him out to dinner first. It was his birthday and he had brought me to New York to work on my first show. *Cats* was pretty memorable.

———————

I interviewed Steve C. Kennedy and his wife, Loni Ackerman, at the Cosi just across from the Winter Garden. We stared at its blinking lights the entire time. Halfway through the interview, Steve said, "I'd like to work in the Winter Garden again. I still have friends over there."

———————

1988: Memories

Loni Ackerman, Actor

I did *Cats* for three years. I was the third Grizabella, and replaced my good friend Laurie Beechman.

I was excited to do the show, but when they said, "Okay, let's have you go up on the tire," I almost left. I was terrified and shaking! But I thought: *I have to put shoes on my kids' feet*. I'd just had my son, George. But I was always scared to go up in the tire. I used to shake every night! The only time it got easier was when the understudy for Old Deuteronomy went on, because he was more afraid than I was so I would help *him*!

I remember a mouse ran over my foot once, right before I went to sing "Memory". I just thought: *Well, he must think I'm a cat*. But the best thing about that show and the Winter Garden, was that when my husband, sound designer Steve Canyon Kennedy, was doing it, our son Jack took his first steps at the theater! Then when I was doing the show, in the exact same place in the theater—right by the sound section—our other son, George, took his first steps. Theatre babies!

When George was three years old he used to sit on the steps with my dresser and watch the show. I remember one time when the tire was about to go up, he knew the show so well that he said, "Bye bye Mommy!"

My sons grew up backstage in theaters; that's just part of who we are. They also had a regular life, so they have both sides. I find it so special that they took their first steps in this theater where I saw *West Side Story* and *Once Upon a Mattress* as a kid. They've got the same smell in their nostrils.

When I came in, *Cats* was six years old. It was pretty set, but I tried to make the role my own, as far as trying to make the performance real. Unfortunately for me, I got sick a lot. I was a mom with two little kids, so I'd always catch what they had. That was hard. When you don't have kids, you just worry about yourself. I thought I'd lost something, but really I was just in a different place.

I remember someone in the show said to me, "You need to be a diva again. You're too nice when you sing 'Memory.'" And I thought: *They're right. I need to have an edge to my performing again.* I lost the edge. When you become a mother, you have to put parts of yourself away. We never put posters around the house, because we wanted our boys to come into their own, not see our successes and feel like they were in any kind of shadow.

Later on, we did put up posters, and my son George said, "Why didn't you put these up?" But we didn't want that. I did lose a part of myself, in a way, at that time. And *Cats* was a way to try to find it again.

1988: Candy Wrappers

Telly Leung, Actor

The first Broadway show I ever saw was *Cats* at the Winter Garden. I remember seeing it with my mom and my grandmother, who barely spoke any English.

We were right near the aisle where the cats would come into the orchestra section! Grandma had never been to a Broadway show either, so she didn't know the rule about the candy wrappers. I remember in the middle of some quiet ballad, there was my grandma, crinkling and crinkling. The cats were on the aisle, and fully in character, they meowed at her! They hissed at her, like: *Stop with the candy!*

Finally I had to tell her. My grandma just didn't know! She barely spoke English.

———————————

In the early 20th century, the Shuberts, inspired by an idea they saw in France, built a bridge over the audience of the Winter Garden, so that headliners and showgirls could parade over theatergoers. Due to the showgirls' skimpy outfits, the bridge was nicknamed "the parade of thighs." Cats *extended its reach into the audience as well, but this time, audience members would not be titillated, they would be hissed at!*

———————————

1988: Technically An Understudy

Jessica Molaskey, Actor

I was on the road with *Cats* and there was a woman in the show who figured out exactly how many days she could be out before she would get fired. If it was nine, she'd be out for eight and then come back for one. So, they literally added a contract to the show and she'd go on for her one show and I'd go on for eight. I was technically an understudy, but I was on for almost every performance, in one role.

When I got moved to the Broadway company, the first time I went on was New Year's Eve, without a rehearsal. That was a hard show to get thrown into. There's this thing called "The Swirl" in the opening of *Cats*, and if you were three feet off one way or the other, you'd get creamed. I remember walking on Broadway after the show ended that night and looking down and seeing program inserts with my name on them, littering the street.

During one performance, I had a guy put his hand right on my ass. I just turned around and hissed!

The Winter Garden is beautiful. At the opening of the second act, we used to slide out at our own pace, and I would lie there and just look out.

1991: Gutted

Bryan Batt, Actor

The Winter Garden was totally changed and gutted for *Cats*. It was a big junkyard. We called it The Litter Box. There were all these oversized set pieces for us to climb around to make us look like we were the size of cats. It was fun.

All I wanted to do when I saw my first Broadway show, *Gilda Radner Live*, was to be on Broadway. And then the second Broadway show I was ever in, *Cats,* was right there, in the same house. Just to be in it and be part of it, just to go in the Winter Garden stage door every night, was so special.

I did *Cats* for a year and a half. While I was there, Loni Ackerman was Grizabella, then Laurie Beechman, then Liz Callaway, then Lillias White.

Laurie Beechman was one of those great souls who touches your life in a special way and you know you'll never be the same. She was one of those friends who I went to when anything was going wrong, or sometimes just to talk. She always had this clear vision about what to do and she was always right. She had that unbelievable voice, and an unbelievable heart too. She was very ill with cancer for many years, and would get chemo, and then come back. Whenever she'd come back, we'd go to Elaine's and have martinis together.

During the show, when she would come on, that haunting sound when she sang "Memory"... I remember being on stage shaking and my eyes welling up. She was very complimentary to me about my performances too. She would always say, "You are making such contact." It was this belief that, okay, yes, I was a cat, but you've got to be the best cat you can be! You can make connections with people.

My mom sent a king cake during Mardi Gras and the tradition is that in the king cake, there's a little baby. Whoever gets the piece with the baby is supposed to get the next king cake. It's a big tradition in New Orleans where I'm from. We ended up playing "Pass The Baby" on stage after we found it. The cat who had it would put it in their paw and no one saw it in the audience. Then someone dropped it into one of the slits in the stage, and it was in the middle of the track that brought in the tires, so these wheels were gonna crush this little plastic baby! It had its legs and arms up in the air. I'll never forget when Marlene Danielle looked up to me and did the pose of the baby as a cat! It was the funniest thing.

1992: I Was So Scared

Hayley Podschun, Actor

My first Broadway show was *Cats* at the Winter Garden and I remember it because I was freaked out! The cats coming into the audience had me screaming throughout the show.

During intermission you could go up and touch Deuteronomy on stage. I don't know what they were thinking! I went up and touched him, even though I didn't want to because I was so scared. I did it just so that I could be on a Broadway stage and I remember how cool that felt.

1993: They Come Over And Purr On Your Lap?

Justin Paul, Writer

My first Broadway show was *Cats* at the Winter Garden. I feel like the theater was a little bit run down at the time. I was about eight years old.

I thought Broadway was always going to be people running through the aisles, coming up to your seat, and interacting with you. That being my first Broadway show, I thought: *Oh my God, this is cool! People are on stage and then they just come over and purr on your lap? Broadway is great!*

1995: Delay

Shannon Ford, Musician

I did a lot of subbing as a drummer. I did *Kiss of the Spider Woman, How to Succeed in Business, Show Boat, Cats...*

I went into *Cats* a lot and it was weird because in that pit, the horns were up about 100 feet away in the rafters. Because of that, there was a delay. Any time they would play, it was like they were in another theater somewhere. You had to sort of ignore them, but also sort of acknowledge that they were still in the score, the arrangement. I remember being thrown by it.

The rest of the band was on the deck. We were mostly off stage left, in cubicles. I'm sure the horns being in the rafters was a space issue. It's usually a space issue, these days. That's why drummers are sometimes stuck in separate rooms and string players are on the third floor and things like that.

1996: First Time On Stage

Liz Caplan, Vocal Supervisor

The first time I ever went on stage *or* backstage at a Broadway theater was when a student of mine, Heidi Stallings, was playing Grizabella in *Cats* on Broadway at the Winter Garden.

During intermission, the audience was welcomed onto the stage. I was there with a friend who had come to visit from out of town, so he wanted to go on stage. I really didn't want to, but up we went.

Then suddenly I was staring out into that theater from the stage. I stubbornly didn't want to admit it, but it was intense and overwhelming. That theater is gigantic, and just having the perspective that Broadway actors have when they're performing was really something else.

1996: I Just Loved To Dance

Jennifer Werner, Choreographer/Associate Director

The first Broadway show I ever saw was *Cats* at the Winter Garden. I had just graduated from University of North Carolina Chapel Hill, and I didn't even have a degree in the arts. I just loved to dance. I worked on a cruise ship for a while, and then I took the plunge and decided to move to New York when I was 23.

I had a few friends who lived here, and they encouraged me to just start auditioning. I didn't know that much about musical theatre, because where I came from, there wasn't any. But I wanted to learn.

Not only was *Cats* the first Broadway show I ever saw, it was the first Broadway show I ever auditioned for! The auditions were even on the stage of the Winter Garden. What I remember is thinking that there was a lot of crap! There was so much junk on stage, and the whole place was very dusty.

1997: I Was Practically Begging Them

Christopher Gattelli, Choreographer/Actor

I'm from Philadelphia. I moved to the city when I was 16 and a half years old. I got a scholarship to Alvin Ailey American Dance Theater. At first, I was 14 and taking the train to New York from Philly every day. Then at 16, I was also doing the *Radio City Christmas Spectacular*, and told my parents, "This commuting is kind of silly. Can't I just move there? I'll come back on all the weekends." So I moved to New York when I was almost 17. I jumped in.

The first time I was ever backstage, my friend brought me backstage at *Cats* to meet his friends. It was my dream show at the time and I wanted so much to be cast as Mistofelees, because I was really small and I could do all those things! I remember him taking us up this long flight of stairs and seeing all his friends in cat makeup... I know that it seems funny now, but at that time in the mid-1980s, when *Cats* was in its heyday, I was out-of-my-mind excited to be there. To see them with their faces painted but not completely in costume! To talk to people in a Broadway show! And to see the stage from the wings. Oh my God. It was incredible.

I auditioned for *Cats* for years and years and years. Eventually, I was doing *Guys and Dolls* on the road, and Tara Rubin, the casting director, did *Cats* as well. She knew I'd been in to audition a million times, and was practically begging them. Mistofelees opened up on tour and she said, "Christopher, do you want to go?" She had me switched from *Guys and Dolls* to *Cats*. I stayed there for two years on the road and then I came to Broadway and did it here. It was a crazy dream come true.

When you did *Cats* on the road, the theaters weren't all covered in that junkyard set. That's what was incredible about moving to New York. When I was a kid, I had snuck in and second-acted *Cats* one day and I remember watching it from the back of the orchestra, really looking at how much of the theater was covered in the show. It was unbelievable; no one had done anything like that yet. My first night performing in that show on Broadway, I felt: *Finally! I'm crawling out from a pipe and coming out and scaring people! I'm really in the junkyard!* Just to be truly in the environment of that gave me chills. Thinking about it still does. It was very special to me.

My favorite tag line ever was from *Cats*: "Is the curiosity killing you?" It was genius advertising! They set it up so well so that you never knew what it looked like inside the theater and then you walked in and were blown away. It was way ahead of its time. I loved it. I still love it.

One of my favorite things about when I was performing was just going to the theater and being in the back of the house. I always love my casts and I think it's because I'm not one for backstage chatter. I don't sit in the dressing room and talk about so-and-so's relationship or other shows. People tend to sometimes. I love going to the theater and taking that time and doing ballet barre at the back of the house. I would do that every day during *Cats* and then I carried it on when I did *How To Succeed* and *Fosse* too.

During *Cats*, I would be back in the standing room spot in the house, warming up and doing ballet, and just connecting with the theater. It was my own personal time. I would always think: I stood right there and watched this show for the first time, and now I'm doing it.

93

When I was in the back of the house, I made friends with the bartender at the theater, because I was doing barre and he was pouring icy drinks. And that's how I know Jesse Tyler Ferguson, because he was tending bar at the Winter Garden then. I love that. That's what I love about these places. Just being in the space.

———————————

Jesse Tyler Ferguson bartended at the Winter Garden. Lauren Bacall ushered at the St. James. Aaron Sorkin wrote half of A Few Good Men *on napkins while selling concessions at the Palace Theatre. The person that sells you your M&M's might be on stage or on your TV next month!*

———————————

2000: The Follow Spot Booth Mystery

Ken Billington, Lighting Designer

When they were doing the renovation of the Winter Garden in 2000, after *Cats*, the Shubert Organization called me and said, "Come take a look at this. We're baffled by the follow spot box."

They had the original blueprint of the Winter Garden Theatre, and the follow spot booth was in a different location. The current follow spot looked like it had been added on, and they couldn't figure out what had happened.

I said, "I can tell you exactly why this new booth is here!" The theater was built for Al Jolson, who always had a ramp that came out in the center of the auditorium. In the old follow spot location in the blueprint, you would not have been able to light him in the middle of the auditorium. Clearly they had moved the booth forward, because the biggest star in the world had to be lit when he sang to the audience! It all made sense: that's why the Winter Garden Theatre balcony is only seven rows!

2001: A Substantial Facelift

Robert E. Wankel, Co-CEO and President of The Shubert Organization

When *Cats* closed, we did a big takeout and restoration of the theater. We gave the Winter Garden a pretty substantial facelift, because 18 years of heavily sold-out shows meant that it needed it. We did this just in time for *Mamma Mia!* to come in.

Mamma Mia! happened to come to the Winter Garden six weeks after 9/11. People were very happy to have the show at that time, because it was light and lively and fun. We had the benefit of having *Cats* at the Winter Garden for 18 years, and now *Mamma Mia!* will celebrate its twelfth anniversary before it moves to the Broadhurst, to make room for *Rocky*. We have a new big show coming in to the Winter Garden, that I hope will run for a very long time.

2002: *Once On This Island* Spoke To The City

Michael Arden, Actor/Assistant Director

I moved to the city right before I started school in 2001. My first week of school was September 11th.

I came to New York during a very terrifying time, but it was also a really important time. It bonded everyone who was in New York, and united them. I think the most memorable theatrical experience I've ever had was going to an Actors Fund Benefit concert of *Once on This Island* at the Winter Garden around that time.

I was still at Julliard at that time, and I somehow managed to get a ticket. I don't remember how I did it, but I was sitting in the row behind Stephen Flaherty and Lynn Ahrens and I was so starstruck and moved and overwhelmed.

It happened right after September 11th. The original cast came together and LaChanze had just lost her husband in the attack. It was just a very scary and emotional time for everyone in New York. I remember when LaChanze came out to sing "Waiting for Life," the audience erupted into such applause. Everyone was overwhelmed, people were sobbing. Truly, no one could leave their seat after the show was over.

It was almost like the Broadway community had come to grieve and to wail and to find a new hope that day. *Once On This Island* as a show really spoke to what the city and the community needed in that moment. Anyone I've ever met who was there and saw that is bonded. And the show felt like the company hadn't been apart. It was like they had just closed the show yesterday. It was really moving.

2002/2014: And Forgive

Stephen Flaherty, Writer

I came to New York in 1982. Two weeks after I got off the bus from the Midwest, *Cats* opened. It played for 20 years, until *Mamma Mia!* opened. Those two shows have been at the Winter Garden for the entire time that I've lived in New York.

But I did get to have a show at the Winter Garden for one night. In 2002, we did a reunion concert of *Once on This Island* for Broadway Cares/Equity Fights AIDS[18] there. It was really something. *Once on This Island* actually looked good on the set of *Mamma Mia!* And our little family got to come back together.

When we were casting *Once on This Island* at Playwrights Horizons in the early 1990s, LaChanze came to an open call. She was a hoofer, and when she walked in, we felt something was right about her. We said: "Oh dear Lord, please let her be able to sing!" Not only could she sing, she could act, and she was exactly how we'd imagined the character.

LaChanze got the role and she rolled up her sleeves and went into training, like the Olympics. I think she knew. I think most actors know when they get "the" role: *Here it is, and I'm going to go for it.* She was spectacular.

Years later, there we were, doing this *Once on This Island* reunion at the Winter Garden. It was almost a year after September 11th, when LaChanze had lost her husband while pregnant with their second daughter. She had not been back to a stage. And there we all were, coming together. I think it was good for LaChanze to be there. I remember the moment that she walked on stage and started singing that first song. It was so amazing and moving. Not only for the actress, but for the part, for the shared history we had, and for the end of the show.

At the end, she stepped forward and sang, "...and forgive." At that point, it was very hard for everyone to do that. It was very hard for our city to forgive. But there we were, listening to her sing those words. It was an emotionally thrilling and draining performance and all I was doing was sitting in my seat in the audience!

---

[18] Broadway Cares/Equity Fights AIDS: the theatre community's response to the AIDS crisis; to date has raised over 175 million dollars for those suffering from AIDS and other illnesses

Once on This Island was really made out of love. When we wrote it, I was taking care of a friend of mine who was very ill. Until that moment, I thought that what your life is and what you write about were two different things. *Once on This Island* was the first time where it wasn't like that. Every emotion that I was feeling, I took and put into the show. I think the show helped me get through, and I think the show is what it is because of what I was feeling. I helped it and it helped me, and the show became this bigger thing than any of us. I still find it moving every time I see it.

I realize that the great thing about music is to just give it away. Throw it out there, and every time someone grabs it, they have a similar experience. There's something in *Once on This Island*. It's like when you taste a dish, and think: *Why does this one taste different than that one when it has the same ingredients?* It's because it's infused with things you don't see. That's *Once on This Island*. It's infused with so much. There's something magical about the show.

The Winter Garden is such a legendary New York theater, but it's had these long runs of two British shows for the past 30 years! And now, we're going in with *Rocky*. I've always wanted to work at the Winter Garden. It was always on my wish list. I just never thought *Mamma Mia!* would ever close or move. I thought: *We're so lucky. We got to play there for a day.* But now we're going to be putting a new show in there! I can't wait.

2004: Traditions Gone Awry

Josh Marquette, Hair Designer

I'm from Alaska. My hometown is called North Pole. I went to college and got a general theatre degree, and while I was there, I discovered I had strength at making wigs.

I moved to New York in 2000 and went to beauty school to learn my craft. I started working on hair crews on Broadway with *The Lion King*, followed by *Flower Drum Song* and *Gypsy*. Then, I did *Mamma Mia!* for years. *Mamma Mia!* was my "home base." I was able to go design a show, and come back again. It was a really great way to develop a design career. Not just any show would let you do that, but at *Mamma Mia!*, they let me come back whenever I needed a job again.

The Winter Garden is nice, because there's so much history there. Judy McLane has been in *Mamma Mia!* for years now, and I vividly remember that on her first day, she said, "Oh my God! We work in the Winter Garden! Isn't this exciting?" I always think about that.

We had a tradition at *Mamma Mia!* that we stopped after it went wrong once. The character Donna has a three-minute change into the wedding, where she gets her hair put up. Whoever is playing Sophie is in the same room too, getting the wedding dress put on. We had this tradition where, during the final show of the week, the actress playing Donna, the dressers, and me, the hair stylist, would have a little glass of red wine and some cheese and crackers together. It was just a small celebratory thing we did.

Then one day, on her way out of the room, Sophie's dress got hooked on the wine bottle and knocked it over. What was underneath? The spandex costumes worn by the three dads at the end of the show. Luckily, the wine spilled on the red one—but it was terrible! That actor had to go on stage in wine-covered spandex.

———————

Hellzapoppin, which played the Winter Garden from 1938 to 1941, was an ancestor of Mamma Mia! *in that the show found a huge audience in people who might not ordinarily go to a Broadway show.*

96

A smash hit in its time, Hellzapoppin *became the longest-running musical ever to play Broadway, a title it held until* Oklahoma! *(1943-48) came along. A topical revue,* Hellzapoppin *was outrageous and pushed every boundary. It opened with Hitler speaking in a Yiddish accent, and provided a performance outlet for pigeons, dwarfs, and old vaudevillians. Actors ran through the audience selling fake goods and tickets to other shows. A 1977 revival starring Jerry Lewis and Lynn Redgrave closed on the road before its planned opening at the Minskoff.*

One of my good friends, Eric William Morris, was cast as Sky in Mamma Mia! *and played the role on Broadway in 2009. The night that I went to see him, a group of our friends took up an entire row in the mezzanine. After the performance, we went backstage and I got to see the view from Eric's dressing room window: a giant ad for fried chicken on the building next door! My friends walked around and got a tour of the set and sound booths, while I stood on stage and looked out, listening to* Follies *on my iPod.*

2009: Shot Out Of A Cannon

Eric William Morris, Actor

There are nine principal roles in *Mamma Mia!* and when I went into the show in 2009, they recast eight of them. The only person who stayed was Judy McLane, and the rest of us were new. Because of that, we really got to do our own take on it.

We had a couple weeks of rehearsal together, and they'd say things like, "There's a giant 15-foot wall here, so you have to move." You'd try to imagine it, but you really couldn't until you were on the stage of the Winter Garden, going, "Oh my God, that 15-foot wall is rotating next to me!"

In *Mamma Mia!*, there are booths on stage, right behind the set, where the people in the ensemble sing backup. They work their asses off, because one minute they're dancing on stage, and the next, they're changing clothes as they're singing backups for all of the songs behind the stage.

The booths are soundproof, and they're the entire length of the stage, so if you want to go from stage right to stage left, you have to walk past this row of cubicles. It's become this lecherous, horribly fun place filled with pictures of old cast members, disgusting signs and people who are half-naked. The principals would always go back there to see what the ensemble was doing because it was hilarious. They knew exactly when they had to start singing for each number, so when they weren't singing, they would do crazy things. There they were, three feet from the action of a Broadway show, in a soundproof booth, trying to make each other laugh and pulling pranks. And you can steal Wi-Fi from Applebee's in that spot!

The first big number for my character, Sky, always felt like being shot out of a canon. You wait backstage for 30 minutes, and then it's three minutes on stage, simulating sex and hitting high notes. There's also this fun number called "Under Attack" in the second act. It's the character Sophie's nightmare, and in the middle, Sky comes out in this huge wedding dress. That always got a huge laugh because it's a big dude in a bridal outfit. Our traditions before that entrance were really fun, too. Me, my dresser, Jim, the stagehands, and anyone else who was around in the wings had an entire dance with all this stomping, as I got into wedding garb.

We had a party in the lobby on the night that all of us new folks joined the *Mamma Mia!* company. That was great because my family was there, NY1 was there and we all had champagne. I loved the Winter Garden lobby because there's a piano there. I'd play that piano all the time.

2010: Hey, Up There

Craig Carnelia, Writer

The single best theatergoing experience of my early life was at the Winter Garden. About a year after I saw my first Broadway show, *No Strings,* with my older brother, James, we saw the original production of *Funny Girl.* We had a tradition in those days. We had a book of seating charts of the theaters that we would mark in blue or in black: "Black is where you sat and blue is where I sat."

Flash forward to 2010, when my wife, Lisa Brescia, took over the role of Donna in *Mamma Mia!,* which she ended up playing for two years. One of my greatest pleasures when Lisa is in a show is getting to know the theater she's playing more intimately. I've shared this experience with my daughter, Daisy, who is now 18 and about to be in the business. Whether it's meeting up with Lisa, or visiting a friend backstage, we'll often just take a moment to stand on stage after a show and take in the feel and shape of the house. What you notice about the Winter Garden is the width. The audience feels wide and close.

During *Mamma Mia!,* I once went up to my mezzanine seat from *Funny Girl* and sat there for a few minutes, after having a picnic dinner with Lisa in her dressing room. To get to know this theater and, through my wife, to have it be a little bit mine, felt special. It's an amazing theater.

2002/2014: A Prayer Circle

Lynn Ahrens, Writer

The night of our *Once on This Island* concert at the Winter Garden was one of the most memorable experiences of my entire life, not just my theatre career.

Once on This Island started at Playwrights Horizons in 1990. When we were off-Broadway, it was a very small company of only 11 people, and we would always do a prayer circle before they went on stage. You'd stand there and hold hands, and anyone who wanted to could join. We'd say a prayer for the safety of the actors, and their hearts, and it was a beautiful moment of togetherness before they went on stage to perform together every night.

When the show moved to Broadway, they continued the prayer circle. Any time I could go there—if I was going to another show that night, or if I was in the area—I would run in before show time and just join the prayer circle. I loved being with them and I loved that moment of community.

About 11 years later, we had September 11th. It was a tremendous tragedy for everybody in the theatre community. LaChanze lost her husband that day. She was pregnant with her second child at the time. She gave birth, and life went on as best it could.

In 2002, we did that reunion of the original *Once on This Island* company for a concert at the Winter Garden, and before the show, we all formed a prayer circle. There we all were, back together again. It was really extraordinary.

The company went out and began to perform, and when LaChanze got to her first song, "Waiting for Life to Begin", she got a huge, huge standing ovation.

At the very end of the show, there's our song, "Why We Tell The Story". The actors sing the lyric: "Pain is why/ Love is why/ Grief is why/ Hope is why/ Faith is why," and the very last lyric of the song is: "So I hope you will tell this tale tomorrow/ It will help your heart remember and relive/ It will help you feel the anger and the sorrow."

Then, LaChanze sang the solo: "And forgive." And everybody sang together, "For out of what we live and we believe/Our lives become the stories that we weave."

It was right then that I realized truly what the theatre is all about, which is that it's a prayer circle. It's just a big circle: we tell stories, and maybe we heal a heart or two, and we put something positive into the world, and we just do it—you know, we just create our circle with actors and collaborators and friends who take part in this art form.

That night was very, very meaningful to me. It was stunning. And the whole theatre was involved. Everyone in the whole giant Winter Garden Theatre was there for LaChanze, and for the show, and for what the show was saying at that point in time in New York City.

Our new show, *Rocky*, is coming to the Winter Garden, and I know that the minute I walk back in there, I'm going to be thinking all about our *Once on This Island* reunion. There's a powerful feeling that lives inside of that theater.

The Marquis Theatre

Built: 1986
Location: 1565 Broadway
Owner: The Nederlander Organization
Longest-Running Show: *Me and My Girl* (1986-1989)
Shortest-Running Show: *Nick & Nora* (closed after nine performances in 1991)
Number of Productions: 32

Shows in the Marquis usually have pretty happy companies, because the theater is modern. It has a lot of space—there's real breathing room. Usually the casts there are happy, because they've got the room to sort of spread out a little bit.

–**Kathleen Marshall**, Director/Choreographer

Introduction: Protector Of The Marquis

Rey Concepcion, Door Man

I was born in Puerto Rico. I moved to New York in 1972.

In the 1980s, I was working as a private security guard, guarding the Marquis Theatre. On the last day of my contract, the door man left for a new job, and I got to take over. I was blessed. That was 25 years ago, and I've been at the Marquis Theatre ever since.

The first Broadway show I ever saw was the first one I worked for: *Me And My Girl* (1986). Great show! It made me a fan of musical comedies.

At the Marquis, we've had some great shows. We had *Shogun* (1990), *Victor/Victoria* (1995) and *Thoroughly Modern Millie* (2002) which I loved. We had *The Woman in White* (2005) and *The Drowsy Chaperone* (2006) which was awesome. And recently we had *Evita* (2012) and *Jekyll & Hyde* (2013). Those were good shows.

During *Shogun*, they did a salt ceremony! All of the stagehands and everyone on the house staff thought that the salt ceremony jinxed the theater. The shows right after that weren't very good. And on *Come Fly Away* (2010), Twyla Tharp did an earth ceremony to bless the show.

One time, they rented out the theater for an event, and Bob Hope came into the Marquis. He had a tradition of making the first person that he saw laugh. That's how he knew that he was going to have a good time on the stage. He saw me first, at the door, and he had me laughing until he got all the way to the top of the stairs! He was pleased.

But it's so nice to meet *everybody*. To me, everybody's important, including yourself.

Bernadette Peters has done three shows here. I love that lady. And during *Follies* (2011), she and Jan Maxwell were both here together! Jan Maxwell is an incredible woman too. That number she did, "Lucy and Jessie", I saw that number 40 times.

Jan was actually a bit of a practical jokester. One time, the night door man, Cisco, accidentally cut someone on the knee with a knife, and Jan came down and gave him a safety kit and some plastic knives.

During *The Goodbye Girl* (1993), Carol Woods and Scott Wise used to love fighting with water guns. You had to walk around with an umbrella.

My routine is usually that I walk into the theater, and open it up. If it's a non-matinee day, I bring my Playstation or my X-Box and I play games. I work out. Once the show is in production, you can have a routine and do these things.

As a door man, sometimes you see a show that isn't perfect, but you also see everything coming together little by little. You see the hard work these actors do, and how much time the writers spend here. And because of that, every single opening is special. For *Annie Get Your Gun* (1999) and *Damn Yankees* (1994), on opening night, the whole staircase was covered in flowers.

With Ricky Martin in *Evita*, the audiences were crazy. We had one guy who was drunk and started screaming that Ricky was gay, during a performance. There was a young lady who decided to jump on stage and go after him and grab him. And at our stage door, there was hair-pulling, and pushing, and shoving, because they wanted to see Ricky. It reminded me of one time during *The Capeman* (1998), when a young lady wanted to bite Marc Anthony's neck!

But on the flipside, sometimes the stage door is great. There was this one person that made me laugh so much. Reba McEntire came out the stage door after *Annie Get Your Gun*. And he yelled out, with a nice Southern accent, "Reba! We named our horse after you!"

During *Me and My Girl*, my first Broadway show, Jim Dale had a swordplay sequence. One day, he threw up his sword and missed—and the sword ended up in the pit. A little old lady came running up! She was very short, maybe 4'9", and real slowly and gently she said, "Are you alright down there?" The mic picked it up! It made the whole audience explode with laughter. And thank God everybody was alright!

———————

Me and My Girl was the first Broadway show at the Marquis Theatre and it was a smash hit, running for three and a half years. The plot followed the exploits of a cockney fellow named Bill who found out he was heir to the Earl of Hareford and tried to become a proper gentleman. The rousing first act closer—"The Lambeth Walk"—had the entire cast dancing up the aisles in a frenzied cockney bonanza.

———————

1986: She Took Me To Broadway

Donna Vivino, Actor

The first Broadway show I ever saw was *Me and My Girl* at the Marquis Theatre. I was eight years old.

I had been doing some work in television and film as an actor, and I loved watching TV. I was watching with my grandmother one day, and a commercial for the show *Me and My Girl* came on. I said to my grandma, "What is that? I want to see that!" And she said, "I do too!" We got all dressed up, and she took me to Broadway.

We were at a matinee, and sitting very far away. I remember Maryann Plunkett singing, and I remember her holding the last note of "Once You Lose Your Heart" for a very long time. You could hear a pin drop, and I thought that was so magical. Also, she was such a great tap dancer, and there was an article in the Playbill about how she'd learned to dance just for the show! I thought to myself: *If Maryann Plunkett can learn how to tap dance and then get this role, surely I can try my hand at some Broadway!*

To this day, the longest-running show to ever play the Marquis is the first!

The second never even happened.

The sequel to Annie, *called* Annie 2: Miss Hannigan's Revenge, *was set to start previews at the Marquis in February of 1990. It had a four million dollar advance, an impressive amount at the time.*

The marquee went up, but the show never came in.

This happens occasionally on Broadway. The marquee for The Baker's Wife *(1976) went up at the Martin Beck and never came in. The marquee for* Busker Alley *(1996) went up at the St. James.* Mambo Kings *(2005) at the Broadway.* Lone Star Love *(2007) at the Belasco.* The Miracle Worker *(2003), starring Hilary Swank, at the Music Box. Most recently, in 2012, the musical* Rebecca *had its marquee up at the Broadhurst for weeks while the fate of the show was in flux.*

None of those shows ever made it to New York, but people who walked by the theaters on the street sure thought they did!

Annie 2: Miss Hannigan's Revenge *picked up where* Annie *left off. It turned out that Warbucks could not adopt Annie unless she had a mother, so he went on a worldwide search to find a wife. Hannigan tried to win the search, while also plotting to drown Annie and drop a piano on Warbucks' head. The orphans were nowhere to be found.*

At one point in the show, The Head of The United Mothers of America told Warbucks, "You need to become a married billionaire like John D. Rockefeller. But then again – he had hair!"

The show was eventually scrapped almost entirely, and a much-improved sequel called Annie Warbucks *opened off-Broadway in 1993.*

After Annie 2: Miss Hannigan's Revenge *skidded to a halt out of town, the word was that the creative team would try to bring it in at a later date. But ironically, at the moment, Charles Strouse, the composer, was committed to* Nick & Nora, *which was also going into the Marquis.*

1991: Everybody Wants To Do A Musical

Daryl Roth, Producer

I was a co-producer on the ill-fated *Nick & Nora*. We all live and learn.

It was very early in my career, and I had become friendly with Richard Maltby Jr. We worked together at City Center on a committee that ultimately became the Encores series. Richard's musical *Closer Than Ever* was the first show I ever produced, off-Broadway, and it was a result of getting to know Richard and David Shire. Richard was the lyricist of *Nick and Nora*, and he got me involved. And while it wasn't a success, I adored the experience and all the people who worked on the show.

As I was not very experienced on Broadway yet, I had very little to say creatively. I was there to listen and learn. They say that things that don't go wonderfully teach you more than things that do; this was a good example of that. What I learned is how important it is for the creative team to all be in-sync and on the same page. The storyline was wonderful, as was the music, but the overall vision was not totally shared by the creators, and I think that made for some discord that ultimately prevented the show from coming together as everyone hoped.

————————

Nick & Nora *closed after 71 previews and nine performances.*

————————

1991: Our Future Begins Tonight

Joanna Gleason, Actor

Opening night of *Nick & Nora* had its own—how shall we say—charm, in that we had 71 previews, and the show never got fixed. Then we had opening night, knowing we were pretty much doomed to be closed by the end of the week. At the opening night party at Sardi's, we were all sitting around, waiting for somebody to come in with the paper, until suddenly, at 11:15pm, the room cleared.

A couple days later, we were packing up our dressing rooms. That show is where I met my husband, Chris Sarandon. He and I got together during *Nick & Nora*. And I remember we just looked at each other that day and we said: "Okay. Our future begins tonight at 6:00 when we've packed up our dressing rooms and loaded everything into your ancient Audi. We're getting out of town." I mean, we just drove off somewhere.

First though, we went to Joe Allen, because they wanted to put up the poster, the "failure poster" on the flop wall. We sort of endured that. I can have a great sense of humor about it now, but that night, it was still a little raw.

But then we looked at each other and said, you know, "Now, real life." And we left the city.

————————

It seems that more couples meet and get married from working on Broadway flops than Broadway hits!

The first show ever to play the Nederlander in 1921 was a 36-performance flop called Swords, *the debut of playwright Sidney Howard (who would later write the movie adaption of* Gone With The Wind*) and where he met and married leading actress Claire Eames. Husband and wife musical duo Jessica Molaskey and John Pizzarelli got together during the three month run of the Broadway musical* Dream. *Multiple weddings were the result of* Good Vibrations, *which lasted less than three months. Even Barbra Streisand and Elliott Gould met and fell head over heels in love during* I Can Get It For You Wholesale, *amidst lukewarm notices and threats of firing from David Merrick.*

————————

1993: *The Goodbye Girl* Costume Shop

Penny Davis, Wardrobe Supervisor/Dresser

During *The Goodbye Girl*, designer Santo Loquasto was doing the sets *and* the costumes. He focused mainly on the sets, since they were so complex. The wardrobe room became a costume shop, and we were making things from scratch, day by day.

In the old days, that just wasn't done. Costume shops delivered the costumes completed. Maybe you'd have to change a hem, or you'd change this or that, but basically the costumes were created in the costume shop. And that's not the case anymore on big shows.

Luckily, I had some really talented people. We could accommodate that. We were a good team.

1994: The Blooper Ballet

Michael Berresse, Director/Choreographer/Actor

Damn Yankees was my third Broadway show, and the Marquis was the shiniest, cleanest theater I'd worked in. I shared a dressing room with Jeff Blumenkrantz. Jeff and I actually did three shows in a row together: *Forever Plaid* off-Broadway, *Joseph and the Amazing Technicolor Dreamcoat* in Toronto and then, right after, we got to do *Damn Yankees* together on Broadway. He's one of my dear friends to this very day.

It was a terrific company. I loved being a part of a big male ensemble in both *Guys and Dolls* and *Damn Yankees*. It was the first time I got to tap into that specific comedic style, and there was also such a specific kind of power in all those men performing together.

One night we were doing the "Blooper Ballet," which was a big number with lot of pratfalls about these bumbling idiots on a baseball field who just can't do anything right. Scott Wise and I were doing lots of flips, lots of gymnastics. I had this one moment where I'd run and dive on the stage and do this 30-foot stomach slide, with a glove in one hand, supposedly to catch a ground ball.

That night, as soon as I hit the stage I thought: *Whoa, I'm going way too fast!* I was trying to push against the stage but I couldn't slow my body down fast enough. Downstage center was the tip of a baseball diamond and on either side of it were these nets to catch balls and gloves. I kept going and I went right off the stage, past the edge of the stage, past the conductor, over the net! I fell 12 feet into the orchestra pit and landed on top of a French horn player.

It was surreal because when you're on stage in a show like that, you're in this artificial world. To land with a thud on the floor in the middle of the musicians was like landing in an alternate universe. Some were reading books! I was looking at them, and they were looking at me, and David Chase was still conducting. The number was still going! So, I got up, David got off his stool, and I jumped up onto his conductor podium.

I grabbed the back of the stage, and I flipped over backwards up onto it. I stood up and did a big double take, and then I ran off into the wings. Except for the people who were in the front row, the audience thought it was just another pratfall in the show! They all went crazy and started applauding. It was fun.

Halfway through the next number, I realized that I had dislocated two fingers. My ribs were bruised. I *had* hurt myself, and I had to leave at intermission.

The next day, I received a big bouquet of flowers from the people who were in the front row and saw it all happen. They saw me in my next five Broadway shows, and we became friends.

Michael is part of a long legacy of Broadway folks accidentally falling into orchestra pits.

During the 1994 She Loves Me *revival, Boyd Gaines famously fell into the orchestra pit, directly onto someone's lap. During her first performance as Elphaba in* Wicked, *Shoshana Bean ran out on stage and directly into the orchestra pit—and was caught by the net above the musicians.*

Legend has it that when West Side Story *had its pre-Broadway tryout in Washington D.C. in 1957, Jerome Robbins was yelling at his actors, with his back to the orchestra pit, and they silently allowed him to back up and fall into it! And when* Anyone Can Whistle *was trying out in Philadelphia, a dancer fell into the pit mid-show, landing on a musician—who died in an unrelated incident the following week.*

During Allegro's *pre-Broadway tryout in Connecticut, Lisa Kirk fell into the orchestra pit while singing "The Gentleman Is A Dope". Luckily, she fell onto the string section, so the musicians used their bows to hoist her back on stage—and she didn't miss a note of the song.*

––––––––––––––

1994: Locked In The Dressing Room

Rey Concepcion, Door Man

During *Damn Yankees*, Vicki Lewis had dressing room number six upstairs, and there was something wrong with the doorknob.

She got locked in during previews, so she took the doorknob off the door and handed it to the stage manager.

After the show that day, Hector, our night door man at the time, decided to make sure the dressing rooms were locked. He went to turn off the light in Vicki's dressing room, and the door closed. He didn't know there was no doorknob.

He got locked in her dressing room for two days!

It was a Sunday, and since Broadway shows are dark on Mondays, he was stuck from Sunday night until Tuesday morning when the cleaning lady came in. This was before cell phones. All he had was a bottle of champagne that Vicki had in her dressing room. By Tuesday night, everybody on Broadway knew about it!

––––––––––––––

Since the Marriott Marquis was built by architects with primary experience in building hotels, rather than theaters, there are a couple of unusual things you can find... if you know where to look!

As you enter the lobby of the theater, glance to your right. You'll see a glass wall of advertisements. Right behind those glass walls are several dressing rooms!

Legend has it that when the theater was built, the contractors forgot to put in dressing rooms. Shopping on the second floor of the hotel was yanked out of the layout, in order to accommodate dressing rooms for the theater.

Without the advertisements plastered on the glass, you could see directly into the dressing rooms.

––––––––––––––

1995: Wigs And Jumps And Soda Machines

Liz Larsen, Actor

The Marriott Marquis is my favorite theater. I did *Damn Yankees* there, and the green room is sublime. It's huge. There are soda machines, there's a bar, there are mirrors, there are couches, there's a huge television. And I had my own dressing room! I had my own phone! There was space.

I met Charlotte d'Amboise, who is my best friend now, doing that show. She had this wonderful area that I would sleep in. Jerry Lewis also had this great area. We were all so happy, because there was space. I've done other shows that weren't that happy, because there was literally nowhere to be, no place to say "hi" to anybody. At some theaters, people just go to their little corner in their little room, and start getting ready; the only time you see people is on stage, and then you go home. So it makes a big difference to a company to have a community gathering place. I love the Marriott Marquis.

The chorus dressing room during *Damn Yankees* faced 45th Street. If I went into their rooms, we could wave at the people who were across the street at the Minskoff in *Sunset Boulevard*. That was fun.

Vicki Lewis had been doing *Damn Yankees* since the beginning, and I love her. She's so hilarious and very powerful. When I replaced her, I felt intimidated by that energy. Plus, the role of Gloria Thorpe was tough. At the end of a show, when I was wheezing for breath from dancing, I had to jump off a 15-foot dugout into Scott Wise and Joey Pizzi's arms, leading with my coccyx. They were very nice to me, but I do not like heights. My mother said, "Just pretend you're jumping into a pool." So every single night, during the song, I had to say, "jump into a pool" to myself so I wouldn't flip out. But I was glad it was a challenge.

Vicki has bright red hair. When I went into the show, Bill, our beloved hair guy, said to Jack O'Brien, the director, "Shall I give her Vicki's wigs?" Jack said, "No, she's got black hair. Black. It's Liz's part now. She'll have black wigs." And that was really sweet. It's not always like that. "This is Liz Larsen's part now."

So I got these black wigs. Then, later on, Jack came back to see the show. He was very famous for these beautiful pep talks, and he gave me great comments. But at the end of the pep talk, we were going to get ready for the show, and he casually said to me, "Hey, we're going to make you red." I said, "You are? Great! Why?" He said, "Because if you're wise-cracking and you're a redhead, you're funny. If you're wise-cracking and you're a brunette, you're mean."

That was the end for me. I decided: *I'm coloring my hair.* And once I really committed to coloring my hair, it completely changed the roles I was being offered!

I really did love doing *Damn Yankees*, and I love the Marquis so much. It was just a happy place to work. With a soda machine.

The Marquis Theatre has a three-decade history of neighborly relations with the Minskoff. The two theaters treat their proximity much like kids at summer camp would treat neighboring bunks. The inhabitants of the chorus dressing room on the 45th Street side of the Marquis are always waving at the cast at the Minskoff out the row of windows that overlooks the street below.

Liz Larsen mentions the Damn Yankees *cast hollering at* Sunset Boulevard *in 1995. During the 2004 revival of* La Cage Aux Folles, *Harvey Fierstein, the show's librettist, was also starring at the Minskoff in* Fiddler on the Roof. *Dressed as Tevye, he would make colorful signs and hold them up for the Cagelles. The* Me and My Girl *dancers did synchronized dances with the* Sweet Charity *company in 1986.*

The Marquis always has an eye on Times Square, for better or for worse. In 2010, there was a bomb scare in Times Square, and the entire cast of Come Fly Away *crowded around the window to watch the police take action before the show could go on that night.*

1995/2002/2006: Cruise Ship Theater

Casey Nicholaw, Director/Choreographer/Actor

I love the Marquis. I really do love the Marquis.

I know many people say it looks like a cruise ship when you come in. And it kind of does. But it really feels intimate for its size—and the sightlines are so good. It's wide, but it brings you close to the show. And there's room backstage! The happiest companies I've ever worked with have been at the Marquis. Space backstage is a huge thing.

I was in *Victor/Victoria* (1995) and *Thoroughly Modern Millie* (2002) there, and those casts were so happy. You have a green room, you have a common place where people can be together. A lot of other theaters don't have that. You're in your dressing room, then you're on stage.

During *Victor/Victoria*, Julie Andrews decorated the green room beautifully for us. She took very good care of our company. We were such a family there. We had a bond from going out of town in Minneapolis and Chicago. We worked on that show forever. It was wonderful *and* torturous. When we did it in Minneapolis, the first act was 45-minutes long, and the second act was two hours! It was crazy. But, you know, we were doing a show with Julie Andrews, and she was great to us. We loved each other, and it was really fun.

During *Millie,* there was a certain point in the show every night where the girls who were at the turntables upstage at the typewriters would turn around. And then, in the wings, I'd be there with the guys' ensemble and some of the stagehands and we would do a show backstage for them.

It started as a simple thing, and then every night, we'd have to decide: *What are we going to do?* We had a wig tub and a costume tub, and we'd have themes. If it was Halloween week, it'd be horror themed, and we did "12 Days of Christmas" one day. Everyone on the other side of the stage would also gather to see what we were doing.

Every single show has traditions. However, *Drowsy* (2006) had one tradition that as the director, I only sometimes enjoyed. That was the "$50 dare." On each person's last night, Troy Johnson would "$50 dare" that actor to do something outrageous on stage. Bob Martin had a "$50 dare" that on his last night, instead of hugging Troy's character at the end, he had to kiss him. He did it! It was really funny.

Julie Andrews was beloved by the Victor/Victoria *cast and by the entire team at the Marquis, who were a very tight-knit group. When the 1996 Tony Award nominations came out,* Victor/Victoria *only received one nomination: for Julie Andrews as Best Actress in a Musical.*

Two days later, at the Wednesday matinee curtain call, Julie publicly announced that she would decline her Tony nomination, saying, "I could not have done this alone... I have searched my conscience and my heart and find that I cannot accept this nomination, and prefer instead to stand with the egregiously overlooked."[19]

Not having appeared on Broadway since The Boy Friend, My Fair Lady, *and* Camelot *in the 1950s and 1960s, Julie Andrews was widely considered to have been a lock for the award of Best Actress. She had never won a Tony Award before, and she hasn't been on Broadway since.*

---

[19] Robert Viagas, "Julie Andrews Declines Tony Nomination," *Playbill*, 08 May 1996, http://www.playbill.com/news/article/31424-Julie-Andrews-Declines-Tony-Nomination (accessed 13 Oct. 2013)

On a Wednesday afternoon in May 2013, Rey Concepcion, the much-adored Marquis Theatre door man, showed me around backstage at the Marquis.

We took a right out of the door man's room, and we were in a large stairwell, that lead to stage level. On the wall was a gigantic replica of a Tony Award that looked like it weighed a ton. Staring at the huge silver medallion in awe, I asked Rey what it was from.

Rey said, "The stagehands and producers of Victor/Victoria *had it made for Julie Andrews. They took her right out here where we're standing, and gave it to her, saying, 'Who needs a Tony when we've got Julie?'"*

"She's one of the sweetest people you'll ever meet. I always get grief because I've never watched The Sound of Music*. I've never seen* Mary Poppins*. But I'm a big fan of her, because she's just the greatest lady."*

––––––––––––––––

1995-2004: Navigating The Maze

Tim Pettolina, House Manager

I was the associate house manager at the Marquis for a number of years. The Marquis is a little crazy for house managers, because you're in the Marriott Hotel, so you have to be careful that people who are wandering in the hotel aren't trying to get into the theater! You have to be very strict at the door.

When I first started to work there, it was pretty overwhelming because the show was *Victor/Victoria* and it was very, very popular. The backstage was so big that it was like a maze, and I would be running around without knowing where I was going. Once, Julie Andrews was warming up and she almost kicked me in the face! The Marquis is enormous, like the Gershwin and Minskoff, and that's why you have two managers in those theaters. Now, I'm the house manager at the Richard Rodgers, so the Marquis was intimidating, but it was a great way to learn.

I'll never forget the closing performance of *The Capeman*. I was James Nederlander Jr.'s assistant while he was putting that show together. I worked with him on the workshops and casting and then, I also ended up being the associate house manager at the theater. I felt very close to the show, because I worked on so many different aspects of the production.

The Capeman had such a beautiful music, and Marc Anthony and Ruben Blades were great, but the show didn't work, and it was savaged by the New York Daily Press. There were protests and it was very emotional. I was very upset by the closing, but it was also a great experience across the board. I remember during the final performance when Ednita Nazario, who was playing the mother, was performing her final song and couldn't even sing because she was crying so hard. It was one of those heartbreaking shows where everybody tried really hard, but it didn't succeed. That was the saddest closing because it meant so much.

There were great shows while I was at the Marquis, and each one has its own memories. Sutton Foster in *Thoroughly Modern Millie* was special, and the show was one of the best musicals I've worked on. It was exciting for me because for the duration of the run, I was head manager. It was right after 9/11 and it really cheered people up. I've been very lucky that I've been able to work so much on so many shows. Hopefully there will be many more.

––––––––––––––––

The Capeman *was the target of protests in the center of Times Square. Opening night was picketed by those who felt the show was glamourizing its central character, Salvador Agron, the 16-year-old gang member who had murdered two teens in 1959.*

Salvador Agron was a Puerto Rican member of the Hell's Kitchen gang The Vampires. He was called "The Capeman" because he wore a black cape with red lining. His story made worldwide headlines when he became the youngest prisoner ever sentenced to death row.

The murders took place in May Matthews Park, which split the block between 45th and 46th Streets, between 9th and 10th Avenues. The park was surrounded by tenements and known for its drug deals and violence. In the 1950s it was frequented by prostitutes, Times Square roughs, and local teens looking for trouble. It still stands today, and is renamed Matthews-Palmer Playground. Sandwiched between nail salons and shops that sell yoga clothes, it is now often filled with elementary school-aged kids and their parents.

During the summer that The Capeman stabbed two innocent teens, West Side Story was finishing up its run on Broadway. A couple decades later, when Salvador Agron got his own Broadway musical, it would play just two blocks east of where the murders took place.

———————

1998: *The Capeman* And Me

Lin-Manuel Miranda, Writer/Actor

It's hard for me to talk about *The Capeman* because it was influential in both good and bad ways. The show opened during my senior year of high school, and I was directing *West Side Story* when it came out.

The Capeman was written by and starring my heroes, and I built it up to this impossible level in my mind. I loved Paul Simon's album, *Songs from The Capeman*, that predated the show's debut. Paul Simon has just never written a bad song! My dad gave me toxic dosages of Ruben Blades as a kid. Marc Anthony was the Latin guy I discovered for myself. I think if you interview any second-generation Hispanic kid, there's the music their parents listened to that they kind of tuned out, and then there's the first one that made them go, "Wait a minute. What are you listening to? What is he talking about?" Marc Anthony was that for me.

I thought *The Capeman* was going to be the second coming of Christ. That's the only way I can describe it.

... And it just wasn't. It's not the show's fault, but it wasn't.

It made me think. On a moral level, what were the chances that two musicals 40 years apart could depict not just Latinos as gang members, but specifically as knife-wielding murderers from the 1950s? What a tiny subset of the community to get so much treatment on the stage.

That's the greatest blessing and curse of *West Side Story*: it's such a good show that if you ask people all over the world what they think when they hear "Puerto Rican," they're going to say *West Side Story*. And sometimes, they're going to think of a Greek guy with brown makeup. That's the mental heuristic, and it's not their fault. It's a great, popular, enduring show.

I actually took my *West Side Story* cast to see *The Capeman*. I had a cast of white and Asian Sharks, since I went to a mostly white school. I'd taught them all to be Puerto Rican—that was the fun of directing *West Side Story*. I brought my dad in and he did dialect coaching, and I really used the show as a teachable moment, and a way to bring my culture into school.

I saw *The Capeman* three times during previews, and it broke my heart. There was so much good in it, and it died so quickly. It felt like the Great Latino Hope, and they had a float in the Puerto Rican Day Parade. There were a ton of Latino actors getting work and I remember thinking: *I'm never going to have a career in the theatre. That was our one big shot and it went away so fast.*

Then I spent a couple of years just trying to fix *The Capeman* in my head. I tried to find a structure to support all of the songs I liked, and make it work. I thought: *Maybe if you cut the jail stuff and you stick to the 1950s stuff...*

I did that with *Capeman* for two years and then I started writing *In the Heights*. At a certain point, you go, *This is never going to be your dream show. This is what it is. Heights* came out of that in a weird way—at least in the way that I knew no one was going to hold a knife in the show. That story exists, it's a real story, but it's not the story I wanted to tell. It's been very well represented already.

————————

Stephen Sondheim was a gofer on the Rodgers and Hammerstein musical Allegro, *a concept musical about a man trying to stay true to his ideals in the complicated modern world. He has said that at the age of 17, his attachment to this show may have caused him to spend some of his later career, including* Merrily We Roll Along, *"trying to fix* Allegro."

This concept of "loving a show so much that you want to fix it" seems to be a timeless ailment of musical theatre writers through the ages...

————————

1998: *Tango* and *Stomp*

Laura Heller, General Manager

At the time that I was the company manager of *Forever Tango*, I was also general managing *Stomp* downtown. I could do it because I had assistants. Every week, I did six shows of each at each theater—I was just unstoppable.

On Saturdays, I had a matinee of *Tango*, a 5pm of *Stomp*, and an evening at *Tango*, and then a midnight at *Stomp*. Saturdays were booked!

I remember one Saturday night at *Tango*, there was a power outage before the show. The lights went out, and we had no electricity. All of these sweet, wonderful people from other countries were there that night, and they were so frightened by our police. It was really hard trying to get them to calm down. And I had to get to *Stomp* by midnight. It was an exciting time.

I'd bring my daughter, Maddy, to the Marquis with me, and we would hang out in the wardrobe room with all of the female tango dancers. Every time a gem would fall off of one of their costumes, the dancer would give it to Maddy and she would sew it onto a headband. She still has her *Forever Tango* gem headband.

1999: How I Got To Sell Programs At *Annie Get Your Gun*

Amy Wolk, Merchandise Manager/On Site Educator

My dad and his friends owned a theater in Chicago. It was only around for two years, but I used to run their box office during the day, when no one else was there. That was my first job in a theater. I ordered perusal scripts[20], I bartended, I did whatever was needed.

———————————

[20] perusal scripts: materials that theatre licensing companies send out to those who are interested in doing one of their shows

110

When I came to NYU in 1996, I lived in a hotel on 31st and 7th, because NYU ran out of dorm space. Because I was so close to Times Square, and it was the beginning of student rush, I would hit the box offices at 10am, get tickets to something, and then go to class.

The very first week I was in New York, I sat on the street and got *Rent* tickets, before the album even came out. I saw *A Delicate Balance* with Elaine Stritch and Rosemary Harris. I waited outside and Elaine Stritch talked to us! I saw Patti LuPone in *Master Class*, and took a picture with her, and then lost the camera in a cab. Somebody somewhere has a picture of me and Patti LuPone.

I got a job at Theatre Circle, the Broadway store on 44th Street. My first day there, I worked the counter with Jesse Tyler Ferguson. Working there, I met Tony Massey, a merchandise manager from the Marquis. During Christmas, his whole staff left and he desperately needed people to work at the theater. Since I'm Jewish, I said I would.

That's how I got my first job at a New York theater, working at *Annie Get Your Gun*. I remember being nervous. That theater is weird, because the whole thing is inside and upstairs. Selling merchandise there, you don't get the same questions as you would if you were working on the street at *Phantom*. But working at *Annie Get Your Gun* was very exciting because Bernadette Peters was in that show and I had always loved her!

At first, I sold programs. Then, I got moved to the merchandise booth. Eventually, I started cover managing, which is where you go around managing the merchandise for lots of Broadway shows.

Training with Tony, there was not an introductory period. Right away, I was in the house manager's office, chatting with staff members. After shows, we'd end up at the Cafe Edison with a bunch of people from other shows. And every day, I'd get thrown into theaters. He'd be like, "Go to *Les Mis*!" I don't remember being in awe of it, so much as being excited by it. I had been around the theater so much, that it didn't feel that far out of the ordinary.

People would forget sometimes that I worked in the theater. I'd say, "Enjoy the show!" And they'd respond, "Oh, you too." Or they'd ask me, "What do you think of the show?" Well, I'm not going to tell you the truth if I think the show is terrible! Sometimes, they didn't realize that I was connected to the show.

It's been great working with producers who make their front of house staff happy. If the ushers, bar staff and merchandise sellers like all of the people involved with the show, they're going to be happier, and that transmits itself to audience members. It's great working on shows where people are nice to everybody at the front of house. It's important, because they're the first people everybody sees.

———————

With only 32 productions to its name, the Marquis has been home to fewer shows than any other theater on Broadway.

As you walk into the lobby, check above the bar for window cards of each show that has played at the Marquis. And hang a right to see an impressive thoroughfare of even more Broadway posters decorating the third floor of the hotel.

———————

1999: Everything About It Is Appealing

James Woolley, Stage Manager/Usher

One night during *Annie Get Your Gun*, Bernadette wasn't feeling well but she went on anyway. She did her first number, there was lots of applause, and then I looked up at my monitor on the desk and there was no one on my screen!

I couldn't figure out where she was on stage. Then, I turned to my right and she was standing next to me, throwing up. We stopped the show, and her understudy, Valerie Wright, went on.

2000: Susan Lucci's Breakfast

Rey Concepcion, Door Man

I hold Susan Lucci very dear. She's the opposite of Erica Kane, her character from *All My Children*; she's one of the sweetest people!

When Susan was here, starring in *Annie Get Your Gun*, I had just quit a second job that I really didn't like. Susan needed breakfast, but it was right after New Year's, so everything was pretty much closed. I felt so happy about leaving that old job, that I left the stage door, put a note on it, and went to get her breakfast.

When I got back she reached in her pocket and I went, "You can never do that. First of all, my wife is a huge fan of yours. So if I take your money, she would never cook for me again. And second of all, I just left a job that I didn't like. So this is my way of expressing happiness." She gave me a big hug.

———————————

In his Stage Door office, Rey has an impressive wall of headshots. They surround him on all sides. At the end of our interview, he began pointing at the wall and telling me a little bit about each of the people. It's a Marquis Hall Of Fame.

"There's Mia Walker. She was here in Annie Get Your Gun. *She was only eight years old then, and now she's an assistant director on* Pippin! *Isn't that something?"*

"Carly Rose Sonenclar. She was 12 when she was here doing Wonderland. *Now she came in second on* X Factor. *Almost won the whole thing!"*

"Linda Gabler! She amazed me, because in Victor/Victoria, *there was a trick in the show, and she actually learned the trick."*

"That's a photo of me holding Harriet Harris' Tony Award for Millie!*"*

"Beth Leavel. Oh my God. Amazing voice, and so funny. Marc Kudisch—he was so good in Millie. *And this is the* White Christmas *wall."*

"Bernadette Peters, during Follies, *came and looked at her picture from* Annie Get Your Gun.*"*

"There's Megan Hilty. She wrote: 'Thanks for taking such good care of us. I love you, even if you are a filthy Mets fan.'"

"Allison Janney. She was so upset when 9 to 5 closed, that she didn't want to say goodbye. She just gave me a hug and a kiss, and left."

"Danny Burstein. One of the best people you will ever meet. He's my brother. We're different colors, different mothers, different races, but we're still brothers."

"Some of the shows, they last here for years. When these people come in here, you meet them for the first time, but by the end of the month, they're family. Because you get to meet their family, they get to meet yours. And before you know it, you're having lunch with them. You're sharing meals. Sharing stories, laughs, sad moments. And they're part of your family."

2001: Rip-Roarin Red

Tony Massey, Merchandise Manager

The most bizarre item I've ever sold, as a Broadway merchandise manager, was this themed nail polish at *Annie Get Your Gun*. The nail polish came in a saddle bag and the colors were named after the show. "Rip-Roarin Red!"

Annie Get Your Gun was a fun show to work on. I will never forget seeing Reba McEntire on the first night she played Annie Oakley. It was the most electric moment I have ever had in a theater; you felt like you were watching someone become a star. She was already a name, and already established in her field, but you felt everyone in the theater go: *Wow. She is truly a triple threat.*

Reba went on to have her whole television career that I feel she may never have had if she hadn't had the exposure of being so wonderful in *Annie Get Your Gun*. She was the real deal. Her first night in that show felt historic.

The Sound of the Marquis

Abe Jacob, Sound Designer

The Marriott Marquis was the first Broadway theater really designed for amplified music. It was built at a time when amplification on Broadway was becoming the thing to do.

I was involved with putting together some of the systems with the acoustician. And one of the things we did at first was make the room very acoustically "dead," so that any amplification you brought in could be done any way you wanted it, without having the room interfere with the sound design.

Most Broadway theaters were built in the 1920s or 1930s, and they were all designed to be acoustically reinforced, rather than electronically reinforced. So, the shape of the room made a lot of difference. You have to be careful when you go into those theaters because you want the electrical energy that you're creating from loudspeakers and other devices to be aimed into the seating area, rather than into the empty space and walls of the theater. Now, we have better technology to shape sound in that way, but in the 1980s, that was a challenge.

The Marquis was dictated by the fact that there was a hotel going up around it. They said, "This is how much space you have." So, the fly floor[21] is not high and there are no restrooms in the theater space itself. But for many other reasons, it's turned out to be a good theater to be in.

---

[21] fly floor: a platform several levels up, backstage, from which stagehands can operate theatrical components

2002: Free Admission To Those Who Dream

Jonathan Groff, Actor

I saw *Thoroughly Modern Millie* six times. The first time I saw it, I got Standing Room Only tickets in the back of the theater. I was so impressed with Sutton Foster. I thought that she was giving a historic performance.

The show also struck me because it was about her character moving to New York and starting her life. There was so much in it about New York City, and being in love with the city, and leaving your small town and making a name for yourself. As a teenager, that really spoke to me.

I went back and saw it again and again. The fourth time I went to go see it, my friends and I got to New York and stood in line at the box office at 10am. We could only afford Standing Room tickets, and those are only available when the show is sold out—but they told us that *Millie* was not sold out that day.

We decided that we would go to the TKTS line and pass out flyers for *Thoroughly Modern Millie* to try to get the show to sell out... so that we could then buy Standing Room Only tickets. We just didn't have enough money for any other tickets!

We passed out flyers for *Thoroughly Modern Millie* all day, from 10am until 1:30pm. Then we went back to the theater, and it still wasn't sold out! I said to my friends, "We're seeing the show. There's no way we're not seeing it."

Since it was at the Marriott Marquis, we could go up the escalator, into the hotel, and be right in front of the lobby of the theater. We did, and I told the usher, "I will literally give you all the money I have if you let us go in and see the show right now." The usher told us, "I'm sorry, there's nothing I can do. You know, you can stand here on the other side of the glass wall and watch it on the monitor."

The overture started, and Sutton started singing "Not for the Life of Me" and we were just sitting outside the glass, on the floor. We were also starving because we didn't eat all day. We wanted to keep passing out flyers.

Then, an usher came down from the mezzanine, and brought us into the theater.

We sat, and my four friends and I watched the show from the 5th row of the mezzanine.

It was amazing. I don't know who that usher was, but she was an angel.

———————

Sutton Foster was so obsessed with Spring Awakening *(2006), which starred Jonathan Groff, that she had bagels sent to the Eugene O'Neill Theatre for the cast and crew, on several Sundays throughout their run.*

———————

2002: My Eight Minutes On Stage

Anne L. Nathan, Actor

I really loved my role, Miss Flannery, in *Millie*. I also understudied Mrs. Meers.

I was contracted to be the second cover for Mrs. Meers, but I really didn't want to do the role. I knew it wasn't a great fit. Eventually I went on, but I wasn't that good. I think they knew it too, because after they'd seen me do it a bunch of times, they were like, "Anne, we love you but we're going to actually get someone to do more performances." And I said, "Great!" I just knew it wasn't my perfect role, and that was okay.

I do remember a moment on stage that was amazing. Sutton Foster and Marc Kudisch and Gavin Creel did what they called the "Scooby-Doo scene." It was a scene at the end of the show where they did a lot of quick dialogue. "No!" "What?" "Yes." One night, one of them started laughing and they absolutely couldn't recover. They kept laughing and the audience kept laughing and finally they had to stop and start the scene over. The audience loved it.

Thoroughly Modern Millie was definitely the easiest job of my life and so fulfilling too. My character was on stage for eight minutes total, and managed to get huge laughs and exit applause! It was the perfect job for me— for anybody.

I had a little a little tap block that the crew made me, so I could practice my tap dancing in my dressing room. Everybody was walking around in that theater in tap shoes, so when you exited the stage, if you ever didn't feel like talking to people, you had to take off your tap shoes, hold them in your hand and tiptoe to your room.

My second-ever trip to New York City was during the summer of 2002. I was 16 years old. I flew up from Florida for the weekend with my best friends from theatre camp. We had time to see three shows, and we picked Urinetown, Thoroughly Modern Millie, *and* Hairspray.

We were so excited that we barely slept for the entire week prior—instead, we had sleepovers and watched my VHS tape of the 2002 Tony Awards. We learned the choreography for Mamma Mia!*'s "Dancin' Queen", and we nearly broke the tape, rewinding over and over to watch "Run Freedom Run!" from* Urinetown *and "Forget About The Boy" from* Thoroughly Modern Millie.

Our tickets for Thoroughly Modern Millie *were for Friday night, then we were seeing* Urinetown *and* Hairspray *on Saturday. We only had enough time off from our jobs to stay in New York for 48 hours, but we were going to make the most of it!*

We were on a plane to New York City that Friday afternoon, singing along to The Last 5 Years *on our shared Discman, writing in our slam book, and probably making the rest of the passengers wish that teenagers were banned from Delta, when a woman on the flight went into labor.*

The plane landed in Norfolk, Virginia. We were stuck at the gate, eating Pop-Tarts and dreaming of Gavin Creel, for three hours. When we got back on the plane, we were panicked. Would we get to NYC in time for Thoroughly Modern Millie*?!*

We asked everyone in the rows in front of us if we could get off the plane first—we had to get to an 8pm show. Nonplussed by the fact that a woman had just nearly given birth on our flight, we convinced them that seeing Sutton Foster was the real emergency.

We missed it. By the time we got to the Marriott Marquis, it was 9:30pm. We cried at the box office, devastated in a manner reserved exclusively for theatrical teenagers.

We woke up the next morning and had the best weekend in New York ever. Hairspray *and* Urinetown *blew our high school minds. We ran ourselves ragged, exploring every bit of the city we could.*

Somehow, while we were doing this, my mom worked magic. She got nine return flight plane tickets switched, and nine new seats to the recent-Tony-winner Thoroughly Modern Millie. *I had never been so grateful to have an assertive Jewish mother in my life!*

I remember my first time in the Marquis. I remember it because we almost didn't make it. But then we did.

I remember sitting in the rear orchestra, thinking "I'm here, I'm here, I'm here!" My friends were chattering all around me, but this world belonged to me alone. Waiting for the sold-out matinee to begin, I remember touching the arm rests, touching the carpet, clutching the Playbill on my lap. Everything at the Marquis looked shiny and plush. I had spent so long picturing New York, and picturing this show about New York...

And then it started. Sutton Foster walked on stage and sang, "I studied all the pictures in magazines and books... I memorized the subway map too..."

2002: This Seals The Deal, I'm Absolutely Moving Here

Jay Armstrong Johnson, Actor

When I was 15 years old, I came to New York City for the first time and saw three Broadway shows. *Thoroughly Modern Millie* was incredible. I remember Sutton Foster and so many things about her performance. She blew me out of the water! I remember Gavin Creel, his voice. We were in the second row. It was my first trip to New York, and I thought: *Yeah! This seals the deal. I'm absolutely moving here.*

Even in its relatively short life, the star dressing room at the Marquis has had many great occupants: Tyne Daly during Gypsy; *Victor Garber, then later Jerry Lewis during* Damn Yankees; *Julie Andrews during* Victor/Victoria; *Bernadette Peters during* Annie Get Your Gun; *Sutton Foster during* Thoroughly Modern Millie; *Ricky Martin during* Evita; *Constantine Maroulis during* Jekyll & Hyde.

The dressing rooms have numbers on them, carved in wood, but the house crew calls the dressing rooms by the names of the actors who have used them most recently.

2002/2004: The Marquis Family

Gavin Creel, Actor

When I first got to the Marquis, I was completely overwhelmed. It was very fortress-like and bizarre backstage. It took me a little while to figure out where to turn left and where to turn right!

Because the theater is part of the hotel complex, there were some sewage problems. On the first preview of *Millie* (2002), we were all in our dressing rooms for half-hour, getting ready. I was in the shower, and I heard a gurgling noise. Then I heard screaming.

On the second floor, there's a drain in the middle of the dressing room hallway floor. I don't know why it's there! Imagine sewage erupting and bubbling up through that drain and flooding the entire hallway.

We were all screaming, and it kept coming. People yelled, "Get in your dressing room! Shut the door! Keep the costumes away from the door!"

We were just starting previews, and I remember thinking: *Oh my God, this is either good luck or a bad omen.* It was thankfully good luck, but we couldn't start the show for 30 minutes. We had to wait for them to clean up the horrible sludge that was coming up through the floor. After that, whenever I heard the sound, I would run out in the hallway and scream, "Everybody get out!" It was crazy.

116

The great thing about show business is that it's very small. Even though it's a big industry and a huge tourist attraction of New York City, theatre is actually a really small community of people, where loyalty is valued and rewarded.

It was so neat because at the time that *Millie* closed, I didn't even know I was going to be doing *La Cage* (2004), the next show to go into the theater! To this day, I can't remember who worked on which show. I see people and I go: *Did we do* Millie *or* La Cage*?* Because to me it was like I left for a bit, and then came back again to the same place.

It was neat to see Rey Concepcion and the gang all there, you know? The same people at the door, the same crew guys that stay with the theater, and just the same family. There were musicians that played both *Millie* and *La Cage* and also David Calhoun, the house manager. Kim, who was the associate house manager at the time of *Millie*, went on to become the house manager at the Al Hirschfeld when I did *Hair* over there.

That's what it's like on Broadway. You watch people grow up and expand and get promoted and they stay in the community. There were ushers who were like, "Oh, I loved you in *Millie* and I'm so glad you're back!" It's a lucky thing.

I feel very lucky that the community is what it is, but it doesn't begin and end with the actors. It's house managers and ushers and the people who clean the theaters. You know them. You recognize their faces. It's awesome.

2002: They Would Add My Name In

Rey Concepcion, Door Man

Thoroughly Modern Millie was like a family. When they were rehearsing on stage, sometimes I would be cleaning upstairs in the mezzanine, and they would add my name into some of their lines. We all had a good laugh over that.

Sutton Foster was such a sweet young lady. She would bring in Saturday bagels. It was a great group. And on that show, I met Christian Borle. He's such a great guy. He collects action figures and comic books, so we bonded over that. We're both kids at heart.

They filmed the TV show *Smash* here earlier this year, and it made my day to see Christian and Megan Hilty back here. They had *both* worked at the Marquis!

2002: Where I Am Aint Where I Was

Laura Osnes, Actor

I think the Marquis would be fun to work in, because it's in a hotel. That's where *Thoroughly Modern Millie* was, and I remember seeing that show before I moved here, thinking: *Oh my gosh, I could do that.* I feel like playing the Marquis would be wonderful.

2002: My First Time On A Brand New Broadway Show

Ken Davenport, Producer

The Marquis is interesting because it connects to the hotel and there are all sorts of passageways from the dressing rooms right into the hotel itself. It's a maze! All of the theaters have very unique layouts, so it takes a while to figure out each one.

I was the company manager of *Thoroughly Modern Millie*. When the show started previews, I remember thinking: *I don't know if this show is going to make it.* There was something about that first night that just didn't quite gel.

And then the most amazing thing happened: a group of incredibly talented Broadway professionals buckled down and did their jobs, from the producers to the directors to the writers to the actors. Over the next several weeks the whole show transformed right in front of my eyes.

That was my first time as a company manager on a brand new Broadway show, from the ground up. I had never been through the process! Now, I realize that first preview of *Millie* was like all the first previews I've ever had of new shows.

After it opened, a different kind of work began: The Tony campaign... and once again, a group of incredibly talented Broadway professionals rolled up their sleeves and worked their butts off, from the producers to the advertising agency to the marketing directors, etc. Then the show won the Tony Award for Best Musical! They eventually recouped and now the show is done all over the world.

That process was one of the most educational experiences I've ever been a part of. It's one of the reasons I wanted to do produce *Kinky Boots* with Hal Luftig. I knew he knew how to forge a winner. If that first preview wasn't quite ready, I knew that he would roll up his sleeves, and I knew he had the ability to get other people to do the same. And I knew he could win a Tony.

———————————

The box office for the Marriott Marquis Theatre is currently on 46th Street, near Broadway. But before that, the box office was on Broadway, with an entrance right in Times Square.

There is a "phantom escalator," no longer in use, that leads from the old box office location to the theater. Peering into the old box office area now, you can see boxes, ladders, and dust.

In 2006, the TKTS booth in Duffy Square closed and the new, sturdy structure with the red steps that we have today was built. During construction, TKTS temporarily relocated to a spot in the Marquis, near 46th Street.

At this point, the mural in the hotel breezeway, heretoforth celebrating classic Broadway shows, was redone so that The Drowsy Chaperone *might have some pull at the booth.*

When TKTS moved back to their regular location, the Marquis Theatre commandeered the area they had cleared for a new box office. This is now coupled with a new Marquis marquee, opposite the Lunt-Fontanne. The bold red signage for the theater leads into the hotel breezeway, which is now always plastered with a mural advertising a current show at the Marquis or another theater nearby.

Why is the Marriott Marquis box office in such an odd place to begin with? The hotel was originally planned without a Broadway theater in it, but the city demanded that the Marriott must build a theater within its structure since they were knocking down five theaters to construct it. Thus, the hotel's ballroom was redesigned to be a theater.

118

2006: Stuck In Bed With *The Drowsy Chaperone*

Danny Burstein, Actor

About four times over the course of our run of *The Drowsy Chaperone*, the murphy bed that would take Beth Leavel, the Drowsy Chaperone, and me off after we sang "I Am Aldolpho," would fail to flip back into the wall. Sometimes, it didn't even come down, and stagehands would try to push the bed down.

One time, all the stagehands were trying to push the bed down, and the whole audience could see them through the wall! Bob Martin, as Man in Chair, turned and said, "Oh look, the neighbors!" He was brilliant.

The stagehands at the Marquis Theatre are aces. They are great people. It's a family that really cares about theatre. You wouldn't necessarily think that. I mean, they sometimes seem like these hardened, tough guys. And then they go, "Danny, that scene in act two is so beautiful!" You don't expect that.

———————————

The Drowsy Chaperone tells the story of Man In Chair, a lonely middle-aged musical theatre fan, who is obsessed with shows of the 1920s. He shares with us his favorite cast album, from a 1928 musical called The Drowsy Chaperone.

At one point, while telling us about the show, Man In Chair says, "Here's where there would be an intermission, if we were sitting in the Morosco Theatre. Which we're not."

This was a nod to the demolished Morosco, which once stood where many Drowsy Chaperone *theatergoers were then sitting, at the Marquis.*

In reality, in 1928, the only musical that played the Morosco was called Say When, *a gleeful romp with song titles like "Cheerio", "Who's The Boy", and "In My Love Boat". In* Say When, *Diana accidentally promises Count Varelli she will marry him, but eventually ends up in the arms of her fiancé, Gregory. The song "Cheerio" actually had lyrics by New York's Mayor at the time, Jimmy Walker! It closed after only 15 performances. It was the mayor's only foray into Broadway showbiz, although his life would later be turned INTO a Broadway musical, called* Jimmy – *but much like Man In Chair, I digress.*

Doesn't sound too far off from The Drowsy Chaperone, *now does it?*

While not in the script, during the New York run of The Drowsy Chaperone, *Man In Chair would remark off-handedly to the audience: "They tore down the theater and put up a hotel."*

———————————

2006: Oh My God, I'm Going To Get Fired

Josh Marquette, Hair Designer

As a hair designer, I always try to get a sense of what the actor's going to be doing with their character, and what they're comfortable with. A lot of people will come to the table with, "I only look good in this color," or, "I think she should have this."

For Danny Burstein's character in *Drowsy Chaperone*, the team said, "We want him to be in a wig. It should be an obvious wig, but not necessarily have a totally hard front." Then Danny said, "I think it should be black. And I think—" There was a grand piano there, and he suddenly remarked, "I think it should be shiny, just like this grand piano!" *Like patent leather*, I thought. And then, I thought: *What's better than a white stripe in a black, shiny wig?*

I pictured that wig so completely in my head. I told the wig maker, "I don't want it to be nice, fine, little hairs in the front so that it looks natural. I want big knots, so it *looks* really hard but it's still a lace front wig. Black. Shiny black, with a white stripe."

The wig maker sent it to me. I pulled it out of the box, and I thought: *Oh my God. I'm going to get fired! This is so terrible. What was I thinking?*

Then I thought: *No, but it's exactly what I want. It's what Danny wants. It's outrageous, but it's what we talked about. Just do it.*

I took the wig to the theater, and told Danny it was there. I warned him that it was bold. He was excited so I pulled it out and I put it on him. Right away, he yelled, "This is perfect! This is it!" *Well, the actor likes it, so...*

Casey Nicholaw walked into the hair room, saw Danny in his wig, and said, "Um... Let's look at it on stage." I thought: *Oh God. The director hates it. And I'm fired.*

Danny found his character. Once that wig went on his head, suddenly he just became Aldolpho. He's been kind enough to say how much the wig helped him. He walked out on stage and it was not even a question. Casey said, "Wow! Perfect! That's done."

————————————

I was a sophomore at NYU when The Drowsy Chaperone *opened at the Marquis. I won the ticket lottery for the first preview, and sat front row center for the show. I loved it. After curtain call, I noticed a stray stack of papers under my chair. It was a script! Clearly left there by a staff member who was frazzled by previews, it had a couple notes on it in red ink.*

I took it. I was 20 years old and stage-struck, and it seemed to have been left there just for me. Thus began a long career as a Robin Hood of Broadway history, only stealing that which has been abandoned or discarded. (I'm not saying I have ever climbed into a dumpster the day after a show closed, but I'm not saying I haven't either...)

Doing interviews for this book, I was half-terrified that Casey Nicholaw, Danny Burstein or Josh Marquette would say to me, "After the first preview of Drowsy Chaperone, *I lost my script!" and I would have to confess.*

————————————

2006: This Is How They Do It In Utah!

Eddie Korbich, Actor

Drowsy Chaperone was such a special show. I have so many favorite memories.

The first day we moved into our dressing rooms, Georgia Engel found that she was assigned to a huge dressing room opposite Sutton Foster. And she said, "No, no, you can't give me this. Bob Martin should have this dressing room." She saw that his room was small, and he was Man In Chair and the writer! She insisted they switch, and then she painted her little room pink. I'll never forget that generosity.

I remember everyone's last performance in the show, because Troy Britton Johnson would give us a challenge to do and we got money to go through with it. Sutton took a tumble down the entire length of the stairs. Georgia did this huge ballet number. Angela Pupello grabbed the curtains, flung them around herself, and did a slow, slow walk. After that, stage management said, "We have to approve these!"

At the end of the show, there was this joke about all of the characters getting married in one big clump. And the line was, "That's how they do it in the army!" One day, they had me say instead, "That's how they do it in prison!" Crickets. No one laughed. For my last show, I said, "That's how they do it in Utah!" *That* got a huge laugh. Bob Martin and Casey Nicholaw heard about it, and that line became part of the show from then on.

2008: Writing *Glory Days* And Performing In *Cry-Baby*—At The Same Time

Nick Blaemire, Writer/Actor

During *Cry-Baby*, I walked into the Marquis for the first time with Chris Hanke and Peter Matthew Smith. They knew that I was a newbie and they brought me over. We had just finished in the rehearsal studio and pulled all the tape off the floor.

I walked over with them and went to the stage door. The stage door guys at the Marquis are two of the nicest dudes on Broadway.

I'd actually been backstage before at the Marquis because Gavin Creel had taken me back when I was still in high school and came to see *Millie*. Before I had gotten into the University of Michigan or he had any reason to be nice to me, he just was.

We walked in, and I remember thinking: *Whoa. This is so big.* My friend Brian Spitulnik calls it "vibrating"— when you're standing there on Broadway and you become one with your dreams and the universe and the lights are shining and there are people there... but you also kind of feel like you're alone and you're in your bedroom. I definitely felt it that day.

During our five-week preview process, they changed the lyrics to Cry-Baby's first big song about 700 times. One night, presumably before someone important from the press was coming, they changed it a couple hours before the show, leaving James Snyder, who was already dealing with a million and one changes, with no time to relearn a song that was surely soup in his head already.

So, the stage manager made huge cue cards with the new lyrics on them, SNL-style, and like a true pro, James, in his Broadway debut, surreptitiously read and performed the lyrics simultaneously, as we all tried to act angry at him, in character, while secretly staring in awe. A true Broadway moment.

The best moment of all was during our third preview, when we found out that *Glory Days,* the show I'd written, was going to Broadway. I was thinking: *What am I supposed to do?!* I walked down to talk to the *Cry-Baby* team.

I didn't really know Mark Brokaw, the director, or Rob Ashford, the choreographer, that well. I was the ensemble guy they had given a chance to, and I was like, "Can I have some time off from your important preview process of your multi-million dollar show to go do my little show that you don't know anything about?" They were truly awesome about it. They just said, "You have to be here when we need you."

Glory Days needed work. That's a whole other story. In any case, they needed me over there one night to fix a song, so I called out of *Cry-Baby* and went to Circle in the Square. Who was in the audience that night? Adam Epstein and Allan Gordon, my *Cry-Baby* producers, and Rob too. They saw me there.

The *Cry-Baby* stage manager pulled me over the next morning and was like, "You're gonna get fired. You can't do that. That's terrible." Then Rob came up to my dressing room and said, "Don't worry. It's fine. You're in the weirdest position of any human being in this building now, so I get it. Don't do it again, or if you have to, just tell me." I remember just falling in love with them so much during that process. It was such a stressful month, and everybody was awesome to me.

We were at the top of the theater, in the sixth floor dressing room. It was me, Peter Matthew Smith, Eric Sciotto, Charlie Sutton, Michael Buchanan, and Stacey Todd Holt. They hazed me! I got Broadway ensemble college initiation.

I used to curl under my desk and watch *Lost* and sleep and write and eat delivery Kodama. The best thing in the world was Chester Gregory, who was down a floor. He wasn't in the show until 30 minutes in so he would always get delivery at "Places!" We would be on our way down, and there would be a dude waiting there with a sandwich or sushi for Chester. Then Chester would come out in his slippers, as we were getting ready to start the opening number, and be like, "Hey guys!"

I raised a fair amount of money for *Glory Days* in the bathroom backstage at the Marquis, overlooking *The Lion King*. I'd go there when I needed to be on phone calls, and people would come in and take poops. They knew I was on the phone with somebody important, and they'd make noises. I'd be like, "Guys, I'm kind of on an important phone call!"

My favorite part of *Cry-Baby* was getting to do "Squeaky Clean" with the boys. Every night, we'd go down to Hanke's dressing room and run that song. The harmonies were hard! We all made up names for our characters. Colin Cunliffe was "Btom," but the B was silent. And the tap number was crazy! We had to jump off a balcony every night.

It was such a *big* Broadway show! It was a great one to come in with first, like: *This is 11 million dollars and we're here to like spend it.* It was fun, it was really fun.

––––––––––––––

When I worked on [title of show], *I remember being backstage in Jeff Bowen's dressing room, looking under the tables. He'd discovered that other people who'd played the Lyceum had signed their names.*

It said "Danny Burstein." It said "Brian D'Arcy James." They'd had his dressing room in years past, in shows now closed.

Throughout the run, sometimes people would come backstage and ask, "Is my name still under the table in the 2nd room on the 3rd floor?"

That was my first taste of what I call the Dressing Room Legacy.

When I interviewed Rey at the Marquis, I found out that in the chorus dressing rooms, the drawers are covered in signatures. On their first day, when any new Marquis cast member opens a drawer, they see squiggles commemorating Follies *and* White Christmas *and* La Cage Aux Folles *and more.*

Many Broadway theaters carry on this tradition. Between The Little Mermaid *and* The Addams Family, *an overzealous cleaning man painted over decades of signatures on the dressing room tables at the Lunt-Fontanne. The uproar could be heard down 46th Street.*

––––––––––––––

2008: Abandoned Escalators

Austin Nathaniel, House Manager

The first Broadway show I ever saw was *Les Mis* at the Imperial. I'm from Connecticut, and a friend of mine had gotten to go into the city and see it. I wanted to see it so much, too. I memorized the cast recording. I begged and begged my mother to take my sister and me into the city to see the show, and even though it was out of her comfort zone, she did.

The show was life-changing. I remember going for dinner on the eighth floor of the Marriott Marquis afterward and my sister and I were still sobbing. We were still at the show.

Then, the Marquis ended up being the first theater I ever worked at on Broadway! Every day, going to work, I would think about that.

I moved to New York City five years ago because I landed a job in house management. I wanted to be a company manager, so I thought I'd come to the city and get on my feet, and then transition into that. House managers and company managers actually have similar jobs in some ways, and they're in the same union, so you can go back and forth.

The first show I worked on at the Marquis was *Cry-Baby*, which opened and then closed right after the Tonys. Suddenly, I was left living in the city with no employment. With some help from people, I got connected with an assistant company manager job on *Tale of Two Cities* at the Hirschfeld. That closed quickly too, and I came back to the Marquis to house manage *White Christmas*. Now, I'm at the Palace. Over the past five years, I've worked on 11 shows at three different theaters.

The most interesting thing about the Marquis is the old escalators that are sort of half there and half not-there anymore. When you'd walk into the front parking area at the Marquis, there were two escalators. Those were sort of the main entrance to the theater. They were connected to the old box office. At some point between when I saw *Les Mis* as a kid and when I started working there for *Cry-Baby*, those escalators were removed— but only the lower half of them!

The upper halves of the old escalators are still there. They're locked off from the public, but they're in the theater space. If you work at the Marquis, you can eat lunch in this creepy landing on the top section of the abandoned escalators, with big windows and a view of Times Square all right there.

2008: I'm Dreaming Of A Magically Designed *White Christmas*

Anna Louizos, Scenic Designer

In *White Christmas* there were some moments where I was ecstatically happy with the design.

When the show starts, we're in a barn in Vermont. The curtains rise, and within minutes, instead of flying up, the set pages open in a very elegant way, and suddenly, where there was a barn, there's this elegant New York skyline. There are white, sparkly palm trees, and patrons sitting at tables dressed in gowns, and a big arch on the stage, where an actress is singing. The transformation happens quickly and drastically.

There's another moment where we're crowded in this train, with all these people singing, "Snow! Snow! Snow!" The iris[22] closes down on the train, and when it opens back up, you're in the interior of the big Vermont inn, with the staircase, and Christmas decorations all the way to the top.

Those are the kinds of transitions that can be surprising. In my head, I saw it, and in my model I saw it, but it's not until you see it on stage that you can be like: *Wow! That really worked. We did it.*

---

[22] iris: a piece of scenery that blocks out everything behind it, leaving only a small circular section in sight

Those who have worked at the Marquis talk about the "secret pass-door" to get backstage. I won't be sharing the exact location, because I don't want to be responsible when Bridesmaids The Musical *is playing at the Marquis and a crazed fan steals Leslie Kritzer's weave.*

But for those working at the Marquis, it's another hidden discovery and often used to sneak friends in.

————————————

2009: Workin' *9 to 5*—And Dolly Parton Made Us Fudge In Her Microwave!

Ann Harada, Actor

In *9 to 5*, I would always watch as much as I could of Allison Janney's second act opener, "One of the Boys," which I loved. Even though the run of that show was shorter than we hoped, I just loved the people in the cast. We were so close.

I just do not understand why that show was not successful. It was pretty successful on tour, and it makes me sad that the timing in New York wasn't right.

Dolly Parton would come in and we'd sing the numbers for her—and she'd cry! She was always around, making us fudge in her microwave. She would come and watch the show from the camera in the stage manager's office during a lot of the previews.

If there was a technical problem, Dolly had no problem going out and entertaining the audience. Just the way she could hold an audience was amazing to watch... her whole persona was charming and lovely. She would go out and sing "9 to 5". The audiences loved that; they went mental!

————————————

The Marquis seats about 1,600 people. It's one of the larger Broadway theaters, but not as large as the Broadway, Foxwoods, Gershwin, Minskoff, New Amsterdam, Palace, or St. James. Of the 40 current Broadway theaters, it is the 8th largest.

For that reason, and because of its great location in the bustling heart of Times Square, the Marquis usually houses large musicals or special concerts. In fact, other than an eight performance return engagement of Patrick Stewart's one-man A Christmas Carol *in 2001, the Marquis has never housed a straight play.*

9 to 5 *was the first show that was so big, that for the first time there was no room for the stage manager backstage, and he had to call the show from a box on the mezzanine level!*

————————————

2011: Clicking Heels On Steel And Cement

Mary Beth Peil, Actor

Follies was amazing and incredible and crazy.

I think the thing that was interesting about that production was that as opposed to when I did *Nine*, where there were also a lot of women, the women of *Follies* were old and seasoned. Nobody went off at each other. Everybody was pretty much confident in what their contribution was and what they were offering, so there were no bad apples or problem children.

The younger cast members were all really appreciative of the older actors. They were respectful of the older people, and paid attention to them, and sought them out to talk to them. It was a really nice environment to be in.

I do this old opera tradition, where you spit three times on each shoulder for good luck. I do it in every show, but I don't always do it to every person. But with *Follies*, somehow I had everybody lining up to come to the party. They would get mad at me if I didn't do it, and they'd say, "I can't go on if you don't give me the spit!" It was hilarious and ridiculous. There are just those things that actors get attached to.

Jan Maxwell did a funny thing during *Follies*. She had a backless dress and she had the second-to-last bow, so she would paste things on her back that only those on stage could see. She would do it mostly for the ensemble—for the kids—but she also did it for Bernadette Peters, who came out to bow after her. A series of pranks! The first time, she pasted hair on her back. She looked like a hairy creature—it was creepy!

Jan had a whole shelf of tricks in her dressing room. Sometimes, fake bugs would be coming up the back of her dress. You never knew when to expect it.

During our run, Jan was in an accident where she was hit by a minivan in Times Square. Her first night back in the show, she went on with tire tread marks on her back!

The closing of *Follies* was really deep, because the show had so many rebirths. That was a hard one to leave.

———————————

The plot of Follies *finds former showgirls and their spouses coming together to celebrate the old theater they performed in one last time before it's demolished to build a parking lot.*

Five Broadway theaters—the Morosco, Bijou, Helen Hayes, Astor and Gaiety—were demolished in 1982 to build the Marriott Marquis Hotel.

During the demolition, there were protests. New York theatre producers Joe Papp and Alexander Cohen built a stage in front of the doomed theaters. Luminaries including Susan Sarandon, Liza Minnelli, Jason Robards, Lauren Bacall, James Earl Jones, Christopher Reeve, Elizabeth Ashley, Colleen Dewhurst, Estelle Parsons, Celeste Holm, Treat Williams, Betty Comden and Adolph Green read great plays and made speeches on the stage.

When the wrecking ball came, many threw their bodies on the theaters and were arrested by the City of New York.

Christopher Reeve said at the time, "The first day of the protest... was one time I wished I were Superman so that I could just catch the wrecking ball."[23] *The wrecking was referred to as "The Great Theatre Massacre of 1982."*

Since the Morosco, Bijou, Helen Hayes, Astor and Gaiety had fallen, the city required the builders of the Marriott to include a Broadway theater in their hotel.

While some found the relatively new Marquis to be an odd fit for Follies, *I think it was perfect. There were more ghosts of the theatre present than ever before.*

———————————

[23] Schipper, Henry. (1982, December). Christopher Reeve – Living And Loving With Superman *Playgirl*. Retrieved from http://www.chrisreevehomepage.com/sp-playgirl1982interview.html

2011: Kissing the Beautiful Girls

Danny Burstein, Actor

When we moved to New York, there were lots of changes made to *Follies*, and they were mostly made by Steve Sondheim. He had very strong ideas about the production, and of course he knows the show better than almost anyone. We happily obliged.

99 times out of one hundred, he was absolutely right. When we tried the occasional thing that didn't work, he would say: "Oh, that didn't work. No big deal." It was never harsh. It was never didactic. It was always very collaborative and nurturing. He would tell you why. It was great; he's an absolute joy to work with.

Once you get over the intimidation thing, that he's Steve Sondheim, you start to go: *Oh, that makes perfect sense!* You just collaborate with him. Because that's all he wants. He wants to do the work, and be treated like a normal person. And that was wonderful.

We all had our own little traditions during *Follies*. I'd go and kiss all of the ladies, who would be waiting to enter before each performance began. I was the last one to enter, so I would go down the line, and kiss Rosalind Elias, and Terry White, and Flo Lacey, and Mary Beth Peil—all of them, just because. Because you have to be grateful for shows like that, and for casts like that.

We had seven generations of people in that show. Unbelievable. I know that when I was younger, all I did was sit in the corner and watch and learn. It was all I wanted to do. I didn't care about my part, I just wanted to find out how they did it, and watch everyone else's technique. And I felt like that again, doing *Follies*. I felt as though I was always learning from masters. It was just heaven on Earth.

2011: Finding *Wonderland*

Jose Llana, Actor

Wonderland was hard, because there were so many rewrites. But at the same time, when it's hard, you get really close with your cast. The cast became instantly close, and we became close with Frank Wildhorn too. Everyone in that theater really, truly enjoyed each other's company.

The weirdest thing is that the theater feels just like the time it was built. It *feels* like 1986. You're so used to Broadway being an old theater, where you walk up a million stairs, and then the Marquis is different. It feels like a regional theater in the middle of Times Square.

1995/2011/2013: The Rule Of Three

Frank Wildhorn, Writer

I've had three shows at the Marquis over the years.

Being involved in *Victor/Victoria* (1995), I felt like the luckiest kid in the world. The first song I ever wrote for Broadway was "Living in the Shadows," the 11 o'clock number[24] for Julie Andrews! To be able to work at the piano with Julie Andrews was so amazing, such an honor, so humbling.

---

[24] 11 o'clock number: the second to last song in a show, when it's a major showstopper; term was coined back when Broadway shows began at 8:30pm because the second to last song would then happen right at 11pm

126

Wonderland (2011) was a great experience. I'm sad that it didn't run longer. On the other hand, it's having such an amazing life around the world. It's such a hit in Japan! And it's opening in Korea and Germany in the next couple of years, so it's taken on a wonderful life.

My shows are so much about where they came from—and *Wonderland* was for my kids. Linda Eder and I used to live on 67th and Riverside on the 38th floor. There was an elevator in the lobby that was always broken, so I used to always think in my head that that elevator went down to "Wonderland." I used to tell my kids that. And the next thing I knew, there I was at the Marquis doing the show. That's the craziness of it all. Fantasy becomes reality.

Rey and I have a great friendship. He's a Jets fan and I'm a Cowboys fan so we always have something to argue about, which is fun. Theatre is all about the people. Rey makes that theater what it is. Carol Ann, who runs the theater for the Nederlanders is fantastic. Everyone on staff there is great to hang with, and supportive. We were back there with *Jekyll & Hyde* this past year, and that was terrific.

Your theater is your home. It becomes your home, and then every night, you have company—and you want to make *them* feel like they're at home. In the best theaters, that permeates not from the place itself, but from the people who work there: how friendly they are, and how they make you feel that. Then, hopefully the energy of the show comes together with that and makes magic.

I love the Marquis. I have always loved the Marquis.

But I remember the first time I read about the five theaters being knocked down to build it. I never got to see a show in the Morosco, the Helen Hayes, the Gaiety, the Astor, the Bijou. I never got to explore their backstages, or buy a ticket at their box offices, or wait at their stage doors. I never will.

If I had been around in 1982, I would've been the first person in line to handcuff myself to the Morosco with Joe Papp and Susan Sarandon and Comden & Green and scream bloody murder in the name of theatre history and reckless urban renewal.

People who were around before 1982 generally feel differently about the Marquis than the people who came to New York after. To theatre kids of my generation, the Marquis is the place that made us want to move here and do shows like Thoroughly Modern Millie. *To theatre kids a generation earlier, the Marquis is the reason why stages they knew and loved were destroyed.*

When plans were made to build Lincoln Center for the Performing Arts in the 1950s, there was an uproar from the community in the area. The cultural center changed the community in many positive ways, but those whose churches and schools and homes were eliminated to make way for the new modern theatrical complex were equally as riled as the Marquis protesters of 1982.

There were actors in the early 20th century who refused to work at the St. James, because the theater had booted Sardi's from its original location in order to build a theater on the same spot. Can you imagine?

Any book about the theatre is going to be filled with people lamenting days gone by and missing things that are gone. It should be. How beautiful it is to be nostalgic for the people and places of theatre past and to honor how much they were loved. There are things I miss too, and I've only been part of the New York theatre world for nine years.

But as Bebe in A Chorus Line *so succinctly puts it, "Oh please! I don't wanna hear about Broadway dying. 'Cause I just got here!"*

Every day, there are new kids getting off the bus, ready to conquer the Broadway of today that is here for them to discover.

2012: *Evitamergency*

Hal Luftig, Producer

As I became a teenager, I was allowed to come into the city on my own and see shows. One of the first shows that I ever saw on my own as a young adult because I said, "I gotta do this," was *Evita*.

As a nine-year-old, I would read Playbills. I would read them like they were Bibles. I would read them cover to cover, as I realized that shows have lots of different parts: costumes and actors and musicians and lights.

I would look in the Playbill and see "So and So Presents." Manny Azenberg, David Merrick, Hal Prince. They were my heroes growing up. I didn't know exactly what they did, but I knew that somehow they put the shows together, and I knew that was what I wanted to do too.

When I saw *Evita*, it was so arresting that it was like I got infected with something. I said, "That's what I *have* to do." So producing the *Evita* revival years later was thrilling, scary, everything! It was wonderful to have that memory, and to sit there while it being teched, thinking: *Oh my God, pinch me! Pinch me!*

I had been 22 years old sitting in the mezzanine of the Broadway Theatre watching the then unknown Patti LuPone and Mandy Patinkin rip up the stage, and now here I was, producing the revival and having conversations with Andrew Lloyd Webber and Tim Rice! Who am I? How did this happen?

The scariest part was that on the very first day of rehearsal, Michael Grandage, director of the revival, said to the company that the first-ever revival of anything is always tough. Especially with a show like *Evita*, people come to it with the memory of what they saw. You are telling them continually for two hours: *Okay that was your memory but this is new.* When he said that, I realized it was true.

My first show at the Marquis was as lead producer on *Thoroughly Modern Millie*. The Marquis is a fairly new theater, as these theaters go. All the older theaters have this Hephaestus fire curtain that comes down. In London, at intermission, they have to lower the curtain to show the audience that it's there and that it works.

When they built the Marquis, they built it with a new kind of modern fire curtain. It's called a deluge curtain, and it's basically a huge pipe that runs along the top of the stage. Should there be a fire, 200,000 gallons of water come crashing down on the stage like a deluge, and it creates a wall of water to stop any flame.

When we were doing *Thoroughly Modern Millie*, they were loading in the set and one of the stagehands accidentally hit the sensor and set the deluge curtain off. Thank goodness it was still the load in, but the deck got wet, some scenery pieces on stage got wet, and we actually lost two days of rehearsals while they tore it out. I thought: *Okay, this is catastrophic.* But it turned out not to be.

Fast forward to *Evita*. We have our first preview and it goes smashingly well. The next day, the cast is assembling in the green room for notes before going back on stage.

The Marriott Marquis hotel was testing the batteries in their smoke detectors, and everything was fine. Then the gentlemen came in to test it in theater. No one explained to them that to test the battery you have to turn off the main switch for the deluge curtain.

A man pushed the button and 200,000 gallons of water came crashing down onto that stage. It filled the orchestra pit. It looked like the Titanic; instruments were floating, sheet music was floating, the stage was soaked. I'll never forget this: Kristen Blodgette, our musical supervisor, jumped in the pit to start saving instruments and music! One of the stagehands started screaming, "Get out, get out! That's where the computers live! There are livewires!" She was in danger of being electrocuted. They yanked her out and she was covered in green, slimy water from the roof tank.

Michael Grandage was practically in tears. I had seen this before so I said: "This is old hat!" They started taking the sheet music and laying it out on the orchestra seats, drying it with hair dryers. It was our second preview. It was the only copy we had of this newly orchestrated score.

That night's preview was cancelled, and we thought that we'd be down for days. But God love that crew. The Nederlanders were terrific—they brought in extra crew too, and they got everything out: carpet, walls, drywall. They dried it, put it all back in, and we only missed three performances.

When it finally hit me, I turned to Nick Scandalios, who runs the Nederlander Organization. He was in the same position when *Millie* happened, and he's also a good friend of mine. I said to him, "Nick, I love you, I love the Nederlanders, I love this theater, I'm never coming back here again. Don't take it personally." We had a good laugh about it.

2013: The *Smash* Tony Awards

Krysta Rodriguez, Actor

The Tony Awards on *Smash* were filmed at the Marquis. The whole thing felt oddly real. I've been through Tony seasons on Broadway, so it was interesting to be a part of recreating that.

Josh Safran, the showrunner of *Smash*, even pulled me aside and asked me a couple questions. He was like, "Alright, what's it like? Do you get to sit in the audience if you're in a nominated show or do they just bus you in to perform?"

I explained to him that mostly you just get bussed in, but the two times that I went, I got to be in the audience. There was an attention to detail there that felt very real.

Being a part of *Hit List* in particular hit home. *Hit List* was at the center of this arc about developing a new show, and that's basically all I've done on Broadway in real life. There's been *A Chorus Line*, but other than that, I've done new original musicals: *Good Vibrations, Spring Awakening, In the Heights, The Addams Family, First Date*.

On each experience, we've been developing something new that has changed drastically, and I've gone on that journey. Like with *Hit List*, a lot of times shows would start out with a vision that everyone would try to make happen, and then something would change it. Sometimes, people's parts didn't become what they thought they would. Sometimes, there were casualties. A lot of that stuff on *Smash* felt very real.

Because of its position in the center of Times Square, the Marquis can be glimpsed in many movies and TV shows, including Enchanted, Captain America, *and* The Sopranos.

2002/2013: It's Hard To Separate The Theater From The Show

Christian Borle, Actor

During *Thoroughly Modern Millie*, I initially had a dressing room that had no windows. Then, when Marc Kudisch left the show, I made the desperate plea to get his room, because it looked out over the Minskoff Theatre marquee. It was nice to have a window overlooking the marquees for *Dance of the Vampires* and later, *Fiddler on the Roof*.

I met Jim Hodun, one of my first dressers, on *Thoroughly Modern Millie*. He's a fantastic designer and painter. He's painted almost all of my dressing rooms. I like to decorate, and make it feel like a home away from home.

When *Millie* was at the Marquis, that was around the time that *Lord of the Rings* came out so we made my dressing room a deep green, which made me feel like I was in Rivendell. For *Spamalot*, I went with a dark midnight blue that made the dressing room feel cave-like. And then, *Legally Blonde* was a little brighter.

It's hard to separate the theater from the show. The backstage people at the Marquis are amazing. They care and they love the place. They make it a family and they remember you years and years later.

My last day of shooting *Smash* was actually in the Marquis Theatre. Our green room for the *Smash* Tony Awards was Sutton's old dressing room that she had during *Millie* and *Drowsy Chaperone.* My dressing room at the Marquis during *Smash* was my second *Millie* dressing room that looked out over the Minskoff. And Rey and I were so excited. We collect comic books, so we got to catch up about that.

My very last shot of the entire series of *Smash*, I was sitting in the audience at the Marquis, watching the Tony Awards. They were like "That's the season wrap," and we were sitting in this incredible Broadway house that I had worked in. It was crazy.

One of the craziest audience reactions I've ever seen in a theater was for Sutton, during the first performance back after she won the Tony for *Millie*. That was huge. When that curtain opened and she was standing there on stage, the audience went absolutely wild. I was not in the show yet, so I was able to watch it from the audience. That seat was right next to the seat where I sat at the end of *Smash*.

When I started doing interviews for this book, who was brought up the most out of every Broadway person?

"You've GOT to interview Rey, the Marquis Theatre door man!" Christian Borle, Danny Burstein... everyone I interviewed who had set foot near the Marquis said it to me.

I was really excited to hopefully interview Rey, but I had a hard time finding his contact information. One day, I tweeted that I was looking for how to contact Rey, and I got a bunch of responses from more people who love Rey, saying just to pop over to the Marquis Stage Door.

The next morning, I wrote Rey a note about my book that I was planning to deliver in person after work. Around noon, I got an email from Anne L. Nathan, who had seen my tweet, saying "Here's Rey's number, and call me." I called Anne—who, sometimes I still can't believe I'm lucky enough to be friends with. In addition to being a tremendous actress who I have hugely admired since I saw her on the stage of the Marquis in Thoroughly Modern Millie *when I was 16 years old, she is one of my favorite people, always looking out for others. She's the very first person who let me interview her for this book.*

Anne said that she had gone over to the Marquis that morning, and told Rey about me and my book. He had said that he'd love to chat—but that today, until 4pm, was his last day at the Marquis for now.

130

Since Jekyll & Hyde *had closed, he was temporarily unemployed.*

He gave Anne his number for me to call. After this generous gesture, I decided on a whim to run over to try to say hi in person and give him my note. I walked in the Marquis stage door, planning on dropping off the note and giving him my number, and was immediately greeted by one of the nicest, most excited-to-work-in-the-theatre people who I had ever met. Rey said, "Let's do the interview now! I would love to!" and grabbed a chair for me.

After the interview, he asked if I wanted to have a tour of the empty theater. (YES.) He took me around and showed me every dressing room and every spot I'd heard brought up in interview stories. We walked around on stage in the empty theater, with the ghost light[25] on, as he told me stories.

Nothing has played the Marquis since then. If I hadn't spoken to Rey that day, I wouldn't have been able to reach him.

Rumor has it that a new construction project is happening at the Marriott Marquis in January of 2014. Parking is being turned into a shopping area, and parts of the backstage are being renovated. The souvenir and theatre merchandise shops that have been underneath the Marquis for years have all been closed. The stage door—and Rey—are being moved west, down 45th Street.

Blessed

Rey Concepcion, Door Man

I love my job. I thank God every day for my job. I've been blessed. Everybody that comes in here, they are all nice people. They all have a bit of fun, they come and work. We barely have a bad day.

After *Annie Get Your Gun*, I said: *I'm not going to get attached to another show.* Because I got attached to that one and then they left. I was really sad to see them go.

What happened though, is that *Thoroughly Modern Millie* came in. Before I knew it, I fell in love with them. And then I said, "Well, you know what? That plan is shot. I might as well accept it." Then came *Drowsy Chaperone*. Everybody was so great! So sad to see them go too.

Then I said to myself: *I'll meet the new show.* And that's how I carry on.

---

[25] ghost light: a tall lamp with an exposed bulb, left on stage overnight following each performance; the light is for safety reasons, but many say it is to give theatre ghosts a spotlight to perform in

The Al Hirschfeld Theatre

Built: 1924
Location: 302 West 45th Street
Owner: Jujamcyn Theaters
Formerly Named: Martin Beck Theatre (1924-2003)
Longest-Running Show: *Man of La Mancha* (1968-1971)
Shortest-Running Show: *Ring Around The Bathtub* (closed on opening night in 1972), *No Hard Feelings* (closed on opening night in 1973), *Onward Victoria* (closed on opening night in 1980), *Take Me Along* revival (closed on opening night in 1985)
Number of Productions: 204

At some theaters, you really have to modify your performance to include the balcony, the third level. The Martin Beck is the opposite of that; the mezzanine truly really wraps around and turns into boxes, and the theater all feels part of the same piece. It's a beautiful theater.

In the show I worked on at the Beck, we had a great little moment of community each night because the theater has that special area on the fire escape that's not quite all the way outside. Our ensemble stood there for a moment during the middle of every show and got a little fresh air together.

-Frank Vlastnik, Actor

Introduction: Safe On The Stage

Michael Berresse, Director/Choreographer/Actor

The first time I ever walked into the Martin Beck, it disoriented me for a second. You walk into what you think is the front door, and then you have to make a sharp right-hand turn into the auditorium. There was something great about that. There's a very short front lobby there, which is really cozy. I loved it.

I love the integrity of the exterior of the structure. I've had several different dressing rooms in that theater, doing *Guys and Dolls* and *Kiss Me, Kate*, and I love that they face the street.

Also, it's my favorite stage door on Broadway, because it's slightly elevated—so it gives a chance for people that are crowded to see the actors. When you step out the door, you're slightly elevated, so they actually can see you for a moment, and then you can disappear down into that crowd. And it's on a side street! A lot of the stage doors on Broadway are either hidden or a crowd control nightmare, but for some reason, that one has always felt very welcoming.

Then you open that stage door, and you walk in, and it's just a perfect little theater. It's a jewel box. Of all the Broadway theaters I've played, it's the theater where I enjoy being on stage the most, looking out at the auditorium.

For some reason, the actors' view is different in every theater. Even though you're not focused on that in performance, when you're leading up to it, when you're walking across the stage and rehearsing and warming up... you really absorb the energy of what it means to look out from the stage into the space.

Every time someone comes to see me in a show, especially if it's a kid, I love bringing them up on stage. When I was doing *A Chorus Line,* it was especially great. I would bring young artists up and let them stand on the line, just for my sake, because I saw this crazy shot of electricity and awe go through them, being almost dumbfounded by what it felt like to stand on the stage, looking out.

I think that's what I liked most about the Beck. I loved the way it felt to be there. I always felt very safe on that stage, looking out at that house.

1960: Nobody Wanted *Bye Bye Birdie*

Charles Strouse, Writer

I remember the first performance of *Bye Bye Birdie* in Philadelphia vividly, because I hid in a closet. At the time, the Shubert Theatre had a marble lobby and a staircase—and underneath was a broom closet with old towels and things. Old cleanser. I remember going in there because I couldn't face the audience coming out.

I closed the door behind me, and in the darkness, I heard someone whisper, "Get out! This is my closet!" It was my collaborator, Mike Stewart.

I have a lot of memories of the Martin Beck in New York, too. Securing a Broadway theater was, as now, impossibly difficult. It's like climbing Everest. That's because if a theater is dark, empty, it costs each theater owner a lot. So their gamble is much like putting a chip on a number, when they pick which show they'll take. They want to make sure they gamble on something that'll run a long time.

At first, there were no theaters open to us. We couldn't get any investors interested except for Goddard Lieberson. Still, we had to beg him. We went back and played *Bye Bye Birdie* for him numerous times, and he always had reactions like, "Let me know. There's still something I'm considering." But he was nice. We felt alive and kicking.

Nobody wanted the Martin Beck in 1960. The man who managed it, Louis A. Lotito, was very nice. He was the first person, aside from Goddard Lieberson, who even thought our show had any possibilities.

Finally, through much pleading, he gave us the Martin Beck, which was not considered a major coup as far as theaters. Then, to our absolute stunning surprise, our show became a hit.

I must have watched *Bye Bye Birdie* 100 times. To see my show there, on Broadway... it was really something.

I was a single guy, and I used to bring dates to the show. It was hot stuff. And I was making money for the first time. My accountant used to beg me to get married. He'd say: "You must know some nice girl!" Because we had Broadway and we also had three touring companies, and I used to give all my money to the government every year. It was funny.

While Bye Bye Birdie *was a hit at the Martin Beck, it didn't stay there for long.* Birdie *occupied the Beck for only six months before moving on to the 54th Street Theatre (now demolished), and then spending ten months at the Shubert.*

Back in 1960, shows were moved from theater to theater more frequently than they are now, to accommodate new bookings. It was just cheaper to move them around if "better" theaters became available. The original production of Annie *played four Broadway theaters, and the original production of* Once Upon A Mattress *played five! Because the scenic elements were simpler, the customary amount of time to switch theaters was about two days.*

In fact, Bye Bye Birdie *closed at the Beck on October 22, 1960, and on October 24, 1960, you could see it at the 54th Street!*

Prior to Bye Bye Birdie*, the most recent musical to run as long at the Beck was the original production of* On The Town*, which called the Beck home 15 years earlier, for the final six months of its run, after playing two other Broadway houses first.*

1964: Not For Me

Louis St. Louis, Writer/Arranger

Before I became a writer and an arranger, I auditioned a bit as a singer. I auditioned for the musical, *I Had A Ball*, on Broadway. My audition was with the infamous Shirley Rich, who practically invented casting.

I got down to the final 12 guys for the role and Shirley came to see me in the wings, at the Martin Beck. She said, "Can I talk to you? They're never going to cast you. It was a fabulous audition. But you're too original."

She asked me, "Is there other stuff you can do?" She was very heartfelt.

At one point, I took a class and we had to perform a song in front of the group. On my show-and-tell day, I got laughs, I got zings from the audience, I got big applause! I sat down, and the teacher's critique simply was, "Well, I think Mr. St. Louis was more interested in the action and the applause." I got up and grabbed my bag. I left and never went back. I thought: *This is not for me.*

I was just meant to work in a different role in the theatre.

1965: A Press Agent Stuck With A 26-Word Title

Harvey Sabinson, Press Agent

I had one advantage, and David Merrick resented that advantage: I had a lot of other producers hiring me. And I would be fired by Merrick, oh… every other show!

He would fire me and then at the end of the day he would send a note. Merrick was really jealous whenever I was working for anybody else. At one point, the producer Alex Cohen wanted me to work for him full-time. He said that he would pay me more than all the other shows I worked on if I would never work for David Merrick again. When I told him how much I was making, he looked at me and said, "I could never match that!"

Merrick was a brilliant producer. He had a great sense of humor, but there was a terribly dark side to him. He had a frightful childhood, and I think that scarred him for life. I understood the guy, and I certainly appreciated the fact that he had such great taste.

I was once in London on a vacation, and I went to see Peter Brook, who was about to direct *The Physicists*, a Broadway show I worked on that starred Hume Cronyn and Jessica Tandy. Peter invited me to come over to the rehearsal hall, where he was rehearsing another play. I climbed a flight of stairs to the rehearsal room, and there I saw about 24 actors staggered around in various stages of catatonia. It was quite weird.

I watched about an hour of this play being rehearsed and I thought: *Oh my God, this play is wonderful!* He was rehearsing *The Persecution and Assassination of Jean-Paul Marat as Performed by the Inmates of the Asylum of Charenton Under the Direction of the Marquis de Sade.* How do you like *that* for a title?

134

Peter was 88, no less! I went back to my hotel, and I got on the phone. I called Merrick, and said, "David, you've got to get over here right away and look at this play that Peter Brook is directing." You know what he said to me? "I've already optioned it." And he had! When he produced it on Broadway, it was a great success!

We cut the title in half, and abbreviated it as *Marat/Sade*. In those days, press agents typed their own releases and made carbon copies and all that. It was very primitive; it wasn't like it is today, of course, with the technology that I can hardly keep up with, by myself at home. I'm surrounded by a computer, an iPad, an iPhone. That would have been my life if I were a press agent today. In those days, you did it all by yourself. I said to Merrick, "I can't type that title out over and over again, no newspaper's going to run it." So we cut it down to *Marat/Sade*.

The Physicists opened at the Martin Beck in October of 1964, and closed after 55 performances. Marat/Sade *opened at the same theater in December of 1965. In the intervening year, four musicals all managed to play the theater:* I Had A Ball, *a return engagement of the original production of* Oliver!, Drat! The Cat!, *and the last two weeks of* Baker Street.

The Beck wasn't known for opening shows that had very long runs. Despite that, the theater could boast the premiere of many important works on Broadway, from Candide *(1956, 73 performances) to* The Iceman Cometh *(1946, 136 performances).*

1965: My Education

Peter Link, Writer/Actor

When I was young, I learned how to second-act a show. For many years, I knew all the second acts of Broadway shows because I knew how to stand around with the crowd and then move into the theater. It was a great way to learn about theatre when you couldn't afford tickets. Eventually, I got to the point where I could first-act a show too!

I studied at The Neighborhood Playhouse, and my job at night was selling orange drink[26] at Carnegie Hall. For two years, I saw every show at Carnegie Hall, and it was a great education. The people who ran the concession stands were these businessmen brothers. They were Russian Jews, and they were the sweetest guys. We became good friends when I worked for them. Later on, when I "made it," they were so proud of me.

The brothers knew I was studying at The Neighborhood Playhouse, so one night, they asked me if I'd like to work somewhere else. I said, "Oh no, I love working here!" And they said, "No, you could work a week at this show, and then a week at this show, and then a week at this show. We'll help you with your education."

The London company of *Marat/Sade* was here, at the Martin Beck. I worked two weeks at that show and saw it 16 times. It was the most powerful thing I think I've ever seen in the theatre. It was amazing! Peter Brook was one of the great, brilliant directors of the time. At one point in the show, everybody was under the stage, and you saw their hands all come up through grates. When they asked if I wanted to come back to Carnegie Hall, I almost said, "No, I want to stay here!"

---

[26] orange drink: a special sugar-water beverage first concocted by the Shuberts and later sold in other theaters

1968/2002: This Is My Quest

David Stone, Producer

For my fifth birthday, my mother took me to see her favorite show, *Man of La Mancha*, at the Martin Beck Theatre. I remember bits and pieces. At the very end, when Don Quixote/Cervantes was walking up the stairs, I tapped my mother on the shoulder and said, "I can't swallow." Of course, I was choked up. I don't think I understood that he was going to face the Inquisition, but I knew something bad was happening.

Then, 31 years later, I produced *Man of La Mancha* at the Martin Beck Theatre, and in the Playbill, I dedicated my work on the show to my mother. On opening night, she asked me if I remembered where we'd sat, and I pointed up to where the seats were. It was around Row J 7 and 9. And she said, "I have no idea how you remember that, but you're right!"

———————

In 1966, the four shows up for the Tony Award for Best Musical were about an eccentric Manhattan aunt and her grand adventures, a dance hall hostess with a heart of gold, a daydreamer scheming to save her brownstone... and Miguel Cervantes in prison telling the tale of the mad knight Don Quixote during The Spanish Inquisition. While Mame, Sweet Charity *and* Skyscraper *all had their dark moments, there was no question that the show that won Best Musical,* Man of La Mancha, *was a notably dark choice for Broadway audiences.*

Although perhaps it wasn't surprising that the show was a success, since the original novel, Don Quixote, *by Miguel Cervantes is considered the second highest selling book in the world, after the Bible!*

———————

1969/2002: An Israeli *Man of La Mancha*

Annie Golden, Actor

The first Broadway show I ever saw was *Man of La Mancha*. Richard Kiley had already left. My parents bought me tickets for my birthday. There was an Israeli actor, Gideon Singer, starring in it, and the reason I remember that is because during the curtain call, the cast sang "Impossible Dream" with a pro-Israel spin. My date had a problem with this and I didn't really understand what was going on.

Israel wasn't that old, and this guy rallied and started singing. It was like in *Casablanca* when they sing "La Marseillaise", you know? I was like, "Oh wow, they're doing a reprise of "The Impossible Dream"!" and suddenly my date said, "No, you don't get it."

I was maybe 17 or 18. I was fascinated. I was wide open and enthusiastic, and then something happened that made me understand the power of theatre, and the responsibility of that power: using it to make a political statement—and also how not everybody has to be on the same page, because my date was not having it.

Many years later, I went to the opening night of the revival of *Man of La Mancha* at the Martin Beck—no, it was the Al Hirschfeld then. It was decades later. The show was such a happy memory for me. But it was interesting, I still remembered that.

———————

The Martin Beck was no stranger to controversial political statements. In 1927, the government interfered when a drama entitled Spread-Eagle *was presented at the Martin Beck. Deemed un-American, the play, about Wall Street greed affecting relations between the United States and Mexico, was said to contain several inappropriate slurs at the army. Even though it received great notices from the critics, it was protested and chased out of town in ten weeks.*

136

1977: *Dracula* Saves

Elizabeth McCann, Producer

When I worked for Jimmy Nederlander, he produced an English play by Alan Bennett called *Habeas Corpus* in 1975. It was directed by Frank Dunlop. Because Jimmy didn't have a theater of his own open for it, he put it in what was then the Martin Beck, owned by Jujamcyn Theaters. I used to sit in the Martin Beck with Frank Dunlop and he'd say, "This place is tacky. You can't produce comedy in this house. You can't!" It had a very gothic interior. It was starkly gothic.

When I got involved with producing *Dracula*, half the rights were held by Jujamcyn, chiefly by Stanley Schwartz, who was running it at the time. He said all the same things about the Beck. And his company owned it! He said, "The theater is just tacky. Nobody plays the Martin Beck."

I said, "I want to play the Martin Beck." That remark of Frank's was sticking in my mind, that it had a sort of gothic feel to it. That felt right for *Dracula*.

We went into the Martin Beck and stayed for about two years! It felt marvelous to have a success like that, right out of the gate as a producer. When you're young, you're a fool. You think you're always going to have success, but you don't. But with *Dracula*, we were young, we were at the Beck, and it was a smash.

———————————

Frank Langella won acclaim in the role of Dracula in the revival at the Martin Beck, and then reprised his role in the hit 1979 film version, which catapulted him to stardom. The film happened because producer Walter Mirisch was so impressed with the Broadway production of the show—and the director of the film, John Badham, saw the Broadway production multiple times.

The original Broadway production of Dracula *had also been a smash hit, in 1927, and it was the show that led directly to the movie in that case, too. Universal purchased the film rights after seeing that production, and its Dracula, Bela Lugosi, also reprised his role on screen. When it was released in 1931, a touring production took advantage of the publicity and came to Broadway for a quick run at the Royale (now the Jacobs).*

Before Dracula *in 1977, bookings at the Beck were bleak. In 1972, one new show opened:* Ring Around the Bathtub, *the only Broadway play by Jane Trahey, one of the most successful, pioneering female ad executives of the 1960s. The play was semi-autobiographical and featured Carol Kane's Broadway debut. It closed on opening night. The theater was empty for an entire year, before* No Hard Feelings—*featuring Nanette Fabray, Eddie Albert, and a 29-year-old named Stockard Channing—opened in 1973. It also closed on opening night. The next four shows at the Beck played a total of 202 performances over a course of more than four years. Then,* Dracula *opened.*

———————————

1980: I Can Go Sit Under My Picture

Jill Eikenberry, Actor

It was unbelievably depressing to have *Onward Victoria* close on opening night. If you've worked in theatre, you know that even if there are so many things wrong with your show, by opening night, you just believe.

We believed. And it was really depressing when it closed. The good news is that 31 years later, the poster is still up in Joe Allen and I can go sit under my picture.

1981: A *Bye Bye Birdie* Sequel?

Michon Peacock, Actor

I stood by for Chita Rivera in *Bring Back Birdie*, the sequel to *Bye Bye Birdie*. I also assisted the director, Joe Layton. I consistently saw the show, because I had to take down the notes. I kept track of all of the blocking, which was tricky, because it changed so much.

I thought the kids in the show were great. Chita did a song, "I Like What I Do" that was absolutely hilarious. I had to do the number once in a rehearsal—and wow! There was so much going on in it! Joe's work with Chita was the best. I'm sure it was because she was so much fun to work with but always the ultimate professional. They came up with great ideas together.

Audiences loved the kids and the musical numbers. I just don't think they were able to get the story to unfold the way they needed it to. It was quite expensive, too. I'm sure they lost an enormous amount of money!

1981: Bigger, Better!

Jeb Brown, Actor

It's 1981. I'm 16 years old, and I'm going to be in *Bring Back Birdie*. Our designers wanted to grab what was going to define that decade at its outset, so the scenery for the show was made up of TV sets. It was going to be a video decade. MTV hadn't even happened yet but everything on the *Bring Back Birdie* set was a picture of the thing on a television.

David Mitchell designed those sets. He had just won a Tony for *Barnum* the season before, so we were in great hands. It was gonna be fantastic, and the set was out of control.

Looking back it seems clear that Broadway was kind of on the cusp of a new sort of musical theatre. In the seasons before us some of the big hits had been smaller shows, but now there was this 1980s appetite for "Bigger, better!" and that was seeping into musical theatre. Consequently, the ambitious sets for *Bring Back Birdie* threatened to devour the actors whole. It kind of got the best of us.

Granted there were other problems with the show. But it's harder to remind people that we also had a lot going for us. When I get a chance to look back on the show now, and talk about it, it brings up a lot of warm, positive memories I associate with that time. As an actor, you really do have to believe in the thing you're doing, right up to the very last minute. You find something to hold onto. Even as the ship is going down, you're hoping that maybe it'll still come together. We, a young cast, definitely believed.

Working with Chita Rivera was unbelievable. What a company leader. She was so gracious. She would come in early to rehearsals, so she could watch us kids work, and she'd just guffaw at everything we did. Donald O'Connor was a true gentleman, and here he was, making his Broadway debut, helming a show that wasn't always working well. He was a little bit deer-in-the-headlights, but he was very brave and a legendary talent.

I remember very well when we were about to do the "Filth" number for the first time, and we hadn't rehearsed it a lot, and our director told us to be "real punk." We did that number at the end of the first act, and the audience booed! We wear that as a badge of pride.

In the first big scene with all of us kids, the "Movin' Out" number, we were dancing all over, on roller skates, and with cordless phones. This was going to be all that the 1980s was about...which, of course, didn't turn out to be entirely true. One particular night, a group from my high school attended the show. There were 25 of my pals in the mezzanine. About 20 seconds into "Movin' Out", a number we'd done a lot of work on that afternoon, I rolled out on stage with my electric guitar, and there was a sudden cheer from the mezzanine. It was sweet. We did the show, and then the next day, at our noon rehearsal, Joe Layton gathered us all in the lobby and began by saying, "As you can see from last night's response, we finally landed the opening number." There I was, 16 years old, thinking: *Do I tell him? Do I say: sir, excuse me, but those were just my friends cheering?*

I never told him... and I always wondered.

———————

In the sequel to Bye Bye Birdie, *Albert is offered $20,000 to quit his job as an English teacher, find the long-disappeared Conrad Birdie, and get him to make a comeback on the Grammys.*

His wife, Rosie, isn't thrilled, but they find out that Conrad was last seen at the El Coyote Club in Arizona. Albert and Rosie have a rebellious teenage daughter, Jenny, who wants to move into a Soho loft with her boyfriend, and a rebellious teenage son, Albert Jr. They leave them behind and head to Arizona to find Conrad.

At the El Coyote Club, Albert and Rosie meet the bartender: Mae Peterson, who fans of Bye Bye Birdie *remember as Albert's mother. Meanwhile, Jenny has run off to join a cult and Albert Jr. has run off to join a rock group called Filth, who performs on toilets while flushing in rhythm. (This number—which Jeb mentions hearing boos during—was cut during previews.}*

At the club, Albert and Rosie discover that the overweight, burping mayor of Bent River Junction, Arizona is The Artist Formerly Known As Conrad Birdie.

Conrad does not want to perform at the Grammy Awards but Albert does not want to give up his advance, so with Mae's help, they fake Conrad's death in order to get Albert out of his contract with the Grammy Awards. Conrad tries to observe his own funeral, but gets locked in a closet. When he calls a press conference to announce his recovery, viewers are so relieved that they want him to run for President of the United States.

But the President of the United States could never swivel his hips on the Grammy Awards. Mae asks if they would take instead, the most famous star of the 1920s, Delores Zepol? Turns out, not only was Mae in showbiz, she was Spanish! (Zepol is Lopez spelled backwards.) Mae and Conrad both ended up doing production numbers on the Grammy's!

The score of Bring Back Birdie *was filled with updated versions of songs from* Bye Bye Birdie. *The teenagers' "Telephone Hour", about going steady, became the teenagers' "Movin Out", about moving in together. The grownups' lament, "Kids", became the grownups' lament, "Middle Aged Blues". Rosie's admonishing solo to Albert, "An English Teacher", became Rosie's admonishing solo to Albert, "20 Happy Years".*

Bye Bye Birdie *is one of the most-licensed shows of all time in schools and community theaters. Can't you picture those folks having great fun putting on the wildly tongue-in-cheek sequel?*

So could the creators. And that's where the trouble began.

———————

1981: A Swig Of Liza's Drink

Michael Mayer, Director

The first time I ever got to spend time backstage at a Broadway theater was when my friend Julie Cohen was cast in *Bring Back Birdie*. It was at the Martin Beck, and I went to see it a lot! I loved watching Chita Rivera and Donald O'Connor walk by, and I became friends with some of the other people in the cast.

Bring Back Birdie was the first Broadway opening I ever went to, and it was at the Milford Plaza. I remember that Liza Minnelli was there, and I didn't have the guts to go over and talk to her! But when she left, I went over to where she'd been standing. She left her drink, and it had Liza Minnelli's lipstick on it. I took a swig from her drink! I thought: *This is as close as I'm ever going to get to Liza, so I have to do it.* I told her that story many years later.

I still remember some of the songs from the show! And *Bring Back Birdie* was the first time I ever saw TVs on stage. It's funny to think about how we used all those TVs years later in *American Idiot*. Early things that you see come back into your work like that. *Equus* was very influential when I saw it as well; I put the audience on stage in *Spring Awakening* just like I'd seen them do in *Equus*.

1981: Opening Cold In New York

Charles Strouse, Writer

Bring Back Birdie was a funny, funny show—and the director Joe Layton and book writer Mike Stewart fought from day one to day final. The production was full of fights.

One of the reasons was that Joe had the idea to make the set a mass of television sets. It was brilliant, but it used up every hour of rehearsal. Every minute, there were electricians and technical things that had to be the priority.

It was a funny script, but we didn't want to do it on Broadway. A producer saw the script, and said, "I want to produce this." We were idiots to let him do it. But it really is amusing. If somebody did it again, I think it would be highly appreciated.

Most shows I've done have opened out of town. That one didn't. Today they open cold in New York. And that's hard.

Working on a show is like surgery. It's that intricate. It's that careful and sensitive. The real pros train themselves to listen to every rustle of a program during a scene. Alan Lerner always said that audiences have idiot genius, and it's true. If you listen, you can hear when they're absorbed, and when they're not. And the difference is small: the rattling of a program, coughing, a laugh from the balcony where you know they're taking it the wrong way. There are so many things.

1981: A Sizzling 1980s Party Joint

Jeb Brown, Actor

During *Bring Back Birdie*, the Martin Beck was right next door to Ted Hook's Backstage. That was our hangout. And Ted Hook himself was around, which seemed impossible, because it just seemed like it had to be a fake name. But there he was. I was 16, so it was just cokes and hamburgers, but we hung out there a lot as a cast.

It was a restaurant, but the place also felt like a club. It was a cabaret space sometimes. And this was the early 1980s—AIDS hadn't happened, Studio 54 was still going strong. Ted Hook's felt like a hardcore party spot. There were some real bashes there. And we were with Chita, who was very friendly with Liza, so Liza was around a lot. It was Chita and Liza and other notables—and all of us kids—at this sizzling early 1980s party joint. The party that had been the 1970s that went into the early 1980s was still going on in New York. And that scene felt a little unregulated.

―――――――――

The spot to the right of the Al Hirschfeld, now occupied by the Private Eyes Gentlemen's Club, was once the popular Ted Hook's Backstage.

Ted Hook was a chorus boy who appeared in over 400 Hollywood movies before he opened the restaurant and piano bar with his name on it in 1973. Because of his showbiz reputation, the establishment was filled with stars of Broadway and Hollywood, seated right next to chorus kids, seated right next to tourists with eyes agog.

Andrea McArdle and the orphans from Annie *liked to grab a bite there with their parents after the show. A Chorus Line's cast and creative team were frequent visitors. Meryl Streep liked to pop in after a performance of* Happy End *at the Beck in the summer of 1977.*

On an average night at Ted Hook's, Liza Minnelli might get up and sing a number, or you might find Richard Burton seated next to Robin Williams. The chorus kids in the show at the Martin Beck would often make it to Ted Hook's and order a drink before the last patron had even left the theater.

Each table at Ted Hook's Backstage was dotted with a lamp with a star's name on it. When a star came in to dine, the wait staff would be sure the lampshade with their name was switched to their table. Ted himself would often lead customers to their tables and surprise them with a pirouette.

Ted Hook's Backstage was one of the most popular post-show hotspots for Broadway folks for a decade. Ted Hook died of an AIDS-related illness in 1995, and a memorial was held for him at the Helen Hayes Theatre, where friends and diners from Jerry Herman to Dorothy Loudon, spoke and performed.

―――――――――

1981: *The First*

James Woolley, Stage Manager/Usher

Everyone has that one show they worked on that they loved that just didn't last. *The First* was mine. It was a musical about Jackie Robinson. I loved that show, and it had a wonderful cast. It was a totally underrated show: exciting and fun, with a great score. It closed right before Christmas, so that was sad for all of us.

―――――――――

David Alan Grier made his Broadway debut in The First, *which told the story of Jackie Robinson, the first African-American to play major league baseball.*

One interesting thing about the musical was that it had a book by theatre and film critic Joel Siegel. This wasn't the first time that a theatre critic had turned the tables to write a Broadway musical. In 1958, critic Walter Kerr collaborated on the musical Goldilocks.

Of course, it also wasn't the only time a Broadway show found itself with a sports backdrop. From Damn Yankees *(1955) to* Take Me Out *(2003) all the way up through the recent* Lombardi *(2010) and* Magic/Bird *(2012), the all-American past-times of sports and Broadway have meshed time and again. Up next:* Rocky.

1984: Going 'Round *The Rink*

Jason Alexander, Actor

The Rink is the one time that I have been totally blindsided on an opening night.

The Rink was a lovely, small, mother-daughter story, with a really fun, good score, and a very theatrical style on the page. It was one of those occasions where we got into rehearsal, and the page actually came alive. Sometimes you go to work on something and it works really well on paper, but it doesn't seem to translate onto the stage. This was not the case. Everything was humming along. We began previews, and the audiences went crazy.

First of all, they loved the ladies, Chita Rivera and Liza Minnelli. They just adored them, and both of them were in great form as we began the piece. *The Rink* was a little bit like a theatrical soap opera. The audiences laughed and cried. It was shmaltz in the best sense of the word and the crowds roared and they cheered and they stood up. They did everything but shout out to the stage during the show and we all felt: *we've got a monster hit here*. We started to relax in it and enjoy it. There was day-to-day work to be done on things, some tightening here and some trimming there. But it was so different from my previous experience on *Merrily We Roll Along*, where they rewrote half a show on the fly. *The Rink* stayed relatively intact all through previews.

We opened with tremendous fanfare. It was a great opening night show and a great party, and then all of a sudden reviews stated coming out and we couldn't buy a vowel. They loved Chita, uniformly. There were a lot of critics that admired what it was, but I don't think there was a single rave. And there were a good many out and out pans. But God knows there were "the Minellians." Had we not had Liza, we would've probably closed within weeks. But because of Liza, we had a huge advance at the box office.

From that point on, the buzz was gone. We spent weeks with audiences coming in, and sitting there with folded arms, like "Yeah, you show me." It took a while for the show to get going every night. It was my first experience with *that*, a show changing with an audience that had been told that they weren't going to have a good time. They came in with a different attitude. It was a huge switch from previews to post-opening night.

There were two parts that were just yummy for me to perform. One was my song, "Marry Me". I got a lovely, beautiful solo song, more or less a wedding proposal set to music that I would sing to Chita. I adore Chita Rivera like very few people I have met. I actually hold her as my role model for how to be a working professional for a life in the theatre. She is so kind, so funny, so charming, so wonderful. When I was singing that song to her every night, she would look back at me and she would just beam. Sometimes she would tear up or she would laugh, but she was always so in the moment, and it was such a delight to have that moment with her every night.

I was 24, and even then, I realized, *This is huge. She is one of the great, iconic legends of the musical theatre and I'm on stage with her and we are having this relationship*. I got it. It was not lost on me.

The other part that was fun was the actual rink number! All six of the guys in the show lied our asses off in order to get cast. When we got to the audition and they said, "You roller skate, right?" we all went, "Oh yeah, absolutely, sure!" I had never been on roller skates! I think Scott Ellis was the only guy who had been on them at all, and he was no wiz either.

They put us into a couple of months of training for roller skating. Roller skating hadn't been on Broadway before. It became passé after *Starlight Express*, but we were the first roller skating show on Broadway. It had a little element of danger. You could go into the pit, you could smash into the wall, you could fall on your ass—there were all kinds of things that could happen.

That whole company just adored each other. The show was our little party. There was a whole bunch of hullabaloo between verses of the rink number where we were supposed to be razzing each other and we would say the most god-awful things. If any audience member actually heard what we were saying, we would have been fired immediately. That was great fun.

When we were doing *The Rink*, because it was such a small cast, we had a lavish set up. If you came through the stage door and went up the stairs, you would get to the dressing rooms of the guys. We each had our own dressing room—two to a floor, unheard of! We had always been shoved into the chorus rooms. I had my own room!

In order to get to Chita and Liza's dressing rooms—which is where everybody that came backstage wanted to go—you had to go across the stage, because the star dressing rooms were on stage right. Everybody in the world came to see *The Rink* because those two ladies have the highest powered and most celebrated friends in the world!

Beverley Randolph, our stage manager, had this little thing that she would do. When she was returning valuables at the end of the show, she would knock on our doors, we'd say, "Who is it?" and she would announce herself as whatever celebrity had been in the audience that night. So if Angela Lansbury had been there, she would say it was Angela Lansbury, if it was Dick Van Dyke she'd say Dick Van Dyke, you know, whoever it was.

We did a performance about five months in, and Elizabeth Taylor came to the show. I went up to my dressing room after the show, and I was just coming out of the shower when there was a knock on my door. I go, "Who is it?" and I hear, "It's Elizabeth Taylor!"

Now, there's no way Elizabeth Taylor's coming to my dressing room, so I go, *Okay, you know what? I'm gonna teach Beverly a lesson once and for all!* I drop my towel. I am butt-ass naked and I open the door and go, "Hello, Elizabeth!"

And it is Elizabeth Taylor, standing there in front of me. I guess there was nobody at the stage door when she walked through, so she walked up the stairs on the wrong side.

I remember thinking: *Oh my God, she really does have lavender eyes and she really is stunning.* And she didn't miss a beat. She stuck her hand out and said, "You were wonderful this evening!" I'm standing there, butt-ass naked, shaking Elizabeth Taylor's hand, going, "Well, you're wonderful, too! You're probably looking for Chita or Liza's room. Let me tell you how to get there."

What bothers me more than anything—it bothers me to this very day—is not that I greeted Elizabeth Taylor while I was butt-ass naked, which is totally inappropriate, but that I opened the door and said, "Hello, Elizabeth!" like she was my neighbor. Not "Ms. Taylor," not "Your Highness," not "Mrs. Burton". "Hello, Elizabeth!" The arrogance of my 24-year-old self.

The title of that story is "Why I Was Totally Nude When I Met Elizabeth Taylor."

———————————

Five productions before The Rink, The Little Foxes *played the Martin Beck Theatre. The show starred Elizabeth Taylor, in her Broadway debut.*

I can't say for certain, but perhaps she did *know the theater's layout well enough to know that Liza and Chita were probably in her old star dressing room area, and she was in fact hoping to meet Jason Alexander!*

1987: Rapunzel's Tower

Randy Morrison, Stagehand

When *Into the Woods* was being loaded into the Martin Beck, they had to deal with Rapunzel's tower. It telescoped up from the stage, and the basement wasn't big enough to accommodate that, so they had to dig into the bedrock underneath the theater!

They went down eight to ten feet below the basement, to give Rapunzel's tower enough room to come up. They accidentally went below the water table, so the whole theater began to flood! They put in pumps.

1987: The Martin Beck Ghost

Joanna Gleason, Actor

Because of the memories and because of the time I spent there during *Into The Woods*, I love the Martin Beck, which is now the Hirschfeld.

Any time you're previewing, you need to do work. It's necessary to have that time in front of an audience to work on things. It was different back then, because now there are the dreaded chatrooms. Now, after the first preview, everybody decides that they're going to weigh in, and not give you any privacy. It's always been hard to be private when you're charging ticket prices and people are coming to see you, but now it's even harder. The word gets out.

We didn't have that with *Into The Woods*. We had some air and space. At first, the show was too long, and some songs didn't work perfectly. Steve Sondheim and James Lapine had their noses to the grindstone, and they'd come in the next day and say, "This is going, this is new, this is being replaced." Staging got changed. But I never felt rickety; I never felt there wasn't a very strong team at the helm, and I knew we could handle anything they gave us. It was all there in James and Steve's very fertile brains; we just needed time to do the work.

Into the Woods was the most memorable first preview of any Broadway show I've ever worked on because of the audience reaction at the end. It was stunning. I had never heard a sound like that.

You sometimes get lost when you're in this process and you get Stockholm Syndrome. But *Into The Woods* was received exactly the way we hoped it would be received. We felt that what we knew to be true about the piece did make it across the footlights. It was very heartening.

The Martin Beck has a ghost, and the Martin Beck Ghost found her comfort in my dressing room. During *Into The Woods*, Bernadette Peters and I had the two dressing rooms stage right.

Every Sunday, after the matinee, I would close all the lids of my makeup and I would group everything together in the center of the table, so that the housecleaning staff could come in and dust without having to fuss with my stuff too much.

About three months into the run, I came in and two of my blushers were all the way down at the end of the table. I thought: *That's strange.* I'd put them back, a week would go by, I'd clump everything together, I'd come in on Tuesday for the new week, and two blushers, again, would be all the way down at the end of the table.

Nobody was using my makeup. It wasn't open, it was just all the way down at the end of the table. Then one week, on the mirror, there was the letter "M." I thought: *Oh, it's just a thing on the mirror.* I wiped it off. A couple weeks later, the letter "M" appeared again.

144

I thought: *Someone is messing with me, and moving my makeup, and having a great joke at my expense.* I still didn't think anything of it—and it went on until I finished the run.

Flash forward many years, and I was doing an episode of a TV show. I was picked up at my apartment by a teamster, and we went through the theatre district. I said, "Oh my God, I played that theater," and I pointed to the Martin Beck. I said, "My favorite time was there in that theater."

He said, "Yeah, my mother worked in that theater too." And I said, "Oh, she did?"

He said, "Years and years ago. She's long gone. And her name was—" It began with an "M." I said, "What did she do?" And he said, "Well, she was on the housekeeping staff. She cleaned the dressing rooms." I said, "Really?" and he said, "Yeah, she loved the stars' makeup. She loved to just go and look at all the makeup." "Okay, okay! Well, your mom visited my dressing room, that's all there is to it."

———————

The dressing rooms at the Hirschfeld go up many floors, and mostly overlook 45th Street.

*The two "star dressing rooms" on stage right have been populated by everyone from Daniel Radcliffe (*How To Succeed *in 2011) to Cher (*Come Back To The Five & Dime, Jimmy Dean, Jimmy Dean *in 1982) to The Martin Beck Ghost!*

The Hair *revival cast members who filled the dressing room all the way on the top floor affectionately referred to it as "125th Street."*

———————

1988: High School-Style Meltdown

Hunter Bell, Writer/Actor

I came to New York City on a trip with my high school and all I wanted was to see Bernadette Peters in *Into The Woods*. I was obsessed with the show and with her. And then Bernadette Peters left the show right before we got there. I found out at the theater and had a full-on hysterical, high school-style meltdown. I was devastated. Like: *Why is this happening to me?!*

Then we saw the show, and Betsy Joslyn served it up. She was amazing. I've never met her but I want to see her one day and tell her that she rocked my world. That's my memory of the Martin Beck.

1989: Three *Grand* Songs At Once

Maury Yeston, Writer

The Beck was a great theater for *Grand Hotel*. I was originally brought into the show because it was in trouble in Boston, and I mean that with no aspersions cast at anybody. God knows that Robert Wright and George Forrest were brilliant. They wrote the great *Kismet* and *Song of Norway*. It's simply that there was a disconnect between the vision and style of the authors and the vision and style of the director. Tommy Tune actually called me up and said, "I have a room for you with a piano at the Ritz-Carlton Hotel. Come save the show."

I had lunch with the authors, and they were adorable. I suggested that I was there only to give them advice and then to go home. I explained to them that I thought that they were not on the same page as the director, and that it would be a choice of whether to replace the director or reconceive the show as much as they could to align with the director's vision—which was of dancing and singing all night. They said that they would never be responsible for closing a show and putting actors out of work and they asked me to join the team.

After that, my job was basically to rewrite the score in three weeks. Having said that, it was not only in the Colonial Theatre out of town that that happened, it happened a lot at the Beck in New York, too! I literally wrote a new number for every major character in the show.

I remember my one great moment at the Beck and it had to do with the interior architecture. There was a song called "Roses at the Station" that David Carroll sang in the second act. One day, Tommy was staging it on the stage of the Beck. At the same time, Liliane Montevecchi was in the basement rehearsing her song. And thirdly, there was a dance ending being choreographed by Thommie Walsh for part of the company and Jane Krakowski that was being rehearsed on the mezzanine level, where the snack bar is.

Those three numbers were being rehearsed simultaneously at the Beck, while I was in the back working, and I got a message from the stage manager that Michael Jeter was crying in his dressing room because he had not yet gotten a new song and he knew that his song wasn't working. I said, "Tell Michael that I am working on his song. I had to do these other things first. I promise I'm working on it."

I'll never forget that as long as I live, because I *was* working on it, and it all did come together. The greatest moment was when all of those things came together and the show clicked, when Michael jumped over the bar in "We'll Take A Glass Together". Writing *Grand Hotel* was thrilling because there was literally no time to do anything. I just had to do everything that was practical: add endings to songs that didn't have endings, very quickly replace songs that weren't working. It's a source of great pride to me that every character for whom I wrote a new character song for was nominated for a Tony: Michael Jeter, Jane Krakowski, Liliane Montevecchi, and David Carroll.

That year's Tony Awards were a horse race between *Grand Hotel* and *City of Angels*. That night, before the ceremony, I went to visit my mom at 200 Central Park South. I got in the elevator in my tuxedo, and was face to face with Gerry Schoenfeld of the Shubert Organization. He looked at me and said, "I think tonight is your night!" As it turned out, it wasn't, but that was okay. *Grand Hotel* ran well over a thousand performances, and it was a great experience.

The show moved to the Gershwin after two years, and it didn't feel like it changed at all. I was shocked! There was one moment in the show where one pair of actors unrolled a thin, red carpet from one wing to another and another pair of actors rolled one from downstage to upstage; it suddenly truly looked like a place in a hotel, and it also separated the stage into these four black areas that were very clearly read as four rooms. It was magic—nonliteral magic!

The theatre is a lie in which we harpoon the imagination of the audience into creating the illusion that's on stage. The lucky thing about the move to the Gershwin is that the show, the scenery, all of Berlin, resided in the lyrics and the music, "Come begin in old Berlin, you're in the Grand Hotel." It didn't change.

———————————

Pippin *had the first television commercial that advertised a Broadway show by actually showing scenes from it. That commercial was a 60-second clip of the song "Glory" with the announcement, "Here's a free minute of* Pippin, *Broadway's musical comedy sensation, directed by Bob Fosse. You can see the other 119 minutes of* Pippin *live at the Imperial Theatre, without commercial interruption!"*

It worked. Pippin *ran for five years. And that* Pippin *commercial changed Broadway advertising forever. Immediately after it aired in 1972, other Broadway shows rushed to put 30 or 60-second glimpses of their show on the tube.*

While Pippin *may have been first, it has been followed by many shows with brilliant television commercials. Unlike any other is the* Grand Hotel *commercial. You get 30 seconds of footage from the dazzling musical, and 30 seconds of a fabulous blue-haired theatre lady, outside the Martin Beck, after having seen* Grand Hotel. *While she bellows the following at a bemused cameraman, the number for Ticketmaster flashes below:*

"Cyd Charisse is fabulous, wonderful! I'd like to see the show TWO more times. I loved it so much! She is fantastic! Her movements. Her dancing. Her voice. Everything about her is terrific! I loved her! I'm going to see it twice more. I'm going as soon as I can get tickets. My husband works in this area!!!"

What could sell the show better than that?

1989: Learning On The Job

Brig Berney, Company Manager

In 1989 I had the opportunity to work for Judy Jacksina, the Broadway press agent. Judy worked on *Grand Hotel*, and I remember being at the Martin Beck when a news crew came to shoot footage of Michael Jeter doing "We'll Take A Glass". So I sat up in the mezzanine with them for an hour and a half waiting to say, "Now is when you guys turn on the camera."

I'm a company manager now and having that year in a press office was so helpful. All of the jobs I had before certainly prepared me in different ways. My first job in company management was on the road with Tommy Tune in *Bye Bye Birdie*. I didn't know what a company manager's job *really* was, but the manager said, "You should go do this on the road because you're so good with details." That's how things happen.

The Martin Beck was built by its namesake, a theater owner and producer. Born in Slovakia, Martin Beck arrived in New York when he was 18 years old without a penny to his name. He built himself up from an actor to a manager to a theater owner, and founded the Orpheum Circuit, one of the most successful vaudeville and movie chains of all time. He discovered and launched Harry Houdini and he built the Palace Theatre, the beacon for vaudeville performers for the first half of the 20th century.

Later on, he built the Martin Beck on 45th Street, which he proudly boasted made him the only Broadway theater owner without a mortgage on his theater. He was actively involved in every aspect of the business at the Martin Beck, from the day it was built in 1924 to the day he died in 1940. His obituary in the New York Times[27] shared that he was often found in his office at the theater—which had three phones!—saying, "I am the staff of the Martin Beck Theatre!" In his time, the theater housed several notable hits.

1990: The Cut List

Alex Rybeck, Musical Director

Grand Hotel had a beautiful orchestration by Peter Matz. There were eight string players—a double string quartet! That's a luxury these days and almost unheard of. The show had a beautiful, lush sound because of the full orchestra, which—instead of being in the pit—sat upon a high platform that provided the second story to the set. We had to climb ladders to get up there, and were in full view of the audience. The platform itself was

---

[27] "Martin Beck Dies; Theatre Veteran," The New York Times, 17 November 1940, http://query.nytimes.com/mem/archive/pdf?res=F40615F63955177A93C5A8178AD95F448485F9 (accessed 13 Oct. 2013)

an iron grid, strong enough to hold all of us and two grand pianos. It was a fun show to play, because we could look down and see the entire show playing below our feet! There were certain moments where I'd lock eyes with members of the cast, and we'd have nightly "bits"—which became little rituals. There was a cast member who would always "toast" me with his beer stein at one point in the show, and I'd mime a toast in return. Eventually, as a surprise, I brought in a very ornate German beer stein, and the next performance, when he made his toast, I lifted up my actual stein and toasted him back!

At one point, I came back to the show from a vacation, and there were only four string players! What happened? The show had been running a while, business had dropped, and it turned out the string players had been hired on a "cut list." That meant that if the show started making less money, they could be cut. So, Peter Matz's job as orchestrator was to see that the orchestration sounded the same without those four people. As the synth player, I sometimes doubled the strings softly on my keyboard, but most of the time, the strings played alone. We sounded thinner, but made do. More time went by. I came back from another vacation. Not only had they cut ALL the string players, but I had an additional keyboard at my station, in order to play all the string parts! There were many new notes written in my book, where previously there had been rests.

I had no choice but to play what was in front of me. Of course, a synth doesn't sound exactly like a real string section, and the first night I played their parts, one of the trumpet players behind me muttered "All skaters move to the left!"

The musicians' union stepped into the situation, and we went into arbitration. When musicians are cut, there's a rule that no one else in the orchestra can play their parts. I volunteered to go to the meeting and bring my score as evidence that I was now playing new notes. On the way, I told the just-fired concert master, "I not only feel bad for you and the other string players; I feel bad for Peter Matz that his beautiful orchestration has been disemboweled. I bet he's upset." He just stared at me and said, "First of all, Peter is on management's side." That was a shock. When he saw I was speechless, he added, "Well, you know, he's also the guy who orchestrated *No Strings*." That show famously had an orchestra that had no string players!

In the middle of the arbitration, *Grand Hotel* itself was cut from the Martin Beck Theater! *Guys and Dolls* was poised to move in, so we could either close, or the producers could try to get some major star replacements and move us to another theater. We ended up reopening *Grand Hotel* at the Gershwin Theatre with Cyd Charisse. And here's the kicker: the Gershwin Theatre, being a bigger house than the Beck, has a larger musicians' minimum! They had to hire back all eight string players who had been fired!

However, our arbitration affected *Guys and Dolls*. They used the same kind of "cut list" contract, but now their orchestrator knew the synth player would have to play the notes of the string players at a very soft level all the way through the show if they wanted him to continue doing that after string players were cut. The point is that the audience should be hearing the same show that the opening night critics heard. It's a good rule.

1992: Sit Down, You're Rocking The Boat!

Walter Bobbie, Director/Actor

Frankly, I was having a very hard time with my part in *Guys and Dolls* during rehearsal. I thought that our director, Jerry Zaks, was going to fire me. I had a difficult time defining the role of Nicely Nicely Johnson because it had become known as this heavyset, character actor part. While I may be temperamentally a character actor, I don't look that way. In the original script, a lot of Nicely's stage business had to do with entering eating hoagies and various foods. None of that stuff suited me, and I wasn't landing the material.

Jerry came up to me as we were leaving the rehearsal hall, and asked, "Do you mind wearing padding?" I replied, "Jerry, if this isn't working, it isn't working, but putting me in a fat suit isn't going to make it funny."

148

The dress rehearsal was one of the most excruciating nights of my life. I was uncomfortable on stage, and I could feel that the show wasn't working. The next day, we dumped most of the big ballet that started the show and we decided to begin right with "Fugue For Tinhorns". Then they let go of one of our actors and I thought: *I guess I won't be fired because they can't fire two of us!*

Jerry left me alone for that first week of previews. And around the third preview, it clicked for me. I just understood the role. The show was a pure joy from that point on, and I had a remarkable time with the company and with the audience. But it was a very odd experience to do a classic show where we spent so much time wondering if it was going to work. You're doing *Guys and Dolls* for God's sake... that show works! It's a classic. But for some reason we had trouble at the beginning of previews, and then one day we just turned the corner.

Everything about that production was joyous: Nathan Lane and Faith Prince and Peter Gallagher, the late Chris Chadman who was our choreographer, Jerry's direction, William Ivey Long, and Tony Walton's designs. The whole thing was thrilling, and I was so glad Jerry had the wisdom to talk to me and then just leave me alone with Nicely Nicely for a couple days. It was a great act of trust.

1992: He Brought The Entire Cast Out Into The House

William Ivey Long, Costume Designer/Chair of the American Theatre Wing

Guys and Dolls was at the Martin Beck. The production was very heightened. Tony Walton had done this extraordinary set for Runyonland: Times Square in Technicolor. I had to live up to that with the costume design.

And boy, oh boy, living up to anything by the great Tony Walton... I was heart-stoppingly nervous at moments. And with *Guys and Dolls*, with Nathan Lane and Faith Prince as Nathan Detroit and Miss Adelaide, they landed at this great level of heightened reality.

I'll never forget, director Jerry Zaks wandering around pensive and holding his forehead in the back of the house. Before previews, in press rehearsals, it was just a lot of big, bold design. Heavy on the design, with a capital D. But the show itself just wasn't working. And I remember one day Jerry just had this inspiration.

He brought the entire cast out into the house. They were in costume, getting ready to do a number. Jerry had Faith and Nathan perform the song, "Sue Me". Jerry said, "Now *this* is the level of heightened reality to which we all aspire. Watch it." And then we all really focused, and watched it.

It was amazing. Nathan and Faith had worked it out, and Jerry had directed it, and it set the tone. Immediately, the actors all went up on stage, and began a scene, and the glimmer of falling into place had begun.

The Al Hirschfeld is one of the only Broadway theaters to have an outdoor box office window. On the exterior of the Hirschfeld, there is an old-fashioned ticket booth that it says "Martin Beck Theatre." When the house was renamed after the famous Broadway caricaturist in 2003, this feature was kept, in honor of its original namesake.

1992: Our Moment

Chris Boneau, Press Agent

There was a moment that put us on the map. Before it, we were these guys, and people thought: *Oh there's this nice publicist, Chris, and he does a lot of off-off-Broadway things, and Adrian, who is great—and now they've formed a company and don't even have a name yet.*

Our first show was *Our Country's Good*, which didn't last very long. Then, Adrian and the office were doing *Guys and Dolls*, and I was doing Faith Prince's personal press. *Guys and Dolls* became a New York sensation in a way that I can't even describe. It was sort of like what *Book of Mormon* and *The Lion King* were like in their moments. It took New York by storm because it was so good.

Faith came from off-Broadway and was a star, and blew everyone away. We had an incredible time, because they were on "The Tonight Show" and the cover of New York Magazine and Faith got this gigantic story in the *New York Times*! It was nuts.

Now, press reps get the review at 10:07pm on their smart phones. But in the old days, you would go to the *New York Times* building and wait. At 10pm, the cart would come down with the next day's paper.

When *Guys and Dolls* opened, we were all standing there—three or four of us from our office—waiting for the cart with the stacks of newspapers. There were all these weird people standing around the *New York Times* lobby on 43rd Street at the time. Some of them were waiting for the advertising section or the business section to come out, and some people were waiting for sports to find out how the horse races had done. It was this crazy, motley group of people.

Typically, our office would grab four or five copies. You'd pay the guy 50 cents in quarters, and you'd stand there, getting rid of the other sections except the Arts, literally ripping pages out, and yelling "I'll take that!"

John Barlow and I were working on *Guys and Dolls,* and I was waiting with him. A guy came downstairs who we recognized as one of the reporters. He was holding the *Times* under his arm, and we saw that it was the cover. Nathan and Faith were on the cover of the *New York Times*.

We were staring at this guy, and he hollered, "Oh! You guys work on *Guys and Dolls*? Here!" Not only was the picture on the cover, the review started on the front page. It was one of those moments.

We were filming a live special for Fox TV at the time about the making of *Guys and Dolls.* The final image is John Barlow and myself running to 45th Street, waving the *New York Times*. We're yelling, "It's a hit!" screaming at the top of our lungs and looking like lunatics.

———————————

Jujamcyn not only owned the Martin Beck, home of Guys and Dolls, *they were also producers on the show. When the show was being put together, it was intended for the Martin Beck. However, no one expected* Grand Hotel *to become such a massive hit!* Grand Hotel *had no stop clause in its contract, so the theater owners couldn't kick them out for dropping below a certain level of sales.*

There was a theater booking jam, as often happens in the spring, and so, Guys and Dolls *was tentatively designed for the Beck, the Virginia, the Marquis and the Gershwin! The Virginia was still occupied by* City of Angels, *teetering on the brink of closure—and* Jelly's Last Jam *was making bids for it, too. The Marquis was occupied by final previews of* Nick & Nora, *and the owners were waiting to see how that went—although they'd already tentatively booked* The Goodbye Girl *for the fall. The Gershwin was deemed too large for the show.* Guys and Dolls *won out, and* Grand Hotel *moved to the Gershwin.*

150

It was reportedly the first time that Jujamcyn had "booted" a show since purchasing the theater in 1968.

———————

1993: The Hardest Show I've Ever Done

Michael Berresse, Director/Choreographer/Actor

Between *Fiddler*, my first show on Broadway, and *Guys and Dolls*, my second, I did my first couple of principal roles in smaller productions, and I started to understand that I had a skill set that had never been tapped into. It was triggered by this desire to tell a better story by being in a Broadway show.

The truth is, I didn't have that conservatory education that a lot of Broadway performers have. I didn't understand the history. I went and I did a production of *West Side* with the original Jerome Robbins choreography at Papermill Playhouse, and then I did *Forever Plaid* off-Broadway and then I went to Toronto and did *Joseph*. All three of those things were very, very informative for me.

The first day I got back to New York, I went in and auditioned for Chris Chadman to replace the Crap Shooter Specialty in *Guys and Dolls*, and to this day, it's the hardest show I've ever done, physically. That Specialty number was a huge challenge. Every guy in that number was exhausted by the end of it, but the guy who had to do what I had to do... I was tumbling upstage on a raked stage!

It was insanity, but it was the thrill of pushing yourself as hard and as far as you could possibly go. Even by the end of that audition I was like: *Oh my God I don't know if I can keep doing this.* When they offered me that job I thought: *I have to.* The experience was very different from my Broadway debut with *Fiddler*. I went into a show that had already opened and won a slew of awards. It was a very highly respected production, with the original cast still largely intact.

The Martin Beck Theatre felt different from the Gershwin. It represented so much of the romance and the integrity and the truth of what I felt like truly arriving on Broadway meant. I felt like I went from being a stepchild to living in a premiere guest suite, and I was super, super proud of that show.

Before "The Crap Shooter's Specialty" number started, there was a scrim down, and a ladder that hung down. I was preset, concealed, halfway up the ladder. Before I was revealed, I was always just clinging to the ladder, wanting to cry, filled with such anxiety about what I was about to do.

I've never had that kind of adrenaline rush, ever, before or since in a show. That excitement and dread, like a roller coaster. That curtain went up and the reveal of the set was impressive, the colors of the costumes... the audience was already on board. Then the number started and it never ever stopped. I was jumping and flipping and climbing and spinning and singing.

Chris Chadman was a genius. The choreography of that show was astounding. He was also a task master and came from that old school of: If you're not hurting or angry or mad, something's wrong. He worked us hard.

I remember finishing the number on my first night, and hearing the audience go bananas. Bananas! Applause like I had never heard before.

Everyone was so proud of me, and happy to know that this number, which had been such a highlight of the show, was going to continue to be a highlight. I loved doing every minute of that number, despite the fact that it brought me to tears every night.

1993: I Have A Picture Of Me Standing Out Front Of The Martin Beck

Amy Wolk, Merchandise Manager/On Site Educator

The first Broadway show I saw was the revival of *Guys and Dolls* in 1993. I have a picture of me standing out front of the Martin Beck.

It changed my life. I was obsessed with Faith Prince; I wanted to be her. And we had house seats. My dad had a friend who set that up because in 1980, my parents invested money in the Broadway production of *Seven Brides for Seven Brothers*, which ran about eight shows. Every year, they'd get a check for about $15. It was ridiculous. My dad said they finally, on the last check, made back their original investment. That was our connection to Broadway.

At *Guys and Dolls*, I remember that they were collecting for Broadway Cares, and Ernie Sabella was at the door. He had just been in that episode of *Seinfeld* where he was naked, and we were excited because my brother talked to him about it. I was 16.

———————

In the first act of Grey Gardens, *Joseph Patrick Kennedy Jr. sings to the young would-be ingénue performer Little Edie: "I need a leading lady with me, neck in neck / To help me lobby for a campaign check," and she sings back to him, "The only lobby I know is the Martin Beck!"*

In 1941, when this scene takes place, Little Edie might have been dreaming of a role in the theater's current show, a Lillian Hellman-penned war drama called Watch On The Rhine. *Chances are, she wasn't dreaming of a role in either of the Beck's two previous tenants:* Cabin In The Sky, *the all-black musical, or* Lady In Waiting, *a play about a mother constantly upstaging her daughter!*

———————

1995: Closing Performances

Jack Viertel, Creative Director of Jujamcyn Theaters

The closing of *Guys and Dolls* was very emotional for me. I was by myself, and I sat on the stairs. I just wept and wept and wept, because *Guys and Dolls* was a record that I listened to when I was five years old.

———————

The spot now occupied by the Al Hirschfeld Theatre was, prior to 1924, six three-story Astor family homes.

Before the theater was officially named, its nickname around town was "the West Side Theatre" because it was the only Broadway house west of 8th Avenue.

At the time it was built in 1924, it was the ninth Broadway house on 45th Street! The illustrious list comprised the Beck, Lyceum, Music Box, Imperial, Klaw, Morosco, Bijou, Booth, and Plymouth. Three years later, the Theatre Masque (now the Golden) and the Royale (now the Jacobs) would also open on 45th Street.

———————

1995: Carol Burnett Saves The Day

Ken Billington, Lighting Designer

On the first preview of *Moon Over Buffalo*, the set broke down. The actors knew it broke down, but they kept performing!

The stage manager said, "We're going to have to bring the curtain in." I grabbed Tom Moore, the director, and we went backstage. He said he was going to go out and talk to the audience, and I said, "Have Carol Burnett go out!"

Meanwhile, there was an army of stagehands, and anyone in the building who could assist, trying to push the set.

We asked Carol and she said, "Oh! I'll do a Q&A!" The stage manager, Steve Beckler, was about to bring the curtain back up, and I said, "Steve, take the curtain up three feet. Make her go under the curtain."

So the curtain went up three feet, and Carol Burnett went under the curtain. The audience started to cheer. She did a great Q&A for about ten minutes, and the scenery was shoved around. We turned a disaster into a great moment in Broadway history.

———————————

Moon Over Broadway was a 1997 D.A. Pennebaker documentary that followed all of the behind-the-scenes madness of Moon Over Buffalo *on its road to Broadway. The show marked Carol Burnett's return to the Broadway stage after 30 years! In one memorable scene, one of the producers considers bringing in his "funny dentist" to help with the show.*

———————————

1998: I Have Confidence

Hayley Podschun, Actor

When I was a kid, my friend Kyle and I were hired as local actors for the Big League production of *Oliver!* that came to Kansas City. Then, Big League was doing *Sound of Music*, so we flew to L.A. to audition. I didn't get it, but Kyle did.

He went on tour with the Big League production of *Sound of Music*. After he finished, he came home. Shortly after, his mom found out that the Broadway company was having auditions for *their* upcoming tour. The company we both danced with was actually going to New York for spring break, so it all worked out. Then, Kyle decided he was sick of "Do Re Mi" and didn't want to audition. But I did.

My mom isn't a stage mom, but while we were there on spring break, she found the number for Binder Casting. We bought a dress at the Gap and went into their office—and I got a callback! We had to fly back the next weekend, and that time, all the creatives were there.

One of the casting agents, Jack, pulled my parents aside and told them that they weren't considering me for the tour—they were considering me for Broadway. He said, "Don't tell Hayley, because in case she doesn't get it, we don't want to get her hopes up."

After the audition, they took me to the Martin Beck and measured me against the proscenium to make sure I was the right height! It was so cool because there was nothing else going on in the theater. It was just us, on stage.

We went back to our hotel room, and that night, we got a fax under the door. My parents wouldn't let me read it at first; they read it in the hallway! Then they told me I was still in consideration for Broadway. I freaked out.

We flew back to Kansas. Then, we got a voicemail on our home phone. They said I was a fourth of an inch too tall, and they couldn't use me. They said they were so sorry, and would keep me in mind for the future.

Then, two days later, my parents surprised me at school. They came to my middle school and brought me into a conference room.

Sound of Music had called back. I had gotten it. They changed their minds. We were moving to New York in two days!

It was so great. We moved to New York very quickly, and I started getting tutored during the day, then going to rehearsal, then going to the show. I understudied Luisa and Brigitta, and so I was sitting off stage every night with Bobby Wilson and Vanessa Brown, my child wranglers. They're both still working today! They're amazing. They made the experience unforgettable and fun. They were always parental, adult figures, but they also had fun with us. You never felt like you were being babysat. You were just hanging out with these awesome people, who you'd play video games backstage with. And Joe, my dance captain, really took care of me when I came into the show. I was trained in dance, and most of the kids there had been more trained in acting or voice, so he was impressed that I learned the show so quickly. He told me, "Don't do cheerleading. Really stick with your dancing, because you're very good at it." Vanessa, Bobby, and Joe changed my whole experience.

I went on for Luisa first. When the whistle blows, the character is supposed to enter from a trap door behind the house. I remember waiting back there, and I looked up into the fly, and one of the crew guys waved at me! I thought: *Oh my gosh, this is so cool.* Then, I ran up the stairs, came through the big door, ran down to my spot, and got so excited. *I'm here!* I was so nervous and excited that I couldn't remember when to step forward to say my name at first! After that moment, it was all great. I knew what I was doing and felt confident.

I love the Martin Beck, because that was my first Broadway house. I can't wait to do another show there. That one to me, always smells exactly how I remember it as a kid. I don't know if it's the cleaning materials they use, but every time I go backstage there, I go back into my 12-year-old self.

In interviewing for this book, I got the chance to speak to so many adult Broadway professionals. And so many of them said that what inspired them to want to be part of Broadway was seeing other *kids on stage when they were still kids themselves.*

Lonny Price saw Oliver! *as a five-year-old, and wanted to get on stage and dance with the other kids. Ken Davenport waited at the* Secret Garden *stage door to get Daisy Eagan's autograph. Steve Rosen saw* The Tap Dance Kid *and thought:* How does he get to do that, I want in on the action! *And every girl and boy who grew up in the 1970s who even got near the Alvin Theatre begged their parents for singing lessons so they could sound like Andrea McArdle.*

This past Broadway season may have set a record for kids appearing in Broadway shows. Between Annie, Matilda, Motown, Kinky Boots, A Christmas Story, Mary Poppins, Newsies, Once... *how many kids sat in the audience at a Broadway show this year, saw another kid on stage, and said: "Mom, I want to do that"?*

A lot. And some of them will *do it. In 20 years, I hope we read in a book about how they discovered Broadway for the first time while sitting in a seat at the Palace, watching Lilla Crawford sing her heart out in* Annie *this past season.*

2000: Climbing And Flipping And Swinging Back At The Beck Again

Michael Berresse, Director/Choreographer/Actor

I had this giant number in the second act of *Kiss Me Kate* that I couldn't fully do in rehearsal because a large part of the number involved the set. Until we were on the set, I couldn't do all the climbing and flipping and swinging. I had looked at the set design with Kathleen Marshall and Robin Wagner, and we had ideas of what I would do. But we knew that in tech, we wouldn't have that much time and we'd have to work on it quickly.

So we got to the theater, we were in tech, we got to the number... and I couldn't do any of the stuff I wanted to. There were cables on the backs of poles, one thing was higher, one was lower, there had been adjustments to the set design, the phone wasn't supported enough so that I could stand on it... there were all these issues and I started to freak out.

Kathleen was very level-headed, and Robin Wagner was ever-accommodating. They were like, "What do you need?" And I said, "In a perfect world, if you could cut out the base of one step on these staircases, and solder in a three quarter inch pole... if you could remove the cables from this and replace them here... if you could reinforce the payphone on the wall..."

I gave them a list of all this stuff, and I went to dinner. I came back two hours later and 80 percent of it was done. Over the course of the next two hours of our tech, they finished everything else. Literally, by the end of the night, I was able to do almost everything that I had planned to do. We got it done. To this day I'm astounded.

I've always been interested in all the backstage aspects of what happens. I love the way that a story comes to life through the use of design and the incredible intelligence of people on the team. That was an astounding thing to see on *Kiss Me Kate*. Their work made that number exactly what we had wanted it to be, and that was joyful.

By the time we got to opening night of *Kiss Me Kate*, there was a lot of buzz, but we didn't really know what would happen. There were two factions: one was saying the book was outdated and no one would ever be able to make it relevant, and the other half was saying that the buzz around the performances and show was really great.

I had been in shows, including *Fascinatin' Rhythm*, where we got to opening night and were convinced that people were going to go crazy, because we knew the level of talent involved. That show was not received well, and it closed.

So, on *Kiss Me, Kate*, we really didn't know. I had learned not to take anything for granted, so I reminded myself: *Just do your job, have a good time, enjoy everybody.* But not everybody was quite that calm. I remember a lot of nerves, a lot of anxiety and Michael Blakemore, the director, walking around.

I was sort of a fly on the wall, because I would always warm up on stage. I watched Michael negotiate different anxieties and needs so effortlessly that night. He floated from person to person, would talk a lot if they needed that, would say nothing if they needed that.

He said to me at one point, "The physical stuff you do is a total mystery to me. You're a smart guy, and you're telling a really clean story, so my job isn't going to be to tell you where to go—it's just going to be to nudge you back on the road if you veer off." That's how he handled me. And then he would talk to Brian Stokes Mitchell or to Marin Mazzie or to Amy Spanger and he had completely different languages every time.

He intuitively knew how to keep people confident and relaxed, and to direct them to do what he knew they could do. I think that's because he's utterly confident in his own capability, so he's not pretentious, and he doesn't have ego about his work.

I remember thinking: *That's a major part of why this show is great, because of that vibe, that humility and that trust in everything we were doing.* I think that was really what had been missing from *Kiss Me, Kate* in the past. It had always been commented on and hadn't just been trusted. In our production, we just did it. People saw it and thought: *Oh! Sometimes, great theater can be super fun and transporting and not necessarily brain surgery— but at the same time, still have integrity and joy.* That was a great show and a great experience.

————————

Kiss Me, Kate *was nominated for 12 Tony Awards – more than any other musical revival in the history of Broadway. The original production in 1949 won the first-ever Tony presented for Best Musical. Cole Porter's most successful musical, it includes the songs, "Another Opening, Another Show", "Too Darn Hot", "Always True To You (In My Fashion)", "Brush Up Your Shakespeare", and a slew of others that have made their way into the popular vernacular.*

————————

1999: A Chance For Stage Folks To Say Hello

Merwin Foard, Actor

Because I live in Winchester, I come into the city through Grand Central. I had a deal with *Kiss Me, Kate* that if I wasn't on, I called into the show from the 125th Street stop, which is the last stop before you get into Grand Central. I could do that by taking a late train, which would put me in the theater right around places.

One day, in the ten minutes that it took to go through the tunnel, something happened. As soon as I came out into the lobby of Grand Central, my phone was buzzing with messages. "You're on!"

It was five of two on a Wednesday before the matinee, and I was at Grand Central! They sing "Another Opening", and the character walks down the aisle onto the stage. So I was *hoofing* it across Manhattan. I entered the building, the guy at the stage door announced, "Merwin's in the building, Merwin's in the building!" over the intercom and they threw me onto the stage. Crazy.

Kiss Me, Kate was happening when 9/11 happened. The night before, September 10th, my wife and I went to a friend's wedding. They had a lovely reception at the Boat Basin, and they were going to fly to Italy the next day to go on their honeymoon. We drove home. I remember I was so excited for them.

The next morning, Tuesday, I was sleeping in, and my wife came in and turned on the television. I remember thinking: *Why are you waking me up? Who's on the Today Show?*

She turned around, and she was just sobbing. I didn't know what to think. She said, "We're being attacked," and I didn't understand what that meant.

Broadway, of course, shut down—as it should. A couple days later, we had to go back to work.

9/11 kept tourism from being a big thing in New York at that time. Our audiences were just not coming. The theaters were empty.

One of the backstage crew guys, Joe Maher, came up with this idea that we would donate money from our salaries. The money that we donated was used to buy tickets for the first responders, the volunteers, the Red

156

Cross, anyone down at Ground Zero, so that they could take their mind off of what they were dealing with, and just come and be distracted by a Broadway show.

His creativity was not only so touching to us, it put money back into the coffers for the producers so they could keep the show running. It put butts in our seats and helped out people who were helping out downtown.

That was pretty remarkable. I'll never forget that gesture. He just kind of, off the cuff, said, "What if we did this?" It was brilliant." It was a win-win-win-win-win-win-win. Good old Joe.

We're still here. Everybody's going to be okay.

2001: September 11th And *Kiss Me, Kate*

Chris Boneau, Press Agent

After September 11th, we all came together—*all of us,* across the board. There was no competition. The idea was, "Broadway has to survive." Giuliani made a big difference when he said, as a public service announcement: *Go see a Broadway show.*

We formed committees to come up with ideas to incentivize New Yorkers to come to the theater. That's when the "Tuesdays at 7" idea was hatched. Nancy Coyne and I were walking down the street one day, and we started talking about it. "What if we had one night a week where you could go to a Broadway show at an early time and get home at a decent hour?"

In addition to all of the horrible stories at that time of the attack, I remember the generosity of all the musicians and actors and everybody across the board at shows. So many people took 25 percent off their pay, so that shows could keep running.

Kiss Me, Kate was very close to closing. It was our second year, and we had announced a closing date. After September 11th, business dropped off, and it was *really* bad. I got a call on a Saturday, asking if it was possible for me to come over to theater because the company wanted to talk to me about an idea.

It was a stagehand who thought of this idea, and took it to the whole company of *Kiss Me, Kate*. He said, "What if we went further and took 50 percent so the show could survive?" They had to get everyone to bless it: the theater staff, the unions. Absolutely everyone working on shows had to agree. They did.

After that happened, I came up with an idea for the Sunday that we were supposed to close. I said to Roger Berlind, who was one of the two producers, "This is gorgeous what they're doing. I know we're supposed to close tomorrow, but I have an idea. Let me write a script for you."

He walked out on stage before the performance and pulled from the breast pocket of his suit a piece of paper. He said, "Ladies and gentlemen, as you know, today is the final performance of *Kiss Me, Kate*. This is a closing notice. We have to post it backstage to let the cast know that we're going to close. Ladies and gentlemen…" and he tore it up into a thousand little pieces and he literally threw it up in the air and went, "Welcome to the not-final performance of *Kiss Me, Kate*!" We managed to run for another couple of weeks.

The show always began with "behind the scenes," the characters getting ready for a show and singing "Another Op'nin'". First, a stagehand came on mopping the stage, and on that Sunday matinee, he came across with a push broom, pushing these little pieces of paper, and he gave a big wink to the audience. They were erupting with excitement.

I had tipped off camera crews that we were going to do this, so it was a big news event. I don't usually love stunts, but that was an appropriate stunt. It was a part of the fabric of things people were doing in all areas of New York. To me, that story captures the good part of September 11th: the bonding. There was so much generosity and all these people just wanting a show to go on.

———————————

The entire Broadway community came together to do whatever they could and help wherever they could, after the September 11 attacks. As chronicled above, it took a while for people to return to the theatre, and indeed, to New York City. Urinetown's opening night on September 13, 2001 was postponed. Many shows closed and never reopened, or stumbled along for a couple weeks before closing.

In the previous season, Broadway had contributed over 650 million dollars to the economy of New York City, and provided tens of thousands of jobs. This amount dropped significantly that season, for the first time in recorded history.

All of Broadway came together to tape an "I Love New York" commercial. It opened with Bernadette Peters singing "New York, New York" a capella, as the camera zoomed in on a group of people in the middle of a Times Square slowly coming back to life. "I'll make a brand new start of it, in old New York," Bernadette sang and danced, side by side with Valerie Harper, Michele Lee, Elaine Stritch, Alan Alda, Joel Grey, Bebe Neuwirth, Adolph Green, Harvey Fierstein, Tony Roberts, gazelles from The Lion King, *show girls from* The Producers, *street folks from* Rent, *factory workers from* Les Mis, *and hundreds of others. At the end, Nathan Lane's unmistakable voice urged, "Come to New York—and let's go on with the show!"*

———————————

2002: Looks Like We're At The Fountain

Craig Carnelia, Writer

When you do big productions of shows, the things you end up remembering tend to be small. Not that they're anticlimactic, but they rarely will have to do with 12,000 people cheering. They will often have to do with a conversation in the men's room.

My absolute favorite thing is being on stage with no one in the theater. There's an aspect of being in an empty theater that must be similar to what people who truly have a church feel when they're in that space. There's a grace and a calm and a silence and an excitement and a sense that things have happened and will happen in the air that is unlike anything else. I've always felt it.

There was a particular day at what was then called the Martin Beck. *Kiss Me Kate* was in its last six months, and the theater owners had just committed to us that we could have the Beck for our show, *Sweet Smell of Success*, which was very exciting news. The final thing to be answered before the theater could be solidified for our show was whether or not there was enough space in the pit for what Marvin Hamlisch was envisioning with Bill Brohn, our great orchestrator.

Marvin and I went to the Beck alone one day. There was no one else there except the door man. There was a ghost light on the stage. We were down in the pit, and had a conversation about the number of musicians. Then, Marvin got to measuring, on his own.

I went up to the stage and spent about ten minutes there, just enjoying the feel that this theater would be mine for a while. It would be ours. There was also a great feeling between Marvin and myself that day. There always was, but this time, we actually spoke about it when we left, that we were really happy with our show and with our collaboration.

Marvin was always effusive in his praise of my work and less so in his affection because he was—what was he? He was onto the next subject before he was finished with the one he was dealing with. That didn't leave a lot of time for love notes, but I didn't need them because we knew that we did love each other. That day, we actually acknowledged how good this all felt. How good the collaboration felt and how good the theater felt and how good the show felt.

There were a number of things in the show that I really loved, and that Marvin and I loved together. Brian D'Arcy James singing "At the Fountain" was very, very special. Nick Hytner did a great job with that song and really let it take the stage in a way that allowed a response that one only expects to get from a musical. The song "I Cannot Hear The City", performed by Jack Noseworthy and Kelli O'Hara, was a highlight. Everything in that song: Bill Brohn's orchestrations, Natasha Katz's lighting, Nick's staging... everything conspired to truly make you feel like you were in this big world, and then it turned into this small world. All the elements seemed to do that at the same time.

The song was saying: in this noisy place, there's this peace and it's caused by what we feel for each other. There's something about the completeness of that. What worked were all the elements doing the same thing, which is odd because very often in a musical the elements work best when they're working in contrast to each other. Here, everything was saying the same thing. It was beautiful.

Our producers were great. Marty Bell and Beth Williams were just fantastic, as were the rest of them, a wonderful group of people. You see ten names above the title and you assume it's about money—and it is—but we knew every one of those people, and they were all in love with our project. Marty Richards was in there, and Ernest Lehman, who had written the screenplay. They loved what we were doing. We were all in it together. The closing day, John Guare was the only writer who went to the performance, but I went to the theater before it started to thank everyone. Then I stood on the stage, before the show, said "goodbye" to Bob Crowley's set, and left so quickly that it surprised me.

2002: Bittersweet Smell Of Success

Kelli O'Hara, Actor

Going over to Marvin Hamlisch's apartment so that he could sit and play some of the music of *Sweet Smell of Success* for me is one of the biggest things that has happened to me in my life. It's one of the things that I hold onto still, just his excitement and zest for all of it. He and Craig Carnelia were so excited.

By the time I joined the show, they had been working on it for a while, but they were still tweaking. To sit with Marvin at a piano and to have him go over keys with me... When songs were cut, he called me on the phone to apologize. It was just a very sweet, personal way of going about things that made me feel important and part of the process, which was really nice. All of those creators were working so hard.

I was really young and kind of naïve to everything that was going on. I remember feeling that our opening night was bittersweet. It was my first lesson on how important critics can be to a show. I didn't understand.

I remember doing the opening night performance and just wanting it to be the very best it could—and there's the audience and they're clapping, and we were feeling so celebratory and so happy. And then I remember going to the Waldorf Astoria in my brand new dress, with my family there, and somewhere in the evening, everyone clearing out all at once.

Sweet Smell of Success is a little bittersweet for me because I didn't understand those things. It was heartbreaking. I just thought we were doing a great show and it was going to be a celebratory night no matter what. Little did I know that the business side of it was very, very important.

159

2002: Out On 45th Street In Our Costumes

Frank Vlastnik, Actor

When I did *Sweet Smell of Success* at the Beck, we had one tradition after the song, "Laughin' All The Way To The Bank". The number went on and on, and we were doing some hard dancing! After it ended, we'd run off stage, rolling Bernard Dotson off on the piano, and we'd be in the wings, schvitzing while Brian D'Arcy James started "At The Fountain".

At one point, we were told we were too noisy, so when we ran off stage, we'd just keep running and go all the way out to 45th Street! We'd stand out there during every performance at that point in the show, in our 1950s outfits. It was hilarious, because particularly during the Wednesday matinees, people would be walking by and wondering *what* was going on.

————————

The Stephen Sondheim-John Weidman musical Bounce *had tentative plans to open on Broadway at the Martin Beck during the 2003-2004 season, but when* Man of La Mancha *closed earlier than anticipated, the theatre owners needed a new tenant and couldn't hold the venue. The show's winding path ended up steering away from Broadway, and it made its New York debut under the title* Road Show *at the Public Theater in 2008.*

Other notable shows announced for the Beck but halted over the years include the commedia dell'arte musical Comedy, *which was announced for November of 1972, but closed out of town, and* The Baker's Wife *whose marquee was up when it closed out of town in November of 1976. Had David Merrick brought* The Baker's Wife *in, it would have marked Patti LuPone's first leading role on Broadway in a commercial production of a musical.*

————————

2003: The *Wonderful Town* Wine Spill

Penny Davis, Wardrobe Supervisor/Dresser

In *Wonderful Town*, the suit that Peter Benson's character wore got wine spilled on it during one scene. Luckily, the prop man was great. He and I discussed it well ahead of time—and that doesn't happen very often.

When I see a potential issue like that in a script, I'm the first one, as wardrobe supervisor, to go, "What happens costume-wise? What's with the wine spill?" Marty Pakledinaz was the designer, so I said to Marty, "What's happening with this wine?" He went, "I don't know."

So I got the contact sheet, and called the prop man. We discussed him taking care of the inventory and management of the "wine" and me taking care of the clean-up each night. I went out and got some swatches of the fabric that Marty was going to use for that costume. I brought them home and started playing until I worked out a realistic substance that I could wash out.

Then I went to Joe, who was building the suit, and said, "We have to make this completely machine washable." The interfacing of the material, anything that was going into that suit, had to be pre-shrunk and pre-washed. It was great teamwork, really, between props and me and the costume shop and everybody.

It was still tricky, because then we were *all* worried that something awful would happen to the suit! Nothing did. One night, the wine got mixed up, and the actors had to drink stuff that had soap in it—but the suit was fine!

————————

160

The Beck has a long history of "sister acts." The original production of My Sister Eileen *played a stint at the Beck in 1942 and a revival of* Wonderful Town, *based on that play, was at the theater from 2003 to 2005. In 1924, the theater's first production,* Madame Pompadour, *had two breakout stars in Irma and Dorothy Irving, twins who had come to the big city from Texas.*

———————

1999/2003: Little Things That A Director Grows To Love

Kathleen Marshall, Director/Choreographer

I love the Hirschfeld Theatre. I've worked there a couple of times because we did *Kiss Me, Kate* there, and *Wonderful Town,* which was my Broadway debut as a director as well as a choreographer.

I love the house itself. It's sort a perfect house for a musical because it's about 1,400 seats, but there's not a bad seat in the house. Compared to most theaters, it's pretty comfortable backstage. It's the only theater I've ever worked in where I've had a dressing room as a director/choreographer. It's the only one where there have been enough dressing rooms so that I could have a dressing room up until opening night. That's pretty amazing. The dressing room tower goes high up, so there's a lot of space there.

There are little things as a director that you grow to love. In the Hirschfeld, there's a little pass-over underneath the stage at the back of the house. A lot of the theaters have pass doors where you can get from the back of the stage to the front of the house and walk along the side at the orchestra level to get to that door. The great thing about the Hirschfeld is that you can actually stay underneath and get to the back of the house. So you can kind of come and go.

———————

The second floor of the Al Hirschfeld Theatre is decorated with dozens of drawings by the late Al Hirschfeld, the famous caricaturist who was at the center of the theatre world from the 1920s through 2003. Hirschfeld drew nearly every theatre personality and every show that came through the Great White Way. His caricatures chronicled all the great stars and theatrical moments of nearly the entire 20th Century. At one point, Hirschfeld would create caricatures for every highly anticipated new show, and the New York Times *would run them prior to the shows' openings, to build buzz.*

Mere months before the Martin Beck was to be renamed the Al Hirschfeld, he passed away, at the age of 99.

If you get a chance to see a show at the theater, make some extra time to head up to the mezzanine level, and look at a real live Hirschfeld.

———————

2006/2013: 1980s Hair

Josh Marquette, Hair Designer

The Wedding Singer was so fun to work on as associate hair designer. I had worked on David Brown's hair crews before, but to actually design a show with him was invaluable. He's my hero. He taught me so much, and I got to see the whole process.

The 1980s is where my heart belongs, whether it's 1980s hair or music or clothes. I think 1980s hair is so fun! It breaks my heart when I watch a TV show or a musical that takes place in the 1980s, and the hair isn't right. Are you kidding me? So it was awesome to be able to do it right.

Amy Spanger had an act one and an act two wig. She had the moment when the wig got drenched in "Saturday Night in the City". That was tricky, and when we were doing it out of town, she leaned back, the water came down and hit her, and the wig went flying off the back of her head! David turned to me and said, "That should never happen to the leading lady." That has always stuck with me. We really had to pin it properly and essentially nail it down to her head.

Seven years later, and I'm back at the Hirschfeld, designing *Kinky Boots*! When I'm designing by myself now, I like when people don't know that there are wigs on stage. When people say, "There were wigs in that?" that's the biggest compliment, because it means I did my job.

I think theatre in general has come to accept "hair hats." Those are wigs that we *know* are a wig. I like my shows not to have those. David was always the same way. So even if I'm creating something like this brown wig with shocking fuchsia highlights, I still want it to look like it could have possibly grown out of someone's head. I still want it to hopefully look like Cyndi Lauper's hair in the 1980s!

———————

This interview was conducted at Hudson Wigs. We were surrounded by wigs designed by Josh for his newest musical, First Date, *which had just started tech at the Longacre.*

In 1981, the creators of Bring Back Birdie *were trying to put on a show about what they thought the 1980s would be* like, *and in 2006, the creators of* The Wedding Singer *were at the same theater, trying to put on a show about what they thought the 1980s had* been *like.*

———————

2007: People Didn't Miss Shows

David Loud, Musical Director and Supervisor/Conductor/Actor

Curtains was so fun. I conducted the show and I had a few funny lines. Then, at the top of the second act, I would rise up on this podium and turn around and sing a song! It was such a funny idea that I would always get great laughs, even though I wasn't particularly funny. The idea was so clever, and Scott Ellis, our director, and Rupert Holmes, our writer, made it so unexpected and delicious.

On *Curtains*, which is a dance show, Noah Racey's hat would come into the pit regularly and I would always try to get it and throw it back to him. The button of the first act was Noah throwing the hat back to Karen Ziemba, who would catch it on the last chord of the song. So if that hat wasn't on stage, the button was sunk. I was always catching that damn hat, and trying to throw it back while still conducting!

It was just heaven conducting *Curtains*. The dancers were so fun, and David Hyde Pierce created this atmosphere of extraordinary trust and kindness and grueling work ethic. He never ever missed a show. He worked harder than anybody else in the theater. So, people didn't miss shows in *Curtains*. For the young dancers in their first show, you felt like they were learning from the best people in the world, right out of the gate.

David set a tone that we all tried to live up to in that show. Never mind that he's the funniest actor ever, and the funniest human being ever, he was a great role model for all of us.

———————

My interview with David Loud took place where over 20 of my interviews took place: just one block away from the Al Hirschfeld, at the Cafe Edison.

A favorite casual dining spot of all creatures of the Broadway jungle, the Cafe Edison on an average day feeds producers breakfast, New York Times reporters lunch, actors a pre-show meal, and crews a post-show dinner.

In 1931, when the Edison Hotel opened on the block splitting 46th and 47th Street, Broadway and 8th Avenue, it boasted an intricately designed dining room.

In 1980, the original dining room at the hotel was converted into the Cafe Edison, opened by Harry and Frances Edelstein. Almost immediately, it became a haven for show folk. August Wilson reportedly wrote several scripts on Cafe Edison napkins. Neil Simon was always around, and immortalized the café in his play 45 Seconds From Broadway. *(Faded posters and clippings from that play currently dot the walls of the venue.) A VIP table, with a red velvet rope in front, boasted the key players of Broadway, usually the Shuberts or the Nederlanders. Both Doug Henning and David Copperfield were regulars at the "Magic Table" in the corner, where a playing card was above on the ceiling as part of a trick occasionally done for the unassuming tourist.*

I discovered the Edison, as I'm sure many avid theatergoers do, when looking for a bite to eat between shows. There's nothing like it in the theatre district. The features of the 1931 dining room are prominent and wildly enough, they haven't been lost to time. Beautiful beige and tan columns and wall carvings give the room a distinctively 1930s feel, but the lunch counter is purely 1950s. The ceiling is ornate, and the chandeliers are the original fixtures! Homemade signs announcing the specials in black marker and a now-defunct balcony area looms—filled with storage—above the lunch counter. Since Harry and Frances were immigrants from Poland, and the menu has an Eastern European slant, the Cafe Edison is affectionately referred to by insiders as "The Polish Tea Room." Its two most famous dishes are the matzo ball soup and the blintzes.

Always teeming with life but never too crowded, the Edison has a magic ambiance that's a mixture of old and new. I had never seen the Edison empty or still until I interviewed my dear friend and mentor Mana Allen, and we closed down the place! Mana tells me that in 1986, when she was doing Smile *next door at the Lunt-Fontanne, the "Smile girls" would come to the Edison between shows, and often be sitting between the theatrical elite and Times Square's transvestite hookers, who also loved the soup.*

A few years ago, I was eating the famed blintzes with Larry Hochman when Jeb Brown sat down at the table next to us. Larry had just finished orchestrating The Book Of Mormon *and Jeb was in the thick of previews for* Spider-Man. *By the time 30 minutes had passed, they were both regaling the nearby table of hotel guests in their 80s and each other and the Edison staff and me with tales about working on each of their shows.*

There's just something about the Edison. When it was reported that Neil Simon had written a play chronicling the Cafe Edison, August Wilson simply replied: "He beat me to it."

2008: A Hundred Pieces They Don't See

Michael Arden, Actor/Assistant Director

As assistant director on *A Tale Of Two Cities*, I learned how many pieces of the puzzle there are to making a show, especially a musical.

For every one thing the audience sees, there are a hundred pieces they don't see that have to come together. For every time you think, *Oh I hear a trumpet*, you have to think of the music contractor, the trumpet player, the sub for the trumpet player, the person who did the orchestrations, the sound mixers who set up the mic for the trumpet...

It really puts things into perspective, as opposed to: we just do our show and people watch and then we go home. There's so much that goes into it: the marketing and the publicity and so on. I think that was what was most surprising to me: just how intricate of a tapestry the making of a Broadway show is.

———————————

Words and Music, the sensational and fictionalized Hollywood version of the story of Richard Rodgers and Lorenz Hart, was released in 1948. The movie starred Judy Garland, Lena Horne and Gene Kelly as themselves, and Tom Drake and Mickey Rooney as Rodgers and Hart.

The last Rodgers and Hart collaboration to play Broadway while Hart was still living was a revival of A Connecticut Yankee *at the Martin Beck. By this time, Rodgers first collaboration with Oscar Hammerstein,* Oklahoma! *had just opened on the next block at the St. James. It was a project that Hart had turned down. Rodgers hoped that working on the revival of* Yankee *together would help Hart get on a straight path and shake the alcoholism that he had struggled with for so long.*

Rodgers' wish came true and throughout the rehearsal period, Hart was the cleanest he'd been in years. Then, after the show opened out of town, his severe drinking problem returned. On opening night at the Beck in November of 1943, Rodgers had to ask two men to control Hart if his drunkenness caused him to disrupt the action on stage. Indeed, it did, and he had to be taken home. Five days later, he passed away.

The final scene of the movie Words and Music *is a fictionalized view of a sick Hart leaving his hospital bed to attend his opening night at the Martin Beck, leaving the theater in the rain, and dying in a ditch.*

———————————

2009: Our Sleep-In At The Hirschfeld

Gavin Creel, Actor

We rehearsed *Hair* in the Union Square Theatre downtown, so that we could get a feel of what it was like to go out into the audience. I was like, "I'll go up to the balcony, I'll run up there for this, that'll be fun!" you know, "Peace now, freedom now!"

Oh my God, what a mistake, because at the Hirschfeld I had to go up a ladder and then all through the balcony and all the way up to the top. I had said I would do the back half of the balcony! It was exciting and important, but holy shit, it was a lot—and tiring!

Hair was the most life-changing experience in the theatre that I've had yet. I found my voice as an artist and as an activist in a way that no show or experience had ever done for me. It was the show itself and also the experience surrounding it: Oskar Eustis and Diane Paulus and the Public and Jenny Gersten putting their weight behind us, and rallying for marriage equality. It was just incredible.

The whole concept of our production of *Hair* was that all the hippies got in a truck and came down from Central Park and found this abandoned theater and then drove the truck on stage, and just set the band up.

We painted the back wall of the theater, and the director, Diane Paulus, made us do these exercises where we had to say what part of the theater we had worked on. Did we lay the rugs down or did we drive the truck in or did we sew the costumes? We had to take ownership of the space.

The idea was that when people showed up in the seats, we just walked out, hit the gong, and started telling them our story. At the end, we went back and slept in the dressing rooms. We felt really strongly that if we were going to do that, we had to spend the night in the theater as a cast.

Our sleep-in, our lock-in... that was one of the greatest nights of my life.

We felt it was really important, and we wanted to do it before the show opened. We knew that once the show opened, it would be taken by the public either as a failure or a success, and it wouldn't be ours anymore.

So we picked a night, and we tipped our door man hundreds of dollars, and he locked the door of the theater.

We ordered pizza, and got booze. Some people may have brought some illegal substances. We blasted music and brought paint in and painted the walls. Everybody took off all their clothes and we were just in our underwear. We said, "We'll ask for forgiveness, not for permission," and we painted suns and quotes from the show.

We ran around, and got drunk and high, and people bonded. We took pictures, and listened to music, and sat on the stage together and just talked. It was so hippy dippy doodle, but it was imperative to the show. I think it was the reason that we were so tightly knit, that we bonded backstage *in* the theater. Everyone came in on Tuesday, and there was just paint everywhere, suns and clouds and sunshine and flowers and peace signs. It was incredible.

2009: You Better Believe In Love

Caissie Levy, Actor

Our night taking over the Al Hirschfeld Theatre during *Hair* was amazing. We had thinking-outside-of-the-box producers and we had an incredible stage manager who supported us, and because of them, we got to have the most incredible bonding night. We think it served the show in a really great way. We really were a tribe, and maybe from the outside, to the rest of the Broadway community, we looked a little obnoxious at times. But really, we were just trying to integrate the show with our lives. We were doing a lot of social activism and outreach for gay rights. We all really felt that embodied what we were doing on stage every night.

Jim Rado was around a lot. *Hair* was his baby, and he tries to see every production around the country, so he was always there with us. He rewrote some things, right up until the time we opened on Broadway. I remember years later, running into him outside the Lunt-Fontanne when I was doing *Ghost*. Every so often, he'll text all of us, "The moon is high, and I'm thinking of you."

Our original cast closing performance of *Hair* in New York was out of control. The show was like a rock concert. There was a 15-minute standing ovation afterward, everyone was crying, people were rushing the stage. It was so electric. We were so close for that entire season, and we ended up winning awards, and we felt like we'd all done good in the community, and there was this connection. And most of us were headed to start *Hair* in London together, so we were so sad to be leaving that era and that theater, but so excited about what was coming next for us, together.

When we were in previews for *Hair*, one of my best friends was very ill. She was an actress in Canada, and she had cancer. My whole cast rallied around me, and we did a huge benefit for her, and we raised about $20,000 to help her. Her fans were amazing, and she was just fighting and fighting this disease.

Between shows one Saturday, I got a text at half-hour from my friend in Toronto, saying: "I'm so sorry, let me know if there's anything I can do." I had no idea what it meant. And I couldn't get reception in my dressing room, so I thought: *I'm just going to bring my phone to places with me and hope she gets back to me, if I'm able to text her from there.* I asked what she was talking about, and she called me and told me that our friend had passed away. We were right at "places" to start the show, and I was a wreck. I just remember saying to somebody, "I can't go on."

They held the show, and they put my cover on, and I remember my whole cast surrounding me, on the floor, before they went on. The crew brought me a glass of whiskey, and I sat outside the theater while my cast started the show. Sadly, that's my strongest memory of being backstage there. But also I remember how much the cast really helped me get through that.

When I saw *Kinky Boots* this year, I went backstage and walked by that little area where I got the phone call. I hadn't been there in forever. And I just thought about the unity that cast of *Hair* had. They held the curtain, and they all just sat with me.

2009: The Theater Felt Like Ours

Jay Armstrong Johnson, Actor

I was on the road doing *A Chorus Line* and my agents called and said, "We have an audition for you, for *Hair*." But I couldn't be in the city for it. So I thought: *Well, that sucks. Missed opportunity. But I'm on the road.*

Then, when I got back to the city, they still hadn't found the person to understudy Claude, so they asked me to come in again. And they gave it to me! Then I found out Gavin Creel was playing Claude and I flipped out. I *flipped* out.

When we were in the third week of previews for *Hair*, none of the understudies or swings had had any rehearsal time yet. All I'd done was watch.

I got a phone call at about nine in the morning that third Saturday from my stage manager, who said, "You're on for the matinee. Get to the theater as soon as you can." I got in a cab, got to the theater, and had about an hour to go over my placement on stage. I hadn't had a rehearsal! I looked at the cast of *Hair*, and I said, "Shove with love if I don't know what I'm doing." And they sure did.

That's about all I can remember from that matinee performance. I don't remember a thing. I just went on total adrenaline. It was maybe one of the coolest experiences of my life so far.

Later in the run, I had 40 people fly in from my home state of Texas, to see me go on for Claude during a week that Gavin had a vacation. When I made my entrance as Claude, it was a stand-still for about 30 seconds. They screamed for me. And everyone in the front row, who didn't know who the hell I was, was looking around. They started going through their Playbills! They had no idea what was happening—that it was just a bunch of loud, rowdy Texans cheering for their boy on Broadway.

Gavin is one of the nicest human beings in the world. He has been a source of advice and comfort for me, and he's so open and happy to just be there. I strive to be like him. He told me one day, "Don't lose what you have, because a lot of people do, in this business. Stay sweet. Stay nice." That's really stuck with me, since *Hair*, and I'm going to try my damndest.

"Walking in Space", the trip, was so crazy! It was almost improv every single night. Everyone had their places on stage that they needed to generally be—but anything can happen when you're tripping on acid! That was probably the most fun to perform, in any role that I went on for.

When you've done *Hair*, there's this really weird thing that happens. It's just written into the show. It feels otherworldly in a sense. "Once in the Tribe, always in the Tribe," is what we'd say. Any fan or friend that would come and say they did a production of *Hair* at such-and-such theater, we'd be like, "Once in the Tribe, always in the Tribe."

166

The revival cast had been working together for years before the understudies and swings even came in, to start the Broadway production. You could tell that there was such a group camaraderie there, but the openness they had to let us into their family was incredible. A lot of people say that swinging a show on Broadway is thankless and a little sad and negative. At times, it absolutely is because you aren't involved in a lot of things. But that cast was special. They truly believed in the show and what it was saying—and we all truly believed in peace and love. I will always keep every single person from that cast in my heart.

In the Hirschfeld, I was able to run up and down aisles, and climb on things, and be in the audience with everybody. The fourth wall wasn't there. So the *theater* felt like ours, not just the stage. Every theater is so beautiful, but there was something special about the Hirschfeld with *Hair*.

———————————

I met Jay Armstrong Johnson when we were both in college at NYU. I hadn't found a lot of friends in New York yet who really, truly loved musical theatre in the way that I loved musical theatre. But Jay did. And he was an incredible performer.

We were two people in a student group that put together a couple of concerts for Broadway Cares/Equity Fights AIDS. One of the most vivid memories I have from college is of a Sunday morning rehearsal in the basement of an NYU dorm on 2nd Avenue. The basement had a piano so we could rehearse there. I had decided that Jay should sing "Why" from Tick, Tick... Boom!, *as the 11 o'clock number of our concert.*

That morning, I sat in my sweatpants with a clipboard, in a gross-smelling, fluorescently lit basement, and I watched Jay sing the song with two other people in the room.

I had never seen talent of that level that close to me before. I cried. I listened to him sing "I'm gonna spend my time this way," and I cried. Jay was the first person I met in New York who truly made me believe: You're going to meet people, and they're actually going to get to Broadway. And you are too.

Fast forward to 2009, and Jay was making his Broadway debut as the understudy for Claude in Hair. *I couldn't wait to see him go on for the role, and all of his friends were staying tuned for the alert. On the Saturday morning chronicled above, I ran down 8th Avenue at the speed of light and got a ticket to* Hair *at 1:58pm for the 2pm matinee. The show that afternoon would star my college pal, Jay Armstrong Johnson, making his Broadway debut.*

I cried a lot that day too. What I mostly remember, though, is feeling like I understood a part of Broadway, a camaraderie, that I hadn't really understood from the inside before.

When you're part of the theatre world for long enough, you get the privilege of watching people who you had always believed in, for years and sometimes decades, achieve their dreams. You get to see them do that on Broadway. And you get to carry around inside of you the fact that it all started in a dorm basement.

After Hair, *Jay was part of* Catch Me If You Can *and* Hands on a Hardbody *on Broadway. As of this printing, he is currently playing the lead role in a new musical that is aiming for Broadway this season.*

———————————

2009: Make It Your Own

Diane Paulus, Director

When we were thinking about bringing *Hair* to Broadway, with every theater we looked at, it was always: *How can we have the actors climbing into the audience here?* We were looking at the placement of the boxes and the balcony in each house, to see if it would be possible for the actors to move from one to the other. We were looking at the aisles to see how actors would be able to maneuver through the audience. It was so funny; we'd walk into a theater and, rather than look at the stage, we looked at the auditorium.

I'll never forget going to see the Hirschfeld, which was the theater where *Hair* ultimately played. Walking in that theater, I thought: *This is it!* It's a one-balcony house, so there's a huge orchestra. And the whole theater feels like one community rather than like a multi-tiered wedding cake style of audience, with separate groups, one on top of the other. You can really move from the balcony to the boxes effortlessly at the Hirschfeld. And the whole theater was designed in this Byzantine style, with stars on the ceiling. The theater felt cosmic, like a spiritual palace that would be the perfect home for *Hair*.

When we moved *Hair* from Central Park to the Hirschfeld, the idea was that the hippies were coming to Broadway. They were going to take over the Hirschfeld, and camp out in the Hirschfeld. We really adapted the show from how we did it in the park. At the Delacorte, these characters' performances took place in Central Park. At the Hirschfeld, it was really like the show was taking place at the Hirschfeld. It was a be-in.

I know our actors had a be-in overnight at the theater. They were hippies! The whole point of it was to live the show from the inside out, so their rebellious spirit to do that was very appropriate. The hallways during *Hair* were painted with flowers and peace signs and plants. There were beaded curtains everywhere. And you could look out the dressing room windows and see everyone lining up on the street, and they could see everyone in their dressing rooms! There really was this narrative, like hippies were living in the Hirschfeld.

I first heard from Jim Rado, one of the authors, that during the original production at the Biltmore, the actors had invited the audience on stage to dance. I said, "Well, we have to do that!" I'll never forget the first time we did it in Central Park. Jim had told me that on Broadway, a couple people would get up and dance. The first time at the Delacorte, hundreds of people got up to go on stage! We were all sitting in the back, going: "Oh my God, what is happening?!" One of the production managers ran to look underneath the stage of the Delacorte, because he was nervous about it holding the weight of so many people!

It became such a part of the show. The audience coming on stage wasn't a post-show thing. To me, the whole event of *Hair* was driving to that moment when the audience became a community on stage and sang "Let The Sunshine In". When we brought the show to Broadway, it was the first thing I said. "We must be able to do this on Broadway." And there was this issue of: well, who's going to let us do that? There were insurance issues, liability, practicality! But Jordan Roth and Jujamcyn were so behind it. They understood that our audience was going to flood the stage every night. It was just the most incredible transformation of a traditional Broadway theater stage, to be a community be-in of actors and audience, side by side. Over the course of the run, people would come on stage with protest t-shirts about the Iraq war, or signs about marriage equality. The cast went to march on Washington for marriage equality, and the post-show made this transition from the show to modern life, now.

It was so great to get to move into the Hirschfeld and break down those boundaries. It was thanks to Jordan and Jujamcyn. I'll never forget Paul Libin on our first day of rehearsal. He came to our first rehearsal for *Hair* on Broadway, and everyone was like: "Uh oh, what's the theater owner going to say?" And Paul said, "Tear up this theater. Make it your own."

2010/2012: A Christmastime Challenge

Casey Nicholaw, Director/Choreographer/Actor

Elf was challenging because it was a Christmas show, so we didn't have any time! We had about three previews, because we had to get the show up for that holiday window.

The movie is so ridiculously funny, and just the fact that people sing in the musical, and that it's Christmastime makes the show sweeter. That was great, but it was a tough balance to negotiate. And the movie has so many sight gags that we couldn't do on stage! The second time we did the show was easier.

2013: We Couldn't Tell With *Kinky Boots*

Hal Luftig, Producer

We couldn't tell with *Kinky Boots*. In the rehearsal room, without the sets and without the full orchestrations and without the costumes and without an audience... we didn't really know.

At the first preview in Chicago, we did not have a big audience because it was a show without a star called *Kinky Boots*—in the Midwest. It wasn't exactly like they were flocking to the box office! Then they leapt to their feet at the end, and you just knew that they were moved, that the show had moved them to just be who they wanted to be. I felt like: *Wow. This is why we do what we do. Because we're touching people and we're stirring emotion.*

I'd actually never experienced anything like the audience reaction at the Hirschfeld. It was like a tidal wave that came over us. The first couple of times it happened, I remember I was standing in the back with Harvey Fierstein and Cyndi Lauper and Jerry Mitchell and we just looked at each other with tears in our eyes. We couldn't quite believe it.

Being of the theatre—dare I say it?—you don't quite trust. You think, *Okay, these people, they're our friends right?* Or, *They must be comped houses* or, *Billy Porter must've invited all of his friends, right?* You spend several performances doing that, and at some point, you let all of it sink in. No, they're not a comped house. No, these aren't 400 of Billy's friends. You see the box office growing, and you realize these are people who are being stirred and moved, and going out and telling people to go see the show. It's the way it's supposed to happen. It is just thrilling. I hope this never changes.

When I need a pick-me-up, I go to that theater and I just stand in the back. Or I stand in the lobby, and I watch these people come out. For two and a half hours, whatever is going on in their lives is gone. That's part of what theatre is supposed to do, and it's unlike anything else that we have. That's why it's a wonderful thing.

It is really one of the things I set out to do when I was a kid. Theatre did that for me. When I saw *Mame*, or when I saw *Applause*, or *George M!*, I was transported. I was transported! I was someplace else watching these people, and that's what's happening at *Kinky Boots* for people, and I love it. I especially love when I see kids who would've been about my age and it's just like: *Thank God I got to do what I wanted to do and make this happen.*

Kinky Boots fits so beautifully into the Hirschfield. One of the things that we didn't know or think about... the set, because it takes place in a factory, has these old stained glass windows, and when you go into the theater the orchestra doors have stained glass too! We didn't even realize that when we chose the theater. The Hirschfeld is just the perfect, perfect fit.

2013: A Stage For Equality

Daryl Roth, Producer

My Hirschfeld experience has been extraordinary and emotional for so many reasons and on so many levels. The first time I worked in the Hirschfeld was on *Curtains*, the wonderful musical created by Rupert Holmes, John Kander and Fred Ebb. It starred two of my favorite people, David Hyde Pierce and Deb Monk. That production created a wonderful family, which brought together the amazing company and the staff of the theatre, many of whom are still there today.

And then, last September, the Hirschfeld took on a whole new meaning for me when my son, Jordan, who is the President of Jujamcyn Theatres (which includes the Hirschfeld) married his husband, Richie, on that stage. We had the most beautiful setting, including the chuppah, which we all stood under to witness this momentous occasion. Seeing Jordan and Richie exchange their heartfelt vows on that stage truly made that house a home. All of the guests who were in the audience felt the warmth, emotion, and significance of the ceremony.

February 21, 2013 was our first day on stage at the Hirschfeld with the *Kinky Boots* company, and I was overcome with emotion. So much had happened in that theater, and there we were, after I had been developing this show for seven years. To reach this day all on stage together for the first time was the beginning of another journey, which has turned out to be one of the best in my 26 years of producing theatre.

My son and the Jujamcyn staff have a very special way of being gracious and inclusive in all of their theatres. When you go to the Hirschfeld to see *Kinky Boots*, you truly feel like you're being welcomed into someone's house. The ushers are excited for people to see the show, and they are in it with all of us. They are part of our team. They stand in the back and dance, and they're just as proud of the show as we are; they're part of the family. When theatergoers come into the Hirschfeld, they feel that energy. They feel welcomed.

Kinky Boots is a big hearted musical that celebrates acceptance, compassion, and understanding. "You change the world when you change your mind." People leave *Kinky Boots* feeling joyous and uplifted, but also with a sense of how to respect one another's differences. The story really resonates, though, because it is personal. It's about family, it's about friendship, it's about love.

And our company has truly become a family, sharing each other's highs and lows, and celebrating in each other's joy. Most of our original cast has been with us since a workshop in January 2012, and then performed in Chicago before we came to Broadway. Over that time, our beautiful Annaleigh Ashford got married, and many of our company members have gotten engaged. In fact, one of our cast members recently proposed to his girlfriend on stage through song with our entire cast singing backup for him. It was the perfect moment, which typifies the love and support this company has for one another.

I am at *Kinky Boots* as much as possible, and the feeling at the Hirschfeld is a very joyous one. You walk into the theatre, and you just become happy. After you have seen *Kinky Boots*, you walk out onto 45th street and you carry that joy with you. It's the perfect "pair." The theater and the show are the perfect fit, and I hope that *Kinky Boots* lives at the Hirschfeld for years to come.

In 1961, Bye Bye Birdie *won the Tony Award for Best Musical. In 1968,* Hallelujah, Baby!, *another Beck tenant, won. It took 45 years for the next Best Musical Tony Award-winner to open at the theater, with* Kinky Boots.

Kinky Boots *recently broke the box office record at the Al Hirschfeld Theatre—for the fifth time.*

The Neil Simon Theatre

Built: 1927
Location: 250 West 52nd Street
Owner: The Nederlander Organization
Formerly Named: Alvin Theatre (1927-1983)
Longest-Running Show: *Hairspray* (2002-2009)
Shortest-Running Shows: *The Little Prince and the Aviator* (closed after 16 previews in 1982), *Senator Joe* (closed after three previews in 1989)
Number of Productions: 132

I'll never forget going backstage at the Alvin for the first time. I was so stage-struck as a kid, and I thought it was going to be very glamorous. Then I walked through the stage door.

What really happens is that you are surrounded by burly stagehands and metal staircases and mechanical things. Backstage at a Broadway theater is not a home unless you make it one. It is the bare minimum of what you need to put on a show. Broadway is certainly about dreams, but it is also about the gritty reality of how to make them happen. Broadway is about machinery and how it moves.

-David Loud, Musical Director and Supervisor/Conductor/Actor

Introduction: Sondheim, The Alvin And Me

Ann Morrison, Actor

The first Broadway show I saw was *Company* at the Alvin Theatre. I was a teenager, and my family came into New York for the first time ever. We were all very excited about seeing the show.

We sat up in the mezzanine for *Company*, and I was absolutely enthralled to be getting to see a real, live professional play of this nature. It was spectacular. I'd been listening to Sondheim for so many years; I had danced around to *West Side Story* at age seven in my living room. So I was sitting there in the mezzanine, and my family and I were loving it. When the show got to "Ladies Who Lunch" and Elaine Stritch sang, "Everybody rise! Rise! Rise!" a bunch of people in the theater stood up and we did too. We were absolutely spellbound.

The fun thing about the Alvin is that years later, I made my Broadway debut in that theater with *Merrily We Roll Along*. Every time I went on stage for *Merrily*, I'd always look at the seat I sat in, way back when I was watching *Company*, as a kid. I played especially to that spot once in a while, because I knew that there was going to be a kid up there who had probably never seen a Broadway show before, and they were going to get to have the same thrill that I had when I saw *Company* right there.

1954: My Time Machine Dream

Jeff Bowen, Writer/Actor

If I could go back and see any Broadway show I missed, I would take a time machine to the Alvin during the summer of 1954 so I could see *The Golden Apple*.

I knew a lot of musicals before I was exposed to *The Golden Apple* in college. I saw a production at Florida State University, and it was the first musical where I really felt I had been transcended in a different way. I thought: *It's a sung-through musical that's not an operetta[28]? With comedy and drama? And no one has heard of it?!*

It's not a well-known show, even though it won the Drama Critic's Circle Award for Best Musical that year. It had all of these people in it who were amazing—Kaye Ballard, Portia Nelson, Stephen Douglass. *The Golden Apple* had a cast of people who were awesome, but who not everyone knew were awesome. It wasn't Julie Andrews and Rex Harrison, it was Kaye Ballard and Portia Nelson. Not that Julie Andrews isn't interesting—of course she is. But these were great actors who hadn't been remembered like they deserved to be. I would love to time travel and see them.

My head popped off about ten years ago when I got access to an audio bootleg of *The Golden Apple* that was recorded backstage at the stage manager's station, on stage left. It was mind-blowing because you could hear the show, and also the stage manager calling the cues! That was a thing I used to dream existed.

Getting that bootleg was literally like having a Broadway nerd dream come true.

The funny thing is that when I came back from my *Golden Apple* time travel trip, I don't know who I would talk to about it. It wouldn't be the same as, "Oh my God, you went back in time to see the original *Oklahoma!*? Tell me all about it!" People would be like, "What?" And I'd say, "*The Golden Apple*. At the Alvin. Pay attention! It was awesome!"

———————

The early years of the Alvin Theatre boasted a bevy of charming musical productions from the Gershwins, Cole Porter, and Rodgers & Hart.

The theater opened in 1927 with the Gershwin musical, Funny Face *starring Fred and Adele Astaire. The Gershwins would also open* Girl Crazy *at the Alvin, with Ethel Merman making her Broadway debut singing "I Got Rhythm". Their last show before George Gershwin's death was the premiere of* Porgy *and* Bess *at the Alvin in 1935. (Ira Gershwin would return for* Lady in the Dark *in 1941.)*

Cole Porter's reign at the Alvin began with Anything Goes, *which opened to tremendous praise in 1934, with first-nighters loving songs like "I Get A Kick Out Of You" and "You're The Top". He followed it with the show* Red, Hot and Blue, *starring Jimmy Durante, Ethel Merman and Bob Hope. Durante and Merman fought over who should have top billing, resulting in a compromise where their names were crisscrossed. The show poster essentially read "Jimmy-Merman-Ethel-Durante," and each walked away thinking they were triumphant. Merman might as well have lived at the Alvin during the 1930s and 1940s, because she was back with yet another Cole Porter show,* Something For The Boys, *in 1943.*

Rodgers & Hart had quick runs of their shows Spring Is Here *and* Heads Up! *in the late 1920s, but they returned to the Alvin in 1937 for one of the starriest Broadway opening nights of all time: George M. Cohan playing current President Franklin D. Roosevelt in the musical* I'd Rather Be Right, *written along with George S. Kaufman and Moss Hart. Rodgers & Hart followed that up at the Alvin with the original production of* The Boys From Syracuse.

———————

[28] operetta: a light opera; an early ancestor of the musical

1955: Toilet Salute

Maury Yeston, Writer

The first Broadway show I ever saw was *No Time for Sergeants*. My mom took me to see it when I was a little boy.

The show was Andy Griffith's Broadway debut. He was hilarious! I will never forget the show or his performance. I think it's the reason I'm in the theatre today.

Andy Griffith's character was a private, and there was a bullying sergeant. At one point, he's punished and told that he has to clean the latrines.

He started cleaning these toilets, and then the sergeant came in and yelled, "Attention!" Andy Griffith stood up and clicked his heels to attention, and as he did this, all five toilet seats went up at the same time in salute too! I'm still on the floor about that. It brought the house down. I think that's why I'm in the theatre. To make something like that, that just knocks people out.

1962: A Very New York Show

Harold Prince, Producer/Director

There's a story about the rooftop of the Alvin from *A Funny Thing Happened on the Way to the Forum*.

There was an actress playing Philia, who eventually was fired and became a movie star. One night, she climbed out of her dressing room, onto the marquee. She was kind of eccentric, and she locked herself out. We had to get her down off the marquee of the theater!

We did a gypsy run of *Forum* that was a smash. No scenery, no costumes. Then, we went to Washington with it, and got the worst reviews you've ever read in your life. We didn't get any laughs. I said to the cast, "You know, you just did a gypsy run-through that was a huge hit. New York is going to love it."

That's very hard to say to people when they're playing for three weeks to dead silence. It just killed the timing of the show! But that group was indefatigable; they worked really hard. And we got to New York! We called Jerry Robbins to come in, and he gave us a new opening number, which was hugely important. But the truth that's been forgotten is that they loved the show before we'd done that! We had gone over well in New York. Then, when we officially opened back in the city, we were even better, thanks to Jerry.

One interesting thing about that show is that it was a hit in New York, and it was always a hit in the West End, but it was never a hit on the road. And when they made the movie, that wasn't a success either. It had a sense of humor that played better in the city.

———————

Hal Prince told me his story about the rooftop of the Alvin Theatre during A Funny Thing Happened on the Way to the Forum *because I had asked about the rooftop of the Alvin Theatre during* Merrily We Roll Along. *Did they ever actually go up there? I had to ask.*

When I told Mr. Prince that Merrily *was my favorite show of all time, I couldn't resist adding, "And I was once Mary Flynn for Halloween." He chuckled and said, "That's my wife. The show was really written about me, Steve, and my wife, in some ways."*

———————

1962-1973: Part of This World

Ted Chapin, President of The Rodgers & Hammerstein Organization/Past Chairman of the American Theatre Wing

A Funny Thing Happened on the Way to the Forum at the Alvin Theatre. I was taken on a Saturday and loved it so much that I went the next Saturday and got a standing room ticket. I did the same thing for *How to Succeed in Business Without Really Trying*. I loved the idea of going back the next weekend to something I really liked, and standing room was a great way to see shows.

For some reason, I always loved the Alvin. I think it was partly because I saw a lot of shows there—*Forum* was one, *Company*, *Flora the Red Menace*, *High Spirits*—I just had a very good feeling about it. There's just something about that theater that I... it just feels the right size, it feels friendly.

When I worked with Alan Arkin, we took over the musical *Molly* which was previewing there and it was a very, very cool feeling to work in a theater that I had just instinctively always loved. It probably was—as much as any other single thing—the moment that made me feel as if I could be part of this world, that I could actually walk into this theater that I'd been in a lot as an audience member.

––––––––––––––

During the 1960s the Alvin's stage was mostly filled with musicals, but the theater did manage to squeeze in bookings of two straight plays: Rosencrantz and Guildenstern Are Dead *by Tom Stoppard, and the Pulitzer Prize-winning* The Great White Hope, *starring James Earl Jones. Both won the Tony Award for Best Play in subsequent seasons.*

––––––––––––––

1966/1977: *Superman* and *Annie*

Charles Strouse, Writer

I attended the closing of "*It's A Bird... It's A Plane... It's Superman...*" That was a show that was the most fun I've ever had in my life. From beginning to end, all the authors, and Hal Prince... it was wonderful to work on.

I was thrilled with the recent Encores! production because that's the show we wrote. They didn't understand back then, the frame we were putting the show in, but the audience this time was sensational. I was into comic books when I was a pre-teen, and we tried so hard to bring back that feeling. David Newman and Bob Benton wrote the book and were just great. My memories of *Superman* are all good, except for the fact that it was underappreciated—but now it's very much appreciated!

Then we did *Annie* at the Alvin later. Those kids were wonderful. They felt they had inherited a world of glamour. They all bought rabbit coats. And Martin Charnin, who directed the original, was wonderful with them. They were the happiest bunch of people you can imagine.

My favorite memory of *Annie* is that it was an overwhelming hit in Washington. Overwhelming. I'd never experienced anything like it. And when it opened at the Alvin, there were lines that went from the Alvin, all the way around Broadway, almost to reach the Alvin again! Three and four deep.

I remember standing there, with Mike Nichols, and my back was against the Union Hiring Hall. That's a place where we used to go—where musicians went—if you were looking for jobs. I mean, the really good musicians, they were working at the hotels already. But guys like me, I was trying to make a couple of bucks when I just got out of college. So I used to go down to the Union Hiring Hall at four in the afternoon, and there would be a call for a piano player. That kind of thing.

And I thought: *Here they are, pouring money into my bank account, and I'm standing, leaning against the Union building, where I used to go and wait for someone to yell, "25 bucks to go to the Catskills!"* And I was so eager to go for that.

That was a very big moment in my life.

———————

The Roseland Ballroom on 52nd Street once acted as a dance hall or skating rink at night, and during the day, it was home to the Local 802 Union Hiring Hall, for musicians who wanted to make a couple bucks playing an audition or society event.

———————

1969: Headlining Across The Street

Len Cariou, Actor

I auditioned three different times for *Applause*, traveling in from Stratford, CT where I was doing *Henry V*.

I had never done that kind of audition process before; it was new to me. The first time I came in, just the director, Ron Field, was there. I sang for him and read. And he said, "Thanks very much. We'll be in touch." I heard nothing.

A month later, they asked me to come and do it again, only, this time, composer Charles Strouse and lyricist Lee Adams were going to be there. I came back and I did a second audition and everybody said, "Oh, very nice. Thanks. We'll be in touch." I heard nothing afterward.

They called me a third time, a month later, and I said to my agent, "What is going on?!" He said, "I think they want you, but now Ms. Bacall is going to be there. She has to approve you next. This time, the whole team is going to be there, all the producers. There are going to be ten people in the room in the Alvin Theatre." We were in the Alvin Theatre which is now the Simon Theatre.

By the time August came around, I thought: *If they can't figure this out by now...* But I said, "Okay, I'd better play the game." By that time, we'd decided to bring *Henry V* in to Broadway at the ANTA Theatre, which is now the August Wilson. We were going to be there for a short six-week run.

I came in and did the audition, and everyone was screaming and saying how wonderful it was. I was really proud. Ron Field came up to me, and he said, "As far as I'm concerned, you're the guy, but I don't get to say that. But I really want you to do it—and I'm pretty sure Ms. Bacall does too." Then he said, "Now, remind me what it is you're doing at the moment."

I said, "Okay, Ron. Come with me." We went out the stage door of the Alvin Theatre, which faces the ANTA Theatre. I brought him out onto the street and I pointed across the street at the marquee where there were three six-foot posters of me as Henry V. I said, "That's what I'm doing." And he went, "Oh, God. I'm so embarrassed." I said, "So, tell them to come out the back door. That's what I'm doing over there."

———————

The Guild Theatre on 52nd Street was built in 1925, and the Alvin was built not long after, in 1927. For almost 90 years, the two Broadway houses have faced each other on 52nd Street. From 1925 to 1943, The Guild Theatre was owned, operated by and named for the Theatre Guild, who produced non-commercial work on Broadway. Across the street, the Alvin was owned and operated by commercial producers Alex Aarons and Vinton Freedley, who took the first few letters from each of their first names and made the name of their theater.

The Theatre Guild had their offices on the 8th Avenue side of their theater, while Al and Vin had their offices on the top of the Alvin. Those offices on top of the Alvin eventually became the offices of Manny Azenberg, producer of many Neil Simon hits. They are now the offices of Audience Rewards, the discount theatre ticket service. To get to the offices, you have to walk in the stage door and take the elevator.

———————

1970: Our Theatrical Salinger

Harold Prince, Producer/Director

For *Company*, George Furth wrote the best book of a musical that has ever been written.

My wife worships J.D. Salinger, and last year, she said to me, "George is our theatrical Salinger." She's dead right.

George wrote the greatest book of a musical ever, Steve wrote a great score, and the idea for making the whole thing a musical was mine. I said, "Let's do a musical about this," and then those guys wrote as good a musical as I will ever work on.

1970: In Good *Company*

Joanna Merlin, Casting Director

I had been an actress all my life. Then, I stopped because I wanted to spend time with my two daughters when they were little. I was starting to get a little bit itchy, because I wanted to do something, and Hal Prince called me out of the blue. He changed the course of my life in such an incredible way. He brought me in as a casting director, so I got to be a part of that golden period of those Sondheim-Prince musicals.

Company was the first show I got to work on casting for, at the Alvin in 1970. It was a privilege and it was really hard. Every show was a challenge to cast, because everyone really had to be able to act and sing. It was joyous and a wonderful period of my life. Hal and I had a very collaborative relationship, and I had a good sense of his taste. He trusted me, and I also had a great relationship with Paul Gemignani. As musical director, he was always willing to work with actors who I liked on their singing. I did the same for him, with singers he really liked for shows. We all had a great back and forth.

Hal and I just hit it off from the start. I think he felt that I was a Jewish mother and that I would take good care of the actors, and that was what he was concerned with. He had very good relationships with actors, always. He respected them and treated them well and rarely, rarely fired anybody.

1970: A Walk Home Through The Village

Peter Link, Writer/Actor

I remember seeing *Company* and walking all the way home to the Village afterward. I was just so thrilled with the concept and the idea and I soared home, through New York. I remember walking and walking and thinking: *I really want to be a part of that.* It was a powerful experience.

1970: It's Supposed To Be Great For Kids

Lonny Price, Actor/Director/Writer

On my eleventh birthday, my grandmother and I couldn't get tickets to *Applause*. The ticket broker said to us, "Well, this new show just opened. It's supposed to be great for kids." That's how my grandmother and I ended up at *Company*.

It changed my life. The sound of that music somehow sent me into a hysteria or something! I just loved the sound of it. I still do. That show was special, and it seemed more monumental than any of the other ones I had seen up to that point.

I remember the elevator in the set, and I remember "What Would We Do Without You" with the hats and canes, and I remember that they bowed downstage of the curtain and then the curtain came in upstage of them and it bounced! You saw the curtain come down and expected it to obliterate them, but instead, they were in front of it. It was very exciting. I'd never seen anyone do that before. And we don't use curtains much anymore, because it costs an extra $70,000 a year. You have to get a guy specifically to pull it.

But I'll always remember that *Company* curtain coming down.

1973: Playing *Tricks*

Christopher Murney, Actor

The first Broadway show I appeared in was a musical called *Tricks* at the Alvin Theatre. We had done the show at the Actors Theatre in Louisville and at Arena Stage and in Detroit, and then we came to Broadway.

We were at the Fisher Theatre in Detroit for a month, and my dressing room there was bigger than my apartment once we got to New York! At the Alvin, it felt like we were on a merry-go-round. We concentrated really hard on getting the show right, and it was really one of the first musicals to come from regional theaters like that. There was a lot of pressure for it to succeed.

Tricks was based on *La Fourberies de Scapin* by Molière, and it had music by Jerry Blatt, who was also writing for Bette Midler at the time. Rene Auberjonois played Scapin, and I was his second banana, Sylvestre. At one point during the show, I walked into the middle of the audience, and started walking on the backs of seats. That was a lot of fun to do, because people didn't expect it!

The audiences were into it, but as soon as the reviews came out, they changed. They grew cold. I don't even remember our closing performance, because I was thinking so hard about what I was going to do next. I had a family, and they had stayed in Louisville while I did the show, so I had to decide whether to go back to the Actors Theatre or stay in New York. I finally decided that I had gotten here, so I might as well stay. So I did.

———————

Christopher Murney is the father of Broadway actress, Julia Murney. In addition to Tricks, *Christopher was in the Broadway musical* Mack and Mabel *and has had an extensive film and TV career. In his early years, he appeared in a musical called* Holeville *with Don Scardino, the Broadway actor who later became television director/producer of 30 Rock. Don would direct Julia in her Broadway debut in* Lennon.

———————

1975: The Asbestos Curtain

Randy Morrison, Stagehand

When I was a little kid, I started thinking I wanted to be a sound man. My dad was a theatre critic for *Variety*, and he was good friends with Brooks Atkinson, so we used to go to his house in the country. At this house, he had a bunch of broken electronic equipment. I would play with it, and end up fixing things. Brooks said to my dad one day, "You should get him into the stagehands' union."

My first show was *Shenandoah* at the Alvin Theatre. I was a carpenter, and I was in charge of the curtain. I would pull a rope down, and another stagehand would pull a rope up, and the curtain would come in.

One night, before bows, the stage manager started yelling at us, "Stop the curtain! Stop the curtain!" An actor had accidentally triggered the asbestos curtain to come in! The asbestos curtain weighs about six tons, and none of us knew how to make it stop. So, John Cullum went into the house through the pass door, and bowed in the audience.

I remember standing outside the stage door one night after pre-set, and seeing a ton of policemen run into the theater across the street. *Bubbling Brown Sugar* was playing there, and two people in the company had gotten into a fist fight! They ended up taking them out of the theater, and we watched them get put into police cars.

1978: More Auditions At The Alvin

Jessica Molaskey, Actor

I remember auditioning for *Annie*. Marty Charnin was infamous for his auditions for *Annie*. They'd bring, like, five girls off to the side so they could hear you, and it was so unnerving. And there was the ghost light, which was straight out of the movies.

I guess they don't do that anymore because it's too expensive. But it's one thing when you see someone in a room—you don't know if they have a size. There's just something that happens to certain people on stage.

1979: *Annie* Then And Now

Merwin Foard, Actor

I went to a community college in Charlotte, North Carolina. My major was broadcasting. When they asked whether we wanted to focus on music, sports, or news broadcasting, I told them I was interested in music. I could play music, but I didn't really sing. They put me in a class to learn the basics of singing before I could major in music broadcasting.

I was in that class singing my first assigned song, a capella, and a teacher walked by and heard me. He approached me after the class and said, "Have you ever done theatre? We're doing *Pirates of Penzance* in the theatre department and I'd like you to be in it."

Suddenly, I got the theatre bug. I left broadcasting behind. Later that year, the thespians were going on a trip to New York to see shows. I got to see *Annie, Ain't Misbehavin', Dracula*… great shows.

Annie was enthralling. We were up in the mezzanine, and it was all brand new to me. They had a set piece called a travelator, which was like a people-mover at the airport. Characters would freeze and be carted across

178

the stage. I'd never seen technology like that before! Seeing a dog on stage was unique, and I was just so impressed with everything these kids could do.

I didn't grow up as a theatre kid. Theatre didn't even exist in my high school. It was amazing to discover all of that in college and then be up in New York seeing my first Broadway show. It still didn't really occur to me that this was something I could do. I was just enjoying watching them.

———————

Merwin starred in the 2012 revival of Annie *at the Palace, his 14th Broadway show.*

———————

1981: Closing *Merrily*

Jason Alexander, Actor

There were a lot of tears at the closing performance. The thing I remember most about the closing is when the curtain came down. For the audience, that show had ended, but it was just beginning for us behind the curtain. There was a whole other three-act event going on behind that curtain after the show.

Hal and Steve and George came to talk to us. At the time, there was some talk of moving the show to an off-Broadway venue, and they were trying so desperately to keep hope alive and keep us children from having broken hearts. There was such an attempt being made to keep us hopeful. There was a lot of mayhem backstage and nobody knew what to do. I've been part of lots of shows that have closed, but this was different. This was everybody going: "We'll be best friends forever!" but somewhere, in the back of your teenage head, you realized that you might not see this person again, and whatever relationship you had, this is its final moment.

There was a lot of that going on. It was very emotional and nobody really wanted to leave the Alvin, and no one knew quite what to do once we left the stage. Going up to our dressing rooms to pack up our stuff and leave seemed alien to us, and a nearly herculean task.

David Loud, Musical Director and Supervisor/Conductor/Actor

I was 18 for most of the experience, but I turned 19 on November 28, 1981. *Merrily We Roll Along* closed on my 19th birthday. I got a great birthday card signed by the whole cast that said: "Happy F---ing Birthday."

Lonny Price, Actor/Director/Writer

Closing was just very upsetting. All of us cried through the whole show. I'm sure "Our Time" was inaudible, and we didn't even bother to smile at curtain call. We were just crying and crying.

They put the notice up, but Hal kept saying, "I'm going to take the notice down!" He was trying to make plans to scale the show down and move it to the Entermedia Theatre, which is now a movie theatre but used to be a legit house on 2nd Avenue called, at one point, the Eden Theatre. That didn't happen.

But Hal saved the record. He told the powers that be at RCA "You'll record this, or you'll never get another one again." That's why the *Merrily* record has this memorial-looking photo of Steve in the middle of it, because they didn't think anything having to do with the show itself would sell. They wanted to distance themselves from *Merrily*, and say that they were putting out this album just because of Steve. That cover is weird. It looks like he died.

Liz Callaway, Actor

The closing performance was sad, but the next morning we recorded the album. So I remember we couldn't—it was very emotional, and incredibly difficult at the same time, to record the next day. But thank God we had that!

Terry Finn, Actor

A lot of kids went back to school after we closed, and a lot went out on tour. I might've been able to go on tour, but I figured it would be a good idea to stay in town for auditions. I felt like there would be something bigger and better that came along. And it took me two or three years to get my next job. I had constant auditions but didn't book anything, and my momentum seemed to stop.

Mana Allen, Actor

After it became clear that our show would be closing, Hal got many of us auditions. Hal asked, "Where do I have openings?" He wanted to give us jobs. On our final Wednesday, between shows, Hal had Larry Fuller audition us on the set of *Merrily*! We didn't have to sing; they knew we could sing. Larry taught us combinations from *Evita*. Four of us—Maryrose Wood, Mary Johansen, Clark Sayre and Steven Jacob—were given jobs on the *Sweeney* tour, and Donna Marie Asbury and myself were put into the tour of *Evita*.

Mary Johansen, the original Mrs. Spencer, came to visit the city recently. She stayed at the Milford Plaza and we met right here at the Edison for dinner. She brought her 18-year-old son, who had never been to New York City before. Mary met her husband on that *Sweeney* tour that Hal put her and the others on. He's now the technical director at the University of Michigan, so they live there. Mary looks exactly the same! I don't know if you can really hear her on the cast album of *Merrily*, but I'll never forget her saying her line, "Well, at least she's not pregnant!" She still sounds exactly the same too.

At the closing performance, the crew played a joke. They hung a giant beach ball up in the house at the spot where we were supposed to look for Sputnik. They thought that would be really funny, but it wasn't, and they got in trouble.

It was wild when a bunch of us original cast members went to see this production of *Merrily* at Pace University this year. Lonny said, "Do you think those kids will be friends in 2044?" Because a lot of us are still close. It's 32 years later and Maryrose Wood is still my best friend.

Jim Walton, Actor

It was only a couple days before we closed that we heard that Thomas Shepard was going to record the album. There was no deal yet, and we were thinking: *This could be it. No one else might ever get to hear it.* And then once we heard that we'd get recorded, that was huge. I knew that the score was magnificent, and that the life that the recording could generate for the show was going to be amazing. I was heartened for the entire last week, knowing that the show would run forever, in its own way, in that recording.

One of my saddest memories from *Merrily* happened during closing day. At the end of act one, I'm singing "Not A Day Goes By" to Beth on the steps of the courthouse. My character is trying to save his marriage. As I was singing it for the last time, I heard someone sobbing and sniffling in the wings. Someone crying backstage. I thought: *Who is doing that?* And when I finally got a chance to look off stage, there, with his shoulders shaking like his heart was breaking, was David Loud.

I still meet people who say, "I loved *Merrily*" or "I was there on closing night." There are die-hard fans. There are people who are almost as proud to have seen it as I was to be in it. "I was there. I thought it was great." There's this weird posthumous glory that accompanies the show. People hear that terrific album and think: *Why did it only run two weeks?! I don't get it.* That's how transcendent those songs are, so theatrical and so profound, and so witty. When I heard the lyric "Leontyne Price to sing her medley from Meisersinger," I wanted to ask Steve, "Did you have that in a notebook from the time you were 20 and you were waiting, or did you just stumble upon that one? Was it luck? How did you do that?"

In 2002, we all came back together to do the *Merrily We Roll Along* reunion concert. That was one of the most special nights of all of our lives. We felt like the judge came back and said, "You know what? You were all right. You are talented and worthy, the show is profound, and we were wrong." It felt like the world came back and gave us another chance, and said, "Sorry, we got it wrong and you do win." That night was one of a kind. Sondheim and Prince were both there and they came up on stage and embraced. It was just phenomenal.

Merrily We Roll Along *changed my life.*

I listened to the cast recording for the first time when I was 12 years old, sitting on the flamingo-pink carpet of my humid house in Florida, dreaming of a place called New York City that I'd never seen. I fell in love with theatre for the same reasons as almost everyone else in this book did: seeing shows as a kid, being in shows as a kid... and Jewish theatre camp, of course! But cast recordings made me realize that shows weren't just The Pajama Game *and* Cats—*sometimes, they were* Henry Sweet Henry *and* Dude*. There were musicals beyond what the local community theatre did, and what had been made into movies. There were shows with riskier stories, and funkier styles, and off-beat attitudes—and I could learn about them from listening to cast recordings!*

Merrily We Roll Along *tells the story of Frank and Charley (would-be musical theatre writers) and Mary (a would-be author) starting out in New York City together. The show followed the three best friends from 1957 to 1976 as they grew up and went from dreaming on rooftops together, to collaborating on "a revue of their own" at The Upstairs Room at the Downtown Club, to opening a show on Broadway to, in Frank's case, abandoning the theatre for Hollywood.*

The thing about Merrily *was that the story was told backwards, so the audience got to see the characters' lives play out in reverse! They saw Frank and Charley dissolve their famous partnership on national television in "Franklin Shepard Inc." before they saw them banging on doors to try to get someone—anyone!—to listen to their first songs. They saw Mary, in love with Frank, heartbroken at his wedding, before they saw him meet her for the first time and say, "I just met the girl I oughtta marry."*

Told chronologically, Merrily We Roll Along *would be a musical about broken dreams and relationships gone bad—but told backwards, it was about the possibility that you could stay true to your ideals and your loved ones and yourself. By the end of the show, you were watching young people sing about the future and thinking: The story could turn out differently! It's up to me!*

As a young person, no story had ever reached me like that before. No show had chronicled the complicated trials of real life that powerfully. Merrily We Roll Along *shaped my entire sensibility of what musical theatre could be.*

And it broke my heart when I learned that the show, starring a group of real-life young people just starting out, had closed after only 16 performances on Broadway.

1970/1981: The *Annie* Girls Put A Curse On The Alvin Theatre

Liz Callaway, Actor

The first Broadway show I saw was *Company* at the Alvin Theatre. I was maybe nine or ten, and my parents saw the show first, loved it and brought home the cast album. I memorized the cast album and they took my sister and me to see it. It raised the bar pretty high, and the fact that I made my Broadway debut at the Alvin Theatre in *Merrily We Roll Along*—a show by Stephen Sondheim, directed by Hal Prince, with a book by George Furth—was crazy. I mean it was so cool.

I remember the Alvin and just being very excited. I was first hired as a swing, and then put in the chorus. *Annie* was before us, and some people think that the *Annie* girls put a curse on the Alvin Theatre! After them, there was just this incredible track record of shows that closed quickly.

In the chorus dressing room, the *Annie* girls had left something in one of the bathroom stalls. There were mean things that they wrote on the walls! They were unhappy they had to move from the Alvin. They're probably all high-powered businesswomen now.

I did some understudy rehearsals on stage. Thank God I never went on as Mary, but during rehearsals, I would sit in the front row of the house and sing for Annie Morrison sometimes. She got sick, so she had to save her voice. I remember running through "Opening Doors"... but we didn't do a whole lot of it, because we spent all our time doing changes. So there really wasn't much in terms of understudy rehearsals. We were there a lot. It was such a great experience.

Before that, we had our "*Merrily* waiting parties." We would get together ahead of time, and I remember going to a party at Lonny's house. Steve was there and he played us one of the songs. That was right out of a Hollywood movie musical. And we were all very close before we started rehearsals. I loved working with choreographer Ron Field, who was eventually replaced. We had dance classes, we got to do this great—he taught us "One" from *A Chorus Line*, and just great choreography that many of us had no business doing, but we kind of rose to the occasion. I loved the stagehands. It was a very, very close group. And it is nice that we still stay in touch. A lot of us do.

I do remember one of the final previews, feeling like we had solved it. Steve came back in tears, and we all felt we had solved it. We knew there were a lot of problems with the show, but we had worked so hard, and we finally felt like: *we did it! We fixed it!* You get to that point with every show. Even if initially you go: *oh this isn't very good*, or: *this isn't going to work*, at some point you believe in it.

And in *Merrily*, I remember that moment, after one of the final previews. We just felt great. Then the reviews came out and it was like: *Oh. Yeah.*

But we had a good run, in terms of two months of previews. And I always say it was the ideal first Broadway experience. Because if you start with a big hit, you have nowhere to go but down. And in this, I was working with the absolute greatest people on something that wasn't successful. So it was fascinating.

It just kind of made you go: *okay, this is the business*. And I never was that wide-eyed anyway, when I started, for some reason. I wasn't as innocent, maybe, as some people in the cast. I was innocent, but I wasn't: *golly gee, this is great! It's gonna be a hit!* I was able to be practical. I could see that it needed work. But still, it's a great show. I thought it was a great show.

Annie had played at the Alvin for more than four years, when it was booted to make room for Merrily We Roll Along. *The orphans packed their bags and moved across the street to the ANTA, where they were still playing for the first three weeks of* Merrily *previews.*

The next five shows at the Alvin after Annie *played a total of 27 performances. They were* Merrily We Roll Along *(16 performances),* The Little Prince and the Aviator *(closed in previews),* Little Johnny Jones *(one),* Do Black Patent Leather Shoes Really Reflect Up? *(five), and* Seven Brides for Seven Brothers *(five). At the time the fifth show closed,* Annie *was still packing them in at the larger Uris (Gershwin) Theatre.*

*There's actually an audio recording of the "*Merrily *Waiting Party" that Liz refers to. It was Lonny Price's 22nd birthday party, and Stephen Sondheim played several of the songs from the show for the cast for the first time. On the recording, he sits down at the piano and dedicates "Good Thing Going" to Lonny for his birthday. At the end, there is cheering and someone yells, "Encore! Play it again!" In response, you hear Lonny's distinctive voice yell, "This is just like what happens in the show!"*

1981: Opening Doors

Joanna Merlin, Casting Director

In 1981, we worked at the Alvin for *Merrily We Roll Along*. During auditions, we were looking at mostly non-professionals. We were looking at high school students. At some of the open calls, we had kids come from all over the country. I remember one open call when they were sleeping in the hallways. One actress came into the theater to audition and started singing and she threw up.

It was this amazing process. Because just like on *Pacific Overtures*, these were people auditioning for *Merrily* who had this great desire to be in the theatre, but who hadn't had that opportunity yet. It was very exciting doing a show with so many young people. It was unfortunate that it didn't work out, but it was exciting because we were discovering wonderful talent. All of those kids. Kids! And Lonny, who had been in the office, helping me with casting and getting coffee during *Pacific Overtures*!

1981: It Totally Prepared Me For The Rest of My Career

Tonya Pinkins, Actor

The first Broadway show that I ever saw was *Sweeney Todd*. It was extraordinary. It's still one of my favorite shows. That chorus, the music, the orchestra, and the story... that's my kind of story, a thriller. And that big, beautiful sound. A real, full, complete orchestra which you don't get often anymore.

It was miraculous and a dream come true to have admired Hal and Steve and then to have my first time on Broadway be with them. I got *Merrily* while I was away at college at Carnegie Mellon. It was over the Christmas break that I auditioned.

On opening night of *Merrily*, George Furth gave us all a picture. I remember opening mine, reading what he'd written on it, and putting it away. Then all of a sudden, Maryrose Wood opened hers and just started cracking up. She read hers out loud. It said, "You are by far the best one in the show." Then, everybody brought their pictures up—and he had written the exact same thing on every one!

I was in the chorus essentially, but we got gifts! I remember getting a big bottle of champagne and incredible gifts that came to us from people I didn't know. They don't do that anymore. I haven't had that, even starring in a show.

There was just a feeling that I can't… it was a dream in many ways, even though everything that could possibly go wrong went wrong. I feel like, in that sense, it totally prepared me for the rest of my career. There was nothing that could happen ever again in a show that… it was like, "Yeah, and what else?" Been there, done that.

1981: I Want To Be That Guy

David Loud, Musical Director and Supervisor/Conductor/Actor

I was a student at Yale when I got *Merrily*. I moved to New York and took off from school for what I thought was going to be two years, to go do the follow-up musical to *Sweeney Todd*. It turned out that I only had to take one semester off because we closed in two weeks. I moved back and finished school, and then moved here for good on New Year's Day in 1984. It just worked out that way.

They were interested in me playing a pianist in the show, who could also sing. Then, I ended up covering Lonny Price as Charley Kringas. At one point during previews, Lonny got very sick and he went on steroids to get through the last few previews. Hal Prince and Ruthie Mitchell took me down into the lower lobby of the Alvin, and they had me sing "Franklin Shepard Inc." I was fully prepared, and sang the song, and when I was done, Hal looked at me and said, "That was swell."

And then he left. And I never went on. But I did rehearse! I rehearsed with Liz Callaway who was the Mary cover, and with David Cady, who was covering Frank, but the run was so quick that of course, not a lot of time was spent preparing understudies.

Paul Gemignani was our musical director on *Merrily*. He was the reason that I changed my life. I went from being an actor to being a musician and a music director. He was so inspiring that I just thought: *As fun as it is to be up here on stage, I want to be down there. I want to be that guy.*

Whenever I conduct a Broadway show, I always love to have the assistant conductor take over for a night so I can stand by the stage manager and watch from the wings. That's the most truly amazing place to watch a show from, to get to watch the rituals of actors before they go on stage, and then what happens when they are in the show. I remember standing next to Beverley, our *Merrily* stage manager, later, when we did *Curtains* together, watching each of the actors touch her before going on. There's this little line in the air between off stage and on stage where the magic happens. It's an incredible thing to watch.

During "Good Thing Going", we were all on stage, while Jim Walton sat at the piano and Lonny sang this song. My particular position was that I was facing straight out into the house. It was a magical moment in the show. It was such a beautiful pop song that Stephen had written, unlike anything he'd ever written before. It was just a gorgeous, restful, artistic moment in the middle of a very chaotic second act. And I would notice each night that for some reason, the exit signs were flashing during that song. I didn't want to focus on that, but night after night, I would see them flashing and not know why. And then I finally figured out that it was because heads were going past the exit lights as people exited the theater. People walking out were creating that effect!

People would also come down to the pit and yell at Paul Gemignani, because he was the one person they could access. "This is terrible, what are they doing?" they'd say. It was so sad.

1981: They Tried To Keep Us Hopeful

Jason Alexander, Actor

I was submitted for *Merrily*, and then I went into an audition. I did a reading for Joanna Merlin and Hal and Steve and Paul Gemignani and Ron Field and George Furth. *Everyone* was in the room. I remember vividly that Joanna took the time to so graciously introduce me to everyone at the table. I was so blind with fear, and that was so kind.

After it was over, I ran out of the audition and straight to a water fountain, because I was so cotton mouthed! Paul Gemignani came out in the hall and happened to pass me and said, "That was terrific, kid!" I had no idea who he was, even though I'd met him a second before, because I was so terrified that I couldn't see straight. Other than that, there was nothing remarkable about my audition process. Nothing other than that it was the most intimidating audition room I have ever—and probably will ever—step foot into!

I was going to Boston University, and I left to do *Merrily*. I remember the first time we walked into the Alvin, because even though I had been on the audience side of so many Broadway houses, I had never stepped on the stage of one. It felt similar to how it did when I walked on the great stage at the Huntington, where we performed our B.U. shows. So I thought: *Okay. It's pretty much the same as any theater, the difference is just that the stakes are higher.* A bunch of the *Merrily* gang went back a couple weeks ago, and I thought the same thing: *From this view, they all look somewhat alike.*

Once we got into the theater, my part didn't change much. Joe was probably the least problematic character, and he was the oldest—other than Geoffrey Horne as older Frank—so the audience could spot me. The big change I do remember is when Ron Field was fired and Larry Fuller came in as choreographer. We started having more dance rehearsals, and some of them were in the lower lobby of the Alvin, where the restrooms are. Some of them were on the stage. But it was hard to get the stage, because poor Lonny and Ann and Jim were learning half a new show every day on the stage.

But there were many times we rehearsed the new dances in the lobby. I remember thinking: *We're dancing on carpeting. I don't think this is gonna work.* We were all petrified, because except for a couple of us, none of us were primarily dancers. And we were dancing one version of the show at night and learning a new one by day, and they were in no way, shape or form similar, and I think we were all just terrified that any day, they were going to say, "It goes in tonight!" and we were going to screw it up. We all lived in fear of that.

1970/1981: It Started Out Like A Song

Lonny Price, Actor/Director/Writer

I saw *Company* on my 11th birthday and I remember Elaine Stritch scared the shit out of me! I thought she was terrifying. I went and got autographs at the stage door after the show, and she came out with her little dog.

And of course, that was me standing outside the Alvin Theatre, where I would do *Merrily* 11 years later. It's weird to think about because *Company* feels like my early childhood and *Merrily* feels like the beginning of my adulthood.

I remember very well the first time I ever walked onto the Alvin stage. Frank Sinatra had recorded "Good Thing Going," and *Merrily We Roll Along* was going to do a radio commercial where I had a little voiceover as Charlie, saying, "That's Frank Sinatra singing *my* song in *Merrily We Roll Along*!" We recorded this when the show was in the rehearsal room, before we had moved into the theater yet. Hal was with me at the recording studio, and then after we recorded it, he said, "Come on, kid. We're going to lunch."

He took me to lunch at Un Deux Trois, and he said, "I want you to see something." We walked over to the theater, and they were still putting pieces of the show in. He said, "This is your theater now."

I remember walking on the stage, and just being overwhelmed by feelings of excitement. That whole experience I was just pinching myself all the time, and thinking: *really, this must be a dream because I couldn't possibly have gotten this lucky in my life. Nobody gets this lucky.*

Ann Morrison and I had dressing rooms that were back-to-back, so we opened the door and made it a suite. We ran back and forth from one to the other. The theater was beautiful. On the closing night, the stagehands made a Sputnik for us house left, where the lights were in the corner. They made a balloon thing to say goodbye to us, which was very, very, very touching.

There was a part of the show where Terry Finn, as Gussie, had to jump into this fake pool covered by blue construction paper. She was nervous about it, and Beverley Randolph, our stage manager, said, "There's no problem. I'll show you." And crash! She went into the fake pool, the construction paper ripped as it should have, but she hit her head and there was blood all over the place. She had to get taken to the hospital, and came back with a tourniquet around her head. And the pool went. Also the pool got a laugh that they didn't like.

All through rehearsal, it was five weeks of "Lonny sings a song here" during one specific part of the show. And we'd move on with rehearsal. I didn't know anything about the song I was supposedly getting, but Daisy whispered to me that she had heard it around her house, and that it was "a tour de force." I didn't know what that meant, but it sounded very good.

I was very excited, and then Sondheim actually called me on the phone and said, "Come over. I want to play you something." I went over to his house, and he played it. It scared me. We were so close to previews, it was so many words, and it was so complicated! But I was okay. I just became fearless, and the part was so right for me that whatever they gave me somehow ended up falling out of my mouth easily. It was like the greatest tailor in the world making you a suit. I had three good notes, and he just kept putting them in the song. It felt like he went, "What does he do well? Let's make that a song!" I was really flattered and lucky.

I remember him coaching me on the song in the Alvin's lower lobby, and I pretty much did the song just that way. I hear him in my head doing it. He was very specific and he grounded you with it. He was just brilliant. Like Shakespeare, if you just kind of do it, it takes care of itself. You just have to trust what he wrote, and you'll be fine.

I think a lot of people rooted against Hal and Steve. They had become so successful by doing art and not commerce. They were doing really interesting, brilliant stuff and it was succeeding and making money. Because of that, there was a lot of bitterness and jealousy toward them. There were some people who weren't like that though. Michael Bennett was there closing night, and he said, "This is a crime. There's so much here." He was very supportive.

Several years ago, at the Laurie Beechman Theatre, where my friends and I were always doing "revues of our own," I saw Lonny Price from afar. Lonny Price! I was nervous, but I knew this could be my one chance. I approached him.

"Excuse me, I just wanted to say hello. My name is Jennifer, and Merrily We Roll Along *is my favorite musical of all time, and I love your work so much, and..."*

As I gushed, Lonny smiled knowingly at me and he said, "We'll have to work together sometime!"

186

I floated on air all the way home, and a few weeks later, we were having coffee. Lonny was working on a documentary about the original company of Merrily, *and to my delight, he asked me to help him with a couple of tasks for it.*

That was the beginning. I met original cast member Mana Allen, and she became my mentor. I met original cast member, Terry Finn, and her husband, David Snyder, and we became virtual pen pals. I met the original Franklin Shepard, Jim Walton, and he re-created his Merrily *performance in a concert I produced. I even got to be a production assistant when Lonny directed Stephen Sondheim's 80th Birthday Concert at Avery Fisher Hall.*

When you start to hear the voices that you grew up obsessed with on cast recordings, on your voicemail… when you start to talk about life with the people who created the piece of art that changed yours … there's no word to describe that.

1981: People Are Ready For You To Take A Fall

Harold Prince, Producer/Director

It's very hard to have a favorite memory of *Merrily We Roll Along*. The rehearsal period was the most fun I ever had in my life, putting on a Broadway show with those kids—one of whom was my daughter, Daisy. Steve and I were so celebrated that there was a picture of us in Time Magazine, saying: *What Will They Come Up With Next?* We were riding for a fall.

Instead of going on the road, we opened cold in New York. Everybody treated our very first public performance ever, our first preview, as if it were a finished show. The newspapers the next day were filled with columns saying what a bummer the show was. Then, everybody had to play the show at night, knowing that the papers were reporting every day that it was a failure.

We continued to work on it. Steve and I felt, and still feel, like if we had come into New York with the show we ended up with at the end of previews, on opening night, the critics would have had a different response. They would have gotten what was good about the show. But *Merrily* was complex; it could never be perfect.

They've done a lot of revivals. I've never seen any of them. But the show will never be totally pulled off. We did a good job of being professional and making the show what we wanted. If they had left us alone and let us work during previews, I think it would have been flawed, but also successful. But some people were really against that. When you get so much success over a span of ten years, people are ready for you to take a fall.

I think I also failed the show terribly, visually speaking. I never knew how it should look. At the time, I had a meeting in the office with my staff. I said to them, "The only way I can see this show is on an empty stage, with a lot of costumes on racks, and a bunch of kids putting it all together. But it costs $15 to see a Broadway show! And I'm not sure the audience will stand for that."

My staff told me, "Do what you think is right." They said the right thing. And I was a coward, and I didn't do it. It's one of the rare occasions of my professional career where I was a coward, and I blame it all on me.

The kids were terrific. Lonny had been my office boy, and he was perfect for his role. Daisy was just wonderful. And I still think it was an interesting concept: having kids telling the story. But it's all probably too complicated. The idea of going back in time is probably too complicated for an audience to grasp. It wasn't successful in its original form as a play by George S. Kaufman and Moss Hart—and then I made the whole thing even more complicated by having the roles played by kids! I blame it all on me.

But that was my idea. I thought: *let's tell people about what happens over the course of a lifetime, to kids. To young, promising, ambitious, idealistic people.* And that was the way to show it. It is, oddly, the adverse of *Follies*.

1970/1981: The Music Is The Reason

James Maloney, Stagehand

My dad was a stagehand, and I would sometimes get to go to work with him when I was a young boy. The show I enjoyed most when I was a kid was *Company* at the Alvin Theatre. I was ten or 11 years old, and I would sit up in the front light booth some nights, and lend a hand around the theater.

The reason I loved *Company* was because of the music. The music was so great. A decade later, at the same theater, I was fortunate enough to do *Merrily We Roll Along* with Mr. Sondheim—and wow! That music is still in my head. The show only lasted a couple of performances, but it's one of the best scores ever.

Merrily We Roll Along was directed by Hal Prince, and it was amazing to work with the actors in that show every night. I was a young kid too, and I had the amazing opportunity to run the lighting consoles. The music struck me most of all—and what strikes me most of all on most shows these days is the set.

David Hersey was the lighting designer of *Merrily*, and it was one of the hardest shows I've ever had to do. It had all of these lighting specials and spots that we put on the balcony rail, specifically to light the actors' faces during the graduation scene. Those things were all very difficult back in the day: little switches and carousels. It was a hard show, but it was fun and I really enjoyed it.

It was one of the first times I did a show without my dad. He was supposed to do *Merrily*, but he was working on *The First* at the Martin Beck before that, and he fell off the stage and broke his ankle. That was a little intimidating to me, but there was a great crew of guys at the Alvin and we got through it.

I really thought the show was going to run forever, and it closed so quickly. The music was in your head all of the time.

1981: We Felt Like We Were In A Washing Machine

Mana Allen, Actor

I had been to shows at the Alvin before *Merrily* and actually my dad, mom and grandfather had worked there. I remember the day we moved into the theater, we went right up to our dressing room. I was in the girls ensemble room with Maryrose Wood, Abby Pogrebin, Liz Callaway, Tonya Pinkins… *Merrily* had moved *Annie* out of the Alvin theater, and when we went into our bathroom, the toilet seat was up, and in lipstick, there was a note that said, "The Orphans Welcome You!" with an arrow, pointing into the toilet! It was not a good sign. Our dressing room window was cracked, so I got sick because I had the table by the window.

I remember that *Oh, Brother!* was playing across the street, and both of our shows were struggling. I remember this hotel bar on 8th Avenue right near us that would let us kids in. I was over 18, but not everyone in the cast was, and most of us didn't drink but we just went over there for French fries. We were in 10-out-of-12s[29] for a

---

[29] 10-out-of-12s: rehearsals where actors are allowed to work for ten hours during a 12-hour period

very, very, very long time and we were exhausted. So we never got to have that long-run party kind of atmosphere.

I had my own dresser because I had 16 changes; my dresser had previously been Betty Bacall's dresser for *Woman of the Year*!

On our second day in the theater, a guy from the fly rail called down to me, "Hey, are you John Allen's daughter? I looked up, and couldn't really see who I was talking to, but I said, "Yes, I am." He said, "You forget the assholes in this business and remember the good guys. Your father is one of the best." And then we had to rehearse, and I never found out who that guy was.

My parents were really proud of me at the show, but I think their proudest moment was when George Abbott came to see one of our rehearsals in the studio and then wrote my dad a letter that said, "I just saw Marianna in the show and she was very good. I think she has 'it.'"

We never had any downtime. We really didn't. It felt like we were in a washing machine, and we were all getting to the theater really early in the morning and leaving late at night. All my memories from that time feel like they were put through a spin cycle too. We were handed lyrics and told they were going in that night. "Learn these on your dinner break." There were new lines written on napkins on stage during the "Like It Was" cafe scene. Some of us had lyrics written on our hands. Right after Larry Fuller came in, one of his first tasks was to cut and restage the transition after "Franklin Shepard, Inc.". The creative team made an internal cut and the kids who were in it had to learn the new music and staging that was going in that night. We were all putting good energy towards this big change going in. As fate would have it, that night, right before this new transition, a bank of lights hit the lockers on the set upstage and there was a crash just as the nervous kids were running on to do the new stuff! Then when that new moment came in the music, all hell broke out in the pit! Apparently only half of the orchestra parts had gotten the cut so Paul Gemignani started yelling bar numbers to them! Everything soon got back on track. Live theatre, there's nothing like it.

I was a huge fan of the movie *Harold and Maude*, and Ruth Gordon, who played Maude, came to our show all the time. She became a *Merrily* groupie. She would sit in the front row and at curtain call, she'd stand up to clap, but it didn't really look like she was standing because she was so little! I was just thrilled to meet her. She and her husband, Garson Kanin even came to the recording session to cheer us on.

A lot of the celebrities who came were brought backstage to say hello before the show. It was lousy standing at places, at the top of the bleachers, for the original opening scene of *Merrily*, because I never got to shake anyone's hand! Everyone would be on the deck meeting Anthony Perkins, and I'd be at the top of the bleachers, waving, "Hi!"

One night, Hal came backstage and said, "I just want to let you know that Ginger Rogers is sitting in the orchestra tonight—larger than life." He instructed, "Whatever you do, don't all look at her!" So, when that opening graduation scene happened, and we were all supposed to be pretending to look for our parents in the crowd, we were really good about not looking at her. But at the same time, we were able to kind of acknowledge that she was there out of the corners of our eyes. Ginger Rogers had big hair that made her look like an ice cream cone. We got on with the show, but it turned out that someone in Ginger Rogers' row was late. She had to stand up and let the late person pass her. So then, we couldn't help but look, and the entire audience then saw that it was Ginger Rogers, and we all were in that moment together. You could see Hal shaking his head, in his usual seat in the box near stage left. The one thing he didn't want to happen just happened, because of the late woman in Ginger Rogers' row, and that was funny.

My favorite part of the show to perform was when I got to be the "Girl Auditioning" in "Opening Doors", and I would give a terrible off-key audition... originally they wrote it for a shrill soprano but when I got sick, I lost my top register and I had to improvise. Luckily they liked it. I also had another bit that was fun—until it started getting the wrong laugh, and got cut during previews. After "It's A Hit!", David Cady and I would be leaving the theater after Frank and Charley's show and he would say something to me, and then my line was, "You *liked* it?" And then I paused and screamed with laughter. You can hear it on the recording someone made of the second preview performance. It's there.

Our opening night party was at the Waldorf-Astoria and I remember how much everyone spent on their opening night outfits! I wore this lovely Laura Ashley outfit, with gold pantaloons and this little white lace collar. I looked very 1981!

I remember when I first heard about the costume plans, I wondered how anybody was ever going to be able to clean them. They were hand-painted. We all looked so great. Our dress parade day in the studio at 890 Broadway was thrilling, because we were these kids who were getting to wear these dozens of wigs and fancy Broadway costumes. We were all thinking: *Hal will love these! They're great!* Our dress parade took a long time, just going in and out of the room with people saying, "This is this costume for this scene," and I remember in the studio at one point and Hal said, "I've lost my kids." He was unhappy. We all suddenly looked too grown-up.

From that point forward, the costumes changed to t-shirts and jeans and leotards with the letters on them to say who we were. I would always go home and tell my father what was happening, and I remember his reaction. "Tell me that again. *What* are you wearing?" "A t-shirt with the name of my character on it, and painter's pants." He didn't say anything, but I knew he was concerned.

I ended up in a shirt that said "His Secretary," but before that, I had this green sweatshirt that said "Fashion Plate". When it was cut, I took it home. In the early 1980s, I tore it up and put safety pins in it and wore it to dance class for years and years after. Now, I have no idea what happened to it. When any of *those* costumes were cut, they said, "Take them home, you can have them." They were dispensable.

At one point, there was this whole 1960s scene where our costumes were supposed to be for a sophisticated cocktail party during the Vietnam war. It was a really dark scene, I looked like Jackie Onassis. I had a Paul Huntley wig that made me look just like her, and a cocktail dress, and these kitten heels, and a stole that was of camouflage material, but instead of a fox head and tails, like those fancy stoles of the day, it was a dead body...it looked like a puppet, with its head, hands and feet hanging down! The boys' tuxedos were made of camouflage material, and instead of handkerchiefs, they had a little body jumping out of their pocket.

Part of our opening night gift from Hal and Steve was a piece of our costume that had been cut from the show. They gave me that dead body stole! When the *Merrily* cast members went to the Encores! production together, I almost wore it. Then I realized: it really looks like a dead body! I can't. I almost brought it today, and then I thought: *You can't bring this thing out at the Edison! Matzoh ball soup will end up on it!*

———————

Mana is part of a Broadway family legacy, as her father, John Allen, mother, Mary Stanton, and grandfather, John Dunsmure, were all on Broadway as well. There are a remarkable number of legacies on Broadway—not just families of actors, but families of stagehands, box office treasurers, and ushers as well. Many of the theatre trades are truly passed on from generation to generation.

Mana's grandfather was in Treasure Girl, *the Gershwin musical that was the second show to ever play the Alvin, in 1928. With its famous creators at the helm, everyone thought* Treasure Girl *would be a huge hit—but it flopped, closing after only 68 performances. Sound familiar?*

———————

1981: Give Me More Pages! I Can Do This!

Terry Finn, Actor

I got a job in *Merrily We Roll Along* in January, playing Gussie, and then rehearsals didn't start until September. In the meantime, because I was in the new Sondheim-Prince musical, I could finally get an agent. Then, I was finally able to get seen for things. I met with Austin Pendleton about doing *The Little Foxes* with Elizabeth Taylor at the Beck. Then, I made the mistake of actually letting him know I was doing the new Sondheim-Prince show in the fall, and I saw his face fall—and I didn't get it. That show only ended up running from April to September, so I actually could've done both! Who knows the life I might've lived if I had just kept my mouth shut that day? But I didn't. And that's the end of that.

I shared a dressing room with Sally Klein, who played Beth, and for some reason, we took to singing that old Cole Porter song, "Don't Fence Me In". We'd goof around. But there was nowhere that was more fun in the building than where Mana Allen was, the girls' dormitory on the other side of the theater. That always seemed like the best place to hang out.

I was one of the older ones, so I could drink. And drink I did. I always had this notion that I wanted to be a Barrymore or something, when I was younger. That was my thing. Abby Pogrebin told me yesterday, "I thought you were so sexy!" Oh God. I can't imagine any of those 16-year-old girls having looked at me and thought that. But we were all impressionable.

We shared something special, and you can really tell because of the way that we respond to each other when we're back together now. We were all really, really nice to each other for the whole process. We really loved each other.

I remember one night on the bleachers, Jim Walton and I spotted a kid in the audience in the most ridiculous outfit of all time. We were looking at him and trying not to laugh, and we saw Steve, in the audience, catch us! But my worst mishap in the show was one night when I was so taken with Lonny doing "Franklin Shepard Inc." that I kept clapping and clapping, completely forgetting that I had the next line.

I tended to look out and check out the house. All these New York people came! As a kid growing up on Long Island, I used to watch so many old game shows, and people like Phyllis Newman and Kitty Carlisle and Debbie Reynolds all came to our show! They were sophisticated and smart and so New York, and I'd get to sit next to them backstage.

Act two was great, because it was one laugh after another! It was really great to have a part in that, because everyone was miserable by that point. I was happy to go out and cheer everybody up!

I loved learning new stuff during previews. I was like, "Give me more pages! More stuff!" I was a quick study, and I just couldn't get enough of it. Every time they'd hand me a new scene, I would think, "Yeah! Yeah! I can do this!" That was fun. Steve walking me through my song, "Darling", for the first time was one of the best things that had ever happened to me in my life. We ran through that song on stage, and I remember Mana was there taking notes, because she was my understudy. He gave the best "how to deliver a song" lesson that I've ever had in my life. It was so specific. Steve really is good at that because he's such a teacher. He knew what he wanted and was able to express that so well, and I was able to deliver it.

But I did know that it wasn't working, and we were losing the audience. I don't know why, but I felt like it wasn't my fault. I was doing what I could with the song, and it just wasn't happening because the audience wasn't into it. When they cut it, it was almost a relief because then I didn't have to go out there and do something confusing. I was much more comfortable going out there and delivering my snarky Gussie comments and getting big laughs.

191

I was okay when our costumes were cut, because I figured the team knew what they were doing, and our new costumes were so comfortable! It was like doing a Broadway show in sweatpants. I kept my beautiful pink "Bel Air" Jacket, but it was destroyed by a flood at my parents' house years later.

I remember opening night because it wasn't as festive as I'd imagined. My acting teacher from college came backstage and up to my dressing room and stood there for a long time, telling me how much he hated the show. "How could *this* be Hal Prince and Stephen Sondheim? What an abomination." And it was my opening night, and I was late for the party, and I listened to my old teacher carry on about what a piece of shit he just saw.

It wasn't as if I didn't know people thought that, because the show had been in so much trouble. But the whole thing really did make me late to the party, so when I walked through the door last, everybody started applauding, but I didn't understand and I looked behind me to see who was coming in.

———————————

The song "It's A Hit!" actually takes place at the Alvin Theatre, in the story within Merrily. *Frank and Charley's first Broadway show, called* Musical Husbands, *opens at the Alvin. When Charley's wife, Evelyn, goes into labor during the performance, the gang gets her into a cab and Mary says "I'd hate it if she'd have the baby right here and they'd feel obligated to call it Alvin."*

———————————

1981: It Felt Like Summer Stock

Larry Fuller, Choreographer/Actor

I did three shows with Hal Prince prior to *Merrily*, where he brought me in as the replacement choreographer. I had seen their invited dress rehearsal at the Alvin, so I knew that they were in trouble.

About a week into previews, I got a call from Hal's office. It was his general manager, Howard Haines, asking, "What are you doing now, Larry?" I hadn't done *Merrily* in the first place, because at the time, I thought I would be directing and choreographing my own show, but then the financing fell through. I was unemployed. I told Howard I was free.

The next day, Hal called and said, "Would you be interested in coming in to help us out on *Merrily We Roll Along*?" I said yes. He said, "Well, come see the show tonight, and we'll talk about it after, if you think you can do anything." That night, we had a drink after the show, and talked. I said, "I can't do what I think needs to be done in the amount of previews that you have left." So he said, "We'll extend them an extra ten days or so." And I replied, "Okay, let's go!"

It almost felt like summer stock. I did a number a day. I re-did everything, except for the *Frankly Frank* Greenwich Village revue section, because that was great. I didn't touch it. I re-did everything else. Those kids were young and they were so full of energy. By that point, they were like deer in headlights. They all had thought that this was going to be such a big success, and then there turned out to be so much turmoil going on, that they were all a little bit in shock.

I replaced Ron Field, who I knew pretty well, and who I have great respect for, as a talent. What happened is that he had asked people who weren't really dance-trained to do technically difficult dance, and they didn't look good doing it. So what I did was to take all of that out, and do more behavioral choreography. There were only about five cast members who were actually dance-trained and I would count on them whenever I needed someone to step out and actually dance. That concept-shift changed every big number in the show. Over the course of about a week and a half of previews.

192

1981: A New Franklin Shepard

Jim Walton, Actor

I wasn't playing the role of Frank Shepard at the beginning of previews for *Merrily*. I played Jerome. Then, during the third week of previews, I graduated into the part. It all happened so crazily, that all I remember from my time as Jerome was that the show was long and audiences didn't get it. I can't even remember where my dressing room was when I played "his lawyer, Jerome." I always try, and I can't remember.

I do remember the very first time that the overture happened. The audience went crazy! The songs were immediately accessible, and they loved the brassy, Broadway sound of the score. And here we were, in the theater where Sondheim did *Company* and *Forum*? Talk about history, my God!

But after that, it was tough. A lot of audience members would leave during performances, and then other people would move down from the balcony, so by the middle of act two, there would be nobody in the balcony.

One of my favorite memories from *Merrily* happened near the end of previews. There was a revolve on the stage, and when the second act started, we would be turned around on the track, timed so that we could step off the platform just as the show began. Because of that set-up, we could peek through and see the audience. I remember one night, Lonny peeking through and going, "Oh my God! There are still people in the mezzanine right now!" We all said, "This is it! We're gonna run! People are finally staying." By the time the show opened, it had changed significantly, but it was still a tough sell.

I think I got my job on *Merrily* because of Ron Field. I made my Broadway debut in his show, *Perfectly Frank*, which played at the old Helen Hayes Theatre, one of the ones that was torn down shortly thereafter to make way for the Marriott Marquis hotel and theater.

I had been doing *Scrambled Feet*, a successful off-Broadway revue, at a place that was, at the time, Art D'Lugoff's Village Gate. It's now a CVS, so you can still get your drugs there. Because I had that gig, I got to audition for Ron Field for *Perfectly Frank*, and I just wanted to meet him! He had directed the first Broadway show I ever saw, *Applause*. I was so excited that I could go in and sing for him.

Well, this was all back in the day, when people had Quaaludes. Quaaludes was the party drug. It's a barbiturate. It just kind of mellowed you out. Well, I had gotten some for a friend, and I thought: *Well, this is perfect. I'll take them, to make sure I get enough mellowed-out sleep before my important audition.* That was my idea of a party drug! Something to make me sleep.

So, the night before my callback for *Perfectly Frank*, I took a Quaalude. I had no idea what it would do. I overslept my alarm, and I woke up 45 minutes before my audition. My voice was shot. I got out a different song, that had only an F top note instead of a G. I remember walking to the audition and my fingers were numb, still, from the drug. I thought: *Oh Walton, what have you done?! You're gonna meet Ron Field, and sing for him, and you're a drug addict!*

Well, they wanted someone who could play the piano *and* sing, so I came up with this kooky idea where I sang two songs that Barbra Streisand made famous. I said, "I wanted to sing two songs, but there's not enough time, so I'll do them as a medley." So I sat down, played an intro, and then sang the lyrics of "People" to the tune of "On a Clear Day"—talk about "drugged out"! And the whole number ended in the middle of a sentence!

I think that's what got me the job. We previewed and opened at the old Helen Hayes, ran for two weeks, and closed. The whole time, I was thinking: *It's my first Broadway show, and I have drugs in my system. And it's because I used them for an audition!* I'm so nerdy. And it backfired on me.

I never told Ron that story. Now, I would. I wish he were alive, so that I could tell him. We joked. He was a very, very talented and an understandably complicated person, but I think he liked me. He was the original choreographer of *Merrily*. He took me aside one day, and we went far house right, near the orchestra pit, way against the wall. It was a quiet talk, and he said, "I just want you to know, there are some changes that are probably about to happen. I was fired." I said, "Fired?!" And he said, "Well, Hal and I agree that it's best that I walk away." I said, "Oh no, that's terrible." And then I actually thought about it, and we hadn't talked about it at the audition, but I realized that Ron was really probably responsible for me getting the show, because he'd directed *Perfectly Frank*.

So, I felt bad for him. And then he said, "And Hal's going to talk to you today." I said, "Alright." I had no idea what it was about. I thought: *I stink as Jerome. They're gonna give the role of Jerome the lawyer to someone else, and I'm gonna clean the toilets.* And Ron said, "They wanna put somebody else on as Frank." I went, "What?!" I thought he was kidding. And then, sure enough, stage management came to me an hour later and said, "Jim, can you come talk to Hal? He's in the lower lobby."

We were in the lower lobby which is sort of underneath house right. I went and talked to Hal, and he told me that the producing team had requested to see someone else on as Frank Shepard. I think he was a bit torn himself, because he liked James Weissenbach as Frank, but clearly there were others involved in the decision too, and he lost out.

This was a Monday, and then that Friday night, I went on! Hal said, "We'll give you two shows to do it. You can have Friday and Saturday night. In case you're nervous the first night, just know that you've got two chances at it, and we'll judge the situation. And if you don't get it, you'll keep the part you have, Jerome, and we'll keep James where he is too, and no harm done."

So, I learned the part, and four days later, I was Frank for the very first time. I remember that after bows that night, the curtain came in, and on stage left, Hal was right there. He shook my hand, and he said, "It's yours."

I think we all struggled with feelings of responsibility after the show was unsuccessful. It's almost like when a friend dies. *Merrily* was like your friend had died, and you should have known, or you should have done something, or you should have done better. If only we had all been better, the show would have run. Do you know what I mean? We were all so invested and youthful. We blamed ourselves. When you're older, you learn to separate all that. You learn to not beat yourself up, to just do your best.

I remember a night when Warren Beatty came to see the show. This was right after we had gotten bashed by the critics, and gotten our closing notice. I had just seen Warren Beatty in *Reds*, and he came backstage right before the show started. We were in the graduation scene, on the bleachers, and he stood down center, and said, "I just want you to know that I've come back to see this show for a second time, because it's fantastic. You are all fantastic artists."

I'm nothing but proud of *Merrily We Roll Along*. I loved that show. But back then, when you're young and you're broke and you have to find a job, and you've just spent three months in the castle... well, you really have to have a huge attitude adjustment after going through an experience like that.

I'm still friendly with people from *Merrily*. I don't get to see most of them as much as I used to, but when we all do get a chance to meet again, it's just like it was. Lonny Price is a very dear friend of mine, and I've worked with him a number of times since then, and we'll meet up just as friends. I can't say enough good things about him and his talent and his kindness.

We were all aware that with Hal and Steve, we were in the presence of greatness. I had just seen *Sweeney Todd* three times. We were all fans of *Company*, and not only were we working with the writers and director, we were in their old theater. It was unbelievable. We knew that. But we really didn't know that our show was only going to run for two weeks. How could we have known?

I'm so in awe of Sondheim. I've never really shaken that. I'm not sure I want to. I think it's good to be starstruck by certain people. I remember that back then, I worked with Sondheim in the lower lobby of the Alvin on "Our Time". He wanted to work with me so I'd know the intentions of all of the lyrics. He helped enormously.

Then, during previews, even after I came in as Frank, they were still trying to enrich the role. So, they said, "Jim, we're going to try you singing "Not A Day Goes By"." I learned it. Sondheim changed some of the lyrics, like "thinking and sweating and cursing." He said, "I think that a woman would sing these words, but a man would sing these." He seemed to be asking me to say, "Yes, I approve" or something! That's the way I felt, and I said, "Yes!" That was all probably in my head. He probably wasn't asking for any kind of approval, but I felt like: *Why are you even explaining yourself? You could tell me I had to sing "dog poop" in a lyric, and I would, because I believe you're right.*

One of my favorite memories of *Merrily* was that on opening night, the cast gave the creative team t-shirts with their names and jobs on them. I don't remember how we worded anybody else's, but I do remember that on Sondheim's, we printed "Best Male Vocalist."

1981: A Perfect Storm

Alex Rybeck, Musical Director

My involvement with *Merrily* was the result of a "perfect storm" of things. When I moved to New York, to make ends meet, I played lots of dance classes and auditions. One of my friends from Oberlin asked if I'd play her audition for a new show called *Merrily We Roll Along*. She got a callback. More surprisingly, so did I. "You at the piano, may we talk to you?" The casting director, Joanna Merlin, and the musical director, Paul Gemignani, asked if I'd coach someone they wanted to bring in. Of course, I said "Yes!" It turned out to be Abby Pogrebin, a classmate of Hal Prince's daughter, Daisy. About a week later, Abby gave her audition, which happily went well. Once again, they asked if I would work with someone else they wanted to see—Daisy! Can you imagine how surreal it was for both me and Daisy to audition for her father in his office? Daisy sang like a lark, and both she and Abby were cast.

At the same time, a friend told me about this apprenticeship program they were doing for *Merrily*. Hal was looking for three apprentices who would each keep a journal of the rehearsal process. There was money for this, from the National Endowment of the Arts. But first you had to apply by going up to Hal's office and filling out a form.

Although I had only been in New York a short time, I was already personally acquainted with Stephen Sondheim. It began as a correspondence when I was in high school, seeking college advice. By the time I was an Oberlin student in the late 70s, we'd met, and he'd heard my music. Shortly after moving to New York in 1980, I enrolled in a brand new Masters Program at NYU for Musical Theater Writing. And the faculty for the first year was like a list of people who had invented the art form: Arthur Laurents, Jule Styne, Stephen Schwartz, Leonard Bernstein, Betty Comden and Adolph Green—and—Prince and Sondheim! By the time *Merrily* auditions were taking place, the NYU program was underway, and I had already had classes with "Hal and Steve."

There must have come a day when the applications for the *Merrily* apprentices were sorted and discussed. I can picture the scene, with my application coming to the top of the pile, and in one voice, Hal, Steve and Paul saying: "I know him!" Of course, I wasn't there, so maybe it didn't play out exactly that way, but it makes me smile to think that a perfect storm of interrelated events led them to know me, and choose me.

Two other apprentices were also chosen: a young director from Atlanta, and a young wanna-be producer from Toronto. I was there as a young composer.

I was thrilled to be "on the inside" of this new Broadway show, created by my idols. It was heady stuff, attending auditions, pre-production meetings, and eventually, rehearsals.

I have vivid memories of rehearsing at 890 Broadway, but once we were at the Alvin, my involvement was more standing in the back, watching everything happening on stage. I didn't have a dressing room, I wasn't on stage, I wasn't in the orchestra. I was kind of a ghost.

It was pretty upsetting when the first preview was met with multiple walkouts and even boos. I had never heard boos in a theater before. My NYU class came to see one of those previews, and the next day I had to go to class and listen to everyone tear the show apart. Of course, I was aware that there were problems, and I could be analytical and objective about the show myself. But to sit there and listen to people you respect tear *Merrily* apart, when it was the show you were working on and in which you'd invested a lot of your heart, that was hard.

Prince and Sondheim really thought the show was going to be their *Hello, Dolly!*—a huge, commercial smash. That was their intention. I wrote in my diary that Hal said to the group, "Some people think that Steve and I do cold, intellectual shows. This is the show where we're going to show them that that's not who we are at all. This show is full of heart, warmth, humanity, humor and musical comedy."

The excitement at that first preview was palpable before the lights went down. You could cut it with a knife. People were primed to welcome what they thought would be the surefire hit of the season. The audience went nuts for the overture. But about ten minutes later, people just didn't know what was going on. They got angry and upset because they couldn't follow it.

I knew the show was problematic, but all through the rehearsal process, I was hopeful. I kept saying, "This is Hal Prince and Stephen Sondheim! One of these days, they are going to pull the rabbit out of the hat and we'll go, 'Oh! THERE'S the great show that was lurking inside!'" The first preview felt awful, because there was no apparent rabbit that came out of the hat. After many rewrites, some recasting, and a delayed opening night, it ran for two weeks and closed.

Earlier, during rehearsals, they tried "Not A Day Goes By" for the character of Beth in several different keys. Since I was the music apprentice, I had gotten to know Paul Gemignani and Jonathan Tunick. I was fascinated by the orchestration pow-wows. And when they needed "Not A Day Goes By" transposed, they trusted me to do it. So I sprawled on the floor of the lobby of the Alvin to write the song out in different keys. Sondheim, who hadn't been around all that much during the rehearsals, walked by at that moment, and slyly asked if I was rewriting his song!

Ron Field was the original choreographer of *Merrily*, and by another twist of fate, I now have his piano.

A few years after the show closed, I was playing an audition for a friend. We started chatting, and I found out she was the executor of Ron Field's estate. He had just passed away. She invited me to come down to his loft, where some of his things were being auctioned off. I said sure!

One of the reasons I said yes is that years earlier, I had observed a pre-production meeting for *Merrily*, where Hal said, "I want the rooftop scene to look like the view from Ron's apartment." Now I was finally going to get to see the view that inspired the "Our Time" scene with Frank and Charley and Mary on the roof!

We went up to Ron's loft, and to my surprise I discovered there were no outside windows! It was apparently a room in the middle of the building. How could this be? Meanwhile, I noticed a beautiful, shiny Yamaha piano,

196

that looked brand new. I mentioned that I could use a piano, because the one I had was falling apart. My friend told me I could make a bid on it, but I knew I couldn't offer what it was worth. I was a poor musician and it was worth tens of thousands of dollars. Still, at her urging, I put in a bid anyway, for some pitiful sum.

But where was Hal's window with the fabled rooftop view? The only area I hadn't checked out was a dim little kitchen area. I went into the kitchen, and, as in many old lofts, it contained a combination bathtub and shower. I parted the shower curtain. There, in the shower stall, was a small square window! Could it be? I stepped into the stall and peeked through the window. There was the rooftop, with the water tower!

Some months later, I got a phone call from Ron Field's lawyer. He said he had good news for me regarding a piano. I almost dropped the phone. He admitted that there were two higher bids than mine, but one was from a man Ron hadn't liked much, and the other was from a famous dance school. The lawyer said, "The piano is such a beautiful instrument, and I just couldn't picture it in the corner of a dance studio, being pounded on daily, with people throwing their dance bags on it. I thought it deserved a better fate. I think Ron would want you to have this." Wasn't that nice? And I've had it ever since.

I invested $300 in *Merrily* (it was the lowest amount one could invest in the show, and all I could afford as a poor grad student). When the show closed, all the investors received a poignant letter from Hal, acknowledging that this show he loved hadn't succeeded. All the investors lost their money. But I got a piano out of the deal, so I may be the only investor who came out ahead!

1981: Big Ideas

Michael John LaChiusa, Writer

The first Broadway show I saw was *Merrily We Roll Along*. I saw three previews of it and I was totally smitten.

I was familiar with Sondheim's work; I had started learning all of it very early on. I was amazed at the music in *Merrily*. Lonny Price and Daisy Prince were friends of mine, and they were in it. I loved the entire cast.

All around me, the audience was hating the show. The theater was filled with these haters, and I couldn't understand why they weren't liking this show that I thought was great!

It was being told backwards and the songs had connective tissue and these fascinating motifs. It was deep and dark and so filled with emotion. I knew these people. I knew these characters.

It was a story about the business I wanted so badly to be a part of—show business—and all its ugliness too. I understood that. But it was really something else that tugged at me about *Merrily* too. I went back for two more previews of it, and the audience was hating it even more; I couldn't understand it for the life of me!

I would get a cheap seat in the mezzanine, and then I'd always move down because people would leave their seats during the show. I loved watching how the show changed. I did that frequently then; I also watched how *Nine* changed throughout their previews, around the same time.

Those Broadway houses are there, and you want shows with big ideas to fill those houses. You don't only want big spectacles. That part of it is fine; that's always been Broadway, and I have no problem with the entertainment side of it. I love shows with dancing like crazy. But you want to feel like a show with a big idea could find a place.

After the last time I saw *Merrily*, I came to the conclusion: *I like that this is pissing people off. I wanna create shows that cause that. I really want to cause trouble.* Something about the sweat and the smell and the anger and the chaos of it all made me really taken with the theatre.

1981: Letting Go Of The Ghosts

Ann Morrison, Actor

Lonny and Jim and I all had dressing rooms on stage right. When you first went past the door men, you'd run up those stairs and see our three rooms. The Alvin was my second home. I have this one memory of the stairwell. One day, I had practically a nervous breakdown. It was about a week after the night that Ron Field had his own nervous breakdown in my dressing room, the night before he was fired/walked out. He told me everything was going to be fine, especially with me and my part. Then, I just couldn't take it. We had so many changes, and I was shaking in my boots. We never really got a chance to land on anything, we'd try something new each day. There was just this one day where I reached saturation, and didn't know what to do. Instead of going to my dressing room, I went down to the stairwell to sit. I was hiding, and Beverley Randolph, our stage manager, found me and said, "You've gotta get up there! You've gotta get on that stage. I know you're scared, but you can do this. If anybody can do this, you can."

I put my chin up, and went on stage. I remember the curtain rose, and I wiped tears from my eyes. And it was a disastrous evening for me. My typewriter table tipped over and fell apart at one point. I remember running off stage at the end of the show, and Sondheim standing in the wings, saying to me, "It was wonderful." I said, "No it wasn't," and got out that back door as fast as I could.

I got all this mail when we were doing *Merrily*. It was my first experience of people not being able to tell the difference between the character and the actor. I would get mail from religious fanatics who were trying to save my soul because they read in the paper that I played an alcoholic!

One day, I was getting out of my costume and makeup, and getting ready to go home, and I saw this young African American girl, standing at my dressing room door, looking at me. I said, "Oh hi! Did you see our show tonight?" She ignored my question, and said, "Are you a singer? Because God wanted me to talk to the singers. I have to find the singer." Now I was getting scared. She said that when she looked at people, she saw the face of the devil, and I told her that when I looked at people, I saw the face of God. She said, "I'm supposed to tell the singer that they do it through the singing. They have to pass it on through the singing." And I said, "I promise I'll do that for you, through the singing." I was just saying anything because I wanted her to be gone! I didn't want to meet her again in the hallway. After she left, I knocked on Lonny's door and Jim's door, and said, "Did you guys see that girl in the hallway?" They said, "What girl?" I ran downstairs and checked with Beverley and she hadn't seen anyone. I went down to our stage door and asked, "Did you send a little girl up?" They said no.

When we did *Merrily*, we were made to feel part of a family: the Broadway family. It was non-stop. In the beginning, I really cherished and loved it, because it was the idea that I was brought up on, that theatre is a family. Then, word-of-mouth turned ugly, and I realized that it was some of the same people in the theatre community that were badmouthing. That was devastating to me, that some people would not support their fellow brother or sister in the theatre.

At the same time, I remember making friends with lots of Broadway people. *The First* was down the street, and they knew that they weren't going to last either, so we bonded. The shows that knew they weren't going to be around became great buds. We used to see each other after work and drink and hug and cry and share stories about all of it, like, "This is a roller-coaster. I never thought this would happen like this."

198

We used to go to this bar called Charlie's. It's long-gone. During *Merrily*, I would go in there, and they all knew me and knew the show, so the minute I sat down, some waiter would come over with a bottle of vodka with a straw in it, because one of Mary's lines was that that was what she ordered. I got a lot of bottles of vodka with straws at Charlie's. I loved it.

When we walked in the Neil Simon together recently, I walked into my old dressing room and was shocked. The tables were all different. I had had drawers, but now there was just a tabletop. I had always secretly wanted to write on the bottom of the drawer, "Ann Morrison" with the date and show, but I never did. So I did it. I crawled under the table last month and wrote, "Ann Morrison, 1981, Merrily We Roll Along."

I'd always assumed that when I finally got in a Broadway show, it'd be much larger than it actually was. But it was just a theater. It just happened to be in New York, where they have great history. When you're walking on those stages, you're standing in the footprints of your ancestors, and you have to pay them homage.

The last thing that I did when we were through filming the *Merrily* documentary, and we were standing on the Alvin stage for one last time, was... well, I don't know if I'll ever perform in New York again, and I don't know if I'll ever be in the Neil Simon Theatre again.

Standing on that empty stage, I looked out at the house and said to Terry Finn, "Terry, I know you'll think this is silly, but humor me." And she laughed and said okay. I said, "I want us to call back all the actors that have worked in this theater all these years, all the ghosts of the past, and when we leave here, we're going to take them with us." We closed our eyes.

A few minutes later we walked out of the theater, holding hands. I hope that we did it.

———————

When New York City Center's Encores! series announced that they would be presenting Merrily We Roll Along, *I was ecstatic. A whole new group of people would get to experience my favorite musical!*

A plan was hatched for the entire original cast of the show from 1981 to reunite in 2012 at the Encores! production. And I was invited. Original cast member Forest Dino Ray invited me to be his plus-one because, "After all," he said, "you're really one of us!"

I've had the great privilege of becoming friends with so many of the "Merrily gang." Not only did the show they made in 1981 change my life when I was a kid, they've continued to change my life as an adult with their kindness and their generosity and their advice and their stories.

And perhaps most inspiring of all... all of these years later, so many of them remain the best of friends.

———————

1981: A Galactic Disturbance

Anthony Rapp, Actor

I wasn't originally cast as the Little Prince in *The Little Prince and the Aviator*. I was ten years old, and they were a little afraid that I was too young to carry the show. I was the understudy, but during rehearsals, they promoted me. Ellen Greene played the Little Rose, and this was years before the *Little Shop of Horrors* movie.

We had 16 previews, and then we closed. We never opened! The night before what was supposed to be opening night, we got our closing notice. That was it. After we left the theater that night, I was walking down the street with my mom and I said, "I want to go get drunk." Now, this was Times Square in 1981, but I was still ten.

One song that my character sang was called "Playground of the Planets". I would travel around as the Little Prince, looking at different people on different planets. I got to fly around, with two wires coming off my sides. While I was flying, the planets would come on, on tracks. One night, instead of a planet trundling on, I heard a blood-curdling scream off stage. Apparently, the track had run over someone's foot.

There I was, ten years old, suspended in the air, and I said, "Ladies and gentlemen, it would appear that there's been a galactic disturbance!"

———————

*Ellen Greene is the only actress to close two Broadway musicals during previews (*Little Prince, Rachael Lily Rosenbloom*), and Adela Holzer is the only producer to do the same (*Truckload, Senator Joe*).*

———————

1982: That's Show Business!

Don Stitt, Actor

A few days before rehearsals for *Do Black Patent Leather Shoes Really Reflect Up?* started, I went to the Alvin. I fast-talked my way past Blue, the stage door man, and I went into the theater by myself. I walked on the stage, and it was just me and the ghost light and those 1500 seats. I remember tap dancing on that stage, just for my own enjoyment.

That was as relaxed and happy a time as I had at the Alvin, because *Patent Leather Shoes* was a stress convention.

I had done the show, but when it had plans to come to Broadway, they re-cast my role. For three weeks, I worked in Macy's as a Santa Claus, before they called me back and said, "We want you back." The next *day*, we did our first preview in Philadelphia.

The show had been redone to be more naturalistic. They'd taken out a lot of the show business shtick and gimmicks, that had really worked in Chicago. I felt like this wasn't the right choice, so I toned down my shtick, but I didn't get rid of it. Everyone thought they'd get rid of me.

Then, at our first preview in Philadelphia, I was the only one getting laughs. After that, a lot of the shtick came back. We spent a lot of time changing "Mad Bomber", and it went from a number for Virginia and Felix, my character, to a big group number at a church carnival. We spent hours working out the technical elements of a gag where Vicki Lewis, as Virginia, would throw a dart at a bunch of balloons.

By the time we opened at the Alvin, they had cut the two-hour and forty-minute show down to 95 minutes! There was nothing left of it. It had changed in ways that I felt were dreadfully wrong, and I wrote out my two weeks notice before the closing notice went up.

I've been sort of dismissive about *Patent Leather Shoes* for years. The anniversary of the opening was last week so I put a picture up on Facebook, and I was surprised by the number of people who responded by saying, "I love that show." That was really validating, even all these years later, because we got our hearts broken on Broadway.

We actually got nice reviews in *Variety* and the *Jersey Ledger*, but Frank Rich's review in the *Times* was very disdainful. All through previews and on opening night, we got some laughs for the parts that still played. Then, after those reviews, you could hear crickets. Everyone had read the *Times*, and nobody wanted to look foolish laughing at something that had gotten a bad review. That was a first for me! I didn't realize how reviews could truly kill laughs. That was very sad.

I can't say enough about the talent of that cast. We had Jason Graae and Vicki Lewis and Karen Tamburrelli, who is now Karla Tamburrelli, the creator of the SAG Awards. The show had a lot of really talented people, including our musical director, Larry Hochman. And I'd never worked so hard in my life, I'd never been so excited when something started, and I'd never seen a creative staff make such idiotic decisions so consistently and with such dedication.

I love so many of the people who worked on that show, but it was honestly also the first time that I encountered a group of people who, as a whole, did not want the social aspect of working in a cast. This was all, "Let's just run it, okay?" Up until then, I'd been friends with every actor I'd worked with.

After we closed, I didn't work as an actor for two years. I thought I was a 26-year-old has-been. Then, we put *Black Patent Leather Shoes* back the way it originally was, and took it to Philly. It was a hit all over again, and it kept me working for two years! That's show business.

1982: A Big Chicago Hit

Jason Graae, Actor

I had an audition for *Black Patent Leather Shoes,* for the role of Louie Schlang. That role was usually played by a really big fat guy, because he had all these jokes about food. But fat wasn't fashionable on Broadway then, so they decided they wanted to cast someone thin. It should have been a heavier guy, because it would've been funnier!

They had two dance callbacks, and my roommate Vicki Lewis and I were both called to the second one. Vicki found out the combination from a friend after the first callback, and she taught it to us! When Thommie Walsh was teaching it to us at our callback, we had to pretend that we didn't know it yet. We were doing that, but then I accidentally kept going! Thommie said, "Well! I guess someone's learned this already." We both got the show anyway!

I was going to make my Broadway debut! My agents weren't as excited as I was, but we went out of town to Philadelphia and ran for six months at the Walnut Street Theatre before Broadway. The show was as successful there as it had previously been in Chicago.

The producers wanted to put a sign under the marquee that said the show was a "Big Chicago Hit!" And I remember that our PR people and some agents fought against it, because they said having the sign say that would be the kiss of death in New York. Nobody in New York wanted to be told what had been a hit anywhere else. I do think that has changed since then.

I was already familiar with the Alvin Theatre in New York because I had been at the second preview and the closing night of *Merrily We Roll Along*. The Alvin was very magical to me because of that. Seeing *Merrily* was amazing. I had wanted to be in it so badly, and I actually had a shot at it at the time, but I couldn't get out of the contract for the show I was doing then. I had to let it pass by, and then some of my closest friends ended up being in it. I was crushed.

At the time, it wasn't as cool to be young in New York as it is now. There weren't as many shows for very young people, and *Merrily* was it. It was Sondheim and it was Hal Prince, and it was all anybody my age was talking about. I went to see the second preview, and I loved it. I was confused, but I loved it. The sweatshirts, with the names and everything, sure—but the score was amazing, and to see my friends standing on stage at the Alvin was completely thrilling to me.

So when we got to the Alvin with *Black Patent Leather Shoes*, it didn't feel right. We had gotten great reviews out of town, but people in New York didn't like the show very much. The producers had originally chosen a smaller theater, but then the Alvin opened up, because it was filled with flops that year. The Alvin seemed too big for the show. There were many dressing rooms—I was 24 and I had my own room!

Our set barely filled the Alvin's stage. It was a little cartoon set. I remember the first time the curtain came up, the audience applauded for us, and Vicki and I both laughed, because we thought they were mocking us. But they weren't! It was a really fun show, and some of the audiences got into it. It just should've been in a smaller house.

We had our opening night at Gallagher's next door, and when Frank Rich's review came out, it started, "The poor ushers at the Alvin Theatre..." Then, it listed all of the flops that had been there. It was devastating. The review went on and on and said the show had "untalented and unappealing performers." It was one of those classic, brilliant, horrible reviews.

We had two weeks of previews, opened on a Thursday, and got our closing notice that Sunday. But we were told by the producers, "This will not be our closing day. We have money coming in from an outside source. We just have to put this up for legal reasons. We're gonna make this thing run."

We believed them. Then as the show went on that day, after each scene, they'd throw props in boxes! And the set pieces would be taken outside. By the end we all knew we were closing, and everyone was sobbing. Most of us were making our Broadway debuts, and we knew that short run was all we were going to get. The end.

———————————

Black Patent Leather Shoes *was the last Broadway show for Russ Thacker. Russ has the sad distinction of having had the leading role in six Broadway shows, which played a total of 19 performances all together. A couple years ago, I was looking to contact Russ Thacker and someone told me, "He lives in the 80s!" (They didn't mean the decade; they meant the Upper West Side.)*

———————————

1982/2013: Friends, The Best Of

Larry Hochman, Orchestrator

I'll be returning to the Neil Simon, which was the Alvin, for *Big Fish*. I was there more than 30 years ago with *Black Patent Leather Shoes*.

Patent Leather Shoes was the first time that I conducted a Broadway show. I even had a dressing room! I shared with Don Stitt, and I had no idea before that that you could decorate your dressing room and make it like home. Of course, had I known that and bothered to do it, I would have had to take it all down a couple weeks later.

I'll admit that I cut up a lot in the pit of *Patent Leather Shoes*. There was one part in the second act where Don Stitt had to kneel directly above me for confession, while a serious scene was going on elsewhere on stage. I would try to make him laugh. I don't think we did any harm.

1983/1998: Auditioning On Broadway

Michael Mayer, Director

I love the Neil Simon Theatre. I moved our production of *A View From the Bridge* from the Criterion Center to the Simon, so we worked to make the show environmental in our new space. We had steps coming down from the boxes. Plus, I convinced Equity to let me bring the 35 people we'd had for the crowd scenes to the Simon, on a special contract.

I remembered going to the Simon when I was much younger, and going up in the elevator to Manny Azenberg's offices. And the last time I ever auditioned for a Broadway show, it was over on the stage of the Simon, back when it was the Alvin.

I kept being brought in to audition for all these Neil Simon shows: *Biloxi Blues* and *Broadway Bound* and *Brighton Beach Memoirs*. I was good enough to be brought back, but I never got it.

I remember I loved being on that stage. You can't afford to do that for auditions anymore! It was so exciting back then to stand on the stage of whatever show was currently playing, and act with the reader and the ghost light. It was very romantic.

I got to do it once as a director. For the *Spring Awakening* tour, we got the O'Neill for one day, and we had everyone audition on the stage. It was fantastic to hear everyone singing into mics, and see what they looked like on stage. I got to give 50 kids the opportunity to audition on a Broadway stage, which was pretty sweet.

––––––––––––

In 1983, the Alvin Theatre was renamed the Neil Simon, in the middle of the run of Simon's Brighton Beach Memoirs. *The next show at the theater was his* Biloxi Blues, *which won Simon his first Tony Award.*

––––––––––––

1987: He's Going To Be A Big Star One Day

Merle Frimark, Press Agent

I worked on *Breaking The Code* which starred Sir Derek Jacobi. It was a West End production that came to Broadway, at the Neil Simon Theatre.

One evening after the show, I was in Derek's dressing room and an announcement came over the loud-speaker that he had a guest. His dresser went off to collect this person, and bring him back. Derek told me a bit about the young man I was about to meet, "He's going to be a big star one day—he's got it all." That young man was Kenneth Branagh!

1988: You Belong Here

Annie Golden, Actor

I had the most glorious opportunity to do *Ah, Wilderness!* at Yale Rep. They were doing that show and *Long Day's Journey Into Night* in rep, and the cast had Campbell Scott, Kyra Sedgwick, Colleen Dewhurst, Jamey Sheridan, Jason Robards, George Hearn... I was like a sponge. I spent the whole time paying attention to everything.

I played Belle, the tart who sang an old-fashioned song at the top of the second act. On our first day, Lloyd Richards welcomed us, and I started weeping. Colleen said to Campbell in front of everyone, "That one's emotional, I love her already. I don't know why she's crying, but she's crying." And I told her, "I never went to university, and I'm a rock singer. I don't get to do theatre like this." She replied, "Yeah, you do. Honey, you belong here."

They brought us to New York, and we got to play the Neil Simon Theatre during a very hot summer. It's just the way I roll that when I work in a theater, or at CBGB's, or at a club, I know everybody's names. I know the door man's name, I know the musicians' names, I know the dressers' names. We're all in it together and it's collaborative.

When I first started working at the Neil Simon Theatre, I'd always see Douglas, the door man, sitting at the door with a composition book. He'd be writing pages and pages and pages. I'm a songwriter, so I got that. I'd also walk around with a notebook sometimes, to write down song ideas.

We bonded over our notebooks, and then we also bonded over being like, "Oh my God, it's Colleen Dewhurst and Jason Robards in our show!" I'd always see him writing, and I'd say, "What do you aspire to be, Douglas?" He'd say, "I want to write," and I'd say, "Well, you're already writing, honey!"

I had this copy of *Moon for the Misbegotten* with Colleen and Jason on the cover. I asked them if they would mind signing it, and Colleen asked me if she could sit with it for a while. Then when Jason got it, he said, "Oh! She wrote a novel!" I told him "Don't feel obligated! Your name is enough!" But he sat with it and wrote something too. I knew that Douglas wanted to be a playwright, so I shared that with him. He said, "You bought this after you met them?" And I told him, "No, I just had it!" "Why did you have it?" "Because I felt like Eugene O'Neill was a playwright that I should know." "I guess you should." We looked at it and enjoyed that together. We were beginners, and we were starstruck together. We remember that to this day.

Later, Douglas asked me to do readings of his plays, and then he made his Broadway debut as a playwright, and then suddenly it was "Douglas Carter Beane is writing *Xanadu*, and he wants to know if you'll be in it on Broadway." In the meantime, he met his husband, Louis, and I became friends with him as well. We eventually had a baby shower for the two of them in the basement at the Helen Hayes, during *Xanadu,* when they adopted their daughter. Theatre is family. It truly is.

1989: Closed After Three Previews

Perry Kroeger, Writer/Actor

Tom O'Horgan may be the only Broadway director who had four shows running simultaneously: *Hair, Jesus Christ Superstar, Lenny* and *Inner City*. He wrote the music for and directed *Senator Joe*.

In 1988, Tom wanted to create a theatre company that combined pop music and opera. He wanted to compose music for projects that would be done by this "New York popera" company. He started three projects: one based on *'Tis Pity She's A Whore* written with Eve Miriam, one called *Nimrod* written with Jonathan Walker, and one called *Senator Joe*, written with me.

Senator Joe was never meant to be a Broadway show. We wrote it is a 1980s off-Broadway political cartoon and Brechtian pastiche. Then, Adela Holzer came on board as a producer. There were no off-Broadway venues available for the two shows, and Eve Miriam sadly passed away. So, *Nimrod* and *Senator Joe* were going to have to go to Broadway.

The result was three previews at the Neil Simon Theatre. The show never opened and was never reviewed. Everything ended on the morning of the fourth preview with Adela being arrested at a phone booth and being taken to Rikers Island. To this day, I do not fully understand how she was financing our production.

We thought that would be the end of our show, but we got a second production. In 1992, we were asked to bring *Senator Joe* to the Moscow Art Theatre, and I got to be the show's designer. I was the first American to design there. Sadly, we ended up not having enough money to bring New York actors to Russia, so for the second time, the whole show had to be trashed.

Before we trashed it, on their dark night, the Moscow Art Theatre hung the entire show I had designed so I could see it in their theater. We took lots of photos.

In 2010, I created a concert series with Kevin Michael Murphy and Caleb Hoyer to celebrate underappreciated musicals. Called "If It Only Even Runs A Minute" after a lyric from Merrily We Roll Along, *the series features songs, photos and stories from original cast members about shows that may not have gotten a fair shake in their time.*

In fall of 2011, I was putting together the seventh edition of the concert and I contacted Perry Kroeger about Senator Joe. *I was at the Neil Simon Theatre, seeing the first preview of the new musical* Catch Me If You Can *when during intermission, I received an email from Perry, saying that he would love to come share some stories about his show in our concert.*

I was standing in the theater where his show had closed after three previews, three decades earlier, when I heard from him. It was odd and perfect.

1992: First Previews

Joe Traina, House Manager

First previews are always fraught with people who are on edge and brimming over with great expectations of: *how is this thing going to do?*

During the first preview of *Jake's Women* at the Neil Simon Theatre in 1992, a man had a heart attack during the performance. It happened in the lower lounge, and it was kept fairly quiet. That's always kind of upsetting for everyone, and certainly nerve-wracking for the producer, the general manager and the company manager.

1993: The Heroic Joop Van Den Ende

Ed Dixon, Actor

The producer of *Cyrano*, Joop Van Den Ende was from the Netherlands, and was the greatest man. He was a self-made millionaire. He started off working with rock bands and worked his way up to being a multimillionaire—and then lost everything, had a heart attack, nearly died, started over, and rebuilt his financial empire.

Just before he came to America with *Cyrano*, he did one deal with European television that made him $500 million dollars. So he was flush. He was so kind and so generous. He gave us leather show jackets and parties and free tickets for our friends and he took us out to eat over and over again at Gallagher's, right down the street from the theatre. He just barraged us with gifts and made us feel loved and appreciated.

He also hired the greatest costume designer from the Netherlands, who designed these unbelievably beautiful costumes that were just magical to wear. The set was gorgeous. The orchestrations were gorgeous. The show was flawed, but I really thought that the New York press didn't give him or the play a fair shake—from the minute it was announced that this entrepreneur from Holland was bringing a big flashy show to Broadway, the basic way people talked about it in the papers was, "Who the *hell* does he think he is? He's not Broadway. Why does he think he can do a big show on Broadway?" They basically ran him and all of his millions out of town.

He also had a hit version of *Three Musketeers* that he wanted to bring in and also a *Count of Monte Cristo*—and he cancelled both of them. He has come back as an investor in a lot of American shows, but all those gigantic blockbusters that he wanted to do, they were just... turned away. I thought, *if that had happened in Oklahoma City or Cleveland or Toledo, if the papers had driven away a multimillion-dollar investor, how would those towns react to those papers?*

1996: The Laptop Era Had Begun

Ted Chapin, President of The Rodgers & Hammerstein Organization/Past Chairman of the American Theatre Wing

When *The King and I* came to the Neil Simon in 1996, it was really my introduction to how the technology on Broadway had changed. *On Your Toes* in 1983, when I first got to the Rodgers & Hammerstein Organization and was still done in the old-school ways.

The Alvin was now the Neil Simon, and when I walked in during the technical rehearsals for *The King and I*, there were all these computers all over the theater. I pulled somebody in stage management aside and asked, "Can you just explain to me what are all of these?" And they did. The laptop era had begun and it was really, really fascinating.

The King and I in that theater wasn't as luminous an experience as I'd hoped it would be, partly because I was disappointed they didn't rebuild the set. The production was conceived for major performing arts centers in Australia, where the stages are huge—so there was just too much of it. The scale wasn't right, so it looked kind of squished into that theater. I remember thinking: *This was very powerful when I saw it in Melbourne and, yeah, it's got all the stuff here, but it isn't quite the same.* It was a slightly troubled production but at the end of the day, it was *The King and I*.

1996: Your First One

Jose Llana, Actor

I was a freshman in college when I booked a regional, non-Equity, summer stock production of *The King And I*. Someone at that audition said, "Have you heard about the Broadway production?" I had no idea.

I found out that you could wait all day and be seen at the audition, so I went. Around noon, some guy didn't show up. I raised my hand and pretended I was him and went in. I sang for the casting director, all the while thinking I was going to get arrested. He said that he was going to give me a callback, and I pointed to the headshot he was holding and said, "Great! But that's not me." I got the job.

The Neil Simon felt enormous to me. I had nothing to compare it to. I suddenly went from being a full-time college student to having a Broadway show. I didn't know how to spend my free time in the city yet, so I was alone a lot. I sat in the theater a lot, and I started a tradition where I would go to the last row of the balcony and have coffee there every night before half-hour. I do that before every show that I do now, and I always think about sitting at the very top of the Neil Simon Theatre.

With so many kids in the cast, every Saturday between shows was a potluck. There were 16 kids, and there was always a birthday, and there were always mothers organizing potlucks.

On the night of the first preview, I freaked out about an hour before because I didn't have anybody in the audience. I thought: *Somebody has to be here.* I called my friend Judy, and bought her tickets, and said, "Come to my first preview, please!" I'm still close friends with her today, and I'll always remember that she was the first person who saw me on Broadway.

On opening night, with everybody important in the audience—my family, Stephen Sondheim, other theatre pros—I messed up the lyrics to "We Kiss In A Shadow". I started singing the second verse instead of the first. I don't love that that happened, but for me, it does mark the specific memory of being so young and in my first Broadway show. It was fantastic.

I look back on my two years with *The King And I* as college. It was my learning experience, and I had a lot of wonderful mentors in that company—older brothers and sisters who, to this day, continue to be mentors.

Whenever I see anything at the Neil Simon I get a little nostalgic. Nothing really ever comes close to your first one.

1996: Something Wonderful

Donna Murphy, Actor

When I did *The King and I* at the Neil Simon Theatre, I had a very large dressing room suite because my costumes were so huge! There was one dressing room on the ground floor, on stage right, that was really two large rooms put together. My outer room had a pull out couch, and was decorated; I had to put my dresses on there, because they were too large for the inner room!

That outer room became a play area. I said, "When the kids are not on stage, rather than having them run up and down, they can just be here. They can play games, nap, whatever. We had little parties and holidays for them in there. The whole company always did something for the kids on special occasions, but I made sure to do something special, because we were "Anna and the kids."

We had some very young children in the cast, and I noticed at one point that the kids were going through my lozenges very quickly. Tons of tins of lozenges every week. Then, stage management asked me to hide them. I asked why, and they said, "Well, the kids are taking them out of their mouths on stage and the wives in the show are finding them stuck to their costumes. Or sometimes, right before the king's death, the kids will be sitting there and accidentally letting lozenges fall out of their mouths onto the stage."

When I was leaving the show, and we were coming up on my last performance, the company had a little party for me, and they told me to close my eyes. Then, they presented me with this special dress. Two of the men in the cast had made it, and it was a dress entirely made out of the lozenge tins! It was this flapper dress, with a hat, a purse, shoes... they squished the centers of some of the tiny boxes and made little bows out of them!

At some point, the cast had started collecting the boxes because everyone knew how many the kids and I were going through.

I autographed many of the insides of the tins, and wrote messages inside of them, and we auctioned it off for Broadway Cares/Equity Fights AIDS.

That was a company that was very prone to pranks. I begged them not to involve me, because I was really easy to crack up. But it was all done in good fun. At one performance, there were a bunch of balloons backstage, so some of the cast members decided to place some underneath my giant gown. I didn't notice, and then at some point, I twirled and a balloon just came floating out from beneath me. It was like I had laid a golden egg! There were five or six of them, and as I moved around, they kept being released!

It was all done in the spirit of people having a good time and loving each other, and never at the expense of the performance. Certain show casts are just more inclined to play jokes than others!

1998: Starstruck

Tony Massey, Merchandise Manager

The first show I opened on my own as a merchandise manager was Matthew Bourne's *Swan Lake*.

I had been working at *Phantom*, and at that point, it was around eight years old. There weren't stars coming to the Majestic at that point. Going to do *Swan Lake* was the opposite because everybody in the world wanted to see that show! At every performance, we would have somebody huge there, like Jack Nicholson.

I was so starstruck back then. Now, it seems less eventful to me, but I still get jazzed and excited over certain TV stars who I think are really wonderful. I don't need to meet them, I don't need their autograph, I just think it's cool to see them in person and have that.

Mary Tyler Moore is one of my favorite actresses, and when she came to *Annie Get Your Gun*, I missed her. Everyone kept asking, "Didn't you see her? Didn't you see Mary Tyler Moore?!" and I felt so disappointed. Then, I worked on a show that John F. Kennedy Jr. came to see, and I missed him too. I was a little like: *Oh, well that's kind of sad. It would have been cool to see him, but he goes to lots of shows. I'm sure I'll see him at some point.* Within a few months, he died.

So, by *Swan Lake*, I had learned. If a star comes to your show, you'd better see them. There's a chance that next week, they'll be gone.

1999: Songs That Stand On Their Own

Frank Wildhorn, Writer

The Scarlet Pimpernel spent two years at the Minskoff, and then we had to close the show for a little bit, reorganize, re-cast, refit it for the Neil Simon, and open. It was the Broadway equivalent of having a restaurant that becomes well-known and gathers loyal fans, and then just as it's gaining momentum, you have to move your restaurant five miles.

It was challenging. You have to educate people to know about your show, and when you close for a while, your show becomes very quickly out of sight and out of mind. It was a tough mountain to climb. On the other hand, it did give the show an extended life for another four months. Carolee Carmello, Ron Bohmer, and Marc Kudisch were fantastic in their roles.

The most important moments in the life of a show are not always just what happens on stage. I love that during Desert Storm, the marines took the song "Into The Fire" from *The Scarlet Pimpernel* and used it for videos that were made. I love when a song transcends the show, and hits the rest of the world on a bigger scale, whether the people who hear it were in the theater or not.

We also had that with "This Is The Moment" from *Jekyll & Hyde*, which was used for Clinton's Presidential Inauguration, four Olympics in a row, the World Series, the Super Bowl... it's been played at so many important events. And I love that Linda Eder can stand on a Broadway stage and sing "Someone Like You" and then you can hear it on the radio the next week.

I love that "You Are My Home" captured the emotion of its moment in the show, and drew the audience into *The Scarlet Pimpernel*, and then was also a Top 40 hit. I just love songs that can stand on their own and that people can relate to, though they may never have seen the show.

––––––––––––

Many songs from Broadway shows have crossed over and become pop hits over the years. From the Fifth Dimension's recording of "Aquarius" from Hair *to the Beatles covering "Til There Was You" from* The Music Man, *several Broadway songs have become radio staples.*

Frank Wildhorn's crossover into the pop market with his songs from shows is quite a feat, as this certainly doesn't occur as much as it used to. The writers of musicals and the writers of popular music were often one and the same during the Golden Age of Broadway, but in the 1960s, this began to split and separate.

However these days, we seem to be moving back to an era of crossover artists! From Duncan Sheik to Bono to Dolly Parton, pop writers are starting to bring more original musicals to Broadway. Could a new era of crossover hits be upon us?

––––––––––––

1999: Into The Fire

Casey Nicholaw, Director/Choreographer/Actor

I actually replaced in the second version of *The Scarlet Pimpernel* the week after opening night. That, for me, was a fantastic experience. It was really fun.

"Into the Fire" was so exciting. To step on that platform and to get lifted up for the first time, while you're in costume and everything else... so cool.

That was after *Steel Pier* for me, and after doing four original shows back-to-back, it was so nice to rehearse for three days, and go into the show, and not go through any of the other stuff. I had a good time on that show. It was really fun to just do it!

2000/2013: The American Flag

Susan Stroman, Director/Choreographer

I was at the Neil Simon Theatre for *The Music Man*, and now I'm back there with *Big Fish*. It's lovely to see the same people running the elevator, and running the front of house, and working backstage. I loved walking in there after all these years, and seeing these old friends. I was so happy to see them, and they embraced me. There's something about returning to a theater that really makes you feel like part of this community.

And we love being on the same street as *Jersey Boys*! All of the stagehands meet in the middle of the street to chat. It's wonderful. And there are these big crowds of audiences for both shows, so you feel this great electricity on the street right before show time.

When you're in previews with a show, you always end up finding a nook of the theater to work in. At the Neil Simon, we rehearse in the lower lobby, right outside the men's bathroom. The creative teams of *Big Fish* and *The Music Man* both rehearsed and fixed and tweaked in the lobby downstairs. Also, at the Neil Simon, I sit on house right in this little stairwell behind a curtain. It's become my office before the show. And when the lights go down, I leave my office to stand in the back of the house.

During *The Music Man*, 9/11 happened. Our production ended each night with the entire company coming out and playing "76 Trombones" together for curtain call, followed by a huge American flag dropping down. When Broadway shows started running again after the tragedy, for weeks, that American flag would drop down at *The Music Man*, and there wouldn't be a dry eye in the house.

The Music Man is so Americana. At that time, it was difficult for all of us to understand what was really going on, or try to digest it. But it was clear that the terrorists really wanted to break our spirit. And there we were at the Neil Simon Theatre, playing trombones and displaying the American flag every night. I'll never forget the image of it, and I'll never forget the feeling and the breath of that audience when the flag would unfurl.

2000: My Center Stage Bow

Jim Walton, Actor

I stood by for three roles in the Broadway revival of *The Music Man* in 2000. I stood by for Harold Hill, Marcellus, and Charlie Cowell. The production was at the Neil Simon Theatre, which, of course, had been the Alvin when I did *Merrily We Roll Along*.

Early in previews, I had not yet learned the song, "Shipoopi", that Marcellus sings. He dances a lot in that song too. During act one of the show one night, they told me, "The actor playing Marcellus has a flu bug. You might be on for act two."

That night, while the audience was watching act one of *The Music Man* upstairs, I was learning "Shipoopi" down in the lower lobby of the Simon. I went on for act two, and I was six inches taller than the other actor who had been playing the role. During "Shipoopi" I got the whole thing except for four to eight bars when I just had no idea, so I just danced around, and the cast was all breaking up. We had only done four or five previews together by that point, but it doesn't take long for actors to get comfortable.

There were also days in that show when I went on for Harold Hill. One afternoon, I went on instead of Craig Bierko, who played the role of Harold. I walked out the stage door, and it was like I'd hung the moon. "Would you sign my Playbill?" "Would you take a picture with my son?" "Do you have a website?" I went to dinner and came back to the theater that night, and Craig was back. They said, "Oh, but you're on for Macellus tonight." I went on for Marcellus, did well, walked out the stage door that night, and it was tumbleweeds. Nobody even looked at me. They looked right through me. And I thought: *Oh, right. It's not me. It's the part I play.* I took it personally for two seconds, and then I just realized: *Oh, right. Of course.*

Being back at the Alvin was great. Talk about an awesome theater. That theater is classic Broadway, such a big, historic place. It was 19 years after *Merrily*. I was 45 years old. I was older Frank by then. I had already progressed in my life to the age that the characters are in the first act of *Merrily*.

It was good to work at the Alvin again. I remember Craig's dressing room, from when I played Harold. It had been the hair room for *Merrily*. There's a picture from opening night of *Merrily*, where it's Lonny, me, Ann Morrison, Hal Prince, Stephen Sondheim, George Furth, and Larry Fuller. We're sitting in that room on opening night of *Merrily*. The first time I walked into Craig's room, I went: "Wow. I remember this place." It was weird to be back in a place 19 years later, where I could remember such specific things having happened.

When I would go on as Harold Hill, I would get the last bow as Harold, much as I did with Frank Shepard. To this day, the only times that I have gotten the last bow in a musical in New York City were during two shows—

210

Merrily We Roll Along and *The Music Man*—that were both at the Alvin Theatre. There I was, the first time I went on as Harold, bowing, and it suddenly hit me. *I haven't done this for 19 years, and when I did, it was at this very same location. This very same theater and this very same spot.*

2002: The Gypsy Run Of *Hairspray*

Gavin Creel, Actor

One memory that was a turning point in my life was going to see the gypsy run-through of *Hairspray*. I'd done a workshop of it, so I knew the whole cast. Up to that point, I hadn't really witnessed something in the arts that was truly, mind-blowingly historic. And this was a historic moment for musical theatre.

Knowing who all the people were on stage, and being friends with them... and then seeing it be something that was obviously going to be so huge. It was just like I could step outside myself for a second, and say, "I'm in the midst of witnessing something historic and amazing." And I realized I belonged here. I'm part of this community. I'm not just a guest.

I felt like a guest in *Millie*, even though it was a huge role and a huge break, but *Hairspray*... there was something amazing about it. I was in a Broadway show, and I went to an afternoon gypsy run. I just thought: *Holy shit, I belong here. There are my people. I'm so proud.*

2002: They Wouldn't Go Home

Jack O'Brien, Director

The great defining moment that we didn't see coming was the first preview of *Hairspray* in Seattle. We were busy loving doing what we were doing and having a good time, and then we played our first preview and the audience went wild. We thought: *Wow! This is pretty good!* Then we played the second preview and the audience went wild again, and we thought: *Maybe it's better than we thought!*

On the third preview, a big section was bought out by the Seattle Gay Men's Chorus. We played the third preview and that audience wouldn't go home. Literally. They stood and screamed. The company took their bows and went to their dressing rooms, and Harvey got out of his wig and his padding, and the audience stayed and screamed. Harvey had to come down in a bathrobe and wave to them, and send them home. It was one of the greatest thrills of my life, and we never, ever turned back from there.

By the time we got there, New York sort of knew what it was getting. Previews at the Neil Simon were over-the-top unbelievable, but by that time, we were prepared for it. We certainly weren't prepared for it in Seattle!

2002: A Huge Sensation

Bernie Telsey, Casting Director

That *Hairspray* first preview was crazy. It was just a huge sensation.

The show was really good in Seattle, but no matter how many times you've done this, you just never know. That first preview audience at the Neil Simon had clearly read about what happened in Seattle, but this was still a New York audience, which can be different. That audience went crazy with an unbelievable amount of joy.

Hairspray was one of those shows where many of the people in the ensemble were so special. The show started with many informal readings put together by Jack and Jerry, where they just put people in it that they knew and really loved, and a lot of those people ended up getting Broadway offers.

In Seattle, we lost our Link to a movie, and we plucked Matthew Morrison out of the ensemble. Kerry Butler and Laura Bell Bundy were in supporting roles, and you just knew: *you are both going to be starring in Broadway musicals*. Within just a couple years, Matt, Kerry and Laura were all starring in their own Broadway musicals. We had someone like a Jenn Gambatese in the ensemble, and someone like Jackie Hoffman, making her Broadway debut. It was a cast where you really felt: *Oh my God, there are a lot of surprises in this crackerjack box!* I remember feeling that way from the auditions all the way to the performances.

2002: The Costume World Is Green

William Ivey Long, Costume Designer/Chair of the American Theatre Wing

The costume world was green, before people even knew to use the word "green." We recycle clothes; it's called "vintage." A lot of costumes, like rough-and-tumble street wear, are better if they've been worn. Even shoes are often better if they've been broken in. Sometimes there are shoes in shows I do that have three sets of names inside of them. They could be their own theatre museum, these shoes.

When I did *Hairspray*, a lot of the "Good Morning Baltimore" overcoats were vintage. It adds another level, and helps you stretch the budget at the same time. There's nothing like an eccentric vintage piece where you go, "Really? Someone designed that? And there's a big button right there? Yes!" Vintage is our friend, and it's great when integrated into a Broadway costume design palette.

Vintage is especially helpful when a new song is written, or a new part is put in, and you have to quickly reorganize what characters are wearing. With *Hairspray*, each scene or stage picture had a color theme. In Seattle, we added a lot of scenes and moved other scenes around. Each time, I would put some vintage costumes on characters for that part and see how they worked. If they stayed, often I would adapt the design into an original costume. It would have different fabric, and I'd move the pockets, and change the collar, and so forth. Vintage is very helpful, because it's often where you start.

It's mostly coats I'm talking about, but men's shirts were very helpful during the design process of *Hairspray*. The show took place in 1960s Baltimore, and some of the vintage I found would make me yell, "Really? That's real? That's not a costume?" Vintage encourages you to be more eccentric. Because the clothes actually were!

2002: School Backstage At The Neil Simon

Laura Bell Bundy, Actor

The Neil Simon Theatre feels so much bigger when you're standing on stage with the lights in your face. It's actually a pretty small theater! The backstage is tiny.

During *Hairspray*, I shared a dressing room with Kerry Butler. That room had so much love in it. It was the most joyful little room in the world! We were very messy. And we had to throw things in the fridge away very quickly or it would start to smell. But it was fun. We had these little hallways and small rooms, so we were forced to be sociable all the time. We left our door open, and our floormates, Linda Hart, Matthew Morrison, and Dick Latessa, would come visit. We used to all do a hoedown at five minutes to places every Saturday night! Usually it would be to the Dixie Chicks' "You Can't Afford No Ring". We would blast it and we would square dance. We had so much fun!

212

When I was doing *Hairspray*, I was also going to school at NYU during the day. There was this one set piece that came out during the first act to be Edna Turnblad's little living room. It was for the scene where Harvey as Edna would be ironing and Tracy would be watching TV. When that piece went off stage each night, the crew guys would make it into a little desk for me. The stagehands set up a light for me there, and they would change out the batteries. I had a couple times during the show where I could just bring my books there, and study between cues. The crew was so sweet to me.

When you do a show, you have your routines with everyone. You have your routines with the crew guys, you have your routines with the elevator person. And you have things you always talk about with each person. There's always the one person in each show who has the horoscopes. There are little things you come to rely upon, and when people aren't there, you miss them.

2002: A Blessed Project

Margo Lion, Producer

Hairspray was a blessed project. I was despondent after my last show, *Triumph of Love*, closed quickly, and I thought I might get out of the theatre because I was so down. I remember my friend, scenic designer Heidi Ettinger told me, "It'll take you six months."

I decided I wanted to do a musical that had a lot of dance and a lot of young people in it. We were coming off the era of British musicals, that I didn't feel had that sense of celebration. An American musical, no matter what it's about, celebrates something.

I called Scott Rudin at one point, and I told him I wanted to do *Clueless*. He told me I'd never get *Clueless*, and asked, "Why don't you do *Hairspray*?" It became a running gag between us, because he knew I had walked out when I saw the movie, and he'd always tell me I should do it.

I was down, so I rented all these movies. One of them was *Hairspray* and I watched it and thought: *You know what, this* would *make a good musical. It has a larger than life character who wants something, and it's about something important, and it's peopled with interesting characters, and it has a real point of view. It's not homogenous, and it wouldn't make just a conventional Broadway musical.*

It took me a year to get the rights, and in that process, I learned two things. First, I learned that there had been someone who had the rights before me: Scott Rudin. Second, I learned that Jerry Mitchell was also trying to get the rights. After I got them, in 1999, I called Marc Shaiman and he said he'd do the music, and that he wanted his life partner, Scott Wittman to do the lyrics. I said, "That sounds like a horrible idea!" He asked if they could write three songs on spec[30].

Those songs were "Good Morning Baltimore," "Welcome to the 60s," and "I Know Where I've Been." Clearly, we moved forward! A friend of mine recommended Mark O'Donnell as the book writer, and he had a very distinct voice of his own and knew how to adapt and got along with Marc and Scott.

Rob Marshall was chosen to direct and choreograph. When he took on the job he said, "You know, there's this other project that I'm working on. I can't imagine it's going to conflict, but it's a movie and it's been around for a long time and I just want you to know that it's a possibility." He worked for a year on *Hairspray* and he did a lot of great work. He did three workshops, three readings, and he did a lot of the casting that remained in the

---

[30] on spec: material created for a project as a pitch to get a job writing the entire thing

show. He came to me after the third reading and said, "You know that thing I told you about? Well it's coming through."

We took a walk in this park because he used to live across the street and I said, "Oh, well, in a year you'll have a hit movie and we'll have a hit show." What's the likelihood that would really come true? Of course, in a year he had *Chicago* and we had *Hairspray*.

We wanted Jack O'Brien to come on board as director, and, ironically, he would not do the show without Jerry Mitchell! Jerry had wanted the rights, and Marc and Scott had wanted him on the show, but I had turned him down. It was Jerry who actually encouraged Jack, and they both joined the *Hairspray* team!

It's a wonderful story, and I love to tell it because it's so instructional. I took Jerry out after he and Jack agreed to do the show, and I said, "You must really hate me." He responded, "No, I think you were doing what you thought was right for the show—and I'm going to show you that *I'm* right for the show." What a class act. It was fabulous. When we brought Tom Meehan in to work on the book with Mark O'Donnell, at first Mark hung up on me, and then five seconds later he called me back and said, "What am I thinking? You've given me the chance of a lifetime."

We had two backers auditions in one day in December 2001, and raised the entire ten and a half million dollars then and there. From then on, it was just one of those blessed experiences. You can't say anything except, "I'm glad I was standing in the road when the cars went by."

Our dress rehearsal in New York was phenomenal. You expect that, because it's the theatre community, the gypsies, coming to support each other. We thought the first preview would be good, but we didn't think it would reach the level of the dress rehearsal—then, it just blew the roof off. It literally felt like the theatre was going to explode.

We opened *Hairspray* on Broadway in August and nobody does that. Nobody had opened in August since *42nd Street* in 1980. We were alone, and we had all the press to ourselves. During previews, we went from a two and a half million dollar advance to a 16 million dollar advance. It was amazing. It was just a gift.

1962/2002: The Clothesline Of The Musical

Jack Viertel, Creative Director of Jujamcyn Theaters

In the early 1960s, I saw a few knock-about comedy musicals on Broadway that were unbelievable. I just thought I was in heaven. At *A Funny Thing Happened On The Way To The Forum*, I thought there would never in the world be a better way to spend two hours. The laughter and the excitement and the kind of music, the wonderful staging and the scenery and the costumes and the lights. That show just never left me.

40 years later, I got to work on *Hairspray* at the same theater. There was never a moment when *Hairspray* wasn't a hit. It was a winner from the time of the first reading of the first act. The main thing that happened during *Hairspray*'s process is that the love story got written. The writers were originally focusing so much on the voice of the piece: the satire and the politics, that they forgot to write the love story. And the love story in *Hairspray* is essentially the clothesline on which everything else needs to be hung.

"I Can Hear The Bells" was written rather late in the process, and "Without Love" came together late in the process, too. The raw materials for the scene at the end of act one with Link and Tracy were in place, but the scene wasn't developed. Eventually, this was all written, and we opened to great fanfare in Seattle and New York. *Hairspray* was a pretty smooth ride. There was the usual screaming up and down the aisle from time to time, but nothing about anything that would make the show a hit or a flop—just an occasional hitch.

214

2006: We Grew Up Dancing Together

Hayley Podschun, Actor

I got to understudy Penny and Amber in *Hairspray* on Broadway after doing it on tour. It was fun to go on for those parts because Shannon Durig was playing Tracy. We grew up dancing together in recitals! When I was seven or eight years old, we'd hang out in her mom's store, and she'd teach me how to do wings and bell kicks. It was really fun to play together on stage, because we'd known each other for so long. Shannon was one of the longest-running Tracys on Broadway; we had a party for her 1000th show.

I was always sad that I didn't get to be part of the party with the theater across the street. Our girls' dressing room was on the south side of the theater, which faces nothing. We didn't have a window, or if we did, it was covered in costumes. We were crammed in there, so we didn't see anything.

But if I went on for Penny or Amber, I'd get to be in their dressing room on the 52nd Street side, and then I'd get to see everyone in *Jersey Boys* doing an underwear dance. It was fun to have another family across the street.

2007: You Just Know You Can

Corbin Bleu, Actor

I grew up in Brooklyn, New York. I grew up seeing shows. Then my family moved to the West Coast.

My father and I were back in the city, visiting. We were walking down the street, and we saw... Alexa Vega was playing Penny in *Hairspray* on Broadway! We were just walking past the theater and we saw her picture on the wall!

I grew up with Alexa Vega, we went to middle school together. We of course had to get tickets. And I got to go backstage. I got a chance to be behind the scenes and go into the dressing rooms and all that.

The whole lifestyle behind the curtain... it's just opening the door to a whole bunch of other magic. There are the costumes and trap doors and extra props and the curtains... Everything backstage is always just... it's like something in a movie.

It's quite a feeling when you get to be backstage, and when you get to stand on the stage and look out into a theater. Some people get up there and think: *I could never do that*. And then other people get up there, and you just know you can.

2003: Every Saturday Night At Five Minute Call

Brynn O'Malley, Actor

When I was in *Hairspray* at the Neil Simon Theatre, across the street was *Flower Drum Song* and then *Jersey Boys*.

When J. Elaine Marcos and I met on *Annie*, we were like, "I can't believe we've never worked together because we know all the same people!" Then we figured out that she was in *Flower Drum Song* when I was in *Hairspray*, and we had that tradition of "Saturday Night on Broadway."

What we would do at the Neil Simon, and what they would do over there, was that when they called "five minutes to places," everyone would just open up their windows, and scream at each other! People would take their shirts off, there were a lot of dirty things and nudity. And the funny thing is, *everyone* would participate. Everyone would just do horrible and dirty things. People down there on the street could totally look up and see what we were doing. And then *Jersey Boys* would do it too, they got into it.

Sometimes, *Jersey Boys* would stage things, and I remember one time *Flower Drum Song* did like, a performance for us—they did a bunch of crazy shit. It ranged from the filthy and stupid to the, "They just did an art piece for us!" This was every Saturday night at five minute call.

2004: From Theater To Theater

Julie Halston, Actor

I used to carry on conversation with the *Jersey Boys* all the time when I was doing *Hairspray*. That's how we'd make our dinner plans: we'd shout across 52nd Street, from the Neil Simon to the August Wilson! We'd yell, "Thursday night! Sosa Borella! 10:30!"

That's how we'd communicate, and everyone on the street below was always like: *What's going on up there?* It was fantastic! We were actually so close together, that sometimes I'd just open the window and say, "Tell Richard Hester I said hello." He was the stage manager at *Jersey Boys*, and I did *Gypsy* with him. Talking from theater to theater was just regular!

2005: The First Time Anyone In The Company Saw Me Was On Stage

Donna Vivino, Actor

My very first time performing at the Neil Simon Theater was pretty crazy. I had done the tour of *Hairspray*, and then I moved to California. While I was there, I got a call asking if I wanted to do my *Hairspray* tour track on Broadway. Of course, I was thrilled. The only difference was that on tour, I had understudied Tracy and Velma, but on Broadway, I would also cover Female Authority Figure. They told me that they'd teach me that role once I got to New York.

I hadn't done *Hairspray* in about eight months, and I was excited. I was going to Broadway. I had two months to prepare. About a month later, I got a call from a 212 number. I picked up, and a man said, "This is Frank. Where are you right now?" I told him I was in California, and he said, "I know you aren't scheduled to even start rehearsals for another few weeks, but we have a situation over here. How soon can you get to New York?"

They were down to just one understudy, who was playing the Female Authority Figure each night. They needed a cover immediately. "You probably won't go on," Frank said. "But we definitely need you here learning it now."

I got to New York the next day, and began rehearsals. It was a Wednesday, and after the matinee, the theater called and said, "Donna needs to go on tonight." I went to wardrobe immediately. I wore the character heels I had been rehearsing in. The show had to actually pay me because I used my own shoes, thanks to Equity rules!

The scariest part of it was being in a theater that I didn't know. It really did feel treacherous! I didn't get a meet and greet with the company, I wasn't familiar with the traffic patterns of the Broadway production. But I was on! The first time that anyone in that company saw me was when I was on stage, playing Prudy Pingleton on Broadway. When I was standing in the back of the house that night, getting ready to go through the audience for the finale, I just remember thinking: *The entire cast is going to be looking at me, this girl they don't know, playing a role for a woman 25 years older.* I wanted so badly to pull it off.

The moment came in "You Can't Stop The Beat" for me to work my way through the audience. I was saying, "Excuse me, excuse me! Coming through!" A man in the audience of the Neil Simon made a funny face at me, and I said, "Give me a break buddy, my role is small enough as it is." I don't know where it came from, but it became my line for the entire run. The entire cast on stage started laughing, so I felt instantly like I belonged.

2006: After Two And A Half Years, I Got Moved To Broadway

Caissie Levy, Actor

I moved to New York City when I was 19, went to AMDA, and then I booked Maureen on the *Rent* tour. I'm from Canada, and after that, I was in between visas. I kept auditioning for the understudy to Penny and Amber in *Hairspray* and the standby for Amneris in *Aida*. I ended up booking *Hairspray*, so I moved home for a year to understudy in the Toronto company. Then, I understudied for a year on the national tour. Then, after two and a half years, I got moved to the Broadway company to make my debut! It was exciting.

I knew some of the cast in New York because they had been in the tour cast. My first night was great. I was so grateful that I was doing a part I had been learning for three years, because I was so nervous and excited. I remember the scrim coming down for "Good Morning Baltimore", and thinking: *I'm on Broadway!*

I remember that performance really well. I remember being in the back of the house for "You Can't Stop The Beat", before Penny enters, and looking down the aisle at everyone, waiting to go on stage. I'd seen *Hairspray* a few years earlier, and thought: *I want to be in that show!* So getting to do it in three different companies was amazing.

Jersey Boys was across the street, and they'd hang signs in their dressing room windows and wave at us. There was such a nice camaraderie between the shows, because it's such a narrow street and the theaters were so small.

2009: My Favorite Score

Stephen Flaherty, Writer

Everyone assumes that growing up, I saw a lot of theater. But I grew up in Pittsburgh, and there wasn't a whole lot going on there theatre-wise, back in the day!

So I lived in my imagination—but I really lived in the world of original cast albums. I went to the Pittsburgh Public Library with my little library card, and I would get a show album, and the libretto, and the piano/vocal score. And I would just learn them. I would memorize them, return them, and get more to bring home. So at one point, I knew virtually every show ever written, and I had only seen maybe three.

Porgy and Bess was my favorite score. And then we got to do the revival of *Ragtime* at the theater where George Gershwin had debuted *Porgy and Bess*! We had 28 musicians in our pit, and we had trouble squeezing them in—and I read that the original production of *Porgy and Bess* had had 40! Then I learned that they'd added more and more seats to the theater over the years, taking a way a portion of the orchestra pit, and it made more sense.

I was lucky that we had a full orchestra. I didn't need 40. And there I was in the theater where my favorite score was first performed on Broadway. I was always taking that in, and absorbing that, and trying to talk to the friendly ghosts as they flew by.

2011: Don't Break The Rules

Nick Wyman, Actor/President of Actors Equity Association

Norbert Leo Butz doing "Don't Break The Rules" in *Catch Me If You Can* was one of the most astonishing things I've ever seen at a first preview.

I remember the first time I saw that song in our tiny rehearsal room. I was squeezed between the mirror and the space where the "stage" started, to watch. My jaw kept dropping further and further, and I literally gaped with delight as Norbert kept on with the song. And at the first preview, the entire audience felt the same way. It stopped the show cold.

2011: I Never Went On

Jay Armstong Johnson, Actor

When I got the standby job on *Catch Me If You Can*, I was psyched. To understudy Aaron Tveit was huge, and I didn't have to learn eight tracks on top of a lead, like I did in *Hair*. The workload was almost less, though the role of Frank Abagnale was like a marathon.

I guess it was one of my sadder Broadway experiences thus far, mostly because I never got to go on. But overall, it just had a different vibe to it. Coming from *Hair*, I was a little spoiled by that vibe and that family. *Catch Me* was the opposite end of that spectrum. It was exciting because it felt professional in a different way. We had Broadway royalty as our creative team. We had Jack O'Brien and Jerry Mitchell, and I learned so much from them just because of their sheer professionalism and their eloquent ways of speaking. It was a time for me to grow up a little bit. I learned how to be a leading man through that process.

I remember being in rehearsals and talking to Alex Ellis, who understudied Brenda. We kept looking at each other and saying, "We're going to win the Tony." Our rehearsal process was so exciting, because we were watching the show, and we thought it was beautiful and brilliant. We really, really fell in love with it, so the excitement to go on for the roles we understudied was huge.

I was thinking: *Yeah, I'm sure I'm gonna go on! This show's gonna run for years.* I built myself up... it was a huge letdown when it didn't go well. But we had a tough season. We had *Priscilla Queen of the Desert* down the street, and we had *Sister Act* next door, and we had *Book of Mormon* a few streets away. It was a huge season, with huge producers and really exciting shows, so that was when I learned that it's a business before it's anything.

I felt so awkward at the closing performance because they let me go on stage for the closing number. They put me in a Frank Abagnale Jr. costume, and I got to come in and sing in the closing number with the cast, for the first time.

It was the first time I'd ever gone on. It was closing night and I was waving goodbye with the ensemble to Aaron and Norbert Leo Butz as they exited up the aisle of the theater. Then, because I had on Frank Abagnale costumes, I was escorted back to Aaron's dressing room. On Aaron's closing performance, I was in *his* dressing room and we were getting undressed. I felt weird. I was thinking: *I have to get out of here as soon as possible and give him his space.* That's the thing I remember most from that night.

218

2012: The Side Of The Stage

Tom Hewitt, Actor

I watched Paul Nolan's final scene on the cross in *Jesus Christ Superstar* every night. It was the most beautiful acting I had seen. My picture was so beautifully framed from the side of the stage and there were several of us watching it from the wings every night.

———————————

Last Friday night, my mom and I went to see the Alvin Theatre's newest musical, Big Fish.

I spent so much of my childhood picturing what Merrily We Roll Along *must have been like at the Alvin, that I never call the theater the Neil Simon—even though that's been its name since before I was born!*

We sat in the second to last row and watched a new musical unfold and I thought: Someone sat here and watched *Hairspray.* Someone sat here and watched *Forum.* Maybe I'm where Jose Llana had his coffee every day or where James Maloney took a break between running lights.

Norbert Leo Butz gave his second tour de force performance at the Alvin, over the course of only two years—and I thought: He's the Ethel Merman of his time! *I wondered if Kate Baldwin had Annie Golden's old dressing room, or if anyone had learned new material in the lower lobby where Sondheim had coached Jim Walton on "Our Time".*

When Big Fish *got out, the crowd from* Jersey Boys *was still lingering. I saw a Jersey Boy on the third floor wave at a* Big Fish *girl across the street.*

———————————

52nd Street

Brian Yorkey, Writer

We were in previews with *Catch Me If You Can*, with *Jersey Boys* across the street, when The Pogues did a concert at Roseland. The Pogues!

It was Spring Break, so that performance of *Catch Me* was packed with high schoolers. Intermission at both shows happened at about the same time, and simultaneously, The Pogues show was getting started.

For about 15 minutes, 52nd Street was flooded with high school students from all over the country, older, wealthy *Jersey Boys* fans, and drunk Irish people, all mixing together. They were *literally* mixing together and talking to each other and sharing cigarettes on 52nd Street.

I was with Marc Shaiman. We looked at it in awe, and I said, "This is a hell of a scene!" That's why I love Broadway. That's why I love New York.

The August Wilson Theatre

Built: 1925
Location: 245 West 52nd Street
Owner: Jujamcyn Theaters
Formerly Named: Guild Theatre (1925-1942), ANTA Playhouse (1950-1981), Virginia Theatre (1982-2005)
Longest-Running Show: *Jersey Boys* (2005-Present)
Shortest-Running Show: *The Stitch in Time* (closed before its first preview in 1980)
Number of Productions: 194

I had gone to see shows at the theater when it was the ANTA. I worked there when it was the Virginia. And now, it's the August Wilson.

-**Artie Gaffin**, Stage Manager

Introduction: Swinging At *Jersey Boys*

Jared Bradshaw, Actor

When I was younger, I came into the city to see *The Wild Party* at the Virginia and *Annie Get Your Gun* at the Marquis. I wanted to see Mandy Patinkin and Bernadette Peters in the same day. I remember that there was a big African American audience at *Wild Party* for Eartha Kitt, and when Mandy Patinkin came out in blackface, the lady next to me said: "I don't know what that cracker thinks he's doing!" That made me uncomfortable. The show had nudity, sex, and drugs. Oh my God, *The Wild Party*! Then I got the album and it's the most played thing on my iPod. I love that I saw it here, where I work now.

And I actually remember seeing the Virginia before that. It was my first trip to New York and we were driving down Broadway. I thought all of the theaters would actually be on Broadway, but, of course, they aren't. I looked down this one street and I saw *Smokey Joe's Cafe* at the Virginia. I thought: *Why isn't it on Broadway? What's* this *street!?* Later when I moved here, I saw *Little Women* here, and I saw *Little Shop of Horrors* and took a photo with Taye Diggs in the lobby.

My first contract here at *Jersey Boys*, I was covering a couple of roles. Now, the longer I'm with the show, the more roles I cover! I was hired as a Nick cover because I'm really a bass. But I have falsetto. I've actually gone on for every male role in the show except Frankie. I've played Joe Pesci, I've played the mob boss, I've played all of the other Four Seasons. That's what *Forbidden Broadway* did for me; it got me here. I did *Forbidden Broadway* for a while, and the casting director of *Jersey Boys* figured out I'd be a great fit to cover all these roles.

Some people think covering is death for your career. But I have a baby and a wife and an apartment to pay for. And I do not need to be a star. You know, every time I teach a class, I tell people: nobody grows up wanting to be an understudy. But I get to go to work every day at a job I love. And on a Sunday I get to star in a principal role on Broadway, and on a Tuesday, I get to get paid $1.73 a minute to sit in my dressing room and post pictures of my baby on Facebook. It's a blessing for a kid from Georgia to get to do that and be part of it.

Des McAnuff, our director, who also is known for *Big River* and *Tommy*, did such a great job with the show. There's this one part of the show where you get to see the song "Sherry" three different ways. You see it on the Ed Sullivan Show on screens, you see it sideways and you feel like you're in the studio, and you see them doing it in concert. There's another part of the show where "Dawn" happens, and you see the view from backstage and then you also have a wall of lights hit you, so you feel like you're in a stadium. You don't realize all these are happening, but they are what makes the show the ultimate backstage story. It's not just a jukebox musical; it uses these songs and shows you what it's really like. *Jersey Boys* looks like a screen and some stairs, but it's really a technologically amazing multimillion dollar production.

I can't wait for *Big Fish* to come in across the street, because then we can do Saturday Night on Broadway again! That's at five minute call where the Neil Simon and August Wilson Theatres have this tradition together. Through the windows and past the air conditioners, we'll all just scream bloody murder at each other. We sing each other songs, we do choreography, we blow bubbles. It's a magical thing!

For a long time, *Hairspray* was there, and they'd watch all the flops come through this theater, and now we're here, and we've watched several shows go in and out of *that* theater. We did the tradition with our friends who were in *Scandalous* and *Jesus Christ Superstar*. I don't think Harry Connick Jr. did it when he was in concert there!

I have a friend, John Michael Dias, who I did *Jersey Boys* with in Chicago. He had been playing Frankie Valli on the road for a while and decided he needed to come home to New York. Obviously, he was good enough to play the role on Broadway but there wasn't an open spot. So, he had to get another job. He's also an amazing seamstress and designer, and some of his friends who were in *Scandalous* got him a job there in wardrobe. I think deep down he thought it might suck because he wanted to be performing, but I said, "Man, that's awesome! You got a job dressing Carolee Carmello and George Hearn!" We got to be across the street from each other and would send each other pictures.

Then, *Scandalous* closed and he was out of work—although that marquee stayed up across the street from us forever! A month later, they called John and asked if he would play Frankie in *Jersey Boys* for a month of Saturday matinees. He went from dressing George Hearn across the street at the Neil Simon to starring as Frankie Valli at the August Wilson. It was his Broadway debut! Usually, when you see someone make their debut, it's in the ensemble, because most of us start there and then climb the ladder. But we got to watch John make his Broadway debut as Frankie, carrying this huge show and singing 27 songs. And he had done the show hundreds of times all over America so he was as cool as a cucumber! The stagehands were all like, "Who is this kid?! What a voice! Why is he so relaxed?"

After John's Broadway debut, we all went to Sardi's for dinner and then we came back to the theater for the night show. I made him stand on 52nd Street and take a photo midway between the *Jersey Boys* and *Scandalous* marquees. In the history of Broadway, who goes from dressing one show to starring in the other one across the street?!

John Lloyd Young, the original Frankie Valli in Jersey Boys, *was once an usher at the Hilton Theatre on Broadway during shows like* 42nd Street *and* Chitty Chitty Bang Bang. *He booked the lead role in* Jersey Boys *in 2005, and less than a year later, he won the Tony Award for Best Actor in a Musical. He recently finished filming the Hollywood motion picture version of* Jersey Boys, *directed by Clint Eastwood.*

1961: Conquering New York

John McMartin, Actor

The Conquering Hero was a musical adapted from a Preston Sturges film. Eddie Bracken played the lead in the film and Tom Poston played the lead in our show.

The show was in a bit of trouble from the beginning. When we were out of town, we all knew they were replacing the ingénue, but she didn't know it. They were rehearsing her replacement in another part of town, and we were still rehearsing with her. She was young and enthusiastic and had no idea the doom that was coming. Since it was my first Broadway show, I thought: *My God, is this the way it is?* I just didn't think you treated your own like that.

Then we got strange reviews and they replaced the director/choreographer, who was Bob Fosse! They hired a new choreographer who was a protégé of Balanchine, so you had all these earthbound Fosse dancers up on toe, feeling very dissatisfied about the change. I believe Fosse sued the production because they kept a lot of his choreography.

Then, we went into the ANTA Theatre, and the show closed in five days. That was my first Broadway theater and my first Broadway show. Again, I thought: *Is this the way Broadway shows are?* And of course, some of them are. However, I got to work with Fosse on four other shows, and it started there. We had a very good relationship, and he ended up being instrumental in my career.

———————

In 1925, President Calvin Coolidge announced the arrival of the Guild Theatre on Broadway by flipping a switch in Washington D.C. that turned the lights on for the theater's first production on 52nd Street, Helen Hayes in Caesar and Cleopatra. *The Theatre Guild would occupy the space until 1943.*

———————

1961: How Did They Do That?

Neil Mazzella, Technical Supervisor

I actually still have the Playbill for *A Man For All Seasons,* which was the first Broadway show I ever saw, back in 1961.

I remember that there were a series of blackouts throughout the show—and every time the lights came back up, the set had changed. I was amazed by that. I've spent the past 40 years trying to figure out how they did that.

1974: A Kid At The ANTA

Jeb Brown, Actor

I loved acting in local amateur productions when I was a kid. Then, when I was nine years old, the American Shakespeare Theatre in Stratford, CT announced a summer production of *Cat on a Hot Tin Roof,* and they had auditions for children. For my audition, I did an abbreviated version of the Gettysburg Address that I'd learned for a report on Abraham Lincoln in school. I had never done anything professional before, and I got the job. Thrilling!

I got $5 for rehearsals and $10 for performances. Our show starred Elizabeth Ashley, Fred Gwynne, Kate Reid and Keir Dullea. There were a lot of great people around as it was true rep and we were just one of three shows that summer. Fred was also doing Toby Belch, and Kate was doing the Nurse in *Romeo and Juliet* with Roberta Maxwell and David Birney. Although I didn't know it at the time, our producers Robert Whitehead and Roger L. Stephens were aiming the show for a Broadway run. At that time, *Cat on a Hot Tin Roof* hadn't been on Broadway since the original. When the summer ended, they came to my mother and said, "Would you consider having Jeb go with the show to Broadway?" She was by no means a stage mom, and really had no idea what she was getting into, but she cared about the theatre, and took the plunge, thinking: *Well, this will be an experience.*

We were at the ANTA. I remember it well. I remember the lined linoleum floor, the burlap bulletin board where I signed in, the long climb to our dressing room. I was on the top floor. This was back in the day when the stage managers would also be understudies. One night, I remember the actor playing Doc Baugh went on for Big Daddy, and our stage manager, Bob, went on as Doc Baugh. He had this little kit of mustaches and eye glasses, and I watched him pick which one to use in the show, and then stage manage in character all night long. I thought that was cool, that he still had his clipboard with him, running the show, but was doing it in costume with a mustache.

This was before automation, so backstage there were a bunch of crew guys standing by huge walls of levers. They would put their hands on numbers 19 and 32, and wait for the cue. When the cue came, they'd pull the huge lever down, and that's how the lights changed. That doesn't happen anymore. That's all gone. I would enjoy watching those guys do their thing.

The kids had the green room underneath the stage to ourselves. Right next to the green room was the wardrobe room, run by an older woman whose name was Mary Lincoln. At age nine I thought: *Is that* the *Mary Lincoln?!* She was that old. My mother told me that it wasn't.

I remember all of it so well because it mattered so much to me. That was the beautiful thing. I had been taken to the theatre a lot as a kid, and I was hip to what a big deal it was. I knew how much I already loved it, and there we were, doing one of those shows in one of those houses on one of those streets. It made a huge impression on me.

One of the girls who played my sister in *Cat* was one of the original orphans in *Annie* a couple seasons later. So my family was onto *Annie* before anyone knew what it was. That was neat, because we saw it so early and then it became a mega-hit.

Shenandoah was across the street from us, at the Alvin, and there were a couple young kids in that one, too. We didn't hang out with them, but we were definitely aware that there were other kids on the block. There was a penny arcade on the Northwest corner of 52nd Street and Broadway at that time, and we'd all go there, the *Shenandoah* kids and the *Cat on a Hot Tin Roof* kids. It was a dazzling penny arcade, huge and old-style, with skee ball and air hockey and pinball—a pre-video games arcade. There was an old magician at a little magic counter, there to demonstrate tricks that you could buy and try out yourself. My whole year was spent going from that theater to the magic shop, deciding which trick I wanted to save up to buy next.

1977: Dynamic Material

Stephen Flaherty, Writer

The first Broadway show I ever saw was *Bubbling Brown Sugar* at the ANTA! It was the summer of Sam and I was 16 years old, visiting New York from Pittsburgh, with my friend. His brother lived in a building with a vacant apartment, and that's where we stayed: 1E at the end of the hallway. Not only was there no lock on the door, there weren't even hinges! At night, we'd go in there and my friend's brother would say: "Are you all tucked in?" and then he would lean the door against the door frame. Already, New York was dangerous and wild.

We went to get twofers[31] and saw *Bubbling Brown Sugar*. I just remember feeling like the performers were amazing. I was blown away. There was an actress named Vivian Reed, who was actually from my hometown of Pittsburgh! She was extraordinary, an amazing artist, and I thought: *I should just quit.* What she did was so

---

[31] twofers: slang term for "two for the price of one" tickets

dynamic and thrilling. But then I realized that with my writing, potentially, I could create something that would really give dynamic and thrilling performers a chance to hone in on material. I could live vicariously from the wings or the audience and watch amazing performers. That's what I decided I wanted to do.

1978: A History Of *A History of the American Film*

Christopher Durang, Writer

In hindsight, the title "*A History of the American Film*" is probably a bad one. It's a comic title once you've seen the show, because it sounds so scholarly, although the play itself is so playful and funny.

The show follows four archetypes from Hollywood movies, the girl, modeled after Mary Pickford or Loretta Young, the tough guy like James Cagney or Humphrey Bogart, the tough gal like Bette Davis, and the young innocent man, who I called Hank after Henry Fonda. The style of the piece changes throughout, as the characters go through all of these archetypal film situations from the entire 20th century, from silent film to the Depression with gangsters to this Busby Berkeley musical to World War Two to alcoholism to disaster movies. The characters keep dying but coming back to life.

The play started out in the O'Neill National Playwrights Conference in 1976, and then three regional theaters wanted it, and somehow my agent convinced all three of them to do it as a joint premiere. So the show had productions at Hartford Stage in Connecticut, the Mark Taper Forum in L.A. and Arena Stage in Washington D.C. The show got excellent reviews, and two young producers brought a variation of the Arena Stage production to Broadway.

The show had songs in it, so I actually got a Tony nomination for Best Book of a Musical, although the show was more accurately a play with music.

The ANTA felt like a very big theater to me. The back of the orchestra made you feel like you were in a sardine can because the balcony was so low right over your head. That's what I really remember about it. We actually almost went to the O'Neill Theatre, but we used the set that was built for Arena Stage and it couldn't fit in the O'Neill load-in dock.

A History of the American Film had 32 scenes, which was an enormous amount for a play. When it was done at the O'Neill, we had these convertible set pieces that people could sit on and then turn into tables. It was a very unrealistic way of telling the story, but the set changes were done really fast, and you could always figure out what was going on from the dialogue. In every other production, there was this understandable temptation to be elaborate with the show, especially because the play jumps from vegetables dancing in "*We're in a Salad*" to Citizen Kane's mansion to jitter bug in the canteens to 1950s Academy Awards ceremonies. The Arena production was especially elaborate, and the backstage was filled with these young, bushy-tailed kids hoping to make it in our profession jumping through hoops to make the sets move on time and organizing the just crazy fast changes. On Broadway, there were just so many costume changes that for the first couple of nights the poor professional stagehands were in shock.

Our production on Broadway was not as good as it had been regionally. If the audience was sitting more than two thirds of the way back, they missed a lot of the funny, intricate acting that was happening. Later, I saw other shows at the theater, when it became the Virginia, that I thought fit very well. A larger musical than ours works well there, but we were a quirky small one. It wasn't a disaster, it was a well done show. It just didn't exactly fit in the theater.

Oh if only we could have one of the intimate Broadway houses, such as the Booth or the Golden. (I got my wish for the Golden for my play *Vanya and Sonia and Masha and Spike*—34 years later!)

224

During A History of the American Film, *the musicians only played for about 20 minutes, so every night, the musicians would go under the stage and out the pass door into the lobby, and then watch from the audience.*

To the right of the bar in the lobby of the August Wilson is a door that leads directly backstage. When I interviewed Jared Bradshaw, he took me on a tour of the entire theater, and we walked through. The door leads to the basement, where the wardrobe room, audio booth and crew offices are, as well as several sets that move up and down by elevator.

The lobby ceiling is odd and slanted, and that's because it mirrors the shape of the orchestra seats above. If you're standing behind the lobby bar downstairs, you are directly below the first row of seats in the audience!

1981: Kiss Of Death Davis

Penny Davis, Wardrobe Supervisor/Dresser

Copperfield was quick. We worked like dogs out of town in St. Louis. Then we came in and worked like dogs again. Then we closed.

There were many nice people in that company. Mary Stout was terrific. George Irving was great. Mary Elizabeth Mastrantonio got her start there. Everybody was really nice, and it would have been nice if it had run. But it wasn't a very good show.

I remember John Simon's review that made my costume designer very angry. He wrote, "Too exposed." Leslie Denniston had so many quick changes with these 1840s gowns, so we had a lot of bows in the show. We were masking snaps and zippers and things, and hiding them with bows.

That was the first Broadway musical Peter Lawrence did as production stage manager. That's when he announced that he wanted to one day rule the Broadway world. He did: his career flourished. I did a number of shows with him.

That was the year, from 1981 to 1982, that I nicknamed myself "Kiss of Death Davis." In the wardrobe world, everybody gets to be "Kiss of Death" for a time, when every show you touch closes. That year, I did about five shows in one year's time: *Duet for One, Copperfield*... They all came and went very quickly. I'd have to look at my resume to remember what they were.

In noting the "Shortest-Running Show" at each theater for this book, I only considered shows that closed prior to their first preview if the show had already notably moved into the theater. In the case of The Stitch In Time, *the new play by Pulitzer Prize winner Marc Connelly was to begin previews in January of 1981 and open in February. The show was co-directed, co-produced, and written by Marc.*

On December 13 of 1980, Marc was given an award at City Center in honor of his 90th birthday. On December 21, he died unexpectedly. The show moved into the ANTA on December 29, but did not end up continuing past rehearsals.

1981: We're Closing Tonight

Harry Groener, Actor

If we did *Oh, Brother!* now, we would get bombed! The show basically makes fun of an Arabic revolution. It's an innocent, fluffy piece though, with two actors in a camel suit wearing huge green sunglasses and pink tennis shoes. It's silly! It was extremely entertaining, and the audiences during previews fell out of their seats with laughter. It had great songs by Michael Valenti, and the orchestrations by Jim Tyler had that great, old-fashioned Broadway sound.

I loved *Oh, Brother!* We had a great time doing it. I could've done that show for a long time. Judy Kaye stopped the show every single performance with her number. We would all stand backstage together and look at the clock to time her applause. Five seconds... ten seconds... 15 seconds... it would never be less than 30 seconds of applause! It would go on and on, and we'd be standing backstage saying, "Go! Go! Make it to a minute!"

Then the critics eviscerated the show. We opened on a Tuesday night, and when we came back the next day for the Wednesday matinee, they said, "Well, our reviews weren't very good, and we'll be closing at the end of the week." We did the matinee, went to dinner before our night show, got back to the theater, and were told, "We're closing tonight."

We weren't ready for that. We all adored each other. We all loved the show. And we thought we had until Sunday—then BAM! We were hit in the face with this: "We're closing tonight."

That was a really hard final performance. It was difficult to sing, because we all looked at each other and just cried. And after that third and final performance, we all carried our opening night gifts and flowers out the stage door and took them home.

1986: The Dresses Turned Black

Artie Gaffin, Stage Manager

Wild Honey was the first Broadway show I ever worked on. I went to the theater a lot as a kid, but I never got to go backstage. We didn't have any connections to the theatre, so being at the Virginia was my first time ever backstage. I had this romantic vision that backstage on Broadway would be so beautiful and it would look like an old movie.

But do you know what backstage is? It's like an apartment that you rent, and you know a certain abuse has been done to it, so you put on a clean coat of paint. Broadway theaters backstage are like paint over paint over paint. The pipes are always showing, and you get old-fashioned heating units.

Most of the old theaters were built for drops and not for the complicated sets that we have now. Sometimes, when sets are put in, there's just no room for a crossover, so people have to go downstairs and through the basement to get to the other side of the stage. *Wild Honey* took place in the 19th century, so the dresses in the show had trains on them. After the first dress rehearsal, the wardrobe supervisor took a look at the dresses and burst into tears. The amount of dirt and dust that was picked up when the women went from stage right to stage left in the basement had turned the trains of their dresses black!

———————

I always love walking down the street past the door to the Theatre Guild offices, to the left of the August Wilson. Of course, the Theatre Guild hasn't been there for years, but in the 1920s, the Theatre Guild's leaders built both the theater and the offices attached.

The Theatre Guild was founded to produce non-commercial plays on Broadway—essentially it was the precursor to the modern day not-for-profit. Run in large part by Theresa Helburn and Lawrence Langner, the Guild had many years of plenty, premiering plays by Eugene O'Neill and gay returns of the hit revue, The Garrick Gaieties*. In its driest moment, after more than a dozen flops in a row, the Guild was in danger of closing its doors for good.*

It was in those years that the Guild had a sharp young press assistant named Helene Hanff. Helene was a struggling playwright, who had had no luck in getting Ms. Helburn to produce her plays, but a bit of luck in landing a spot at the copy desk.

During the time that the Guild was in trouble, Helene had been made weary by working on so many financial disasters in a row. The next show to come in was being bad mouthed out of town, with a new writing team culled of one collaborator whose partner was dying and one who hadn't had a hit in years. The night before the show was to open in New York, Helene stayed up from dusk until dawn, stamping hundreds of exclamation points after the name of the show in its program. The creators had decided on a whim that the title needed an exclamation point.

That title was Oklahoma!

Helene tells that story in Underfoot in Show Business[32]*, her memoir from when she was a 20-something, trying to make it in showbiz in 1940s New York City. Her partner in crime is Maxine, a struggling actress, and together, they experience all things theatrical, from the joys of summer stock to second acting to getting the gossip at the drugstore counter.*

The first page of the book reads:

"Each year, hundreds of stagestruck kids arrive in New York determined to crash the theatre, firmly convinced they're destined to be famous Broadway stars or playwrights. One in a thousand turns out to be Noel Coward. This book is about life among the other 999. By one of them."

Years later, Helene Hanff became a successful playwright. Her works include 22 Charing Cross Road*, a Broadway play that later became a movie starring Anne Bancroft.*

1988: You're Never Gonna Last At The Virginia

Charlotte D'Amboise, Actor

I did *Carrie* at the Virginia Theatre, and people always think that place has a black cloud around it. Before I went in with *Carrie*, I remember someone saying to me, "Oh, you're never gonna last at the Virginia! It's too far uptown." And now, *Jersey Boys* has been there for years. We were only there for two weeks with *Carrie*, though.

Because *Carrie* was so fast, I don't remember the theater as well as the other ones I've worked in. I remember we could open our windows and see the show across the street, but I don't remember what was there. I really only remember my dressing room.

My favorite thing was to watch Linzi Hateley and Betty Buckley do their material in the show. They were so spectacular. But I also remember getting booed at by the audience. I called my mom, and I said, "Mom, I think they were booing at us! It's crazy!"

---

[32] Helene Hanff, *Underfoot in Show Business* (Harper and Row, 1962).

1988: The Sound Of *Carrie*

Steve C. Kennedy, Sound Designer

It was interesting working on *Carrie*. We had a load-in and then we had to stop for a week, because they ran out of money or there was another problem. We worked around-the-clock to get to that first preview. It ended up running for five performances.

For Broadway shows, the sound equipment is all rented from a shop, so after *Carrie* closed, we had to get all of our equipment out fast, because another show needed it right away. That was the end of it.

1988: Not Involved

Michael Starobin, Orchestrator

I was not that involved in previews of *Carrie* because they decided that the problem with *Carrie* was the orchestrations.

————————

In 1943, the Theatre Guild leased their house to a radio station. In 1953, it changed hands again, and was placed under the auspices of the American National Theatre and Academy, or ANTA, who ran it until 1981.

In 1981, Jujamcyn, owned by manufacturing tycoon William McKnight and corporation owner James H. Binger, bought the theater and named it the Virginia for Virginia McKnight Binger (William's daughter and James' wife). The name Jujamcyn itself is comprised of the names of the three grandchildren of McKnight: Judy, James, and Cynthia.

Jujamcyn began their reign on Broadway in 1957, when they obtained the St. James from the Shuberts. Around the time that Jujamcyn bought what is now the August Wilson in 1981, they reached a total of five theaters on Broadway. At that point, the Nederlanders owned ten and the Shuberts owned 16 and a half (the Irving Berlin estate owned half of the Music Box), but no third organization had ever reached a count as high as five.

————————

1989: *City Of Angels* Auditions

Frank Vlastnik, Actor

I've spent some time working as an audition reader in theaters. I was the audition reader for all of the original *City of Angels* auditions, and they were in the Virginia, where the show would play.

When we were there, the walls were still painted black from *Carrie*. There were tarps over the house, because they were starting to renovate the theater back to how it was, pre-*Carrie*. Between the tarps, there was one uncovered section of the house where Cy Coleman, Michael Blakemore, Larry Gelbart, and some of the other *City of Angels* production folks would sit. All of the auditioners were waiting in the star dressing room, which has an inner area and an outer area.

Randy Graff came in and she said to me, "What's everything like?" I told her there was plastic all over everything, and the theater looked a bit odd. We chatted. Three different times, I've seen Randy give the best auditions I've seen in my life.

When she walked out on stage, I announced, "This is Randy Graff," and she said, "Oh my God, look at all the plastic on the furniture. It looks like my Aunt Judy's house!" She made everyone laugh, and immediately, she had them in the palm of her hand. She sang "Murder He Says", which is a Frank Loesser-Jimmy McHugh song that Betty Hutton made famous.

The creative team told her the song was fantastic. Then they were buzzing, and Cy Coleman called out, "Randy, do you know a song of mine called "Nobody Does It Like Me" from *Seesaw*?" We found out later it was very similar to "You Can Always Count On Me" from *City of Angels*. Randy said, "Yeah, I do! It used to be my audition song." Then, they didn't have the music—so Cy Coleman came up on stage and played it for her himself.

Her "Nobody Does It Like Me" was incredible, and then she read a scene and was hilarious. I think that they were originally thinking of more of an Eve Arden type for the role of Oolie/Donna. Randy is smaller and more heartbreaking, because she just has that way of making you fall in love with her. She took them in a different direction.

After "Nobody Does It Like Me", she said, "You know what? I got my first Equity job singing that song." The creative team looked at each other and said, "She just got this job singing that song, too."

1989: The Tony Race

Chris Boneau, Press Agent

The August Wilson was the Virginia when *City of Angels* was playing. At the very beginning of my time in New York, I was doing personal press for a lot of Broadway people. I wouldn't call them "stars" because the people who hired me had the featured roles. I had the good fortune of doing personal press for a couple of actors in *City of Angels*.

I immediately bonded with Randy Graff, and she was the very first person I represented who won a Tony Award. Randy and I have the same birthday, May 23rd, and we call each other "Twin." During the Tony season, I was fairly new at this. I didn't really know what you were supposed to do! I helped her find her dress, and I would go visit the Virginia and talk to her all the time. I came up with ideas for press that she would feel comfortable doing; we got her making singing appearances.

We've had many, many Tony wins in my office at Boneau/Bryan-Brown. We've been very lucky. We have been associated with 181 Tony Awards! But when I look back, the one that mattered to me most was Randy's. It's ironic because Jane Krakowski was in the same category that year for *Grand Hotel*—we're very close friends, but I didn't know her as well then.

Looking back on Randy's win, it still gives me chills. I hosted a little party in my apartment for her beforehand and then we went to the Tony Awards and it was just a great, great night. My friend won a Tony Award and it was the first one I was ever involved with.

1989: Reveal Applause

Randy Graff, Actor

We had four weeks of previews for *City of Angels*. The first two weeks of previews, my friends and my agents were coming, and they were saying, "Oh, I don't know about this. I don't know."

The audience reaction was slightly lukewarm because we hadn't figured out the rhythm of the show yet. It was so technical! And there were rumors going around that they wanted to close us. We were in bad shape.

It absolutely came together during the last two weeks because of the genius of Michael Blakemore. We finally found our technical rhythm—and the audience reaction changed as well.

I remember the night after I won the Tony Award, because it was the first time I ever got entrance applause—or reveal applause, because I didn't make an entrance, I was just revealed!

My dressing room was really, really tiny, and I shared it with Dee Hoty. We had a landline! We were catalog shopping all the time, dialing 1-800 numbers. One time, I almost missed my entrance because I was in the middle of some order with J. Crew.

The stage area was a little scary because we needed a bigger space, so all of the set pieces were hung over us. Just hovering over us! I always found that a little frightening. The minute a stage piece came off, the guys would hoist it up with ropes and bring another one down. We were crowded back there.

My idol came. Elaine Stritch! She came up to my dressing room during *City of Angels* and was very, very complimentary. That was a standout moment for me. There were a lot of fancy people during that time. Maggie Smith, Angela Lansbury, Plácido Domingo... it was very exciting. And I've got pictures with all of them.

City of Angels was the coolest, greatest opening night party I've ever been to. It was at Roseland. It was like an old-fashioned, old-school opening night party. Because of the music and because of Cy Coleman, we had a band on stage, and they sounded like a real 1940s big band!

At opening night parties, around 10:30, word gets out of whether or not you got a good review in the *New York Times*. We got a great review in the *New York Times* from Frank Rich! They stopped the party, and they read it to everyone at the party, up on the bandstand. It was very old-school. It was beautiful.

Chris Reeve, God bless him, he was there. And *he* came up to *me*! I actually have a picture with the two of us. He was completely smitten with musical theatre. He said to me, "Oh, Randy, I knew the minute those opening chords of the orchestra began. I knew I was at a great Broadway show."

1989: The Crew Was Choreographed

Michael Rupert, Actor/Writer

When we did *City of Angels* in the early 1990s, the tracking of the sets wasn't computerized yet. Everything was still moved by a stagehand who was at a control. He would actually say "on stage" and "off stage" as the performance was happening. It was right before everything became computerized!

There was one moment in *City of Angels* when I had to come in, in the dark, and two sets would move off as I came out. There was a young, new crew member who was just learning the ropes. He was moving the sets during that performance. Sure enough, he moved them the wrong way, just as I was going through. The sets smashed, and slammed into me—fast. I didn't realize until I was in the middle of the next scene that I had cut my leg badly. All of a sudden I feel something wet on my leg, so I look down and there's blood all over my pants. Those things happen sometimes!

The August Wilson was the Virginia at the time that we did *City of Angels*, and it was a tough house to be in because *City of Angels* was a relatively big show and there was *no* space off stage. It was a big company, for such a small theater. And every set piece had to be rigged in the air. It was fascinating watching how the crew of *City*

230

of Angels was choreographed backstage to winch[33] those set pieces. We had a stack about four high, and they had to get them down at the exact right times, get them on palettes, get them out to the exact right spots. It was really like choreography. It was hard.

Backstage was absolute chaos most of the time. It was actually as challenging getting to the stage as it was to perform the show!

––––––––––

City of Angels had 46 scene changes—and a stage manager calling a cue every seven seconds!

In several interviews at the time, the bookwriter, Larry Gelbart, confessed that the Hollywood hardships endured by the screenwriter trying to maneuver the system in City of Angels *were somewhat based on his own experiences making films, most notably the recent hit,* Tootsie.

––––––––––

1992: Shows About Real Life

Tonya Pinkins, Actor

I auditioned to do *Jelly's Last Jam* at the Mark Taper in Los Angeles on a Friday, and rehearsals started that Tuesday. That original production was very different from what we opened with on Broadway, and Obba Babatunde played Jelly Roll Morton.

When we got to the Virginia, Gregory Hines was our Jelly, and we were making humongous changes in previews every day. Someone told me our first preview was four hours long! There were many parts of the show that were cut, including this extraordinary number I loved, where the cast came out of gorgeous porcelain-looking boxes with masks of Gregory's face on. Then, they'd turn the masks around and you'd see their faces were painted as coons with black, black faces and red, red lips. Before that part was cut, the boxes just wouldn't open one night, and the actors were trapped in them.

Because *Jelly's* was so technically complicated, there were a couple times when scenic failures destroyed things. One night, a hydraulic lift in the show came out when it wasn't supposed to and destroyed the on stage piano. Gregory went into his nightclub act, which was fantastic! He was a consummate performer who had been on stage since he was three years old.

After that, any time something went wrong, Gregory would do his act. The audience loved it. Eventually, George had to remind Gregory that he was playing a character, and he couldn't do that; if something went wrong, he'd have to respond as the character would. He started doing that, but it was a big adjustment for him. He felt more secure as a performer than an actor, and he liked doing all of his tried and true stuff.

My favorite part of the show to do every night was "Lovin' Is A Lowdown Blues". Gregory was very improvisational, so the show was new and fresh and alive every day. We liked to play, so we were always challenging and testing each other. It was great.

The *Jelly's* company would circle up before every show and pray. We did that during *Caroline, or Change* and *Play On!* as well. I've found that happens more in companies of African Americans. My daughter was born during *Play On!* so that was great, because we had a baby in the prayer circle.

––––––––––

––––––––––

[33] winch: to move large pieces of scenery on and off stage, often that have tracking embedded in the deck

The star dressing room at the August Wilson Theatre is often the singular room that is off stage left, directly in the wings. However, currently, during Jersey Boys, *this room is a quick change booth, filled with racks of dresses and holders for wrist watches that the male ensemble members wear in different scenes. That room was once Sutton Foster's dressing room, during* Little Women. *It was once Elizabeth Ashley's during* Cat On A Hot Tin Roof. *Since whoever is playing Frankie Valli in* Jersey Boys *barely leaves the stage, he doesn't need an easily accessible dressing room during performances.*

Other stars at the August Wilson over the years have included everyone from Humphrey Bogart in The Mask and the Face *(1933) to Henry Fonda in* Our Town *(1969). Rosalind Russell made her Broadway debut at the theater, in* The Garrick Gaieties *in 1930.*

––––––––––

1992: *Jelly's* Journey

Margo Lion, Producer

I grew up in Baltimore, and I always loved the theatre. Then, I figured out that I was also very interested in history and politics. I had been an actress, but I knew I wasn't that great, and what I really loved about the theatre was being in the company of artists. I think that's what landed me in this business more than anything else.

I moved to New York in 1967 and worked for Robert Kennedy on his campaign. Through his office, one thing I worked on was a program with a lot of theatre producers to help under-served kids see shows and have opportunities in the arts. When the senator was killed, I didn't know what to do with myself, and my soon-to-be husband said, "Well, you can be a nurse or you can be a teacher." Being a nurse didn't really appeal to me, so I taught school for six years.

When I was married with a child and living in Vermont, my then-husband got accepted at the University of Iowa for playwriting, and I spent the next couple years with my husband's friends who were writers. I really enjoyed hearing about the work they were doing and having responses to it. I thought: *These are the people I want to spend my time with.*

I came back to New York, and I knew I had no particular skill. I didn't write, I didn't direct, I didn't act, I didn't design, I didn't stage manage. I thought: *I love to put things and people together and think of ideas for projects, so maybe being a producer is the thing I'd like to do.* My cousin Martha was the only one I knew who really knew anybody in the business, so I called her. She said, "Well, I know this woman, Lyn Austin, a producer who works for Music-Theater Group/Lenox Arts Center."

I apprenticed with Lyn for five years. I did everything from delivering press releases on my bike with my son on the back, to sweeping dressing room floors, to helping raise money, to coming up with projects. It was a great education. I had a lot of freedom to learn while I was there, and what I learned is that I wanted to work on theatre that appealed to a larger audience. I also learned that I really wanted to combine my interests in American history and theatre.

That was a time when there were a lot of revues: *Eubie, Sophisticated Ladies, Ain't Misbehavin'.* There were shows like that featuring the work of jazz composers and lyricists, and I thought: *Well, I want to do a show that shows where jazz came from.* I asked a jazz drummer I knew, "If we were going to do a show about the origins of jazz through a prism, what figure would tell that story?" He replied, "You should listen to the interviews that Alan Lomax did with Jelly Roll Morton in the 1930s."

That began an 11-year journey to tell both Jelly Roll Morton's story and the story of how jazz started and became the most unique American art form.

In the meantime, I produced a series of award-winning shows off-Broadway that didn't make any money. On *How I Got That Story*, I met Pam Koslow, a producer who was married to Gregory Hines. I proposed the show to her and Gregory ended up being interested in directing. We couldn't find anyone interested in writing the show. I think this was primarily because in the collected Morton interviews, he comes off as a sort-of self-hating person of color, and at that point in the early 1980s, no African American wanted to take on a job writing about someone who hated his own people.

I had split from my husband by that time, and was living with a guy who was a writer. He took a crack at the story and wrote a serviceable script. We did a reading, and Gregory decided he didn't want to direct; he wanted to be in it. So, we did three or four presentations next with Gregory as Morton. Stan Lathan, who works with Russell Simmons, was the director.

Things were different then in terms of rules for presentations, and the attorney general's office tried to shut us down because we didn't have our offering papers out. It was dramatic. And at first, nobody of any weight even came! We invited everyone, and no one came to the first presentation. By the fourth presentation, we couldn't get all the people who showed up into the room. The word of mouth was fantastic. It was largely because of Gregory and Savion Glover, who was also in it.

After that presentation, I said, "This isn't the show I wanted to do." It didn't explore anything in depth. I parted ways with the writer, and then I made a stupid mistake. The hottest African American writer at the time was August Wilson, and the hottest director was Jerry Zaks. Idiotically, I put them together even though they couldn't have been more different. August had only ever seen one musical in his life. This was my education; I was learning on the job.

August Wilson and Jerry Zaks worked for a year trying to create a new script. August wrote a play and then every ten pages, there were six Jelly Roll Morton songs. It just wasn't right. This was around 1987 and then he won the Pulitzer Prize for *The Piano Lesson*, and I had to fire him. He didn't care; I later produced two plays of his and we became good friends. Jerry went off to do *Miss Saigon*, which he later ended up not doing after all.

This was many years into the project and now I had no director and no script. My friend, the press agent Richard Kornberg, said to me, "You should really get down to the Public and see *The Colored Museum*. It was created by a terrific African American writer." That's how I met George C. Wolfe. I asked if he wanted to write the show, and he was pretty broke, so he said yes.

George had no idea how he was going to do it. This was around 1987. He brought in Susan Birkenhead to work with some of the original Morton lyrics. George struggled for a couple years trying to find a way into this story about a very complicated man who denied his roots.

While this was all happening, I had met Rocco Landesman and Jack and Tom Viertel. We did *Frankie and Johnny* and *I Hate Hamlet* together. I was continuing to learn during this period. Of course, there were times when I thought: *Let's just throw this Jelly Roll Morton idea away!* But Pam was a good partner and she always convinced me that we could do it.

Then, in 1990, I did my first big job money-raising as a producer. I raised a million dollars because I was going to do *Annie 2*, which was going to be the next big blockbuster musical.

At the same time, we had a reading of *Jelly's* at my apartment. Gordon Davidson from the Taper was there, because he was interested in George's work. It was so excruciatingly hot that it was unbearable, and it was a horrible reading. I think it was the worst reading I've ever been to in my life.

Afterward, Gordon and Pam and I talked and said, "We've got to let this go." I said, "It's my fault. It was my idea, and it was a bad idea." We went back into the living room to tell everyone else that, and George, in a way that only George can do, leaped up out of his seat and said, "No no no no! I know how I can do this now! I know!" He'd had some conversations with Joe Papp that were helpful, and he had seen this version read, and he was convinced he could do it now. We all were doubtful at this point, but Gordon said, "We'll give you until December and then we'll do one more reading in Los Angeles."

That fall, I was raising the money for *Annie 2* and I thought *Jelly's* was pretty much dead, and that was that. I went to Washington D.C. to see *Annie 2*, and believe me, there is nothing louder than 2400 people *not* clapping. The show was a disaster, and I was pretty bummed. Then I had to get on a plane to L.A. for the last gasp of life of *Jelly's Last Jam*.

I read the material on the plane and I couldn't understand what the hell George had written. I got to L.A. and I got strep throat. My car broke down on the way to the reading.

Then I got to the reading and it was magic. The show had turned into magic. Gordon said he would give us a slot at the Taper the following season. Gregory didn't like what George had done with the material, and he wouldn't star in the show. We had a very hard time raising the enhancement money[34] for the L.A. production, but we did it. Then we were trying for Broadway, and Gregory came out and saw what the show had become, and said, "I'll do it."

We got back to New York and had another workshop and more backer's auditions. Sam Cohn, the powerful agent, said, "If this show is ever a success, I'll eat my hat!" There were all these people who had no faith in it.

Rocco was the president of Jujamcyn at the time, and he did a lot of things to make the show happen. We got the Virginia. We couldn't afford to do another out of town with the new show. The first preview was almost four hours long and during the next couple weeks, we changed the entire second act and all of the scenery.

Actually, we had to cancel the first two planned previews because we were behind in tech and having all sorts of creative disagreements. Paul Libin, who was the producing director of Jujamcyn, is one of the greatest people, and he said publicly, "Well, the lobby is being torn up so we can't possibly have these first two previews." The lobby was being renovated, and he gave us the perfect out. Canceling previews might have caused us to attract some bad word-of-mouth but because of him, it didn't.

Then we opened on Broadway and got very good reviews. Gregory won the Tony and Tonya won the Tony and we should've won the Tony but we didn't. And that was really my beginning.

The creators of Les Mis *and* Miss Saigon, *Alain Boublil and Claude-Michel Schonberg, originally thought that Trevor Nunn would be offered* Miss Saigon. *Cameron Mackintosh felt he needed an American director to take on the more contemporary story, so he offered the job to Jerry Zaks. When there were no large Broadway theaters available,* Miss Saigon's *debut in New York was postponed. The Theatre Royal Drury Lane in London became available, but Jerry Zaks wasn't available to spend as much time as was needed working in London. Cameron Mackintosh offered* Miss Saigon *to Nick Hytner.*

Miss Saigon *opened on Broadway during the 1990-1991 season and ran for ten years. The next season,* Jelly's Last Jam *finally made it to Broadway to great acclaim, as did the landmark* Guys And Dolls *revival, directed by Jerry Zaks.*

---

[34] enhancement money: money that a commercial producer gives to a not-for-profit production

1992: A Drink In The Middle Of The Second Act

Jack Viertel, Creative Director of Jujamcyn Theaters

There are some shows that were basically always hits from the beginning, like *Hairspray*. Then there are other shows that were really in trouble, that could've easily gone down the sewer, but didn't.

The examples of the latter that always come to mind for me are *Grand Hotel, City of Angels*, and *Jelly's Last Jam*. Those three were in serious trouble after the first preview of their first production—and two of those were at the Virginia. They got themselves out of trouble little by little, preview by preview.

Jelly's Last Jam had a second act that went on for days. The show is a rags to riches to rags story, and in those, the fall is always less interesting than the rise, especially when it's driven by ego or substance. We've seen that story so many times. Another problem with the second act is that Jelly Roll Morton had three wives, so we were trying to incorporate that.

Three or four nights before the critics came, we thought: *We've fixed it! It's a great second act.* Then on press night, I was watching the show, and I realized it wasn't fixed. I didn't feel like watching anymore, so I went across the street to Gallagher's to have a drink in the middle of the second act.

Every producer on the show was already there; I was the last one to get there. Everybody had the same reaction to the show that night. There's something that happens when you gather a bunch of people at a show who are going to write about it: you can suddenly see what you couldn't see the night before. When you're watching a show with people who don't have any stake in it, but who are there to write about it, that always happens.

―――――――――――

Gallagher's is where Black Patent Leather Shoes *celebrated its opening night in 1982, it's where the* Cyrano *cast went out with their producers in 1993, and it's where the* Jelly's Last Jam *team went for an act two drink in 1992. Gallagher's has as long a history on 52nd Street as either of the theaters do.*

In fact, Gallagher's and Funny Face, *the first attraction at the Alvin Theatre, opened just nights apart from each other in 1927. The restaurant was initially opened by Helen Gallagher, a former* Ziegfeld Follies *girl. She was married to the famous vaudevillian, Edward Gallagher, when the restaurant opened, but within two years, she divorced Edward and married the infamous gambler Jack Solomon. Gallagher's became a hotspot during Prohibition, as the restaurant was teeming with bootleg hooch and showgirls. After booze was made legal, it became the first real steakhouse on Broadway. Today, it remains a Times Square legend in its own right.*

Before the two current Broadway theaters had been built on 52nd Street, Gallagher's had been a different theatre haunt entirely! In 1927, the room had been Chez Evelyn, a nightclub owned by a former showgirl: post-scandal Evelyn Nesbit, who was then in her 40s.

Evelyn Nesbit grew up penniless in Pittsburgh in the 1880s and 1890s. By 1901, she was the belle of New York City, the image of the new century in America. Her face was plastered on ads for Coke and Vanity Fair; her silhouette was praised in Broadway shows and in the first fashion photography. She was seen in the arms of several famous men, including the infamously womanizing architect, Stanford White—with whom her sexual escapades on a red velvet swing became well known. In 1906, Evelyn's millionaire playboy husband, Harry K. Thaw, shot and killed Stanford White in the rooftop theatre of Madison Square Garden, and she became the center of the most famous scandal of the era.

After a widely publicized trial, Harry was sent to prison. Having received no money to live on, Evelyn struggled to find work in show business. In May of 1921, she opened a place called The Evelyn Nesbit Specialty Food Shop on

52nd Street in order to support herself, her mother and her son. Evelyn lived in an apartment above the store, and the place was said to be a secret cocaine den.

Before the year was up, the place was robbed and a burglar made away with cigarettes, silverware, and roast chickens. Later that week, police came to claim the building from Evelyn, intending to seize it for a real estate entity involving the Shuberts. Evelyn rushed to the Shuberts' theatrical office and got a temporary reprieve for the rent she was behind in paying. Even with the reprieve, she couldn't pay, and when city marshals began putting her belongings in the street, she overdosed on morphine. She was narrowly saved from death and the Shuberts gave her another reprieve.

The suicide attempt earned her enough attention to gain some customers for a time, but before February of 1922, she was permanently evicted and moved into the apartment building next door on 52nd Street. The Specialty Shop building is now a parking garage next to Roseland Ballroom.

By 1927, Evelyn had moved to the ritzier Chez Evelyn across the street, named in her honor. She was playing hostess at the wild speakeasy located at 228 West 52nd Street one night when Harry K. Thaw, then released from jail, came in and made a scene, throwing glassware. By the end of that year, its namesake had quit Chez Evelyn, claiming not to have gotten her share of the club's profits. Gallagher bought the place and the restaurant has remained there ever since.

In 2009, a revival of the musical Ragtime, *chronicling many characters including "the girl on the swing," Evelyn Nesbit, would open on 52nd Street at the Neil Simon, on the same block where so many of her post-swing escapades had taken place.*

1993: My First Job On Broadway

Ken Davenport, Producer

When I was a student at NYU, I took a History of American Musical Theatre class. It was taught by Jack Lee, who was a musical director on Broadway. I did well in the class, but I wasn't a star student. I remember forgetting my homework one day and feeling like an idiot.

I did have a bit of a theatrical past: my great-grandfather, Delbert Essex Davenport, was a lyricist, producer and press agent. I brought his scrapbook into class one time. Because of that, I think Jack knew that I was serious about theatre.

Over winter break, Jack called me and said, "I'm going to recommend you for a P.A. position on the upcoming Broadway production of *My Fair Lady* starring Richard Chamberlain. Do you want to do it? You just graduated, right?" I said yes, but told him I hadn't graduated yet. He responded, "Well then you won't be able to do it," and I said, "If you recommend me, I'll figure it out."

He gave me a number to call. It was Craig Jacobs, the stage manager. I called him. No return call. I called again. No return call. I waited a couple days and called again. No return call, nothing.

I waited for it to happen, and I somehow convinced NYU to give me school credit for a semester-long internship. Still, no return call. I was home in Massachusetts for the holidays, and my friends invited me on a ski weekend. I didn't go because I was too afraid that I was going to miss the return phone call.

I sat by my answering machine, waiting. I must have called Craig Jacobs 15 times. Then, the last day came to register for classes for the next semester at NYU. I went to my adviser and I said, "I don't know what to do!" He said, "Welcome to Broadway. People promise you things and they don't happen."

I got home and my answering machine was doing something strange. It was beeping in a way that it wasn't supposed to. I hit play and nothing happened. It was obviously broken. And I couldn't fix it. What if I missed the call? I finally popped out the microcassette and ran to get a microcassette player that I used for voice lessons.

I played the whole thing and then, at the very end, I found this message: "This is Craig Jacobs from *My Fair Lady*. I'm calling about the P.A. position. Will you call me back right away?" I called him back and he said, "Can you come up here and meet with me right now?"

I met with him that day and he gave me the job right then and there. If I hadn't had a Sony X20 microcassette recorder in my closet that day, I wouldn't be sitting here today.

When *My Fair Lady* started, my main responsibility was lunch. Everybody on that show wanted lunch brought in, so I would take lunch orders from around 20 people every day. I had to start at 10:45 in the morning in order to get food for everybody. I had to take all the orders, get the food from different places, and separate everything correctly—but the worst part was charging everybody. I'd have to go up to Richard Chamberlain or Howard Davies during rehearsal and be like, "I need nine dollars and 33 cents please," and then they'd go, "This is the most expensive sandwich I've ever seen!" That was unbelievably stressful.

Then one day, that changed. It was 1993, and computers were still a relatively new thing. I'm a computer geek, and have been since I was about ten years old. One day, I saw Craig Jacobs hunting and pecking, trying to type out a rehearsal schedule on his Mac. I asked if I could help, and he said, "No, I don't think so. You know, it's a computer." I replied, "I think I can give it a shot." I did, and I added some clip-art or something very simple, and printed it out. It was pretty, and the next day he said, "Why don't you do that again?"

That was when I became more valuable to them. Because of that, they brought me out of town with them. I also did a lot of driving actors around, including David Bryant, the original Marius in *Les Mis* on Broadway. I loved *Les Mis*, but hadn't realized that was him, and we were driving through an Arby's when he told me. I almost choked on my roast beef sandwich.

The Virginia Theatre was the first Broadway theater I was backstage in. The reason I went to NYU was to meet someone like Jack Lee who was working in the business and could help me, and he did. He introduced me to Craig. I ended up being Craig's P.A. on *My Fair Lady* and then *Grease*. Then, I P.A.'d the tour of *Grease*, and that's where I met Charlotte Wilcox. I worked for her and met Dan Sher, who gave me my first company management gig. Then, Craig Jacobs was the production stage manager on *Show Boat*, and recommended me to be a computer tutor for the company manager's boyfriend! Through that, the company manager got to know me, and I was hired as the assistant company manager for *Show Boat* on Broadway. After that came *Candide*, *Ragtime* and *Parade*. I can track every job I've ever had back to that first *My Fair Lady* experience. I still have heart palpitations when I think about trying to find that tape player to play that message.

I worked for Ken at Davenport Theatrical Enterprises from 2010 to 2013. In that time, we produced and marketed Broadway shows like Godspell *and* Macbeth. *I wanted to work for Ken for years before I was hired. In fact, I went to parties that he threw and even wrote him a letter when I was in college.*

One of my favorite memories of working for Ken was a night when we were both working late in the office on 49th Street. It was early Summer, 2011, and our team was waiting for Circle in the Square to open up so our Godspell *could come to Broadway. As I sat there that night, looking at a spreadsheet, Twitter refreshed in the corner of my screen and I saw a new headline pop up from Playbill: "Broadway Sports Drama* Lombardi *To Close May 22." I sent Ken a G-Chat that* Lombardi *was closing and we were both in shock. We screamed a little bit. We had a theater!* Godspell *was really going to Broadway now! But that's a story for another book...*

The technology involved in the situation wasn't lost on me. Of course, I had already heard his infamous My Fair Lady *story.*

1995: Jailhouse Rock

Louis St. Louis, Writer/Arranger

On my way to my first preview of *Smokey Joe's Cafe*, I got arrested.

We had a rehearsal at 3pm that day, and then the first preview was that night. I was driving into the city and redoing the intro to the song, "I Keep Forgettin'" in my head, because I didn't like the way it was yet. I passed a toll, and I rolled my window down with the money in my hand, but I never paid it. I kept driving and then I suddenly looked down and realized: *I forgot to pay the toll.*

I was flagged down by a cop. I said, "I've never done this before. Look, the money was in my hand." He told me he couldn't take it. He asked me to pull over, and I did. Ten minutes later, he said, "Step out of the car. You're under arrest."

I had gotten a traffic violation a year and a half earlier, and then the cop never appeared in court. They told me it was on my record. I said, "But I have to get to the theater!" And he said, "The theater will be there without you."

They took me to the prison inside of Port Authority. They took the shoelaces out of my shoes. They took everything from me and put me in a cell.

They let me call my partner, Roberto, and he and my company manager, Laura Green, came down to the precinct. They got an attorney. They took me down to central booking, with the prostitutes and the pimps and the drug dealers. I was kept until seven the next morning. I was horrified and very frightened.

When I came out of the courtroom at 7am, Roberto and Laura were there. They had stayed up all night. I said, "Well, I'm going to do the matinee. We need to do the matinee! It's our second show."

I got to the theater, the old Virginia, and the props man had made a bloody glove and put it on the piano, as a joke for me. Pattie Darcy Jones did an arrangement of the Cat Ballou theme, the old western about the gunman. They all dogged me for weeks. I got sent to jail instead of our first preview!

1995: Important Music

Jack Viertel, Creative Director of Jujamcyn Theaters

Smokey Joe's Cafe was conceived for the Walter Kerr Theatre. Then, it turned out that it was a little too big and expensive to play the Kerr because the Kerr is small. It probably would have done very happily in the O'Neill, but the Virginia was available. And the Virginia, at that time, was one of the hardest theaters to book.

The Virginia was comparatively far north on 52nd Street, and the size was a little awkward, and for years, people had considered the theater ugly even though it had been redone. It felt a little like a runt-of-the-litter show going into a runt-of-the-litter theater—but we were glad to have a theater! We were glad the show had good gross potential.

238

I loved the songs of Lieber and Stoller when I was a kid, and I always knew that I wanted to make a show out of them. I also always knew it wasn't something that would necessarily make critics rave, but I thought audiences would love the show.

We tried out in Chicago under the title *Baby That's Rock And Roll*. One critic there said, "Even when the show is bad, it's good." He was right. The songs are so good that they got this excited reaction from the audience, even when other things about the show were incompetent.

Susan Schulman was our original director, and she didn't feel she exactly understood the material, so, after Chicago, Jerry Zaks took the show over. We did it in Los Angeles, and then we came to New York.

Again, I always thought the show would get mixed reviews, but I was blindsided by the almost unanimous opinion that this was a crass attempt at marketing rather than a show. That felt personal, because in fact, the whole project had nothing to do with marketing. My brother and I felt this was very important music to us, so we did this entirely out of devotion and passion and wanting people to experience what we loved. To have someone not like it is one thing, but to have someone think you're being crass? When all you've done is gone to that place in your heart that's important to you? That was bizarre, and very hard to get over.

The show played well in the Virginia, and the nice thing about it was that we always had seats there that we could discount, based on the layout of the house. There are lots of seats there that are good, but just aren't premium, because the orchestra is so deep. *Smokey Joe's Cafe* was a show that had a lot of potential audience members who were not regular theatergoers and were not used to paying Broadway prices, so it was great that we always had discount tickets to offer.

Watching that show from the back of the house was really fun and gratifying. You could see how excited the audiences were, and this was way before *Jersey Boys* or any of those other sort of shows. Maybe in a funny way we sort of invented the jukebox musical, or came close. We would just stand in the back of the Virginia and watch all the bodies move. We had the feeling that we were giving people an awfully good time.

Smokey Joe's Cafe was indeed a landmark musical in terms of bringing shows based on writers' catalogues to Broadway. Its popularity in 1995 helped pave the way for musicals from Mamma Mia! *(ABBA, 2001) to* Movin' Out *(Billy Joel, 2002). These musicals all took the essence of writers' work and turned that into the concept of a show. Smokey Joe's wasn't the first to do this—among others,* Beatlemania *(1977) could certainly be considered a creative ancestor—but it did welcome a new wave of these shows on Broadway.*

Many people consider "jukebox musicals," or shows that use the songs of a popular artist in a new context, to be a new development on Broadway. The birth of the jukebox musical is hard to pinpoint, although a lot of its evolution did happen at the August Wilson Theatre since two of the longest-running shows there have been based on pre-existing music: Smokey Joe's Cafe *and* Jersey Boys!

*Jukebox musicals that use the songs of a popular artist can generally be divided into two categories: those that tell the stories of the artists' lives through their songs (*The Boy From Oz, Lennon, Jersey Boys*) and those that use the essence of an artist's work as a jumping off point to tell a new story (*Smokey Joe's Cafe, Mamma Mia!, Movin' Out*).*

The first modern Broadway jukebox musical to tell the story of its songwriters' lives was not Jersey Boys *in 2005, like many think. It was probably* Leader of the Pack *in 1985, a musical that told the life story of Ellie Greenwich through the lens of her songs. It was the first Broadway musical to really take that format and create the type of musical filled with pre-written popular songs. Plus,* Leader of the Pack *had people like Annie Golden and Darlene Love playing themselves, with Ellie Greenwich playing her older self and Dinah Manoff, her younger self. The songs included Ellie hits like "Be My Baby", "Chapel of Love", "Do Wah Diddy" and of course, the title song, and told the story of her rise to fame and tumultuous romance with writing partner Jeff Barry. This was auto-bi-fiction-ography on stage, much like it would be when people like Berry Gordy, Carole King, the Four Seasons, Fela Anikulapo-Kuti and more took to the Broadway stage to illustrate the stories of their lives later on.*

While Allegro *was one of the very first concept musicals, it doesn't get widespread credit as such because it was not a mega-hit.* Leader of the Pack *could be considered the* Allegro *of jukebox musicals. (And I could get beaten up at Sardi's for such an outrageous statement!)*

———————

1997: *Smokey Joe's* Callbacks

Heidi Blickenstaff, Actor

I had a couple of callbacks for *Smokey Joe's Cafe* that were at the Virginia Theatre itself. I was up for the track that swings for the white girls. Never, before or since then, have I been part of an audition on a Broadway stage, and it was just what it looked like in the movie version of *A Chorus Line*.

When I auditioned for *Smokey Joe's*, I was thinking: *It's happening. It's totally happening just like the movie.* There we all were in our suntan Capezio tights and our character shoes and our sexy microfiber dresses that clung to our bodies, that I'm sure I was a little self-conscious in at the time. I was 25 years old and hadn't been in a Broadway show yet. I remember totally going for it on that Broadway stage, and wondering if I would ever actually get the opportunity to perform on a Broadway stage for people, or if this was as close as I was going to get, just being a part of the audition.

I did not get the part in *Smokey Joe's Cafe*. But then four years later, I made my Broadway debut at the O'Neill in *The Full Monty*.

2000: It Was Supposed To Make People Angry

Michael John LaChiusa, Writer

The Wild Party was supposed to make people angry—and it did. We wanted to hold up a mirror to some really ugly things that were happening in New York and the ugly side of our society. It was an angry piece, a violent piece. People did have trouble with that. But you know, *Wild Party* ran about two hours and that's a long time to look at ugly people. So I understand. People were either on board or they were not.

We had no intermission because the story was about a party, and it was supposed to be played out in as close to "real time" as possible. One of our original run-throughs was five hours! That was actually an initial idea: to have the show run for five hours. You'd get up, go eat, and come back, and the party would still be happening. I still have all the material for it.

When we were first putting the show together, George C. Wolfe and I did a spin around town to find an old bowery house. We also checked out some decrepit theaters that hadn't been renovated yet. Then, we learned it was smarter for us to do the show on Broadway than anywhere else because of the price point necessary, considering the stars we already had lined up.

Of the Broadway theaters, the Virginia was the one I was smitten with. It was the only theater we saw that had a pit that wasn't destroyed. Every other Broadway house had a pit that had been shoved under the stage, where you can only see the top of the conductor's head. Acoustically, we didn't want that for the show. I wanted our audience to *see* the orchestra.

I always think that when the audience can see your orchestra, for some reason, they really hear the music. The visual connected with the sound provides a different experience than the one if you can't see the band playing—if they're shoved under the stage, or a block away with the sound being pumped in. The Virginia was as close to an original Broadway house and pit as we could find, and I was smitten with it. Since then, I've always made sure that in my shows, one way or another, the orchestra is seen, rather than disguised or hidden.

There were a lot of cuts during previews because when previews began, we were clocking in at two hours and 30 minutes—that's way too long without an intermission. It was a real battle to get to where we got with the piece—we actually ran out of time before we could finish working on the ending. At one point, I wrote an entire new duet for Toni and Tonya in 12 hours. I wrote "Best Friend" in the lobby of the Virginia in the morning, and it was on stage that night. I hadn't slept, and I wasn't even using Finale[35] yet! The whole song was written by hand.

I also wrote a number during previews called "Gin/Wild", just in case we ended up not being able to cut more off the show, and we needed a song that could be a division line for an intermission. I wrote the song as a backup. I didn't tell George, but he was too smart to be fooled! "Gin/Wild" ended up being put in right before the number "People Like Us", so it leads us into the third part of the evening. "Gin/Wild" ended up being a real big, powerful showstopper, so it turned out to be a great change, even though we didn't have a break.

The lobby of the Virginia was very intriguing. The theater has an "after room" that I was fascinated by and spent some time in, with a door that led to another door that led to backstage. Of course, I particularly loved spending time in the pit. It was a really tough show to play, so I would bring our trumpet players ice packs to cool off their lips! It was fun to sit there with the orchestra and watch them play during the performance; they were one of the best orchestras I've ever heard in my life. Also, you couldn't be seen by the audience, but you could watch the audience.

It was a volatile production, but it was *The Wild Party*. It was supposed to be that. I loved that theater; I loved being in that theater. I loved the ushers; they were so wonderful. They took on a battle because there were hostile customers leaving to go to the bathroom, and they had to constantly say, "You can't go back in during this number," and deal with "I'm going back in now!" I dig ushers. Ushers are our friends or our enemies.

The Virginia was a great space, and there were lots of fun things about it. We were across the street from Susan Stroman's production of *The Music Man* at the Neil Simon. That was like night and day on 52nd Street! They had all these children in their wholesome, all-American show. Our dressing rooms, of course, overlooked the dressing rooms of their theater. We would always wave back and forth. Toni Collette was such a fun gal, and one day, she decided to flash *The Music Man* cast. Not the children. But I think the entire street below saw Queenie from *The Wild Party* flashing the residents of River City, Iowa. That was classic.

2000: Where Brilliance Lies

Tonya Pinkins, Actor

My daughter was born a little diva, and she always loves being around the theater. She's an incredible singer, and we used to dress her up and put her in my wigs backstage. When I did *The Wild Party* at the Virginia, she was about three years old. My dressing room was small and all the way upstairs. She came into the theater, looked at my dressing room, and went, "Oh." Then, she went downstairs and spent the rest of her time with Eartha Kitt in the star dressing room.

---

[35] Finale: popular music notation software

That's one lovely thing about the theatre community, that my daughters and son could always come and hang out at the theater, whether in my dressing room or somebody else's. It's a very welcoming community about kids.

Both *Jelly's Last Jam* and *The Wild Party* were directed by George C. Wolfe and he's the most fun director ever! He's just like a big kid. My favorite quote and motto for how I work is: "Brilliance lies in the moment that might not work." George is like that too; he's forever taking risks. I'm not even interested in getting a project if there's not some risk I'm gonna take. That's what I like to do. I want to find out what's possible that I haven't done, or that hasn't been done at all.

George's vision as a director is always exciting. About *Wild Party*, he told us: "This is about creatures of the night. The journey of this play takes place in real time, and most of these people never see the sunlight. They party all night and when the sun comes up, they go to sleep. They wake up at night to do their work and then party again." We were all so moved by his vision for the end of the play, that at the end of this terrible evening of murder and mayhem, Queenie stays awake for the sunrise. That's like an awakening for her, her moment in the sun.

We had a talkback once, and someone in the audience thought she was committing suicide at the end, and that the sunrise was the lights of the subway coming at her so she could kill herself. Some people loved the show, but some people just didn't get it. I think it paved the way for all of these shows that aren't about an arc so much as about watching real life, like *Next To Normal* and even *Caroline, or Change*.

2000: Dark, Serious-Minded, Huge Show

Michael John LaChiusa, Writer

The closing performance of *The Wild Party* was one of the most amazing things I've ever seen in a theater. I watched from the wings, which was my favorite place to watch the show. I loved being as close to the actors as I could, without being in their way. The wings are amazing; you see the whole show and you're so close to the actors that you can feel what they hear from the orchestra. I think it's very important for every writer to spend some time there, being as close as you can to experiencing the show from the stage.

The audience was crazy for the entire closing performance; the audience and the actors both tore the roof off the place. At the end, we came out and took our bows, and George stood up there in front of the entire place and said, "You know, when they run you out of town, get out and make it a f---ing parade." That brought down the house all over again, because it was really true. We felt like we were being sent away, and we felt like that show was the end of something. I can't put my finger on it exactly, but it was the end of the century and the beginning of a new one. It marked the beginning of these new mechanics of how Broadway works. Broadway has changed so radically since then, in terms of the content available and what people want from a Broadway show. I think it was the beginning of the "on-demand" audience. I get this feeling in Broadway audiences now, of people feeling like: *I want to change the channel now, why can't I? Why are you making me watch this? I want to tell* you *what I want to watch.* It's an ideology that's seeped into our culture. It's going to be interesting to see how theatre and theatre producers play into that in the upcoming seasons. Is everything going to be a circus, where you can put your eye wherever you want? Are we going to have no more directors saying "look here" or "let's put a close-up on this song"? I'm not sure audiences can focus as much anymore.

And *The Wild Party* was one of the last of the big, dark, serious-minded musicals. There have been some. Back then, *Wild Party* and *Marie Christine* were considered to be that and there was some sense of: "We can't have dark musicals! There's no such thing as that! Bad! Bad!" Then, that idea evolved so that now critics and audiences embrace dark, serious-minded musicals to a certain extent, but only if they're small in scope, in size.

The Wild Party was really one of the last shows to be taken to Broadway as a dark, serious-minded, huge show, without the thought of pushing it into the form of a chamber musical[36].

2000: *The Best Man*'s Best Understudy

Ed Dixon, Actor

I got cast in the wonderful role of Senator Carlin in the 2000 revival of *The Best Man*. It was the first time in my career that I'd ever played a person in the 20th century with my own background! It was the first time I was using my Southern accent in a contemporary play, and I was thrilled about that. I was thrilled about being Senator Carlin, who had a great scene.

During the negotiation, they said, "You have to stand by for Charles Durning as Ex-President Arthur Hockstader. Take it or leave it." Charles Durning was a big star *and* the lead of the show. Nobody wants to understudy a role like that, because if you go on, the audience will be disappointed. I said, "I don't want to stand by for Charles Durning. I like my part and I just want to do that." They said, "This is what we're offering and if you don't like it, there are five guys standing behind you."

I took the job and then I had to learn that gigantic part and understudy the star. The first day of rehearsal, Charles went into the hospital. He's wasn't there the first day or the second or the third… I spent rehearsals doing my part and then doing his and then mine, sometimes back to back. I got very close with the company and with both parts and then, finally, Charles got out of the hospital. He came to rehearsal, and I looked into his eyes and knew that I was going to go on for the part.

On the second performance, I got to the theater and found that Charles was out and I had to go on. All of the critics from the Outer Circle[37] were there. I've never been so scared in my life! Since Charles had come in to rehearsal, a lot of blocking had changed. They didn't have costumes for me. At one point in the show, his character wore a tuxedo, and I had to send someone to my house to get my tuxedo so I could wear it in the show. I wore my Senator Carlin suit for the rest of the show.

When Charles made his first entrance, he got entrance applause. I came on and there was dead silence. But I finished the opening scene, and got exit applause! From then on, I was home free. The performance went wonderfully, and it was one of the greatest nights of my life. There were all of these stars in the show, and there I was, taking the last bow, with them applauding me.

Shirley Rich, the famous casting director, was in the audience that night and she wrote me a beautiful letter saying that what happened that night was what theatre is all about. We ended up winning the Outer Critics Circle award! Months later, I was out on the road and ran into one of our producers who told me, "You know, you did that. They were all there that night." The whole night was truly amazing.

Charles never missed another show. That night ended up being my only shot at the part.

———————

The majority of these interviews have been done in person, but at least 50, including Ed's, were done on the phone.

It struck me at some point that not only do I have recordings for life of Broadway professionals telling me fascinating stories, I also have recordings for life of Broadway professionals playing with dogs, turning off ovens,

———————

[36] chamber musical: show with a small cast, usually done in a physically minimal production
[37] Outer Circle: an organization of journalists who write about New York City theatre for out of town newspapers, national publications, and other media outlets outside of New York City

yelling for husbands, eating cereal, icing their knees, ordering coffee, burping babies, picking up dry cleaning, texting back mothers, kicking broken printers, flirting with waiters, smoking, drinking, getting called for half-hour, unexpectedly running into friends, foes, former students, and former teachers... and my personal favorite, pulling Truvia out of a purse.

Real life. It happens.

2001: My Entrance To Broadway Was Different

Damian Bazadona, Digital Marketing Executive

I don't have a theatre background, and the first three shows I remember seeing were *Phantom, Rent* and *The Lion King*. I went to *Phantom* on a date with my wife, I went to *Rent* because my friends said I had to, and I got *The Lion King* tickets as a Christmas gift. I remember opening that gift and being surprised because the tickets were for a date over a year away—it was that hard to get a ticket. That's just unheard of now.

My entrance to Broadway was very different than most people working in the industry. I worked in digital marketing, and at one point, someone had me draw up a banner ad for *Miss Saigon*. Then I ended up working a little bit on IBDB. Then, I met Ben Mordecai. He brought me into the industry, and had me work on *King Hedley*. That was the first time I was in a theater and started to understand Broadway. Before that, seeing shows, I didn't really know why I was there.

Ben was a producer who trusted me with all of his digital marketing. I did websites for his shows, and I did other forms of marketing that were just starting in the Broadway sphere. He thought they were important, and after *King Hedley*, we worked on several other shows together, including *Ma Rainey's Black Bottom* and *Flower Drum Song*. He was an amazing producer. He was still a producer on his deathbed, producing via conference calls from his hospital bed. He was remarkable.

I remember getting the opening night invitation for *King Hedley*, and it said "black tie optional." I rented a tuxedo, and I showed up half-an-hour early. When I got to the Virginia, the only people that had on tuxedos were August Wilson, the executive producer of the show, and me—and I was the first one at the theater. I had no background in theatre, and I had no idea what was expected of me!

That was enlightening for me. In hindsight, it really made me take into account that there are a lot of people in the world like I was that night, who have no idea how to attend theatre. They don't know the etiquette, and they think theatre is an elite activity. I use that experience as a point of reference now, when I tell people how to find and nurture new audiences. Many people who love theater grew up loving theater. I didn't grow up going to see shows. I came in as an outsider, and I looked like an outsider.

Through digital marketing, you can now learn so much more than you once could, before you even walk into a theater. You can look on message boards, check out discounts, read all kinds of information about the show— and afterward, you can talk about the show with a community. That really didn't exist 10-15 years ago. But now, you can watch the Tony Awards in Iowa and then get online and look up everything you thought was interesting.

I remember the first time that I sat in the August Wilson Theatre, back when it was the Virginia. I wondered: do they fill this big theatre every night with people paying $85 a ticket? My background is in live entertainment, and when I started out, I was a DJ and nightclub promoter. So, I understood the idea of getting people off their couch for entertainment, but $85? Then, as I started to see more theatre, I started to get it. Yes, this is remarkable. You can't see this anywhere else. Still though, in order to get people to continue to buy something expensive, we really have to build those new audiences. That's my personal passion: to make new generations see that theatre, or any live experience for that matter, is for them, and to get them to care.

2002: Theater Could Be Like *That*

Alex Wyse, Actor

When I saw *The Crucible* with Liam Neeson and Laura Linney, that was the first time that I ever knew that theatre could be like that. I knew theater could be like *Into The Woods*, and I knew that theater could be like *Peter Pan* and *Beauty and the Beast*, but I didn't know that there could be acting and drama, like *The Crucible*.

The show opened my eyes to a new kind of theatre. It's one of the reasons I decided to go to acting school instead of musical theatre school—because I knew that theatre could be like that, and I wanted to make that.

I remember everything! I remember Jennifer Carpenter. One of the best things was her breaking down in the courtroom scene, screaming, "Don't touch me, you're the devil's man! I'm with God!" It was wildly good. It was so powerful. I was really taken with a lot of the supporting characters.

When the show ended, we all stood up to leave, and I turned to my grandma and said, "That was incredible." Then, a woman in front of us turned around, and she said, "You're young." Those people are the worst!

I was at the show in the first place because a childhood friend of mine, Betsy Hogg, was in it. I thought: *Alright, we're gonna go see Betsy in her show*. I didn't know anything about it, and then it ended up changing the way I saw theatre. Thanks, Betsy!

———————

I was doubly excited to interview lighting designers Ken Billington and Jason Kantrowitz because I would get to interview them and I would get to see inside the old Theatre Guild building!

The building where Helene Hanff once stuck exclamation points on programs that would change the American Musical Theatre forever is still in the hands of theatre people. These days, it is the office of Broadway in Asia, Ken Billington and Associates and several others, including would-be Rebecca *producer Ben Sprecher.*

As we chatted about 52nd Street, Ken and Jason told me that they often heard the casts of the two shows on the block yelling at each other, or the people at Roseland making a racket.

The exact room we were sitting in had been the Theatre Guild offices. I was sitting where Helene sat and dreamt of being a playwright and maybe looked across the street at the Alvin. The office below our feet once belonged to her boss, Lawrence Langner. The floor above was once the Guild's rehearsal rooms. We walked up the stairs and I saw that the floor where Oklahoma! *and so many others had been rehearsed was now abandoned.*

We reached a locked door and Ken said, "Oh, that door leads to the August Wilson! We can't use it, but it's there."

As we marched downstairs, he showed me an ordinary-looking ledge in the stairwell. "In the original movie version of The Producers, *Zero Mostel as Max Bialystock leans out this ledge and throws coffee out the window! His fictional offices were in this building too."*

———————

2002: The Asian Broadway Community

Jose Llana, Actor

The cool thing about doing *Flower Drum Song* at the Virginia was that the dressing rooms face the dressing rooms at the Neil Simon across the street! I had a bunch of friends in *Hairspray*, and my windows were directly across from Clarke Thorell and Marissa Jaret Winokur's, because we were on the second floor of our respective theaters.

I would warm up to *Floyd Collins* in my dressing room, and Clarke would yell things at me across the street while I was doing that. Our ensemble upstairs and their ensemble upstairs were facing each other exactly, so they made up all these games. We were only there for four months, but during those four months, the two companies had all kinds of shenanigans planned with each other.

Working with that group of people on *Flower Drum Song* was fantastic. I've been lucky enough that my career has bounced back and forth from Asian show to non-Asian show, and they're different animals. When you're in an Asian show, you instantly become a family because everyone has a shared, similar history. We all had similar upbringings for a number of reasons. Whether we were Chinese, Japanese, or any other Asian nationality, we all grew up with that tiger mother. We all grew up in Asian families, wanting to do theatre.

Flower Drum Song was a very close cast. To this day, the shows I was in that go out of their way to have reunions are usually the Asian shows. *Flower Drum Song* and *The King And I* have the most reunions. It's great. It's family.

2002: New Friends And New Food

Tony Massey, Merchandise Manager

I worked on *Miss Saigon* on tour, and then *Flower Drum Song* on Broadway. The Asian Broadway community is the most tight-knit group of people! There's such a sense of community in that world.

A friend of mine once called me "an honorary Asian" just because I spent so much time working on those two shows. That community of people is extraordinary to me. They all know each other, and they're all friends. Of course, it used to be that you had to ask who knew each other, but now, with Facebook, I'm always seeing that everybody is connected. If you've worked with Deedee Magno or Lea Salonga, you have a connection to all of them, because every Asian performer grew up a fan of theirs. The Asian community is amazing and just feels so connected!

Food is a big part of the world of an Asian show. I grew up in the South, and we barely even had Chinese food! When I came to New York, all of a sudden I was inundated with all these different types of food. That's been a big change in lifestyle for me, working in theatre in New York and on the road. I always ate dim sum with the company of *Saigon*. I literally ate the same things over and over all the time growing up, but now I've been introduced to so many different foods, and I'm such a fan of all of them.

2002: The Hair Area

Josh Marquette, Hair Designer

The hair area in the theater is often an after-thought. You take care of all the actors, and then, "Oh well, this room is kind of big enough for hair. Barely." On *Flower Drum Song,* we were down in the basement, in a long,

246

narrow space. You had room for a table, and you had a little mirror with lights around it. There were four of us, literally elbow to elbow! At the end of the room there was a bathroom without a sink in it.

I think that's where the hair room usually is for shows at the Virginia. But it's often like that. For *Book of Mormon*, we have a very small space, and there are about 50 wigs in that show!

The most fun thing about the backstage of the Virginia during *Flower Drum Song* was that everyone would do stripteases for the cast of *Hairspray*, across the street. At five minutes before show time, if you were in a room with a window facing the street, it got pretty explicit!

2002: Thank You, Billy Porter

Telly Leung, Actor

During my senior year of college at Carnegie Mellon, Billy Porter came to direct the senior musical, *Company*, and he cast me as Bobby. When we were working on the show, he said to me, "Telly, do you know about this Broadway revival of *Flower Drum Song*?"

Billy's first Broadway show after he graduated was *Miss Saigon*, so he knew the tight network that is the Asian Broadway community, and because of that, he had seen *Flower Drum Song* during their tryout at the Mark Taper. I didn't know anything about it. Billy called Mark Oka, his dance captain from *Miss Saigon*, who was also the dance captain on *Flower Drum Song*, and he said, "Listen, I have three Asian kids in my cast of *Company*. I'm sending them all down on a Greyhound bus to audition for you. When can I send them?"

There was one day we could go audition. I was in tech for *Company*, so, one night, after tech ended at midnight, I hopped on the last Greyhound bus from Pittsburgh to New York. I got into Port Authority early in the morning, and basically gave myself a shower at the sink at Ripley-Grier. The 16th floor was filled with people I didn't know. Because I've been in the Asian Broadway community for ten years, now I think I know every single one of them!

We did a jazz combination and a ballet combination, and then they kept a couple people to sing. They kept me! Mark Oka walked in, and said to me, "Sing high. We need a tenor." I thought: *Great! If I made it through the dance calls, I can definitely sing high*. I'll be okay. After I sang, Bobby Longbottom looked at my resume and said, "Oh, you're doing *Company* right now. That's a nice leading-man role." I didn't know at the time, but he was looking for someone to understudy Jose Llana. He asked if I could sing "Being Alive". I thought: *Great! I sang that a couple hours ago in tech*.

I sang "Being Alive" and then I went back to Port Authority and got back on the bus to Pittsburgh. I got back to school, and went straight to rehearsal! Billy said, "How'd you do, diva?"

I found out later that he had already known! His friends had called him and told him I would be asked to come to the final callback, but that I pretty much had the job. He played it off like he knew nothing, and I told him, "Billy, I'm not sure, but I think it went well. They kept me all day long! Maybe nothing will happen, but thank you for sending me to that. I know that I never would've gotten in the door without you."

I distinctly remember saying, "If I really get this show, I know I'll only get 25 words in my first Playbill as 'Dancing Bonsai #5 On The Side,' but 'Thank You, Billy Porter' will be four of them. And that happened. I made my Broadway debut in *Flower Drum Song*, and those words were in my Playbill bio.

There are so many stories about Billy doing that for people, believing in them. Whenever I tell that one, someone else will add in a time that he helped them too. To see him now in *Kinky Boots*, getting the acclaim we all know he's deserved for so many years? That's the perfect showbiz story.

All of the other Asian Broadway gypsies wanted us to walk into the Virginia for the first time together, so we did. There were so many people making their Broadway debuts! I remember walking in the stage door with everyone, and seeing so many faces with mouths agape. We had never seen a Broadway show from that side before. Later on, when I did *Godspell*, I was doing a video blog for Broadway.com. I remembered that day during *Flower Drum Song*, and said, "I have to make sure I capture this moment for my *Godspell*-mates who are doing their first show." I brought my camera the day we went from the rehearsal room to see the Circle in the Square Theatre for the first time. I shot the four of them standing outside the theater, and then I tried to capture all four of their reactions, going in. Some of it was speechless, some of it was tears. I was just so glad I captured it so they'd have it forever and ever somewhere, because no one was there to do that for us. All I have is the memory, that snapshot in my head of what it was like for all of us, that day at the Virginia.

Flower Drum Song opened in the fall and it struggled to stay open. Across the street from us was *Hairspray*. Those kids had a huge hit with people lining up around the block, and our show was so empty sometimes that you could hear crickets. Two of the main things that hurt our show were the musicians' strike that happened and the crazy blizzards that New York got that winter.

For some reason, our show wasn't cancelled during the blizzards! Now that I know more about how producing works, I wonder why we didn't cancel. I think it would have saved us money instead of keeping the theater open for the 25 audience members who showed up! I remember during one blizzard, I looked out the window at half-hour and the *Hairspray* kids were making snow angels in the street! Their show got cancelled and it probably saved them money in the long run. I wondered, "Why are we doing our show for a couple of people while they're making snow angels?"

So, we were not the winning show in that regard. We did, however, win the strip show.

The ensemble dressing rooms of *Flower Drum Song* and *Hairspray* faced each other exactly, on the fourth floor. At the beginning of the run, we'd always wave hi to each other. One day, we started doing a striptease. From that point, it escalated! It always happened during half-hour, so little did the patrons filing into the Neil Simon and Virginia know that four flights above them, there was a whole other show going on.

The strip show got more and more advanced. *Flower Drum Song* started burning CDs and sending them over to the Neil Simon with notes that said, "Press Play When We Give You The Signal," and we would sync up these dances! We choreographed these wild dances during our dinner breaks on Saturdays.

We had paper fans in the show, so one time, we choreographed this whole strip show with fans. Our lighting guys gave us lamps and our house electricians hooked us up with gels, so we had this outrageous red lighting.

For some reason, there was a blow-up sex doll. Someone had gotten it as a gag gift and it was just hanging out in the ensemble dressing room. At one point, the button of our strip show was this blow-up sex doll, tied to a string, thrown out the window of the Virginia Theatre, and then we shut the window! I remember seeing the *Hairspray* kids losing it across the street. They told us later that Marissa Jaret Winokur got on the loudspeaker and announced, "Guys! Look out your dressing room windows. The *Flower Drum Song* kids have a great show for you!"

The whole thing was so fun, and those guys were so great. It was nice to be across the street from them, but to be honest, we were a little jealous. They had a big hit on their hands, and they'd win the Tony long after we closed. I learned very quickly on that first show that Broadway wasn't as glamorous as I had thought. Our show opened and closed in four months, and not only did it open and close quickly, I stood on a picket line! It was crazy! But it was good. It was a good first show to be in.

When there's a show with so many Asian people, it really feels like family because we all know each other from auditions for the same parts or those few opportunities where there are all-Asian shows. Otherwise, there's the "token" in every show. If there's an ensemble of dancers in a Broadway show, usually there's one Asian or one African American person. The communities are often represented that way in a show, rather than in a large collected way. So, on shows like *Flower Drum Song*, where we all have the opportunity to come together, we understand how lucky we are, both to be working and to be together.

I've been very blessed in that the four Broadway shows I've done have all become tight-knit families. Two were Asian and two weren't, but on *all* of them, we've chosen to spend our downtime with each other. I love that. I know it's not always the case on shows, and it's the thing I'm most grateful for.

2003: Inside The Puppet

Justin Scribner, Stage Manager

I made my Broadway debut as a P.A. on *Little Shop of Horrors*. I did the out-of-town tryout too, which had an entirely different cast, including Alice Ripley. Connie Grappo, who was the original assistant director off-Broadway, directed it. When the producers replaced her with Jerry Zaks, he replaced the entire cast except Hunter Foster as Seymour and Ray DeMattis, who was the understudy for Mushnik. The stage manager stayed though, and so did I.

I got the job on *Little Shop* because I was originally hired to be a P.A. on *Dinner at Eight* at the Beaumont, which would've been my first Broadway credit. At the last minute, there was another P.A. thrust on the stage manager and she had to let me go the day before rehearsals started. It was very upsetting, especially because it happened at the time of my life when I was living on $200 a week, and without that job, I wasn't even able to buy Ramen.

Yet, if that hadn't happened, I wouldn't have gotten hired on *Little Shop*. That stage manager "owed it to me," as she said. She said, "I loved meeting with you, and I really wanted to work with you. I feel so guilty about what happened with *Dinner at Eight*." That's how I got the job on *Little Shop*!

After we opened *Little Shop*, I worked as a P.A. on *Nine*, with the replacement cast led by John Stamos. Then, the show *Jumpers* hired me as a P.A./assistant stage manager for two shows a week. Then, *Little Shop* called me back to sub as an assistant stage manager! I got my Equity card[38] that summer.

The Virginia felt gigantic to me! *Little Shop* was a show where I felt really valued as part of the team. As P.A., I created the run sheets for the show. I was backstage with a clipboard for all of the previews, watching every scene shift on stage, noting any change, making sure I had what every person's exact track was. I would note a prop man one day, and the carpenter the next day. I really felt like I was able to be a part of it. And we had space backstage! We had booths for singing, we had space for quick changes. It felt spacious. It was a good starter theater for me, and the plant was so cool in the space!

I got to ride in the plant, which was awesome. When we were rehearsing, we had two spaces: music/dance/staging rehearsal and puppet rehearsal. When you were in puppet rehearsal, after a lot of safety checks, you got to participate. The puppeteers were these muscle men, and a lot of them had worked on the

---

[38] Equity Card: an identification card given to actors and stage managers by Actors Equity union once they have enough credits to join

original show and the movie. They were fantastic! You got to see them really fixing what they'd always wanted to fix, and seeing these plants come to life. As they were perfecting that, they needed someone to be the guinea pig who would be picked up by the plant and shaken around. Of course, they wanted that to be completely safe, so we tested it a lot.

By the time in the show that Audrey II had grown into the giant plant, there was a puppeteer behind it operating the neck, and a puppeteer in the middle of the plant, right behind the tongue, on a surfboard-type platform operating the jaws. There was a bar in the middle, so when you got eaten, you'd grab ahold of the bar, and it looked like you were in the plant's teeth. There was also a stage manager under the neck, so that when props were "eaten by" the plant, they would be accounted for.

I really enjoyed that plant business, and I really loved the Virginia. I made friends with all of the ushers, because I also took lots of blocking notes in the house. That theater has a great cross-through to backstage. It was a great first Broadway experience.

2003: Generations Of Writers

Alan Menken, Writer

When we opened the revival of *Little Shop of Horrors* at the Virginia, we were across from *Hairspray* at the Neil Simon. Harvey Fierstein and I didn't know each other as well back then, and I remember one time he just came out of his stage door and yelled across the street, "MENKEN!!!" I just love Harvey. That camaraderie is just great about the theater community.

I remember rehearsing *Sister Act* at 42nd Street Studios when Marc Shaiman and Scott Wittman were in the same building with *Catch Me If You Can*. We commiserated about our shows' troubles in a season when we were up against each other. I remember walking by *Book of Mormon* at the O'Neill and bumping into Bobby Lopez. Bobby's mother knew my sister, and I had given him a school recommendation back when he was a kid. There he was under the marquee of his show, and I offered my congratulations. He said, "Oh my God, Alan!"

There's this sense in the community of older writers and younger writers seeing each other and wishing each other well. There are these generations. And that's a cool thing, realizing that you've gone from being the new kid on Broadway to the older generation on the block.

2005: A Changing Sound

Steve C. Kennedy, Sound Designer

I remember being in tech for *The Producers* and thinking: *No way.* There was no audience, so nothing seemed funny! I felt the same thing with *Hairspray*. Most of the time, stagehands are so busy working, that they're not going to pay attention and laugh during tech. But on *Jersey Boys*, everybody was laughing! Des McAnuff has a crew that just laughs. And everyone felt it: the songs and the energy of the piece were so great.

Of course, I had also done *Carrie* in that theater. For *Carrie*, the lighting team had built a huge bridge for follow spots. It was still there during *Jersey Boys* 20 years later.

Our team maintains *Jersey Boys* very well. There are very attentive resident directors and production stage managers. Sometimes, I'll go back to the show if they need me, or if I happen to be nearby. But I do have an associate who constantly checks on and works on *Jersey Boys*. When I was doing *Hairspray, Catch Me If You Can*, and *Jesus Christ Superstar*, all across the street at the Neil Simon, I'd always run over to catch a few numbers from *Jersey Boys*.

Sometimes, you stay away from shows once you've opened. Because sometimes you go back and think: *God, I could have done this, I should have changed that, I could just redo this whole thing.* But at the same time, you were in love with what you did when you designed it, and all of a sudden, you're hearing it in a whole different way. Sometimes, I wish I were a set designer because everything stays static. In sound design, the mixers change, there are different actors on stage, there are new factors all the time.

In 2005, the theater formerly known as The Guild Theatre, the ANTA, and the Virginia was renamed the August Wilson Theatre. August Wilson was a Pulitzer Prize-winning playwright, well-known for The Pittsburgh Cycle, *his ten plays that each chronicle a different decade of the African American experience in the 20th century.*

August Wilson and Neil Simon used to sit across from each other dining at the Cafe Edison, and now they sit across from each other on 52nd Street. Commemorating artists by naming theaters in their honor always seems to give the building a new light.

2006: My First Laugh On Broadway

Susan Blackwell, Actor

The first time I ever performed on a Broadway stage was as part of a benefit concert of *The Best Little Whorehouse in Texas* that Seth Rudetsky put together for the Actors Fund. It played at the August Wilson.

We were brought backstage for the rehearsal, and *Jersey Boys* was playing there, so their set pieces and props were backstage. I came to all of this a bit later in life; I was in my 30s when the concert happened. I was an adult, not fresh off the bus—and still I was just knocked sideways by the privilege of getting to be backstage and then on stage at that theater.

Even though I only had a small part in the benefit, I remember getting a laugh and thinking: *This is the first laugh I ever got in a Broadway house! This is my first time on Broadway!* Getting to have that whole privilege was kind of mind-rocking.

2012: The Underwear Over There Actually Has A Speaker Behind It

Jared Bradshaw, Actor

Our swing room upstairs has this slanted ceiling and it's sort of hidden on the top floor. There are no windows. If it's over 70 degrees, it's baking hot in here and there's nothing you can do, because the heat comes in from the roof. The *Jersey Boys* marquee is actually below us. There are days when we three swings come up here and we kind of act out the whole show. Sometimes other people in the show don't see us at all for a couple days if we're not on.

And this is the room where Mandy Patinkin had his aquarium during *The Wild Party*! I like to think about Mandy Patinkin walking up those same stairs as us, and about all the other people who were in the theater then: Norm Lewis and Marc Kudisch and Toni Collette. All of them sharing rooms like us.

We have a summer barbecue in our little alley every Labor Day. Sometimes, Rick Elice and Marshall Brickman, our writers, will send over ice cream, or beers, or Gatorade. Actually, last week, it was so hot that Jujamcyn sent over a Mr. Softee truck! They parked Mr. Softee right in front of *Jersey Boys* and everyone had a sprinkle cone between shows. We have a birthday club. We had Pioneer Day once, because Heather Ferguson, who was in the cast, is Mormon. She taught us all about her tradition of Pioneer Day, and we celebrated it for the first time.

I understand that some people don't want to see the understudy. Andy Karl and Matt Bogart are in our show, and I love them! If I were seeing the show, I'd want to see them. So I get it. Andy never calls out, but during one performance, after "Big Girls Don't Cry", he smacked himself in the teeth with his guitar. He chipped his tooth off! That was halfway through act one. The stage manager called me to the stage and I got into costume, hair and mic. I thought I'd have to go on within minutes, but Andy is amazing and made it all the way to intermission. He wanted to do act two, but he really had to go get his tooth fixed! So, I finished the show in that role. I've actually gone on in the middle of the show around 50-something times. That's why we have a monitor. That underwear over there actually has a speaker behind it.

If anybody out there is reading this book on Saturday night, if there's a show playing at the Virginia and the Alvin—I mean the August Wilson and the Neil Simon—come over! Come over to 52nd Street, and just listen! At five minutes till 8pm, stand on our street and look up and you'll see both casts screaming out the theater windows at each other. It's an awesome thing.

———————————

On a Sunday afternoon in August, before the matinee, I visited Jared at the August Wilson Theatre. As I waited outside in the sun, dozens of theatergoers bought tickets at the box office.

Stage door security gave me a nametag—the first time that's ever happened to me at a Broadway theater! And with my Jujamcyn sticker on, I followed Jared up one floor from street level, to the stage. We passed a wall covered in neatly arranged costumes and shoes with labels. There was a bulletin board filled with photos of cast members, past and present, with new babies—including Jared himself.

As we walked on stage left, Jared showed me all of the guitars that are used in the show, hung and pre-set on the walls. On the back wall was a row of false mustaches, used by several characters in Jersey Boys. *There were even costumes hung above the stage, in the fly, that would be lowered down during the show so actors could change. Randy Graff had not been joking—the August Wilson needed every bit of space it could get!*

Many times while writing this book, I heard detailed stories about a theater and then found myself backstage at that theater for the first time. As I explored the home of Jersey Boys, *I couldn't help but think of when it had been the home of* City of Angels, Jelly's Last Jam, *and* Cat on a Hot Tin Roof.

On stage right, there was a stage management console, with different monitors, next to an old-fashioned ghost light, sent as a gift from a stagehand in another theater. A heavy door led to an alleyway outside, where I was told several casts have had their summer barbecues.

As we stood on the stage and looked out into the house, Jared told me about all of the technical equipment in the show, how complicated and dangerous some of the mechanized scenery is and how safe the actors and stage management are. I thought of Michael Rupert, getting injured by some of the first mechanized scenery, right where I was standing.

The walls of the house at the August Wilson look as though they've been sponge-painted, and during Carrie, *they were painted black. There are odd, fake boxes at the mezzanine level, and décor that matches the design of the exterior.*

Jared took me up to the dressing rooms, and we looked out the windows. For the first time, I saw the same view as all of those actors who, for decades, have yelled to their buddies across the street. I like to think that even in 1935, when Alfred Lunt and Lynn Fontanne were doing Taming of the Shrew *at the Guild Theatre, they shouted across the street at the Gershwins, working on the original production of* Porgy and Bess *at the Alvin.*

The swing floor was five levels up, and Jared and his two fellow swings shared a small room with a slanted ceiling and no window. The three guys had decorated their dressing room as part frat-house, part Broadway library, and that was exciting enough to me, even before Jared added that the room had been Mandy Patinkin's during The Wild Party. *He had kept his aquarium where we were sitting!*

We walked down the hallway of the swing floor, and on the other side was the fly man. We were so far up, that we were actually in the flies of the stage! Ron let me press a green button and cue the screens to fly them in before the show that night. I looked up at a steep ladder that was there to take the crew further up into the fly.

Near the end of the hall on the top level, there was a door. I knew exactly where it must lead. I opened it, and sure enough, there I was, looking at the top floor of the Guild Theatre building, where I'd stood with Ken Billington and Jason Kantrowitz. We'd unlocked the door!

After interviewing Jared for a while in his dressing room, we were interrupted by the intercom: "Jared Bradshaw, are you in the building? Jared Bradshaw?" We ran down five flights of stairs quickly. Jared was going on that day and needed to check in.

Before I left so that Jared could get into costume, he showed me the stage management office. He opened the door to show me the bathroom, above which a sign hung. It said:

Here, on this spot, on May 17, 2006
Former President William Jefferson Clinton peed.

...Accompanied by a photo of the Presidential Seal.

For me, the August Wilson started with President Calvin Coolidge turning on the lights, and ended with the story of President Bill Clinton peeing. Welcome to Broadway, where even Presidents of the United States feel at home.

"52"

A song by Joe Iconis

Alvin and Virginia were institutions
Alvin and Virginia loved the fall
They lived through epidemics and revolutions
Yeah, Alvin and Virginia had seen it all

They lived on 52nd but not together
They were friends but kinda competitive
Both survived some seasons of dangerous weather
They taught me this lesson on how to live

They'd say
Remember, remember things that now are gone
Remember, remember and carry 'em on
Good buddy
Remember, remember the history
Remember, remember, remember me

Alvin and Virginia were not too fancy
But their tastes often alluded to days of yore
They sometimes played it safe, but were mostly chancy
They were real New Yorkers down to the core

Their tolerance for tourists was always ample
With an ever growing capacity
Alvin and Virginia taught by example
They didn't really speak but they spoke to me

They'd say
Remember, remember things that now are gone
Remember, remember and carry 'em on
My brother
Remember, remember the history
Remember, remember, remember me

Things in New York are temporary
You can beg it to stop changing but it won't
People and places, names and faces
Now you see 'em, now you don't

I've always found that change comes in steps and stages
Alvin left us first, then Virginia went
Now they're just some words on Wikipedia pages
Very few will understand how much they meant

But every time I walk into a theater
I think about the legacy and all who came before
That may sound lame or hokey but it feels like something sweeter
Makes me want to join the legacy more and more

Remember, remember things that now are gone
Remember, remember and carry 'em on
Forever
Remember, remember the history
Remember, remember, remember me

Remember, remember, the things you once admired
Remember, remember and be inspired
Forever
Remember, remember the history
Remember, remember, remember me

The Mark Hellinger Theatre

Built: 1930
Closed: 1989
Location: 237 West 51st Street
Owner: The Nederlander Organization
Formerly Named: Hollywood Theatre (1934-1941), 51st Street Theatre (1940)
Now Known As: The Times Square Church
Longest-Running Show: *My Fair Lady* (1956-1962)
Shortest-Running Show: *The Utter Glory of Morissey Hall* (closed on opening night in 1979)
Number of Productions: 79

I wish I had gotten to work in the Mark Hellinger. But it's been a church. I started doing shows too late. I've worked in every other one, even the Barrymore and the Belasco. I've worked at all those, but I've never worked at the Mark Hellinger, and I guess I never will. Because that 99 year lease will go until I'm dead.

–**William Ivey Long**, Costume Designer/Chair of the American Theatre Wing

Introduction: A Reputation As A Flop House

Frank Vlastnik, Actor

The Mark Hellinger was my favorite Broadway theater.

The first show I saw there was *Merlin*. I saw *Grind* there, I saw *Rags* there, I saw *Legs Diamond* three times because by then, I was working in the business at Gatchell & Neufeld, a general management company.

It's so opulent. That's where *Sunset Boulevard* should have been, because that set would have looked so glorious in that theater! I heard that Andrew Lloyd Webber wanted that to happen too.

It used to be a movie house, and sometimes when you see shows at theaters that used to be for movies, the seats aren't raked enough. The Hellinger was perfect; I just loved it.

The Hellinger had a bit of a reputation as a flop house, because it had so many shows that just did not do well. *Dear World* played there; *Ari* played there. But it was just a stunning theater.

The Nederlanders sold it quickly and surreptitiously. They gave the church a 99 year lease.

1951: Counting The House

Mana Allen, Actor

My Dad, John Allen, was in *Two On The Aisle*. He said that whenever the cast was on break, instead of hanging out with the performers, Bert Lahr would hang out in the box office. Being an old vaudevillian, that makes sense—he was a businessman too.

Dad said Lahr had the amazing talent of being able to do a sketch and count the house at the same time!

256

The Mark Hellinger originally opened as the Warner Brothers Hollywood Theatre in 1930. One of the only Broadway theaters that initially opened as a movie palace, the Hollywood was one of the hottest spots to see a new film in New York City. Warner Brothers built the theater to showcase their new "talkie pictures."

The Hollywood showed movies exclusively until 1934. During the Great Depression, the theater went back and forth between live entertainment and film. The revue Calling All Stars *with Martha Raye and* Banjo Eyes *starring Eddie Cantor were two of its most popular live attractions. Then, for most of the 1940s, only films were shown.* Casablanca *made its world premiere in the theater in 1942.*

In 1948, the theater began housing only Broadway shows, and it was renamed the Mark Hellinger in honor of the famous theatre journalist, columnist, and producer.

1956: Alan Jay Lerner

Maury Yeston, Writer

The second Broadway show I ever saw was *My Fair Lady* at the Mark Hellinger. I was a little kid, and it completely sold me. The two turntables, Cecil Beaton's costumes, Julie Andrews and Rex Harrison, that score by Alan Jay Lerner and Frederick Loewe… it was extraordinary.

Alan Jay Lerner later became my mentor and friend. The producer Herman Levin had heard my song, "New Words", and he was interested in producing one of my shows. He had produced *My Fair Lady*.

Herman's office was on Madison Avenue and 49th Street and Lerner's office was two floors below it. One day while I was with Herman, he called Lerner and said, "You have to come upstairs and hear this kid play this song."

I played my song for Alan Jay Lerner. He told me that when he was younger, Oscar Hammerstein used to drop by and give him coaching and notes on his writing, and that he would be glad to do the same for me. He told me to just stop by every few weeks. That's what I started doing. It was extraordinary.

My Fair Lady was the Hellinger's first true smash hit show, running for nearly six years, four of them at the Hellinger. (The show eventually moved to the Broadhurst and then the Broadway.)

The original Broadway company starred Julie Andrews as Eliza Doolittle and Rex Harrison as Henry Higgins.

On December 23, 1957, Moss Hart played the part of the Escort of the Queen of Transylvania for one night only. My Fair Lady was Moss Hart's 41st Broadway show, and his second-to-last before he passed away at the age of 57. He had agreed to direct My Fair Lady after hearing only two songs.

1956: Direct Current

Jason Kantrowitz and Ken Billington, Lighting Designers

When we first started working in old Broadway theaters, you couldn't plug your blow dryer, or anything else, into the outlets in the dressing rooms. The theaters all ran on direct current.

Direct current is very efficient in operating things like motors and lighting boards. When the theaters were built, we lived in a direct current world. Some things still run on direct current, such as the New York subway system and most elevators. Alternating current can travel longer distances and is more efficient for most other electricity needs besides operating machinery.

You used to walk into a Broadway dressing room and see a sign that said "DIRECT CURRENT, DO NOT PLUG HAIR DRYERS IN." If you were lucky, there would be one alternating current socket. You couldn't plug any appliances in at all. They would blow up!

Everything started to change beginning with *My Fair Lady*. Abe Feder, the lighting designer, used autotransformer dimmers, which needed alternating current. It went into the Mark Hellinger Theatre, and in order for them to use those lighting boards, they had to convert the theater to alternating current. Then, *My Fair Lady* moved to the Broadhurst, so *that* theater got alternating current. It was such a hit, that it played houses all over the country. If you wanted *My Fair Lady* in your theater, you had to convert to alternating current.

Broadway was actually still a little behind the road houses in that regard. Most of the Broadway houses stayed direct current until *A Chorus Line* showed up at the Shubert with its computer controls. At that point, all of the shows began utilizing computers and electronic dimmers, so every theater was converted.

Phantom of the Opera was another show that changed lots of theaters. Because of *Phantom*, new lighting positions for equipment were added all over the country, steel was added to the rigging systems, and trap rooms were rebuilt so that 300 candles could come up out of the floor. If you go into roadhouses where *Phantom* was done, you can still see where lights were hung in order to house the chandelier, the angel, the boxes. You can see where *Phantom* put those points, and now other shows use them all the time.

1959: Courting My Future Wife At *My Fair Lady*

Charles Strouse, Writer

I miss the Hellinger, because I met my wife when she was in *My Fair Lady* there. I used to wait backstage to court her after the show

I first met Barbara Siman at a party thrown by a girl I used to go out with. She and Barbara were friends because they were both dancers. This girl was having a party, and I guess they were lacking a guy so she asked me to come.

I saw *My Fair Lady* so many times. Mostly, I would see the last part of it. The stage door man—I think his name was Jerry—would let me in because he knew Barbara and I were going together. I would always watch from the wings of the Hellinger.

At the time, I was 30 years old. I had written some music for one Broadway revue, and for a play, and *Bye Bye Birdie* was about to happen but hadn't happened yet.

It's a remarkable adaptation that Alan did for *My Fair Lady*, and the score is wonderful. I always watched it and thought that. The theatre is so full of mixed feelings though. Sometimes, I look at or listen to somebody else's show and think: *Why aren't I doing this? Why didn't I write this?* It's a terrible thing. It permeates everything. It's one of the reasons why people call people "Darling" all the time.

I never really knew Fritz Loewe, but that was the first time I met Alan Jay Lerner. 24 years later, we collaborated on the Broadway musical *Dance A Little Closer*.

258

I was always waiting around in the wings of the Hellinger for Barbara. So that theater has a certain kind of nostalgia for me.

1964: My Dad's Stage Manager Script

Mana Allen, Actor

I still have my dad's original stage manager script from *Fade Out–Fade In.* There were lots of good stories about that one.

My dad used to talk about particularly dangerous cues, and there were a few on *Fade Out–Fade In.* They were incumbent upon my father to call the cues right, or someone would get hurt. He talked about those dangerous cues like they were his famous tightrope walking stunts from the circus.

He was in the middle of one of those cues one night, and composer Jule Styne came up to him while he was calling it. Jule yelled, "John, the violins are too loud!" Jule Styne was really tiny, and my father took him by the collar, flung him across the wings, and then finished calling the cue. Nobody got hurt. At that point, my father banned Jule Styne from coming backstage during the show ever again.

When Carol Burnett left the show, Betty Hutton took over her part and they rehearsed at the Hellinger. Daddy remembered that when Betty arrived at the theater for rehearsal, she brought trunks of clothes with her. They'd rehearse her for an hour and twenty minutes and then she'd have a break, and use it to go to the dressing room and change into a completely different outfit. Every outfit was top-to-toe. She'd come back out in a sailor outfit with a little tam and sailor clothes and sailor shoes. And then she'd go on the next break, and come out as the "Good Ship Lollipop" girl.

The first night she went on with Jack Cassidy, who was the other lead in it, he sang a song and Betty Hutton turned to the audience and said, "Isn't he wonderful?" Jack leapt off the stage and told my father, "I am not speaking to that woman. If she ever does that again, I will walk out of this theater." It was one of those moments.

Over the years, several people had offices in the Hellinger Theatre, including Jule Styne. By the account of several people, Styne's office was dingy and often smoke-filled and one couldn't see much out the dirty old window. His piano had burn marks on it from times when he'd forgotten to put his cigar out. But it was a great, cheerful place, always filled with music and meetings.

Not only did Jule Styne have his office at the Hellinger, three of his shows played there: Two on the Aisle *(1951),* Hazel Flagg *(1953), and* Fade Out-Fade In *(1964).*

1965: Bigger Than It Actually Was

Ted Chapin, President of The Rodgers & Hammerstein Organization/Past Chairman of the American Theatre Wing

Although I never worked there, I have many memories of seeing shows in the Mark Hellinger. To me, that theater always felt bigger than it actually was.

I never saw any of the great shows that played there, but I did see *On a Clear Day You Can See Forever*. The actor Clifford David was a friend of our family's, so we went backstage and he walked us out into the auditorium. We just stood in the back and that was very cool. I also saw *A Doll's Life, Coco, Legs Diamond, and The Utter Glory of Morrisey Hall*. I never saw the original production of *My Fair Lady*, alas.

1969: Take Out These Seats!

Red Press, Musical Coordinator

I did *Coco* at the Mark Hellinger. It was a beautiful theatre, just lovely. It had a nice, big orchestra pit.

Even with that big pit, we'd hired too many musicians to fit! Andre Previn, the film composer who wrote the music, said, "Take out these seats! The pit needs more room." So, they did. At that time, if a composer said, "Take out seats!" the production would take out seats. If Richard Rodgers or Irving Berlin wanted a 40-piece orchestra, they got a 40-piece orchestra. Now, composers are so anxious to do a show that sometimes they're told, "We'll do your show with five musicians," and they say, "Okay!"

———————————

During Coco, *the female ensemble had very quick changes in the wings. They had to pretty much strip down to nude to change in and out of Cecil Beaton's costumes. At the Hellinger, the load-in door is right near the stage right wing, and Katharine Hepburn liked to keep it open because she liked it to be cold. The girls were practically freezing to death!*

So, she bought them all cashmere sweaters as a gift. The door stayed open.

———————————

1969: Katharine Hepburn In A Musical?

Harvey Sabinson, Press Agent

Coco, by God, yes! That's the show that had the biggest advance line I ever had for any show. People were clamoring to see Katharine Hepburn in a musical. She was a lot of fun; I loved her. She was supposed to be murder on press agents, and everybody I talked to said they were terrified of her but I wasn't. She was great.

———————————

Coco *was at the Hellinger during an interesting time to be housed on 51st Street: a 48-story office building called the Uris Building (now called Paramount Plaza) was being built next door. It would soon house new Broadway theaters named the Uris (now the Gershwin) and Circle in the Square. Reportedly, Katharine Hepburn did not enjoy the sound of construction during her solo numbers, so each Wednesday, the construction workers would pause so Hepburn could sing her 11 o'clock number, "Always Madame" in peace.*

One of the chorus girls in Coco *was Ann Reinking. While Charles Strouse had once been the stage door johnny of the Hellinger, now it was Bob Fosse's turn.*

———————————

1971: Feller Scenery Studios

Gene O'Donovan, Technical Supervisor

Feller Studios was in the South Bronx. When I first started there, it was right across from Yankee Stadium. The building is still there, although Yankee Stadium is not.

I was just a stagehand. I started out working in a shop. I got there by mistake. A friend of mine knew someone who worked in a scenery shop. They were looking for ten young bodies to load some trucks. We all went up to this scenery shop in the Bronx, Feller Scenery. And off we went, loading trucks. I was the only one of the ten who wanted to go back. I was hooked from day one. That was probably 1965 or 1966.

The great thing about working at Feller Studios was that they did so many different things. We got to work in so many areas! I was part of the group that built all of the staircases, windows, and doors. But I was sent to the drapery shop, and I learned how to sew drapes. And I was sent to the covering shop, and I learned how to build stage floors.

You'd go in there in the morning, and you'd end up in Detroit for four days. When I first got there, I always wondered why people had socks and underwear in their tool drawer. I found out pretty quickly. Sometimes you just didn't go home.

Often, we didn't know where each piece would go, but one of the first times I remember knowing was on *Jesus Christ Superstar*. There was a chalice that we built. I worked on that with a sculptor, and did a lot of the carpentry end of it.

The shows just went on and on and on, working at Feller Studios. When the shop closed, I was kept there—it was sort of a deal between the person I was going to work for and Pete Feller, the owner of the studio. It was really a different day and age. You were sort of an indentured servant. And you were really happy to be that, too!

I learned a tremendous amount from Pete Feller. I still think about him. His son is the prop man at the Barrymore Theatre, and we're good friends. And when you meet people who worked in that shop, we always have Feller-isms: things that were said to us that we say now, or ways things were done that we carry on.

When I came back from the army, from Vietnam, I was asked to come in to work. I said, "Pete, I'm just home for 30 days." And he said, "Be here tomorrow. I was in a real war." Later on, I found out that he was the technical director of *This Is The Army*!

Being a shop guy, I always felt like being able to work with Pete Feller was the be-all and end-all. He had a huge effect on so many of our lives. And younger people who are in the theatre now really don't know who he was.

Feller Studios was an amazing place to work. I worked on the original *Chicago*. Pete was the person who, if you were at that point in your life where you needed a passion, you could find that passion in him. He was passionate about the theatre. I learned so much about owning a scenery shop from him. I learned what I would do, and I also learned what I wouldn't do. He was a yeller and a screamer. I'm not a yeller and a screamer. We felt that his way of motivating people didn't motivate us at all—even though sometimes it did.

As of late, as I get older, I find myself not having the patience that I had in my younger days. I've started to think that Pete held it together very well. He seemed to be enthusiastic until the very end. I think about that.

The great thing about this business is that so many people will teach you. It's the kind of business where, when you show up and say, "I don't know anything about this," people go, "Isn't that great? Let me teach you how to do this." That's the way it was, and that's the way it still is, which is pretty fantastic.

Production photos from the original Jesus Christ Superstar *at the Mark Hellinger prominently display the chalice Gene helped build.*

261

Many who worked at Feller Studios went on to long careers in theatre production. Gene worked side by side with Bill Menchine, who now owns Show-Motion, Fred Gallo, who's now president of Scenic Technologies, Jerry Harris who now owns PRG, and Neil Mazzella, who is now the head of Hudson Theatrical.

Two of the most in demand technical supervisors and production managers on Broadway today are Gene O'Donovan and Neil Mazzella. They met as stagehands on the 1978 Michael Bennett musical Ballroom. *They were the lowest men on the totem pole, and when Michael wanted to make a change in how the scenery moved, Gene and Neil were stuck in a room for several days, unscrewing wheels off the bottom of platforms and changing them to sliders. As Gene said, "You either never want to see that person ever again, or they become your great friend— and we became great friends."*

Ballroom *played at the Majestic Theatre, and today, 35 years later, Gene and Neil both have their offices at 260 West 44th Street, which overlooks the Majestic. They were partners for several years, after founding Hudson Scenic. They still go out to dinner together once a week.*

I had the great pleasure of interviewing both of these incredible gentlemen of the theatre in their respective offices. I'd known their names, and had infinite amounts of respect for their profession... but speaking with Gene and Neil, I got a glimpse into the world of scenic shops and technical direction that has completely enhanced my understanding of how Broadway productions happen.

1971: Saving *Superstar*'s Sound

Abe Jacob, Sound Designer

I was doing sound for Peter, Paul and Mary on the road, and Peter Yarrow was a good friend of Michael Butler's. That's how I got connected to *Hair*, and designed the sound for the San Francisco production. I met director/choreographer Tom O'Horgan.

A little while later, I was on the road and decided to stop in New York to see *Jesus Christ Superstar*. It was going into the Hellinger, and I had a couple friends in it. When I got to the theater, a sign on the door said that the shows had been postponed. I thought I would see if anyone was around anyway, so I could say hello.

I walked into the Hellinger, and I saw Tom O'Horgan. He told me that they were having sound problems, and I began to help. I was in the right place at the right time. It wasn't the fault of any individual, but a lot of things conspired against doing sound the way that they wanted it done in that house.

Jesus Christ Superstar had been trying to use all wireless microphones. In 1971, the technology for this was not developed. The wireless mics would make the sound system pick up taxi signals and other radio calls! They weren't reliable, and the loudspeaker system that could do high-quality playback back then was more suited for home use than for a large theater like the Hellinger. They had enclosed the orchestra pit, to create a recording studio sound, but the fact that there was no air space around the instruments created a very closed-in sound.

The first thing that we did after I got there was to get rid of the wireless mics. Tom O'Horgan re-choreographed the shows based on handheld mics with cords. Robin Wagner, the set designer, said, "Why don't I put fake vines on the microphones? They'll look like they're from the garden of Gethsemane." We all worked together. I changed the loudspeakers. Three days after I got there, they had their first preview of *Jesus Christ Superstar*.

The Mark Hellinger was a terrific theater. I loved the size of the orchestra section, the size of the stage. I also did the musical *Merlin* there, with Doug Henning, Chita Rivera, Nathan Lane, and Christian Slater, who was 13 years old. That was 1983, and the sound in the theater was terrific. Because the Hellinger had such a large orchestra section and small mezzanine, the natural sound is very good. I'm sorry to see it's not a theater anymore.

───────────────

At the beginning of the 20th century, Broadway musicals did not use any microphones. As the sound of the Great White Way evolved, stage mics began coming into play. Microphones would be placed on the stage and hanging in the air, to pick up voices. Wireless mics, or body mics gradually came into play in the 1970s. In 1976, The Robber Bridegroom *was one of the last Broadway musicals to not use body mics. The original production of* A Chorus Line *the year before had also not used body mics.*

In their early days, wireless mics on Broadway were in the FM band of radio. Sound designers needed to adjust the mics in their show to an unused frequency, and that depended on many other factors. If a mixer tuned the sound just a little bit differently than usual, they might pick up an FM radio station during the show! Cabs in those days used illegal radios, and if they were driving by a theater, that could also interfere with the sound. Many times, a baseball game or pop song was accidentally heard coming from the speakers in a show with wireless mics! Microphones have come a long way since the 1970s.

───────────────

1978: Second-Acting, Stage-Dooring And Being A Student

Brig Berney, Company Manager

When I was a student at NYU, I would second-act shows all the time! It was so much easier then. Sometimes, I'd come up to Times Square the night before I wanted to go to a show, when it was getting out, and I'd grab a Playbill or find one in a trashcan so that I could walk back in with the crowd the next day after intermission.

I'd always pick a show that I knew wasn't selling out. I remember second-acting *Ballroom, I Remember Mama,* and *Da.* I probably went to shows more often than I did homework. I learned a lot from going. If I liked a show a lot, I would go back and see the whole thing.

One night, I remember walking around Times Square and I walked by the Mark Hellinger, where *Platinum* was about to start playing. Bruce Vilanch, who wrote the book, was outside, and we started chatting about the show. Then he asked me, "Would you like to come in and watch some of our tech rehearsal?"

I stood in the back of the theater for a while, watching the show with him. There was one funny bit in *Platinum* where Alexis Smith taught some of the other characters how to do a time step. Bruce asked me if I could do one, and I said no, so he taught me a time step, in the back of the house.

I had a lot of fun experiences like that when I was a young kid, a student in the city. I've actually never seen Bruce Vilanch since! I've never had the opportunity to work with him. But I realized early on that so much of this was about contacts. About knowing people your age and also knowing people older. Back then, you could really stand at a stage door and say, "I'd love to meet the stage manager. I'm a kid at NYU and I love theater," and you could get shown around. Because there were far fewer people who went to stage doors back then, you could get noticed by someone—perhaps remind them of their younger self—and learn from them.

I love doing that myself now. I love hearing, "How did you become a company manager?" and then getting to pass on any knowledge I have to people who might find it encouraging.

───────────────

My first time ever going to the Hellinger was in 2006. I was sitting at home one day, and I read on the BroadwayWorld message board that it was possible to step inside 1989. Well... almost. You could step into the Times Square Church, and actually look around at a Broadway theater's lost former glory. I immediately got on a subway and rode up to Times Square. I found out that you had to visit the church only during certain hours on Wednesdays and Fridays. I sat outside for a while and imagined what it would have been like to see Fade Out-Fade In *or* Rags, *and then I went home. Of course, I returned later that week, and I was not disappointed. The Hellinger is palatial in such a way that no other Broadway theater can hold a candle to.*

Recently, after interviewing Wicked's *current Elphaba, Lindsay Mendez, backstage at the Gershwin, I saw handfuls of people entering the theater across the street for church service. I snuck into the Hellinger with them, for a quick peek at our theatrical past. What if the Hellinger could still be a home to big musicals like* Wicked *that now need homes? What if the Gershwin and the Hellinger were meant to be neighbors, like the Simon and Wilson, with show people in each theater bonding with the other across the street?*

––––––––––––––

1979: Scene Shops, Softball, And Tony Awards

Neil Mazzella, Technical Supervisor

You needed some hook to get work on a show. And in the old days, the hook would always be some shop, a scenery shop. When I was working at the shop for the Metropolitan Opera House, I met stagehands there who were working shows on Broadway. They'd say, "Hey, do you want to replace somebody?" So I'd go and fill in. It wasn't a regular job, though.

One show that I filled in for years was *Sugar Babies* at the Mark Hellinger. One of the stagehands at the Opera House shop was the head carpenter there, and he constantly needed guys to come down and fill in for guys taking days off. That's how you'd get in. Then you'd hopefully get a real job—a steady one. You'd look for those opportunities, to work as a replacement, and you'd use them to get to know the house carpenters and key employers down there, and work your way in.

The Hellinger was a great theater. A phenomenal theater, with a lot of things to see, and good sightlines. There were many, many shows at the Hellinger. It was a sought-after theater. In fact, one of the negotiations that fell through was that director/choreographer Michael Bennett was going to buy the theater himself. Unfortunately, that didn't happen.

Sugar Babies was a vaudeville show with Ann Miller and Mickey Rooney. The whole set fit in the first half of the stage. The second half of the stage was used to play softball, football, and any other sport we were doing while we were waiting to change the scene. It was as old-fashioned a show as possible, with enormous stage space.

Ann Miller asked us to stop playing softball because, when she would walk by, she would get nervous about the ball flying by her head. She couldn't see the way she used to. We stopped right away. She was a very sweet woman. It was a great environment to work in.

I ran the light board for the Tony Awards that year, when we did it at the Hellinger. That was the famous year that Liz Taylor mispronounced Jimmy Nederlander's name. She announced him as "James Needleheimer." I got blamed, because they said I dimmed the lights, and, of course, I didn't. It was in all the papers that the crew, being overzealous, changed the lighting. I got a letter later, apologizing.

It was also a memorable Tony Awards because it was the year that David Merrick won for *42nd Street*. We don't have Tony Awards like that anymore. We always used to do them in a working Broadway theater. So we'd have to move the set aside and bring in the Tony Awards set. But it was a really magical time, doing the Tony Awards back then.

––––––––––––––

In 1984, Michael Bennett was one of the first of the Broadway big wigs to try to buy the Mark Hellinger Theatre from the Nederlanders. The powerful director of A Chorus Line *and* Dreamgirls *wanted to expand his empire, and he wanted to become a theater owner. The Nederlanders said yes to Bennett, but at the last minute he cancelled the deal. He would succumb to AIDS three years later.*

Bennett's first choreography credit was on a short-lived musical A Joyful Noise *at the Hellinger in 1966. In 1985, the film version of* A Chorus Line *was filmed at the Hellinger. In 2006, Michael Bennett's lawyer, John Breglio tried to buy the theater to premiere the first Broadway revival of* A Chorus Line*. His efforts failed.*

1980: She Took A Lot Of Energy

Penny Davis, Wardrobe Supervisor/Dresser

Oh, the Hellinger! I filled in as wardrobe supervisor on *Sugar Babies* at one point. I had worked for so long for Ann Miller, but when I turned 25, I became officially too old to dress her. She took a lot of energy. But I would sometimes still come in and help out.

She was doing *Sugar Babies*, and called me to do it, but I had another show at the time. One night at six o'clock, I had people coming over for dinner, and she called me and said, "Penny, girl? I need you to come in tonight. My dresser's out sick." I said, "Ann, no, I can't. I don't know the show. I've never seen the show." "Well you've got to come in and do it." And I said, "Look, I'm sure the wardrobe supervisor has everything under control. And I've got people coming over for dinner." "Well just call up and cancel!"

So I called the wardrobe supervisor, Irene Ferrari, to find out what was going on. She didn't really have it under control. I went in and learned the show later that week. Back in those days, you didn't get paid to learn a show. So it was a freebie. Then I started working on that show at the Hellinger.

1981: The First Thing I Ever Performed On A Broadway Stage

Liz Callaway, Actor

I moved to the city in 1979 with my sister, Ann Hampton Callaway. I went to college for four years, and then I moved to New York. I had the feeling that I had a lot of ability and raw talent—but I knew I had a lot of work to do, and I was definitely a late bloomer.

My goal when I moved to New York was to get into the chorus of an off-Broadway musical in three years. Of course I didn't realize that not all off-Broadway shows have choruses! Then I landed *Merrily We Roll Along* after being in New York a little over a year. I did a lot better than I thought I would!

With *Merrily*, we were all cast in December of 1980, and then we didn't officially start rehearsals until the fall of 1981. In that time between, because I had the credit that I was going to be in the new Sondheim musical, I got *Senior Trip*, a TV movie about a group of high schoolers who visit New York City. It also starred Scott Baio.

In *Senior Trip*, I filmed a song at the Mark Hellinger. I did scenes with Mickey Rooney there. That was the first thing I ever performed on a Broadway stage. I can't believe I remember this because it was so long ago! It was at the Hellinger when *Sugar Babies* was there, so that was very cool.

1980s: Cable TV

Jason Kantrowitz, Lighting Designer

Back in the 1980s, cable TV became very popular, and all of the stagehands wanted to watch it during their breaks. But no one wanted to pay for cable, so they would actually go to the roof and string cables back and forth across the streets between the theaters!

There were cables that you could see, going from the Neil Simon, to the Hellinger, to the Gershwin. One person would be paying for cable for all of Broadway. Don't tell Time Warner!

1979/1982: We'll Never Get It Back

Ken Billington, Lighting Designer

The Hellinger. I forget about the Hellinger.

My friend Arthur Whitelaw produced a show there called *The Utter Glory at Morrissey Hall* (1979). I went on opening night and at intermission, we went across the street to some bar. We came back at intermission and backstage, the wardrobe lady was packing the wardrobe on opening night. David Graden, who did the costume design, said, "What are you doing?" She said, "I've seen it, haven't you?"

In fact, it did close that night. The cast went to the opening night party with their makeup cases.

I did *A Doll's Life* (1982) at the Hellinger, and that was an amazing musical that did not get its due. I'm not saying it was perfect, but it had a lot to say, and the score was just beautiful. It was beautifully designed and directed, too.

I remember all of the theatre queens at the first preview. And by "theatre queens," I mean: people who go to the theater all the time and have many opinions. I remember hearing them in the lobby going, "Oh, it's the worst show I've ever seen. It's terrible. It's terrible!" When the bell rang for intermission, they knocked each other over trying to get back in to see act two. How terrible was it? If it was that terrible, dinner would be more interesting. So that was one I thought was really killed by ill-will. I liked *A Doll's Life.*

We'll never get the Hellinger back. It's a church. A very successful church. We sold out.

In the era that they sold the Hellinger, the Broadway theater owners couldn't get shows to put in their houses. There was talk at one point of tearing down the Broadway Theatre completely. I wish we had the Hellinger now, but 25 years ago, everything was different.

During the 99 year lease, the church is not allowed to present any theatre in there.

It would be great to get it back. It probably looks better now than it did when Broadway shows were going in. I know that when they shot the movie *A Chorus Line* there, they painted it and made it look a lot better than it did. I probably did five or six shows in the Hellinger. I liked it. I thought it was a good theater. I'm sorry that the Nederlanders sold it to the church, but the church is very successful. That church ain't going any place.

––––––––––––––

The Times Square Church is very happy on 51st Street, In fact, it's such a prime location that if you want to buy the place now, you also have to pay to relocate the church. At least, that's what I've heard!

266

Still, at least the Mark Hellinger hasn't been demolished or turned into a retail space (although, years before the theater became a church, its main entrance on Broadway was turned into retail space and is now a McDonald's). The Mark Hellinger is still there, and anything could happen in the future.

1985: A Show About Violence

Harold Prince, Producer/Director

There are some things I wish I had done differently about *Grind*. It's a fascinating show.

I wanted to do a show about violence, because we were living in a very violent period, as we're still living in now. I wanted *Grind* to be about every kind of violence—domestic violence, public violence, all kinds.

Instead, it became a very specific story about a burlesque house and its goings on. That is what Fay Kanin had written as a movie originally—but they didn't make the movie, and I wanted to tear the material apart. I didn't persist. I might have failed, but that's what I should have done.

The score is good, really good. But it was a schizoid musical, and it failed because of it. Still, it had one of the best opening numbers of any show I've ever done in my life, "This Must Be The Place". There are two shows I've done that failed that had incredible opening numbers. The other one was *Tenderloin*, with the opening number, "Little Old New York". They both were musicals where the opening number worked, and the audience thought: *Well, this is going to be the greatest evening!* And then, everything from then on was downhill. That's sad.

1986: One Of The Last Shows

Alex Rybeck, Musical Director

There are so many beautiful theaters on Broadway. To me, the magic of a theater isn't just about the work that goes on inside, but—especially in the older theaters—the actual architecture and design elements that surround you as you look around.

Like so many other people, I really want to see the Hellinger reopened. It was—and presumably still is—so gorgeous. I saw *Rags*, and *Sugar Babies*, and many other shows which played there, but you almost felt you got your money's worth just by walking across that palatial lobby with its huge chandelier and monumental staircase. It definitely made you anticipate whatever you were about to see.

1986: My Heart Was Broken

Charles Strouse, Writer

In 1986, decades after *My Fair Lady*, I had a show of my own at the Hellinger: *Rags*. The musical, about the immigrant experience in America in 1910, had lyrics by Stephen Schwartz and a book by Joseph Stein. It closed after four performances.

When *Rags* closed, my heart was broken. My heart was *broken*. It was one of the saddest days of my life.

I had put so much of myself into the show. I'm Jewish. My ancestors, like everybody's ancestors, came from another country. I have very strong feelings about my identity as an American who's indebted to Native

American and African Americans and Jews and Italians. I paid a lot of attention to the music during the era that the show was set.

I think the show has some of the best, most heartfelt lyrics that Stephen has ever written. I feel the same way about my score. I wrote it for a great artist, Teresa Stratas, our leading lady. She was a bit nuts too, but I really fell for her. When you're writing for a great performer, you tend to love them. You really feel their voice. She was that way about my music too. The show was a great experience. Stephen and I had a great time collaborating, and we remain friends.

It was a very significant project for me. And it has its appreciators. I'm glad to say I get mail about it every once in a while. There are productions of it all the time now. But that's the terrible thing about Broadway. Shows get known to be "hits" or "flops," and that's the last word. It's just terrible.

Your blood is all over the page on one, and that's a flop. Your blood is all over the page on the next one, and it's a smash. That's Broadway.

1986: I Gave A Curtain Speech And We Marched On Times Square

Lonny Price, Actor/Director/Writer

The Hellinger felt too big. The first row felt a hundred million feet away because the pit was really big.

I saw *Timbuktu!* there. *Dear World. Legs Diamond. Grind.* That lobby is so beautiful. I always loved the lobby.

Then I did *Rags* there. I think it may have fared a little better in another house. I do have a feeling that there are certain theaters that don't have a lot of energy in them, and certain theaters that do.

I didn't read the reviews of *Rags* but I knew they were bad. And we had no advance.

I had some notion that we could turn it around, so I wanted someone to do a curtain speech. Teresa Stratas and I were talking about it and I said, "You have to give a curtain speech and tell people to tell their friends. Maybe if we sold some tickets, the producers wouldn't close it so quickly, they would look at it differently."

She said "You do it." I told her, "I don't want to do it, you're the star." And she said "I need to be an enigma. They shouldn't hear me other than as the character." She was an amazing woman, she was also very Norma Desmond-y at times. I adored her and she and I were very friendly. She sent me to pick up the awards that she won that year!

After our final matinee, I stepped forward and said to the audience, "We're closing tonight." They groaned. Then I said "But, perhaps…" They were all yelling, "We hate the critics" and I was going, "No, no, no, let's not do that. That's not important. But maybe we can turn this around. We're going to go to the TKTS booth and try to drum up some business. It would be really cool if you came with us."

We went out the stage door—in our costumes—and marched down to the ticket booth. And we sold out. We sold 700 tickets at the ticket booth in an hour because the entire audience came with us! We had posters and we had given them posters. I was sort of leading everyone.

We stopped traffic, and it was actually mostly the audience that started going up to everybody and saying: "We just saw this extraordinary show, you must buy tickets to it!" They sold the show. Within an hour, we sold out that night. And we still closed.

It was an audience show, and it has a great score—and Teresa was amazing. I thought "Well, if we could have kept doing this, maybe we would have had a chance."

I was just kind of fearless. If I believed in something, I didn't care what the protocol was. The truth of it is that if *Rags* had run another week, I wouldn't have been able to do *Dirty Dancing*. I was praying *Rags* would run so I wouldn't have to do it.

I just wanted to be on the stage. I just wanted to be in shows. I didn't care much about the movies. And I remember thinking: *Oh, God. If it just runs one more week, I won't have to do the movie.* Then it closed and I did the movie and I'm very glad I did the movie! As it turns out, it was a wonderful, wonderful gift to do that film. But that's how I felt and that's what I remember.

───────────────

The Hellinger was one of the largest theaters on Broadway. Holding 1505 seats, it was about as big as the Winter Garden or the Lunt-Fontanne. In the 1970s and 1980s, the big musicals that played the Hellinger didn't stick around for long. Shows like Ari, 1600 Pennsylvania Avenue, Platinum, The Utter Glory Of Morissey Hall, A Doll's Life *and* Rags *all played less than one month of performances.*

Since 1970, the Hellinger had had only had two notable hits: Jesus Christ Superstar *and* Sugar Babies, *and by 1989, that was a big problem regarding the coffers of the Nederlanders. They didn't think that a big hit show was likely to grace the theater any time soon.*

As James M. Nederlander said at the time, "There's no shows being produced. We have to keep the theaters filled. We've got the Gershwin with nothing in it. We'll have the Nederlander as well. We don't have anything on the horizon to put in the theater."[39]

At various points, there were plans to turn the Nederlander into a disco and the Lunt-Fontanne into a multiplex.

The Hellinger's exterior and interior are both landmarked, so the Times Square Church couldn't change the features of it. The church actually rented the Nederlander Theatre from 1987 to 1989, and hadn't changed anything there—if anything, they restored the building to its former glory.

The huge, gorgeous, three-story lobby is as luminous now as it looks in 1956 photos of Lerner and Loewe during the intermission of My Fair Lady. *The entire place is burnished in gold and rose shades, and every room is filled with stunning details, like a fireplace in the lower lobby and an old timey ticket-takers' desk in the main foyer. Many of the people who I interviewed who worked there, and who have since snuck into a church service to get a fervent peek at an old home, attested to the fact that the theater now looks far more beautiful and shined up than it did in the 1980s.*

"In show business," Nederlander said, "You have to take the first booking."

───────────────

1980s: The Last Great Orchestra Pit

Michael Starobin, Orchestrator

They're starting to reduce the state of the orchestra pits. And the state of the orchestra pits, for most theaters, is already very sad. It used to be that orchestra pits were fully in the open, so musicians didn't have anything over them. Broadway pits were like opera pits: if you go see the pit at the Metropolitan Opera, none of the

───────────────────────────

[39] Rothstein, M. (1989, February 8). The Hellinger Theater Is Leased to a Church. *New York Times*. Retrieved from http://www.nytimes.com.

musicians are under the stage. The pit is a long, wide, open area and the players are all out in the view of the audience. You almost don't need to amplify the band in any way. That is how the Broadway orchestra pits used to be.

Two things happened. One: to get more seats, Broadway theaters built their stage forward, over the pit and put musicians underneath, with just a small opening. And two, in the 1970s and 1980s, and during *Dreamgirls,* people wanted to make the pits more like recording studios. Shows wanted to be able to completely manipulate the sound. So the pits were dropped, lowered. Then it actually became almost impossible for any sound to project out of the pit.

Now, you also have many scenic elements being built *through* the pits! When I did a production of *The Grinch,* different stairways and elevators had to go through the pit. Suddenly, it's harder to see the conductor, and even if you're five feet away, you may be watching him on a video monitor.

The union argues for the number of musicians in the pit, which is a whole other issue. But, separate from that, the union has no say over the conditions of the pit, in terms of what's in it. Broadway's never going to go back to being acoustic, but the sound of Broadway shows could be more natural if some of the sound actually came directly out of the pit.

There's only one unaltered orchestra pit I've ever worked in, during my time on Broadway, starting with *Sunday in the Park With George* in 1984. The only pit I ever saw that wasn't covered was at the Mark Hellinger. The Hellinger had an opera style pit where everything was out in the open. It actually ended up causing problems for myself and other orchestrators! We would write for amplified sound, but then end up in the rare pit situation at the Hellinger. There, the orchestrations could use heavier, fuller textures under a voice with amplification.

Suddenly, at the Hellinger, a number of shows felt "over-orchestrated." This was because everyone had gotten used to covered pits! I did *Sugar Babies* there, and then orchestrated *Rags* and *Legs Diamond*, both of which were flops. I saw *Grind* there, which flopped. It didn't have a great track record with successful shows. But to me it's one of the greatest tragedies that that house is gone. It definitely needed renovation. It was old, but it was beautiful old. It was lovely on the inside and it's a complete shame that's not a theatre. It's a church.

Legs Diamond was one of those sad shows that did two months of previews, wherein they kept hacking at the show, trying to make it better. It never really got better. It was upsetting, and Peter Allen was such a sweet man. When you're going through a show in crisis like that, it's like trying to dance in an earthquake, and he was very friendly and nice throughout the whole thing. It was so sad to see him going through that experience. No one knew that it would be the last musical there.

One of the great things about the house is that Jule Styne used to have his office in it. I used to walk underneath this long passageway from backstage, going all the way under the audience and coming out of the lobby at the back of the house. There was another little office off of that passageway and it had a sign that said "Property of Paul Whiteman." I guess Paul Whiteman, the old jazz bandleader had an office there. Perhaps his band was the house band at one time. I never got to find out.

1986/1988: Magnificent

Laura Heller, General Manager

My ex-husband, Eric Stern, was the conductor on *Rags*, and I'll never forget how heartbroken everyone was when it closed. They all got together and marched through the streets. Michael Starobin marched with a drum! It was an emotional show, with a fabulous cast and a great score. It really was heartbreaking.

270

Then I spent some time at the Hellinger later during *Legs Diamond*. And at one point, Peter Allen invited us to Atlantic City. We spent the whole time going through secret passages. It was fabulous. He had just lost his manager to AIDS.

I remember that the lobby was magnificent. Someday, someone could get it back.

1988: One Of The First Automated Sets

Joe Traina, House Manager

Legs Diamond was produced by the Nederlander Organization. Several million dollars were invested by the Nederlanders themselves.

The show starred Peter Allen and was about the famous gangster of the Jazz Age. It was really a pastiche consisting of a number of songs strung together by a fairly thin plot to showcase Peter Allen's talents. Harvey Fierstein had written the book.

One of the problems was that it was one of the first times automated sets were used in a Broadway show. David Mitchell designed them, and they looked great—but they wouldn't move properly. When you're tied to a design with technical problems like that, you're stuck. Since it was automated, you couldn't even solve the problems by getting someone to push the scenery out on stage.

I was standing in the lobby of the Hellinger on many nights, as a representative of the theater. I had to tell people that there would be no show that night and that we didn't know when there would be a show. I remember saying a lot of, "We may have a show tomorrow, but possibly not."

That was challenging, to be on the front lines. Some guy from Denver was really angry that he couldn't see *Legs Diamond*, and told me that if I hadn't been such a nice guy, he would've punched me in the nose.

—————————

In December of 1987, the New York Times *announced that producer Alexander Cohen would open a revue called* Bright Lights, *comprised of songs from the last 50 years of Broadway musicals at the Hellinger, the following summer. On opening night, the theater would be renamed the Richard Rodgers.*

In January, the paper amended this news, announcing that the show would open in the fall of 1988 instead, and that the Mark Hellinger would be renamed the Richard Rodgers as part of a large-scale television special.

Bright Lights *never happened. The 46th Street Theatre was renamed the Richard Rodgers instead.* Legs Diamond *claimed the Hellinger for the fall of 1988, and then the theater was gone.*

This was just a couple short months before Jerome Robbins' Broadway, *a revue comprised of songs from several decades of Broadway musicals, opened and took New York by storm, winning the Tony Award for Best Musical.*

Could Bright Lights *and the Richard Rodgers television special have saved the Hellinger? We'll never know.*

—————————

1980s: I Want The Hellinger Back

Nancy Coyne, Advertising and Marketing Executive

I've worked on over 1000 shows, and oh God—I loved the Hellinger. It broke my heart! I want the Hellinger back. We did Cameron Mackintosh's *Oliver!* there, and for Hal Prince, we did *A Doll's Life*. Losing the Hellinger—that was hard!

The Crime Of The Century

James Woolley, Stage Manager/Usher

I did *Timbuktu!* with Eartha Kitt. Everyone has this image of her as a certain kind of performer, but off stage, she was demure, shy and sweet.

To this day, I'm shocked that the Mark Hellinger is a church. It's the crime of the century. I worked on a lot of Tony Awards ceremonies that were held there. It was acoustically perfect, had perfect sightlines, was a perfect, gorgeous theater. It's a crime that the theater is empty. It pains me every time I walk down 51st Street.

When I was doing *Sunset Boulevard*, we were looking at venues. We even looked at New York City Center. Andrew Lloyd Webber offered the church a large amount of money to use the Hellinger, which would have been the perfect theater for that show. And the church said, "If you can find us a bigger space to go to, we'll go."

—————————

The Tony Awards were held at the Mark Hellinger Theatre in 1970, 1980, and 1987.

On February 19, 1989, after a torturous run, Legs Diamond *closed. Eight days earlier, the* New York Times *officially reported that the Nederlanders had leased the Mark Hellinger Theatre to the Times Square Church for five years. Many theatre folk understood the decision. The Hellinger hadn't had a hit in many years. The Nederlanders had put their own money in* Legs Diamond. *There weren't a lot of shows demanding theaters.*

Some however, disagreed with the leasing of the Hellinger as shows that were big hits were suddenly extending their runs longer and longer.

Producer James Freydberg commented, ""If Cats *continue[s] to play, and* Les Miserables *and* The Phantom of the Opera, *and with* Aspects of Love *and* Miss Saigon *coming, there are going to be fewer large musical theaters available. And if one of the larger and better houses is going to be locked away for five years, it shows very little insight into the future of the theater."*[40]

Miss Saigon *almost opened at the Hellinger in the early 1990s. In fact, Cameron Mackintosh wanted to buy the theater from the Nederlanders. He postponed* Miss Saigon's *Broadway bow when he couldn't find an appropriate Broadway home for the epic musical. There were some rumors it might then go into the Hellinger, but the Church wasn't interested in giving up their lease, and Mackintosh didn't want to wait.*

—————————

[40] Rothstein, M. (1989, February 8). The Hellinger Theater Is Leased to a Church. *New York Times*. Retrieved from http://www.nytimes.com.

The Immortal Theatre

Nick Wyman, Actor/President of Actors Equity Association

I would like to work in the Mark Hellinger Theatre someday. I know it belongs to the Times Square Church, but the theater is also sacred to Broadway. To me, it's the immortal theater. It's gorgeous! It's a great space for musicals, and we need musical spaces. I'm not a big fan of those large, newer theaters. But in the Hellinger, you feel like everybody in the space is in the same room with you. You can feel that you're all enjoying the show together. I would love to see the Hellinger come back to Broadway. It's not torn down. At least we have that.

———————————

With the hoopla over the Broadway theaters that were demolished in 1982, it was no wonder the leasing of the Hellinger was kept quiet and private.

The Nederlanders needed the money, and demand for Broadway theaters was in decline. The organization had been having trouble booking the Nederlander, the Mark Hellinger, and several of their other spaces. They had also purchased the New Amsterdam and were taken aback by how much work needed to be done to return that theater to use. They put their own money into Legs Diamond, *and it turned out that that was the last straw. So they made a deal with the Times Square Church. After the five year lease was over, in 1991, the decree came down—The Nederlanders had extended the lease: The Times Square Church would call the theater home for 99 more years.*

In 2010, Michael Riedel reported that every Broadway big wig had made a play for the old Hellinger at one point or another. The Shuberts even told him that if the church would ever sell, they'd be first in line. But the church says that they will never sell. (And if they do, the Nederlanders have first dibs!)

———————————

1988: The Last Show

Joey Parnes, Producer

When we were doing *Legs Diamond* at the Hellinger, we had no idea that it was going to be the last show in the theater.

At that time, the number of previews we had before opening was unprecedented. We cancelled some of the previews entirely, because we had an enormous amount of trouble with the set. We have better technology today, but back then, it was rudimentary and the demands on it were too complicated. We actually had to throw out some scenery, just because we had to weed it down. There was so much of it.

During previews, the creative team also eliminated an entire character as they rewrote the show. An actor who was on contract lost his job, because they just took the role out of the script. That was one example of the kind of stuff that was going on during *Legs Diamond*.

As tough and troubled an experience as it was for everyone working on it, as much money as we were losing, Peter Allen, who was the star and composer, was unbelievably great. I learned something from that that stuck with me. When the person on the top of the bill is a mensch, it actually makes it impossible, or at least very difficult, for anyone else to behave badly. Every day, people were upset, people were feeling all kinds of pressure and anxiety; but Peter was upbeat and positive. I only saw him lose it one time, and it was earned. Other than that, he never let us know that he was disappointed, worried, embarrassed, ashamed. None of those things ever came past his face. He was always, "Let's keep going! Let's do this!" I've done other shows where the headliner was cranky and difficult, and that permits everyone to be cranky and difficult. Sometimes, they're late or uncooperative and then the entire show and team absorb that. You can't even necessarily address it unless you have the support of the star. And Peter was an amazing leader throughout all of *Legs Diamond*.

When *Legs Diamond* closed, we thought the theater would just be dark for a while, and then another show would come in. None of us saw the sale to the Times Square Church coming. And when we heard, we didn't understand the words. I just remember thinking: *What does that mean, they've sold it to a church? How is that even possible? It's a theater. How could they do that?*

I didn't want to believe it, so I bluffed to myself. *Maybe* it's just a temporary thing. Maybe they're only doing it until the next big musical wants to rent the theater. The more time passed, the more we realized: No, the theater has been sold.

And we were stunned. How could that happen?

The Lyceum Theatre

Built: 1903
Location: 149 West 45th Street
Owner: The Shubert Organization
Longest-Running Show: *Born Yesterday* (1946-1948)
Shortest-Running Show: *Truckload* (closed after six previews in 1975)
Number of Productions: 305

The Lyceum is the oldest continually operating theater on Broadway. And there's something about the personality of the Lyceum that makes it forgotten in certain ways, until you remember it. When you remember the Lyceum, you feel like a child who isn't spending enough time with your grandparents.

It's so obscured from Times Square now, with these giant modern structures around it, so it feels cut off in a strange way. And yet, the Lyceum is a stunningly beautiful building. It's a vibrant, thriving, hidden epicenter of the theatre community because of the Shubert archive on the top floor. There's something about all that history upstairs that anchors the theater, that makes people feel like it's a special privilege to be there.

-Michael Berresse, Director/Choreographer/Actor

Introduction: Everything I Ever Wanted A Broadway Theater To Be

Jeff Bowen, Writer/Actor

When we were looking for a Broadway theater for *[title of show],* our producer Kevin McCollum took us around one afternoon. We went to see the Cort, I believe, and we went to see the Belasco, I believe. We went to see Circle in the Square. Then, we went to see the Lyceum.

We were all together -- myself, Hunter Bell, Heidi Blickenstaff, Susan Blackwell, and Michael Berresse, walking around and feeling what it felt like to be in those theaters. We were going into stage doors and walking around on stages. The Lyceum was the fourth theater we visited that day, and it just felt totally right. For some reason, on that stage, the closeness of the house was perfect. It was a sweet feeling. It was a theater that felt like a little old lady, and it was a great space.

The Lyceum is everything I ever wanted a Broadway theater to be. It's so old-school. It's an underdog of theaters. It's everything I thought was awesome about being on Broadway. It's not even a class officer of Broadway. It's not the president, treasurer or secretary. It's just the class coordinator.

And it would be fun to do a show in the Gershwin, but I'd worry that I'd get swallowed up by it. I'd have to find my own secret corner that could be mine.

Knowing that the Lyceum had a repertory company at one time... knowing about the archives of Shubert history that are up on top... knowing that there was stuff there that made that place more than just Broadway—it was such a *theater*. You just knew that behind every layer of paint at the Lyceum, there were at least ten more layers of paint and another bizarre color from another bizarre time. Everything was so old!

It's this little theater on the wrong side of Broadway, but it's so awesome, and it has so much integrity, and so much history, and it's quiet. There's a quietness about the Lyceum Theatre's bones. That old lady feel. The

Lyceum is that cool old lady in the corner that you don't really know unless you choose to go up and talk to her, and then you find out: "Oh my God, that was the neatest person I've ever talked to in my life." And you just wouldn't know. The Lyceum is the best one.

During my sophomore year of college, I saw a show that changed my life forever. I lived in an NYU dorm on 14th Street and 3rd Avenue, and on my walk home one day, I saw a cool show poster in the window of the Vineyard Theatre nearby. I walked into the theater, bought a ticket, and 30 minutes later, saw [title of show] *on a whim.*

I loved it very much, and as the show's run at the Vineyard played out, it became very popular within the theatre community. The next school year, I was putting on a musical theatre revue with some of my college friends, and we all were obsessed with songs from [title of show], *so I decided to write to the creators of the show and ask if we could sing some of their songs.*

Hunter Bell and Jeff Bowen wrote a kind letter back saying that the future of the show was still pending, so they weren't able to have songs from it performed out of context yet. Jeff and Hunter were so generous and down to earth that I ended up inviting the whole [title of show] *gang to see our production. (This was the same production that Jay Armstrong Johnson and I had been rehearsing in a dorm basement!)*

Not only did Susan, Hunter and Jeff march down to NYU to see our little show, they even called [title of show] *director Michael Berresse and held up the phone during the performance so he could hear one of the songs! We were honored, and blown away by their kindness and encouragement toward all of us.*

1965: The Lyceum Looms In My Imagination

Jack O'Brien, Director

I was the assistant director for the APA Phoenix Repertory Theatre, and we spent many seasons at the Lyceum. My mentors were John Houseman, Ellis Rabb, Eva LaGalienne, Alan Schneider, and Stephen Porter.

It was a long time before I got my own show. Houseman knew that something was going to fall out of the season, and he shoved in this O'Casey play, *Cock-A-Doodle-Dandy*, directed by me. I was 29 years old when I did that. I was not a mover and shaker, or even a voice at the table. I was a facilitator meant to be taken advantage of—in the proper way—if it was possible. And he made it possible.

The Lyceum looms in my imagination for a lot of reasons. First of all, it was our home. It was the APA home and it was dearly bought. We thought we were moving to Broadway, and then the Ford Foundation grant intended for us fell through.

Fortunately, because of the great good fortune of timing, APA's *You Can't Take It With You* moved into the Lyceum and played for a year, so we had a chance to regroup, raise money, and sort of apportion the funding. By the time they closed, the Lyceum was ready for us and we were ready for it.

I have a photograph of Ellis standing on the marquee with his arms open saying "Welcome to the Lyceum!" Rosemary Harris is a faint figure in the window behind. The Lyceum felt like a private playground because it had been conceived as a rep house.

Even when I went to the Lyceum with *The Nance* this year, and took the company through, we could no longer climb up the stairs far enough but we could see a paint frame at the top of the rear of the theater where they could hang canvases to paint scenery. There's a slot in the floor on every subsequent floor of the dressing rooms that flips up so that the paint frames could be lowered all the way down to the deck and taken up and be put into the theater. There's rarely been anything like it.

There's an apartment on the top of the theater that now holds the Shubert archives, but that was producer Daniel Frohman's office. He did indeed have a peep window where he could see what was playing on the stage. There's a secret passage that goes from the men's room underneath the auditorium, to backstage. There are all sorts of wonderful surprises that I know about that you would only know if you were a young person growing up in that theater.

If you were on stage, looking at the house, on stage right—up that staircase—that was Rosemary's dressing room. Up the stage left staircase was Richard Easton's. Ellis had what is now Nathan Lane's star dressing room. Ellis shared his dressing room with Brian Bedford because they never shared a show. And we had a big reception room where we could have company meetings. I can picture the entire company, and where each of their dressing rooms were. It was Sydney Walker, and then it was Keene Curtis, and everybody else above. It's a playground in my imagination.

I returned before *The Nance*, to do *Invention of Love* at the theater. And that was deeply moving. The Lyceum has a very specific place in my imagination, in my loyalty, and in my heart.

───────────

Jack O'Brien currently has upward of 40 Broadway credits to his name, with no end in sight. One of Broadway's leading directors for the past few decades, Jack got his start at the Lyceum Theatre, during the reign of the APA-Phoenix Theatre repertory. The APA-Phoenix leased the Lyceum from 1965 to 1969, and was one of two repertory theaters to call the Lyceum home during the 20th century. Tony Randall's National Actors Theatre had the run of the Lyceum during much of the 1990s.

One aspect of the Lyceum that lends itself well to a repertory company is the backstage set-up. The Lyceum has dressing rooms on either side of its stage, but it also has a large tower of dressing rooms in the back. When the Lyceum was first built, its owner Daniel Frohman created this ten-floor tower to accommodate a scene shop, a costume room, and more additional space that might be needed for a large company. Every time I ran up the stairs in back, I would stare in awe at the narrow open space on each level of the building that Jack mentions, where theatrical drops were once lowered.

There were vents in the floor of the audience, so that the new technology at the time could run fans over ice cubes, pushing cool air through the vents. Voila, primitive air conditioning!

Daniel Frohman also built himself an office on top of the theater, equipped with a small trap door in his study. When his wife, Margaret Illington, appeared in a play at the Lyceum in 1907, he would watch through the trap door, and if he thought she was overacting, he would wave a white handkerchief. The Lyceum's innovative scenery shop rooms are filled with aisles and aisles of theatrical history in the form of old costumes, orchestral books, and libretti.

───────────

Elevator Built For Two

Frank Vlastnik, Actor

I love the old Lyceum. One reason is the Shubert Archive on the top floor. It's amazing, and you get there in an elevator built for two. All of the librarians are so nice and so knowledgeable, and they have these huge old-fashioned office chairs, that look like they're from Frohman's original office!

───────────

The summer after the [title of show] *gang came to see my college show, my path crossed with Jeff Bowen's again when we were both working at The Rodgers & Hammerstein Organization. "Hunter and I are making a couple little YouTube videos to tell people that our show is going to Broadway. Because if we say it, we think it'll come true," he told me. "Do you want to intern with us and help us make the videos?"*

And that's how I came to work on the [title of show] *show, one of the first-ever Broadway web series. I did everything from creating costumes to taking notes to running errands. I hung out with everyone from Lea Michele to Cheyenne Jackson. I spent half of my senior year of college in the back office at Kevin McCollum, Jeffrey Seller, and Robyn Goodman's Producing Office. There were* Rent *posters on the wall and Tony Awards gleaming on the shelves. The back office was filled with all the theatre books I'd spent my childhood reading, when I was 1238.6 miles away. It was the first time I really felt like a member of the community.*

1969: I Sold Programs And I Took Coats

Barry Bostwick, Actor

When I was at NYU, I auditioned for the APA Phoenix Repertory Company and I was contracted to be part of their journeyman apprenticeship program.

First, I did a production of *War and Peace* out in Los Angeles. Then, I said that I wanted to go back to NYU to work on my master's degree, so they said, "Well, okay. We'll fly you to New York—*if* you'll work for us when you're not in school."

So I worked at the Lyceum while I was a student at NYU. I sold programs and I took coats. Because of that, I was able to stand in the back and watch all of their shows that season.

It was a wonderful education for me. I saw *The Show Off, Exit the King,* and *Misanthrope* with Helen Hayes. It was my first Broadway experience and I was able to stand in the back and watch these shows going on. I could watch these wonderful actors do these classic parts, night after night. The next year, I joined the company and made my Broadway debut in *Cock-A-Doodle-Dandy*, playing what I like to call the title role of the cock. I got to do it with Donald Moffat, and some of their best actors. Jack O'Brien directed it, and it was his first Broadway show as a director. He gave me my start.

My first impression of the Lyceum was that there really was a door man in the back! And he really was out of some 1940s movie. "Hey kid!" He was one of those "hey kid" guys.

Because the Lyceum was an older theater, the dressing rooms were small and crowded. I shared a dressing room with Keene Curtis. Everybody there, they were really all mentors to me. Particularly Ellis Rabb. He was one of my real champions and mentors when I was a young person. He was just a genius. My first experiences were in the repertory. They weren't big flashy Broadway musicals. They were serious theatre. That's where I started.

To this day, the Lyceum has been home to over 300 productions. The Lyceum on 45th Street was built by producer Daniel Frohman in 1903, after receiving the news that his first Lyceum Theatre on 4th Avenue between 23rd and 24th Street would be demolished. That theater was built in 1885 and was the first theater to be lit entirely by electricity—under the guidance of Thomas Edison himself! Frohman received several offers of real estate on Broadway to build his new theater—which would at first be referred to as "The New Lyceum"—but he did not want a playhouse directly on Broadway since it was always filled with too much traffic!

Frohman's plans for the New Lyceum were to open each season with an attraction starring Annie Russell, have his stock company play a new production through March, and, in the spring, present E.H. Sothern in a new vehicle. For its first years, the Lyceum spent much time playing several productions in rep at the same time.

When the New Lyceum was built on 45th Street, the area to the west was still called "Longacre Square." The New York Times *would move uptown in 1905 and soon, the Lyceum would be considered part of "Times Square." The New Lyceum was built with several bricks taken from the old Lyceum.*

When the theater was about to open in 1903, the New York Times *declared it a marvel. Not only was the theater exquisitely constructed, it was equipped with every modern theatrical comfort possible. The Lyceum even had a wide enough entrance to accommodate five carriages at once—so theatergoers exiting plays in bad weather could escape in comfort. One of its upstairs accoutrements was a rehearsal room that was an exact replica of the Lyceum stage, so that actors could accurately plot their productions. During* [title of show], *on most nights, you could find standbys Courtney Balan and Benjamin Howes running through the entire show, as it was happening on stage, directly underneath the stage in the basement. I knew that we were doing the exact thing that theatricals had done a century before us a few floors up in the original Lyceum rehearsal room.*

In 1905, Ethel Barrymore appeared in A Doll's House *at the Lyceum. Later that year, a play called* Just Out Of College *told of the exploits of a young man wooing the daughters of several different pickle manufacturers. In 1907, the Lyceum was home to the show* The Boys of Company "B" *which marked the only Broadway appearance by Hollywood's Mack Sennett. At age 27, he played the small role of Servant.*

While the first musical at the Lyceum was Fashions *of 1924, a play with music by George Gershwin, called* The French Doll, *opened in 1922. 91 years later, at the time of printing, the current tenant at the Lyceum is the musical* A Night with Janis Joplin—*which is being produced by George's great-nephew, Todd Gershwin.*

In 2005, the New York Times *called the Lyceum's facade "the most beautiful theater exterior in New York"[41].*

1972: That Old Feeling

John McMartin, Actor

After *Follies*, Hal Prince said, "I'm going to be doing some theater in repertory, and I want you to be part of the company."

We did theatre for three years as part of the Phoenix Repertory Company, and it may be the best time I've ever had as an actor. You would do a farce in the afternoon and a drama at night. It was crazy during rehearsal time, because in the morning you'd rehearse one show, and at night, do another. You wore so many hats. Any young actor would give their teeth to work like that, to get to play these wonderful, classic plays. It was the most productive thing for me as an actor.

We did *Chemin de Fer*, a farce, Moliere's *Don Juan*, *The Visit*, *The Great God Brown*….

I never quite understand people that go, "He does musicals, how is he at plays?" because I find that you're using the same tools. Acting in those shows directed by Hal Prince… he had marvelous imagination. There were things in *The Visit* that were dazzling that I really appreciated. It was a unique and original production. I don't think there's a delineation between plays and musicals; it's all art.

---

[41] Gray, C. (2005, August 14) For 102 Years, The Play Has Been Its Thing. *New York Times*. Retrieved from http://www.nytimes.com

The Lyceum is where my wife, Charlotte Moore, and I got together, working with Hal Prince and Phoenix Repertory. That's how we met, and here we are, more than 40 years later!

When I first played the Phoenix, I was in one of those dressing rooms in back of the theater where the hallway is. Then, in 2007, I did *Is He Dead?* there, and I had a dressing room right off stage.

I was glad to get back there. I love the Lyceum a lot because of that old feeling. It doesn't feel like any other theater.

The Lyceum was the first Broadway theater to ever be granted landmark status, in 1974. It is also the oldest continuously operating Broadway theater! While the Lyceum and New Amsterdam both opened in 1903, the New Amsterdam didn't house a Broadway show between 1937 and 1997.

The Lyceum has a 110-year history of nothing but shows—although, fascinatingly, the Lyceum has only ever housed ten musicals—and five of these were during the 1970s! At around 950 seats, the Lyceum has typically been a better fit for plays—although several special musicals have come in through the cracks.

As our time creating the [title of show] show *web series went on, I got to know the entire team, including Larry Pressgrove, musical director, and Michael Berresse, director, who was also an actor I had loved in many shows and on many cast recordings for years, from* Kiss Me Kate *to* A Chorus Line. *Michael and I began to have discussions about what would happen when the show went to Broadway—in terms of staging, publicity, concepts, everything. Eventually, I would become his assistant.*

I spent most of my senior year of college on 45th Street, in a producer's office that would wind up being just a couple doors down from the Broadway theater that [title of show] *would open in 11 months later: The Lyceum.*

1975: *Truckload* Hurt

Ilene Graff, Actor

Truckload was a show that closed before it opened.

The music was by Louis St. Louis, who had been the original musical director of *Grease*. He was a towering talent, a great singer and songwriter, and so energetic and fun to be with. He decided to write this show about hitchhiking across the country. There was a huge red truck on stage, with a platform on it that held the band. He played the truck driver and he "drove" the band. It was all on a turntable and it spun—the show looked terrific!

Louis wrote all these great songs with his partner, Wes Harris, and he got Pat Birch involved. She was the choreographer of *Grease* and part of our gang too. I did a bunch of backer's auditions for the show. The songs were amazing and Louis played his ass off on the piano. Producers started throwing money at us because the score sounded so great!

We went into rehearsal and the book was problematic. It wasn't as strong as the songs. Maybe if we had done the show as a concert, it would have been a success. The whole cast was wonderful, but the show as a whole was just uneven. We started having trouble with our producers, and when we got into the Lyceum, we had a ton of trouble with the sound system. It was just terrible.

Dick Clark was one of our producers, and he came in to tech one day and said, "This sound system stinks! We're pulling it all out and putting in a whole new sound system." He spent a ton of money and replaced the entire sound system at the Lyceum, and within days, we were closed.

We came to the theater one day and Manny Azenberg, who was our general manager, called us all upstairs into one of those tiny offices at the Lyceum. He said, "I have some news. We're done. We're not doing the show tonight or ever again."

It was the worst disappointment of my life. I had been playing Sandy in *Grease* on Broadway, and I'd left to do *Truckload*. We didn't even get to open. To this day, I've had several series cancelled, pilots that didn't sell, shows that closed, projects that fell apart—but nothing has hurt close to the way that *Truckload* hurt at the time, because we all believed in it so much. I loved it! I loved singing those songs. I loved singing those backup parts—the backup parts in the show were to die for! Then, it was all over and it was horrible. After six previews.

The Shuberts had a hand in producing the show, and Phil Smith knew how crushed we all were. He came over to me and gave me his business card, and scribbled something on the back. *A Chorus Line* had just opened and of course, I knew everybody in the show and in the pit. He said, "Any time you want to go see *A Chorus Line*, show the ushers this card at the door, and they'll let you in." So I would go stand in the back of the Shubert and watch *A Chorus Line* and sob. There were all these people with jobs!

1975: Closed During Previews

Todd Graff, Director/Actor

I didn't see *Truckload*. It kills me! I never missed anything my sister was in. But it closed so early in previews! I never got to see it, to my great chagrin.

1975: A Fire Engine Red Truck

Louis St. Louis, Writer/Arranger

Truckload was similar in concept to what they're doing down at the Public Theater right now with the show *Here Lies Love*. Pat Birch, our director, originally wanted to reconfigure the Broadway Theatre to make it an environmental atmosphere, filled with trees and a road. They all thought she was crazy.

Still, we had inside word that *Candide* was going to close at the Broadway, and if we could wait three months, we could have the Broadway.

We ended up at the Lyceum. When we loaded in, I sat in the front of the fire engine red truck, with the piano bolted into the hood, as they brought it down the hallway through the load-in dock, at the back of the Lyceum Theatre.

The show had an 18-piece orchestra! They were all up on this scaffolding that was behind the big, red truck.

We had gotten all of the money for the show from two presentations. We did the show in a rehearsal room twice, and then we had the Shuberts and Dick Clark as our producers. Adela Holzer came on board later, and many blamed her for the show's quick closing during previews. When it happened, some people went to her town house on East 72nd Street, and covered it in toilet paper! Luckily, no one was charged, but it did make all of the columns the next day.

In all of Broadway history, there have been only six musicals that technically closed during previews, without opening: Truckload *(1975, Lyceum),* The Little Prince and the Aviator *(1981, Neil Simon),* Senator Joe *(1989, Neil Simon),* Breakfast at Tiffany's *(1966, Majestic), starring Mary Tyler Moore and Richard Chamberlain and adapted from the Truman Capote novel,* One Night Stand *(1980, Nederlander), a Jule Styne musical about a comic who planned to kill himself at the end of the evening, and* Rachael Lily Rosenbloom and Don't You Ever Forget It *(1973, Broadhurst), the campiest musical to ever play Broadway.*

1975: Gritty

James Dybas, Actor

The Lyceum Theatre is on 45th Street but the stage door is on 46th. So, for *Truckload*, we had to load in the entire truck across a block, down a long hallway inside the theater.

It's a very old theater, so everything was kind of creaky. That was a good match for the show. *Truckload* was gritty. There was this great big red truck on stage that people could actually get in and out of. Pat Birch, the director, spent a lot of time making sure you could see the people who were in the truck. I was her assistant.

We rehearsed *Truckload* at the Winter Garden, actually. Pat was very cool in rehearsal. She always wanted to go with the flow, and everyone getting along was very important to her. She told the company they could come to her with any problem. She could fix problems in the show easily, too. Most of the cast members in the show were not trained dancers, but she made them all look terrific.

Louis' music was so terrific and contemporary and eclectic. Wow. I'm really sorry that there wasn't a cast album. I did take a lot of home video, though.

Truckload *has a special place in my heart, because it is a key part of one of my favorite Lyceum adventures during* [title of show]. *As Jeff Bowen remembers:*

"And of course, my favorite story about the Lyceum involves you. That day that we decided to get into dressing room G. It was off right, on the top floor, and it was the dressing room that had either never been renovated, or hadn't been renovated since 1920. We were determined to figure out how to get in there, and just see what was there. But deep down, I had this secret goal. I collect Playbills of shows that ran 50 performances or less, and when we first announced that we were going to be at the Lyceum, I thought to myself: Somewhere, in the walls of that theater, there's got to be a Truckload *Playbill. I know there's one somewhere in the building. I'm not leaving that building until I find it.*

"And Jennifer Tepper and I found a way to get into that dressing room one day. It was so dusty and my allergies were killing me, but there were all these old ticket forms—handwritten ones. Honestly, there was literally nothing we could find in that room that could have been put there after 1980. Everything was from a time before that. It was like nobody had gone into that room in 30 years. The old sink fixtures and light fixtures were there.

"I was so glad we did that. And I remember I was in my "Jeff" costume, because we were in the middle of a two-show day. That was funny, because it was so part of the character, something that he would do, too. It made me so excited that night when I was performing the show, knowing that we had done that.

"I wonder if anyone's been up there since us! Probably not. It's really high up, on a crazy high floor, and it gets dark as you go up! I remember the light stopped at the fourth floor, there isn't even a light on the fifth floor, so we

walked up in darkness to the sixth floor, and there was just one working light bulb. There was really no reason you'd want to go up there unless you wanted to shoot a horror movie or something. But it was so exciting, knowing that once upon a time, this was a fancy little dressing room that some little chorine sat in who was doing a turn-of-the-century operetta.

There was a cabinet of old press clippings. We found Something's Afoot *press photos. And somewhere in the long-forgotten dressing room, we scored two mint-condition* Truckload *Playbills—which we might have stolen."*

———————————

1976: He Should Have Won The Tony

Ed Dixon, Actor

The original production of *Something's Afoot* at the Lyceum was really a great production. It's a flawed piece, but that was such a delicious production with such delicious people in it. I think I saw it, full price, three times, maybe four. I just couldn't believe that the critics ran the show out of town. That broke my heart.

Gary Beach should right then and there have won the Tony. I'm not kidding. I will never forget that performance. It was a staggering performance, and I couldn't believe that he wasn't nominated. It didn't make any sense because it was just *that* good. Sometimes when a show is not successful, people won't give the nominations that are deserved, in my opinion.

I've always wanted to work in the Lyceum because I saw Whoopi Goldberg's debut in that house in 1984 when no one knew who she was, and I saw *Something's Afoot* in that house, which I have such fond memories of.

1976: I Saw *Something's Afoot* And You Signed My Playbill!

Ann Harada, Actor

I loved *Something's Afoot* because I loved Agatha Christie novels. I loved the idea of a spoof of that.

My family was at TKTS and we said, "Oh, this looks good."

Later, I met Gary Beach. When I got to work with him, I said, "Oh my God, I saw you in *Something's Afoot* and you signed my Playbill!" He was kind of appalled.

———————————

I spent many hours during the summer of 2008 exploring the Lyceum.

In the lobby, there are two grand marble staircases, dotted with framed photos of theatrical legends of the past. On the first level of the left staircase is a tiny elevator that leads up to the Shubert Archives at the top of the theater! One day, Jeff and I went up to explore with Reagan, one of the archivists. He showed us the trap door in the floor, built into the theater by Daniel Frohman 105 years earlier. I pretended to wave a handkerchief at the stage.

There's a room in the Lyceum below the lobby, on the left—an old-fashioned smoking room, complete with retired fireplace! Clearly out of use for years, the room became mine and our [title of show] intern Leah's own little office. No one else used it.

Every time I return to the Lyceum, I'm terrified that that beautiful out-of-use room will be gone and replaced with a modern merchandise booth, or another ladies' bathroom. I run down the stairs to check for the wooden furniture and seating lining the walls and each time, I sigh with relief. The room is always empty, but it's always there.

1980: Timing In Our Favor

Elizabeth McCann, Producer

The most memorable opening night of my career was for *Morning's At Seven*. The original play had been written and produced in 1939. I worked on a version off-Broadway at some point that got great notices and some press but never did good business. Then, in 1980, there was a production in Chicago that people were talking about. I broke my leg, so I couldn't go see it, but my producing partner, Nelle Nugent, said, "That was a great play!" She believed in it more than I did. It had a reputation as a really lovely play that had a tendency to flop.

We had done *The Elephant Man* and *Dracula* by that point, and both had been hits, so people came up to us during previews of *Morning's At Seven*, and said, "It's really good of you to put money back into theatre after your success, because you know this isn't going to sell tickets." We couldn't get a feature out of the *Times*. The play was dead. Nobody wanted to hear from it. Then, suddenly our press agent got a call from the *New York Times*, saying that they'd like to assign a reporter to be with the writer of the play, Paul Osborn, on opening night.

They hadn't known Paul's name a week ago, but it turned out that critic Walter Kerr had come to the show and he thought it was wonderful. That was the turning point. There was also a transportation strike the week before we opened, and the whole city was a mess. Then, the strike ended on the night that we opened the show. There was a sudden sense that things were simple. The timing worked totally in our favor, and Walter Kerr wrote us a love letter of a review, and that was it.

Morning's At Seven, a play about four aging sisters, actually played two revivals at the Lyceum. The first, in 1980, was the biggest hit the theater had seen in a while. The second, in 2002, didn't run as long, but did star Estelle Parsons, Frances Sternhagen, Christopher Lloyd, and more.

The longest-running show of all time at the Lyceum is not a musical, as is the case with every other theater in this book. The Lyceum's long-runner was the original production of Born Yesterday, *written by Garson Kanin and starring Judy Holliday.* Born Yesterday, *about a corrupt businessman and his smarter-than-she-looks blonde mistress, ran for 1642 performances—no small feat in 1946.*

1982: Apartheid Stories

Lonny Price, Actor/Director/Writer

I loved the purple seats at the Lyceum. I thought they were so beautiful; I just loved them. The purple seats and the wood. It's a beautiful house. The marble staircase. It's really gorgeous.

Our dressing rooms were in the back. That part is not very pretty. And that tunnel is very weird.

"Master Harold"… and the Boys was a very lonely show for me because it was just the three of us. And I played the white boy that spat at the black man so it was depressing. It ran for ten months and it was just hard. But I

was very proud of being in something that I thought was really, really, really good. The writing was terrific and it was about something so important. I felt honored to do it.

I realized the magnitude of the play when I read it. I didn't get the part at first. Zeljko Ivanek got it. Zeljko did it at Yale and then he took a horror movie called *The Sender*. He thought the play would wait for him and it didn't.

I was the second choice. I remember reading the play in my bedroom in my parents' house because I was still living there. It was so clearly an incredible piece of work, and for a young actor to play, to have that many colors to get to play… it was just a gift from God to get to do that with the man who wrote it directing it—and it was about him! It was overwhelming.

I thought that Danny Glover was the bomb. I mean, Danny in that role… he was just crazy-great. And then I directed him in the Broadway revival of the show 20 years later. He's the sweetest man, and he's a citizen of the world. He's in Haiti one day, fighting injustice, and then he's here doing the show. He's a real political force. I admire him a lot.

I knew that Todd Haimes at Roundabout was a very big fan of the play and I said "I would love to do it again, and let's get Danny to do the lead." He said, "Anytime." So I stalked Danny a little bit and I said, "We need to do this for the new generation. We need to show this play." That's how it happened.

The first time—*because* it was a first time—when my character spat at Sam, the gasp was extreme. There was this horrible, horrible gasp. During the revival, apartheid was over, so I think the play had less potency. I think that time is not far enough away—it's in a no man's land right now. It ended up that apartheid stories at that point were not that interesting to people.

1982: A Fly On The Wall

Sally J. Jacobs, Stage Manager

"Master Harold"… and the Boys might have been the most emotional show I've ever been part of. Athol Fugard would sometimes be on the floor crying. I was young, and it was extremely moving to see a playwright have such emotion toward his production. It was his story. That's what's so beautiful about the theatre, you get to have these live experiences, telling stories that actually happened.

I was happy to be a fly on the wall for that. That was at the Lyceum, and it was very special.

1993: Tony Randall, Jack Klugman, And The National Actors Theatre

Danny Burstein, Actor

I didn't audition for *A Little Hotel on the Side* at the Belasco. I had worked with Tony Randall at the St. Louis MUNY, doing *Around the World in 80 Days*. I had these wonderful parts opposite him, and we got along famously.

I said to him, "If you ever do this National Actors Theatre thing…" which he'd been talking about for 20 years before that, "…please let me know, because I would love to be a part of that."

Sure enough, in 1990, I got a call from him. "Danny! Tony Randall!" And there he was, saying, "This is the season. And I think I see you starting out over here, and then growing up in the company. Your assignment this year is that you're going to be in this play, and you're going to cover these roles."

He said, "I love you. And I believe in you. And I hope one day, you'll take over the company from me." I said, "That's amazing. That'd be wonderful." Of course, I knew nothing about running a theatre company, and that was completely off-the-charts intimidating and crazy to me at the time.

It was a beautiful experience. Tom Moore was a wonderful director, and we had a great time doing the show. A great time! And then the reviews came out. The reviews killed us—and Frank Rich went after Tony. That was hard. All of a sudden, literally, the next day after the reviews came out... we had been getting screams, crazy laughter. Standing ovations. Lynn Redgrave and Paxton Whitehead and Maryann Plunkett and Tony were giving fantastic, wonderful, ridiculously funny performances, and Tom Moore had added all these bits in that were piss-in-your-pants funny. The next day after the reviews came out, nothing. It was like a bomb had dropped in the theater. It was heartbreaking. Heartbreaking. Unfortunately, that followed the National Actors Theatre on Broadway. More often than not, the reviews were extra-tough on the company. It was very upsetting.

When we did *Three Men on a Horse*, we were at the Lyceum. Jack Klugman had survived throat cancer, and he was taking a huge risk—encouraged by Tony, who was his best friend—to come back on Broadway. They fashioned a microphone, two mics that were fastened under his shirt, right at his collar, so that it could pick it up when he talked in his gravelly voice.

It was jarring because you were so used to hearing him speak in his normal voice. But he had lost a vocal cord to cancer so he built his voice up on one cord. And he was spectacular in the show! It was just that his voice was very, very different. People needed to get used to that. There was an adjustment period, watching the show. You'd sit there, and go: *It's very different.* And it was. But, you understood him. And he was still as wonderful an actor as ever.

The day after the reviews came out... many of the reviews questioned whether he should've come back. *How could he do this? He really shouldn't have. It was too distracting.* And Jack and Tony, they were both my heroes. Tony took me under his wing, and Jack was the greatest guy. He had survived cancer, and stopped and smelled the roses. That's the way he turned his life around. He just became this wonderful guy who gave back.

He came in that next day, and signed in, and I saw him at the board. He was really down. I said, "Are you okay?" I didn't understand the impact of it, because I thought, you know, why would he give a shit about the critics? I didn't. But he really took it hard. He walked to his room, shaking his head, and he said, "I just don't know..."

I followed him to his dressing room, which was off stage left at the Lyceum. There's only one dressing room right there. I sat in his room, and he said—he was very emotional—he said, "Maybe they're right. I should never have come back—I really shouldn't be doing this anymore, I'm past my prime, and I should just hang everything up on the shelf."

I told him, I said, "Jack! You're my hero. I love you. Hearing these words come out of your mouth—" You know, this is from me, I'm a young kid. "Hearing these words come out of your mouth, it's like I'm listening to something impossible. You know? It's like watching Superman cry, and go 'I'm no good anymore'. Are you kidding? You're Superman!"

It meant so much to me to let him know how much he was respected in the company, and how much he was respected by so many actors, myself especially, at that moment. He was very sweet, and took it to heart, and listened to me, and patted me on the back, and thanked me. I left his dressing room. And he went on.

Tony then convinced him to do something. One night, after one of the shows, Tony and Jack were left on stage. Everyone of course jumped to their feet, because it's Tony and Jack. Tony said, "Would you indulge us for a second? We'd love to do a scene from *The Odd Couple*. But we'd like to do it without this special mic that Jack is wearing. Just us, no mics."

They did it, and the crowd went crazy. They loved it. Because Tony and Jack were brilliant at that, God knows! Then Jack asked them whether they could understand him without the mic, and whether they knew what was going on, what he was saying, and everyone roared their approval. They had just watched it and gotten every joke!

He sort of looked down, and thanked them, and the two of them walked off arm in arm. The whole cast, we were all sitting in the wings , watching them do this, and praying that it would all go so well. And it exceeded all of our expectations. Wow. That's a memory that I had forgotten about. That was at the Lyceum. And it was an amazing, amazing day.

As Danny Burstein told me about Tony Randall and Jack Klugman, on a windy summer afternoon in Riverside Park, I realized that the dressing room where he had told Klugman that he was his hero in 1993, was Michael Berresse's dressing room during [title of show]! *I had spent days on end in that dressing room, organizing opening night gifts, working on sheets of notes, meeting with Michael, learning how to direct a Broadway show. The dressing room opened directly into the wings of stage left, or directly into an alley that led to 45th Street, giving anyone with access to it a very quick entrance right from the street to the stage. And Danny spent time in that room too.*

I can only assume that room has a long history of people talking to their heroes in it.

I grew up obsessed with the original cast recording of A Chorus Line, *so my anticipation for the 2006 Broadway revival was gleeful. I couldn't wait to finally see the show on the Great White Way.*

A Chorus Line *brought theatre history to life for me in a way that no other Broadway production had. I felt like I was really getting a chance to see and feel what the spirit of the original production was like. Halfway through* A Chorus Line*'s run, I started working with the* [title of show] *team. Michael Berresse was starring as Zach, the director in* A Chorus Line, *and he was also the real-life director of* [title of show]. *It felt wildly sophisticated to watch him play a Broadway director on stage, knowing I was about to work for him, as a Broadway director in real life.*

I remember the morning of my 22nd birthday. We were filming a [title of show] *segment for NY1 and I skipped a class so I could be there. Then, after the shoot was over, suddenly Jeff, Hunter, Susan, Heidi, Larry and Michael were singing me happy birthday and I was blowing out candles on cupcakes... and I had an orchestra seat to see* A Chorus Line *that afternoon.*

A Chorus Line *was a show about people wanting to be in the theatre that ran during the very same year I got to be a part of a Broadway show for the first time. Michael left* A Chorus Line *to direct* [title of show] *on Broadway. I became his assistant. It was the beginning of everything for me—the beginning of a life in the theatre.*

For Michael's last performance of A Chorus Line, *the whole gang got tickets to support him. And I was part of the gang now! We sat in the rear orchestra and I watched as attentively as I had the first time while all of the show people fought for their lives. At the end, as one character was raising her arms to the sky, Michael, as director Zach said the very last line: "And I'm so glad we're going to be working together." I knew he was speaking to the characters, but I felt like he was speaking to me, too.*

1993: Respect For Each Other

Brig Berney, Company Manager

I got to work on *Three Men on a Horse* with Jack Klugman and Tony Randall. Everyone worked for minimum and everyone was great. It was such a fun group. They were stars, but they were never demanding. Jack was very lovely to me and gave me a plant that I kept alive for many years after.

Those men were so easy-going, and they loved each other so much. They had such a respect for each other, and they'd go to parties and just be hugging each other the whole time. That was really genuine. Jack was incredibly indebted to Tony for making him realize that he could still perform even though he'd had that operation on his vocal cords.

Tony was just trying so hard to make that theatre company work. He would do anything he could to keep it going. There were rumors that he had sold some of his wonderful art collection to have money to fund it. And I believed that; I believed that he would sell a painting so that the shows could run the ten weeks that they were supposed to. Of course, Tony would never have mentioned that. He would have just done it. He loved this idea so much, of great actors doing great plays for a short period of time.

1995: This Is What The Audience Sees

Tom Hewitt, Actor

School for Scandal was a joint production with alumni of the acting company at the Great Lakes Shakespeare Festival and Tony Randall's National Actors Theatre.

We did the show in Cleveland and then had a limited Broadway run. It never really had a feeling of a Broadway show for us. It was as though Broadway was just one stop, part of a whole co-production with other organizations.

The Lyceum was the first time I had the experience of being in a dingy backstage. It was dark, kind of rundown. That was my world; we were in this dark and dusty place, in a crowded dressing room.

The closing day, for some reason, was the first and only time that I went into the lobby and into the house. I thought: *Well, this is just glorious and absolutely spectacular. This is what the audience sees. This is their experience as they come in. Wow.*

My experience was standing at the stage door and having it smelling of bad Chinese food. My life there was dark and dingy but the audience saw the glamour and beauty of the Broadway experience. That's the first time I had that juxtaposition.

———————————

While the Lyceum entrance is on 45th, the stage door is on 46th, between 7th Avenue and 6th Avenue, an exterior hidden between Chinese food restaurants and juice shops. I loved walking into that stage door on 46th Street! The block is also home to Roundabout's Laura Pels Theatre, and the former home of the New York High School of Performing Arts. (Once the "Fame school," it is now the Jacqueline Kennedy Onassis High School.)

Several cement steps up from an unassuming entrance is the Lyceum stage door. To the right, our door men from [title of show], John and Neville, were always ready to hand you your dressing room key, your mail, and a hearty hello as you walked into the theater. The long hallway, used for load-ins, also had a bathroom, the office belonging to our prop woman, and a large call board, which was often filled with everything from sign-in sheets and Equity

288

announcements to cards from Alice Playten and cartoons drawn by fans. Our sign-in sheet became a favorite "easter egg" to show backstage guests, since at one point, cast members stopped signing in with their initials, in favor of something more creative. The day that Rent *closed, the* [title of show] *cast signed in with graffiti such as "RIP Angel" and "Roger + Mimi 4E".*

When we found out that [title of show] *would open at the Lyceum there was another show currently playing there:* Macbeth, *starring Patrick Stewart. I went to see* Macbeth *alone, and I sat in the rear mezzanine. At intermission, I went up to an usher.*

"I'm going to be working on the next show here!" I told her, with an abundance of absurdly self-oriented joy, like a teenager who expects the whole world to be thrilled that she got her driver's license. As soon as the words were out of my mouth, I felt foolish, but the 40-something woman grabbed my hand and shook it.

"That's wonderful, dear!" she exclaimed, and congratulated me. She pointed at a Playbill in her hand, "You're going to be in here, you know."

During previews of [title of show], *when I would move throughout the mezzanine to take notes on staging, we would wave at each other.*

I spent many pre-show nights chatting with our ushers about theatergoers who ate fried chicken in the front row and shows that deserved to run longer, and I spent many long afternoons during tech quizzing our stagehands about the hardest shows they'd ever worked on and set pieces that had been cut from shows. To me, every single person in our Lyceum Theatre felt like an institution there.

2000: Load-In At The Lyceum

Neil Mazzella, Technical Supervisor

Anybody told you about the load-in at the Lyceum?

You're loading in the stage door! There's no load-in door. At the Lyceum, everything has to be built to fit through the stage door and go down a long hallway. It's extraordinary. It's the only theater without a load-in door.

You have to build a show to fit in its theater. So the first thing you have to do at a theater is to measure the door. If the door is larger than a truck door, then you don't care, because then you just have to fit in the truck. But when it's as big as the door to your apartment, that's a whole other set of rules.

We did a show at the Lyceum called *Rose*, which was all portals and flats. What we did was, we built all the flats at the shop, and then we loaded it in like a K'NEX set. We brought it in piece by piece, and then bolted the whole thing together and covered it.

You can't really load in through the front door, because there's a rail at the back of the orchestra blocking you as you come in, and you have to make a turn to go down the aisle. It's very difficult. You can do a couple of things like that, but the rest is a puzzle!

2003: The Cast Of *I Am My Own Wife*

Doug Wright, Writer

I said to the prospective producers of *I Am My Own Wife*, "Absolutely not. It's a small play, it needs a small venue. It could survive off-Broadway but I don't think it could survive on Broadway. The play is going to get lost in one of those vast, cavernous theaters."

David Richenthal, our producer, very wisely said, "Just visit the Lyceum and see what you think."

We went into the theater, and I felt completely dwarfed by it. I was more convinced than ever that it couldn't work. But our director, Moisés Kaufman, asked Jefferson Mays, our lead actor, to go on stage and start reciting this pivotal monologue from the play. Moisés whispered to me to go to the third balcony, and I did. I sat there in the very last row, and I listened to Jefferson tell the story. And it landed.

I trudged down the stairs and admitted that I was wrong and implored that we go into the Lyceum.

I learned that even if a play is small in scale—a single actor and a single set—if it traffics in ideas that are large enough to fill a volume of space, if it's about things like 20th century European history and the fall of the Berlin Wall and the evolving nature of human sexuality, if it has big ideas, it can fill a big space. That's the lesson I walked away with.

Because a large part of the play was set around the Second World War, we attracted an enormous segment of the Jewish public. I think they embraced us even more vociferously than gay theatergoers, which was surprising to me but obviously very welcome. There were some gay men and women who cross-dressed when they came to the theater. Many would wear a string of pearls which was my character Charlotte's signature symbol. I got emails from people telling me that it had helped them come out of the closet or put them in touch with the history they didn't know they had, which was very moving.

There were also exotic backstage visitations: Siegfried of "Siegfried and Roy" came backstage at *I Am My Own Wife* numerous times, and hugged Jefferson and told him that he recognized strongly in the show the Germany of his youth!

I think the most touching response came from a middle-aged gentleman who came backstage and was still overcome with emotion. He was trembling. He grabbed me, and his eyes welled with tears, and he said, "You don't understand. I am this play. I am a museum curator so I understand it." And I was so touched by that because it didn't have to do either with the historical content of the play, or even my heroine's sexuality, but with one of the play's primary thematic conceits which is the nature of curatorship: how we curate history, how Charlotte curated her furniture, and how I as an author curated her as my subject. So I was very moved by this particular individual.

Jefferson was such an inventive actor that playing all 35 characters wasn't enough for him. He had to make up names and identities for all the phantom actors who he figured were in the cast along with him! There was the embittered old German actress that we called Brigitta Klench, who was doing a cameo and deeply, deeply pissed off about it because in Berlin, she triumphed in *Wer hat Angst vor Virginia Woolf?* And here she was in *I Am My Own Wife* playing a foreign reporter with four lines. We had a wonderful actor from Delhi named Pradeep Gupta who was joining us for the Broadway company, and there was an American actor named Chris who played a soldier at Checkpoint Charlie. He was desperately in love with the actress Ulrique Lich, who played a Hamburg University student who had three lines.

I would come in at half-hour to say hello to Jefferson, and he'd be full of tales about the fights the cast was having. Sometimes he'd also put these other names up on the dressing room doors—because the Lyceum has

290

four floors of dressing rooms and Jefferson was only using one of them. He had a lot of empty ones to fill with other personalities, and he did. With *I Am My Own Wife*, we didn't even have enough people in the theater for the League's baseball team!

It makes me a bit melancholy because as a playwright, the theater doesn't become our home in the same way as it does for the actors. Our visits to the theater are so infrequent once the show is open that we don't get that same everyday sense of neighborhood and community that the actors thrive on.

I do remember being very touched by the tradition of opening night greetings to every new tenant on Broadway. I found that to be a very beautiful tradition. I loved the fact that these baseball games would happen once a week. And I was surprised with my first Broadway show, at how much you did feel part of an instant community.

———————

The Broadway Show League that Doug refers to is a great tradition of the community, begun in 1955. The casts of Broadway shows and other industry folks all get together to play sports in Central Park, including baseball and softball. However, Broadway shows were competing against each other in recreational sporting events even before then. As far back as the 1920s, the Ziegfeld Follies girls had tug-of-war competitions in Central Park with the choruses of other Broadway shows!

On the opening night of every new Broadway show, you can find on that show's call board sheets of greetings from every other play and musical currently playing. Each individual cast and crew signs their sheet and then sends it down the block. I have a "Congratulations [title of show]! From All Of Us At A Chorus Line*" sheet and a "Happy Opening* Godspell*! Best Wishes From The Company Of* Follies*" sheet on my wall to this day. My favorite opening night greeting sheet I've ever seen was backstage at the Brooks Atkinson for* Hands on a Hardbody: *the* Lucky Guy *sheet was signed: "All Hands Together! Tom Hanks." What could be more indicative of the community spirit of Broadway? The opening night greeting sheets are a descendant of the once-popular opening night telegram.*

———————

2008: Part Of It All

Hunter Bell, Writer/Actor

When we were trying to figure out which Broadway house *[title of show]* would be in, we made that all public, via *the [title of show] show* online! It was part fun and part marketing. There was this one episode at the beginning of it all where we ran around to look at stage doors and theaters to see where we might be. The funny thing is that the Lyceum is the first theater we went to that day.

There were all these rumblings about where we'd possibly be able to bring the show. We visited the Cort, and it felt like a southern plantation cotillion inside. Then, all of a sudden, the Lyceum opened up. Patrick Stewart had been doing *Macbeth* there, and our producer, Kevin McCollum, got the theater for us.

We were so excited to be at the Lyceum; it was such a Cinderella story that we had gotten there that the staff felt that too. So, we all tried to soak up and savor the experience. We would do warm-ups together on stage at 7pm, and the ushers would be in the house, prepping the space, and house staff would be around, and we'd sing lines to them. It was so fun to have more people who were part of the *[title of show]* experience. We had a great box office staff, great backstage people, and our great door men!

There was just this special energy at the Lyceum. If I walked into the front of house to get tickets for my family or friends, I always noticed that the box office people were genuinely excited about the show. The door men and security guards were excited for us on nights when we had fans at the stage door. All of those people made me feel so much like a member of the community.

One thing I really couldn't believe about Broadway was that feeling of having your own dressing room key. The door man would hand you your key the moment you came into the space, and every night, handing it to him was the last thing you'd do before you left. It was so special and comforting to hand Neville that key every night. I had my own dressing room on a Broadway show! I couldn't believe it. I'd get my key, sign in, walk down our hallway, and head up to the third floor where my dressing room was next to Jeff's. Jeff had signatures under his dressing room table from previous occupants, and I had fresh paint on mine. I said: "Come on, let's scratch this paint off!"

2008: Run Of The Place

Susan Blackwell, Actor

When we were selecting our theater for *[title of show]*, our producer, Kevin McCollum invited us to visit a short-list of theaters. We went in through the stage door to the Lyceum, and we met one of the gentlemen who would become one of our stage door attendants, named Neville. He was so kind, so welcoming, and he was so much a part of our first moment of visiting the theater that would become our home on Broadway. Neville was a wonderful man. He was an older African American gentleman, with a very distinctive croaky voice. He was so kind-hearted and such a welcoming presence, and shortly after *[title of show]* closed, he passed away. I will always associate him with our entire experience.

I had seen shows before at the Lyceum, and I remembered thinking about how architecturally ornate and beautiful the lobby was. It's something to behold. It's so regal. They literally can't build theaters like that anymore! I saw both *I Am My Own Wife* and *Lieutenant of Inishmore* from the highest balcony at the Lyceum. Those were both good shows, and I had a very positive feeling about the theater.

The Lyceum is really built for a much larger cast than just four performers, one musical director, and our support staff. So, it was kind of great. We are such close friends, and then when we first walked in, we were just like: "Oh, we'll all just share one dressing room! That'll be fine." And all of our agents and managers were like, "Uh, no. You can each have your own dressing room." We couldn't believe that we had the run of the place.

There was a set of dressing rooms stacked on each other on stage right, and I commandeered one to be my nap room. I was working full time during the day at my corporate job, and doing *[title of show]* eight times a week on Broadway. So I would finish my 9-5 corporate work day, get to the theater, eat, sleep, wake up, go down on the Lyceum stage to do a physical and vocal warm-up, and do the show.

Before *[title of show]* happened on Broadway, Heidi was doing *The Little Mermaid* on 46th Street near Broadway and I was doing *Speech and Debate* on 46th Street near 6th Avenue. Having shows on the same street as your friends, and moving from one show to another together gives you the sense that New York is the smallest town in the world. Each time you step out the door and walk down the street, you are greeted by familiar faces who are saying "Hi!" and "You wanna grab a grilled cheese with me?" I think the proximity of those theaters does set up this feeling like it's your street and you're surrounded by friends, just like you would be in a small town.

2008: Crossing Our Fingers And Dreaming The Dream

Heidi Blickenstaff, Actor

When I negotiated my contract to be in the ensemble of *The Little Mermaid* on Broadway, we made sure it said that I had one out: for if *[title of show]* got to Broadway. I thought for sure that they wouldn't allow that, but they said yes fast—because they were certain *[title of show]* wouldn't happen. And I have to say, everybody thought that about *[title of show]*, not just Disney! We thought that ourselves! I didn't think it was going to happen either. The clause was just this safety. In case a miracle happened.

We were always crossing our fingers and dreaming the dream, but we weren't counting on it. And then it all started happening. The *New York Times* said we were coming to Broadway, and I was flooded with all these emails, and then I remember I had to go to *Mermaid* and tell my company manager and my associate choreographer: This is going to happen. This is really going to happen. And everyone at the Lunt was thrilled for me, but shocked. It was something no one was expecting. The show had been open for a hot second, and I was leaving. I exercised my two-week-out and I left.

2008: It Was Like Being In The Beatles

Susan Blackwell, Actor

Before the first preview of *[title of show]* on Broadway, I don't think I realized the extent to which we'd build a very devoted, very rabid following of actual living, breathing human beings. It's hard to gage those things virtually, on the Internet!

On July 5, 2008, when we did the show, the audience was raucous. It was rock-concert-raucous at the Lyceum, and it was overwhelming. After the show, all of the fancy folks who Kevin and people on our team had invited were brought backstage and we were brought up to the green room to meet them. I thought that night: *if this is it, I have won life. This is amazing.*

Then, Seth Marquette, our company manager, came up to me and said, "You need to get downstairs now, before the police come!" I was thinking, "I don't know what your sentence means." But I did as I was told. The cast and Larry Pressgrove, our musical director, were hustled downstairs, out of the room of fancy Broadway guests, and out the stage door—and 46th Street was filled.

Not just the sidewalk, not just the street—even the sidewalk *across* the street was filled with all of these people who had been investing in the fate of the show via the Internet. There were police around, and we came outside, and it was like being in the Beatles. There were barricades, and there were literally hundreds and hundreds of people who had been following our journey, and who were there to celebrate that all of us—not just the performers, not just the people working on *[title of show]*, but all of us in the theater that night, we all made it to the Lyceum. It was one of the most remarkable nights of my life.

2008: This Is Special

Michael Berresse, Director/Choreographer/Actor

Of all of my memories on Broadway, two of the top three happened during *[title of show]* at the Lyceum. The first was our first preview.

I have never, ever experienced such a pure, emotional response from an audience as I did at our first preview of *[title of show]*, because it wasn't about glamour, it wasn't about visibility, it wasn't about awards, it wasn't about money. It was about real emotion. It was about good storytelling and people. It was about connecting and those kids in the audience weren't faking it. They weren't lying, they weren't there because it was a popular thing to do, they were there because the show was speaking to them and saying something very, very specific to them. Something about what was possible for them and their lives.

I'm so emotional thinking about it. I was so proud. I've never been so proud. Ken Billington, our lighting designer, turned to me as I stood in the back of the house before that first preview. I barely ever sat watching that show, maybe once on opening night, I did. It was hard for me to sit, but I would stand often in the back and Ken was sitting in the back row right in front of me, and he turned around during that first preview night and he said to me, "I know that you guys know that this is special,"—and I think at the time that was Ken's 83rd Broadway show—and he said, "But, in 83 Broadway shows, I've never ever seen this before in my life. Until you're 90 years old, you won't realize fully how special this actually is."

I don't think it's going to take me until I'm 90. I think I get it now. But for someone like him to sense that about [title of show]... well, it was special.

No one really knew what to expect. We had a fan base, but we didn't know how far it would go. The whole show was just such an out-of-body experience, in the most delicious way, that I even remember the crew at the first preview, saying to me, "We were watching you guys during tech, and we didn't know what the hell was going on, but then we started really watching the show." The crew guys in that house are just there doing their job. Not too many shows play for too long there, so they don't get too invested in each show, it's all transient. But slowly, they each started to really care, and they were passionate and proud of the show. I think to their surprise, they got jazzed when the audiences received it so well. And I was always walking through that, witnessing that evolve from inside the theater.

It felt like something that was different was happening, and nothing represented that better than the stage door after the first preview. We opened that door out onto 46th Street, and the crowd was so deep and so heavy that they were having to redirect traffic. There were crowds and police barricades and cops. I'll never forget Dale Davis, Jeff and Susan's manager, who is now deceased, sitting there in a chair they'd set up for her, right on the ledge, just sobbing, because for someone in her 70s who had spent a lifetime in the theatre, she just wanted for them to have that kind of joy. She was so proud. She never needed to comment on it, she just wanted to witness it. She wanted to be close to it, so she could feel some circle in her life closing.

It was a highlight of Dale's life to see that happen. Jeff had worked for her as an intern, answering the phones, and then he became her client, and she was also my upstairs neighbor at one point. We had a lot of connections to Dale, and to me, she represents what the Broadway theatre personality is like. She had devoted her life to the theatre. She seemed like the physical manifestation of what the Lyceum was feeling that night. She was so proud to be a part of it. The whole scene was staggering. The shouting and the gifts and the flashes from cameras and the whole thing going up in clips on YouTube. It was magnificent.

2008: Something I Could Say To Liza

Hunter Bell, Writer/Actor

Every night before the show, we'd all circle up stage right. There was a little white door where you could duck into the house, so me, Jeff, Heidi, Susan and sometimes Larry would squeeze into the vestibule next to the door, and we'd come up with a word to focus on that night. One night, it could be "super bubbles" and the next, "Bernadette Peters." We kept a piece of paper hanging there for the entire run, with our word from each night.

Then, Martha, our stage manager would walk in and give us the call, and we would enter from stage right. And away we went! I get stomach feelings still, thinking about it now.

One of the biggest things for me was getting to meet John Kander at the stage door! We had a conversation about something in the show. There's a part where Jeff and I argue whether "theater" rhymes with "sweeter." John told us he'd had that same argument before! That blew me away. We joked about writing, and I wasn't just a fangirl, we could talk about my show. It blew my mind.

Meeting Bernadette Peters was major. I had clocked so many hours with her as a kid, in my mind, in my ear, in my heart. I had spent so much of my childhood listening to *Sunday in the Park with George* and *Song and Dance*. Donna Murphy. Betty Buckley. Des McAnuff. Jack O'Brien. I would always ask the question, "Why are you here?" Sometimes we were so in it and doing our thing that we forgot we were in a Broadway show, with all of the stuff that happens around that. Some nights, it was only after I got home and saw the still pictures of the red carpet or the stage door that I could digest what was happening.

While we were doing the show, I was obsessed with watching *Liza with a Z*, because I'd recognize all of the areas backstage. That's my theater! I even went up to Liza at the Tony Awards press meet-and-greet that year, and said, "Hi! It's nice to meet you. I'm in your theater from *Liza with a Z*." And she said, "Isn't it amazing?" That was all I needed. I just wanted that one moment. I actually had something that I could say to Liza and connect with her about!

––––––––––––

During the run of [title of show] at the Lyceum, Jeff had a list in his dressing room upstairs where he kept track of how many performances [title of show] had run, and if it was more or less than other Broadway shows. The night that we played our fifth performance, he looked at the list and proclaimed, "We've run even longer than Rags!" Because we held onto that, we felt like a part of the larger picture.

From singing at Broadway on Broadway to having a table at BC/EFA's Broadway Flea Market, every tradition that came along during [title of show] was sacred to us. Inside the theater every night, we were getting to experience it through the eyes of these hundreds of young fans, who felt like they were a part of Broadway because we were. They had watched in their bedrooms when [title of show] on Broadway was just a wish inside a YouTube video and they were there every step of the way.

When "Hunter" and "Jeff" were dreaming of Broadway in an early scene, they agreed that the set should be just four chairs. And what if they actually got [title of show] to Broadway? Well in that case, the set would have to be four chairs made out of diamonds.

On Broadway, the show had a different ending than it ever had before. After the finale, the four chairs flew up and what was lowered onto the stage? Four chairs coated in "diamonds."

One of those "diamonds" is framed on my wall.

––––––––––––

2008: It Changed Everything

Heidi Blickenstaff, Actor

We went on our *[title of show]* adventure, and it didn't last long, but it changed everything. We say this all the time, but it's true. Every moment of that experience… I know you can't possibly remember everything, but I think that we were so incredulous that it was actually happening, that we were so grateful and stunned all day every day, so we sucked the marrow out of every single moment of that experience. Because of that, it still remains a very vivid, visceral memory for me, all of it. From rehearsing it again, to moving into the theater, to that first day when we opened the box office for ticket sales, to the first preview night with the fans crowding on 46th Street, to opening night when my dad got stuck in the elevator and the fire department had to come get him out, to the birthday parties we had for people, to the moment when Kevin McCollum sat us down in the stage management office and told us he was going to post the closing notice.

Every single bit of that experience, including the smells and the sights and the feelings from the Lyceum, it's all so crackling and present in my memory because I was just so grateful that it was all happening. All of us were, and I think that fueled us. That gratitude, that disbelief that it was happening, and the shock we felt, I think that was contagious. That's how our fans felt, everybody felt that way. So, it turned into this unbelievable experience, with so much goodwill thrown at it because everybody really wanted it to succeed. Not everybody—it wasn't everybody's jam. But for those people who did take that ride, it was *very* special, and that theater turned into something crazy.

I never even thought I would ever get to play that theater! It's such a beautiful, old, vaudeville-feeling house. I'll always remember what it was like at the end of each performance, when we were all just standing there, and that applause was going on and on and on you just couldn't believe it, and you're standing there looking up at the highest person, in the highest seat in the house. Even though *[title of show]* was not a commercial success, the experience inside of that theater during those performances was once-in-a-lifetime. That moment at the end of the show came together with the theater in every beautiful way. The people who were there seeing it, us, the theater itself, the people who were working on the show… we were all just this blissful, happy family for a moment in time. It wasn't without its quirks and cracks, but I loved being there. I loved how bare it felt, how wide open, because our little set was this nowheresville rehearsal open space. We had this wide open space, and instead of it being packed full of yellow dresses and sea grottos, it was filled with our story.

I loved those stupid chairs that came down at the end. It was Kevin McCollum's idea, for the Broadway run, and we were all like, "No! No! We don't want that! It's too on the nose! It's too first-choicey! It's too happy-ending!" And he won out, and when those stupid chairs would come down, every single night I got a lump in my throat, because it was like I was living my dream in real time over and over, eight shows a week, all summer. It was just magical.

And I say "magical" knowing that it is the dorkiest, most overused word ever, but there's not a better adjective. It was totally magical, and I am so proud to have had that experience with those people. I have had really glorious Broadway experiences, and I hope to have more, but nothing can ever compare to what that was, all of those stars aligning to bring those people together—and I'm talking about the six of us, plus everybody who worked on it, yourself included. Including the door men, the ushers, the audience, our set guys, the people who sold merch, the fans, the people who recorded the cast album.

Everybody who worked on that show and was there for it really became a part of that show and a part of its story. And I don't know if I'll ever have that experience again. I certainly haven't had it since. And I almost don't want to have it again. I want it to live on its own, and be this beautiful island, because I'll always remember it as one of the most special times of my life.

2008: Die, Vampire, Die!

Susan Blackwell, Actor

There we were on a Broadway stage, having these conversations with themes like "Die, Vampire, Die!" about slaying your creative demons, and "I'd Rather Be 9 People's Favorite Thing Than 100 People's 9th Favorite Thing", and "Part of It All", which is literally a song about wanting to be part of this community, and part of this legacy, and what that meant, and what it would take to do that. All these things we were talking about in that show were a direct reflection of these conversations we were having in our lives. These were the things we thought about, that were important to us.

So we really did take our beating hearts and—at the risk of getting our hearts broken or failing or having people take a piñata swing at us—put them out there in front of people. I believe that when you do that, from a place of true kind-heartedness and authenticity and vulnerability, and all the risk associated with it, sometimes people do take a big piñata swing at you. Which is fine. But what happens more frequently, the overwhelming response, is that other beating hearts, other like minds, other members of your tribe hear your beating heart and they extend their own, and they say, "My heart beats in sync with yours."

We've continued the work we started with *[title of show]*. Our show closed on Broadway, and then it was licensed, so it goes out into the world that way. It goes out in the form of the original cast recording, and Hunter and I both go out as representatives from the show, as teachers, as educators continually having conversations about that idea of stopping the thing that is keeping you from being free, so that we can all be as self-expressed as possible in this lifetime, so that we can all enjoy as much creativity flowing through us as possible. So, these discussions we started on our own brown couch and around our own dining room tables in our own crappy New York apartments. These discussions continue, and I'm so happy to be a part of that conversation, because I think it's a worthy conversation, and I think it makes the world a better place.

I also love how on a weekly basis, at least one person comes up to me and says one of the following. Choose your own adventure: "I played Susan in a production of *[title of show]* and the friendships I made doing that and the bravery I experienced doing the show changed my life" or "I just want you to know, I couldn't go to school last year because I was having panic attacks, and the song "Die, Vampire, Die!" made it possible for me to get myself together and go to school" or "I want you to know that when I am struggling, my parents look me in the face and say, "Die, Vampire, Die!", and it's our family code for 'You can do this.'"

I'm so honored by all of that, and all of these messages came to us through *our* teachers. The idea started with Lynda Barry, and we mutated it through our own ideas. We weren't the geniuses who came up with everything, we were just the ones who were interested in using the small megaphone we had to blast it out to the world and fight for the powers of good.

When we left the Lyceum, I left a message under my dressing room table and I drew a monkey next to it, for whoever was after me. For whoever would be in that dressing room, on the second floor, in the back of the theater.

2008: Survivors

Michael Berresse, Director/Choreographer/Actor

The Lyceum feels underappreciated. And *[title of show]* felt a little underappreciated. There was something about the humility of the theater, and the humility of *[title of show]*.

There's a lot of smoke damage. You see decades and decades, a hundred years of smoke scars in that lobby, yet it's also this beautiful, traditional slice of what theatre is, and I think *[title of show]* is that, too. There was an element that was specific, and marginalized about *[title of show]*, but at its core, it was about an absolute, true passion and love for the traditional structure of a Broadway musical, and the art form. It explored the content of creation.

I think they're both survivors, *[title of show]* and the Lyceum. To see so much vibrant youth in that theater, seeing that show, was thrilling for me.

Every theater has these moments of electricity that never leave, and get absorbed into every aspect of everything else that happens inside that theater. The theaters don't forget. They just need to be awakened, to have a witness, and those kids came into the Lyceum during our show, to this theater built in 1903, and they felt like it was their home. There was nothing that felt uncomfortable or old-fashioned about the Lyceum when we were there. People owned it, and walked in, and treated it the way kids do who are super-comfortable with their grandparents—kids who are like: *Your age doesn't scare me, your weird clothing doesn't scare me.* Kids who realize that this 105-year-old grandma, at some point in her life, was 16.

Those worlds collided, and it was good for the story of the show and the heart of that theater. I am convinced that whether we carry it, or whether it manifests in the space, our energy doesn't ever leave. People talk about ghosts in theaters, and I understand what that's about, but for me, it's about the electricity and the joy and how what we leave keeps bouncing around and bouncing around until someone taps into it again. We tapped into it hard that first night ever doing *[title of show]* on a Broadway stage, in a way that was overwhelming. One of the biggest satisfactions in that was my invisibility. After being in nine Broadway shows, I got to direct one, and I got to watch everything happen.

————————

We've lost several people from the [title of show] *Lyceum days—Dale, Jeff and Susan's manager, Roger, one of our ushers, Neville our stage door man and Roy Miller, one of our producers. I'll never forget Dale crying outside the stage door after the first preview, so proud of how her clients had made their dream come true. I'll never forget how Roger had emphatic opinions about every show he ushered, or how Neville was so pleased that I enjoyed his notepads at his stage door man office. (They were understudy slips from other shows!) I'll never forget Roy Miller asking me questions in the back of the house about my opinions on certain scenes in the show, treating me as though I was on the same level as him, a Broadway producer.*

[title of show] was five years ago, and there are so many people who are gone who will always be such a big part of that experience in my head. They live on in the Lyceum for me. I think about them when I'm there, and I see them sitting or standing or cheering or laughing where they once did. Their memories live on in that theater.

————————

2008: Because We Could

Hunter Bell, Writer/Actor

Jeff and I even went to the load-out the day after the show closed. Just because we could! We wanted to take the full ride. We were there to see them put the marquee up, and we wanted to see everything get taken out of the theater too. We savored every moment because we knew: when could this ever happen again? It was super special. And we documented every moment: with photos, blogs, videos—but also we documented it emotionally, we made sure we were always present.

I don't think I've been back in the Lyceum since *[title of show]* closed. I see some of the ushers on the subway though, and I see some of the stagehands walking down the street. It feels like time travel.

————————

Working on a Broadway show for the first time, I learned a million things. I learned how to listen to an audience for different kinds of laughs. I learned how to manage things when there were celebrities in the house. I learned how to navigate my way backstage in a manner both helpful and unobtrusive. I learned about follow spots and seamless transitions and notes sessions and sensing when someone really needed a pep talk.

I never sat in the same seat twice. I wanted to see our show from as many different spots as possible. I wanted the full Lyceum experience. I watched the show from the orchestra, the mezzanine, the balcony. I watched it from both boxes, and from the front row. I watched from the stage right wing and from the stage left wing.

The theater itself really did feel like a strong presence in the show. This totally-outside-the-box-of-what-Broadway-typically-is little musical was being presented on the oldest stage on Broadway! The Lyceum legitimitzed [title of show], *and* [title of show] *gave new life to the old Lyceum.*

————————

2008: Dream Come True

Jeff Bowen, Writer/Actor

We got to the Lyceum, and it was so exciting. People say "live in the moment" and "really cherish this" and "it's fleeting" and "live for the day"—but getting ahold of that was like trying to hold onto a fish with rubber gloves. It was just flailing out of our hands, there was so much buzz and excitement and we were all so proud and so emotional and so nervous to perform. There were all those levels, and you want to hold onto it. You wish to just sit for two seconds and be able to be like, "This is awesome and it's going to be gone tomorrow, so we're going to hold onto it." I remember trying to check in with that feeling.

One thing that was great was that our first day doing the show on Broadway, July 5, 2008, did seem to stretch on forever, even though it was so fast. It was such a big, exciting day. It was also very bittersweet. Probably the hardest thing I ever did in my life up to that point was to start the show that night, because that was actually the end of the show. We had to stop writing, and so much of the joy and the love that I had associated with that show was really part of the developmental process.

Doing the show was fun and I had a blast doing it, but writing it, and promoting it, and getting in fights about it, and working our asses off about it and believing in it… all of *that* was what was awesome about it.

That opening night was great, but there was a moment when we were taking the final bow on opening night where, as much as we were completely washed over with a wave of support and love, there was a little part of me that was sad. Because I knew that the four years we spent getting there was over. I don't know if other people have that same feeling when they work on a show. It was this hard thing, because I wanted to feel all these feelings of excitement and joy and pride and love, but at the same time I had this sad feeling, like: *School's over. We have to graduate. Camp is over, time to say goodbye to all the camp friends.*

And then we walked out onto 46th Street, and there were just crowds and crowds of people there, and then a third crowd of people there who were curious as to why everyone else was crowding. They thought we must've been the Jonas Brothers. Then the machine starting going, and we all jumped on the machine and did our part. The opening blurs in my memory. I don't know if other people say this, but the first preview felt like opening night, because it was like: *Now, we're up on a Broadway stage, telling this story that's about being on a Broadway stage.*

When we went into the Lyceum, stage management had already picked our rooms for us, and they were in the newer wing, which was very far away from the theater but would let us be much closer to each other. So we stayed. Only Michael had a dressing room on a side of the stage, on the bottom floor stage left. Then, we ended up designating other rooms on either side of the stage as "yoga room," "nap room," "nonsense room," "party room," that sort of thing. Our fly guy took over one of the rooms over there, and used it to watch boxing. It was like the set of *All In The Family* in those rooms sometimes.

I've always been such a history buff for Broadway theaters. I'm a nerd for that stuff more than most people. If you say a musical, I can tell you what theater it was in. I don't know if that's good knowledge. Okay, we'll say it's good knowledge to have that.

So, I'm very happy to be part of the community of theatre, and the community of Broadway, but deep down, I think I'm more happy to be part of the history of Broadway, all of those stories and all of those ghosts that are a part of that legacy. I think it's so cool that we have all shared the same building with all these people. Liza did *Liza with a Z* at the Lyceum. She stood on zero at the Lyceum, and I stood on zero at the Lyceum. To tell the truth, I usually had to split zero at the Lyceum with Hunter, but maybe I stood there once.

––––––––––––

Weeks before [title of show] *started previews at the Lyceum, Jeff and I were walking to an ad meeting at SpotCo, and he told me about one of the advertising tag lines they were thinking of:*

[title of show]: *What If You And Your Best Friends Made It To Broadway?*

That didn't end up being our advertising tag line, but it did end up being the truth.

I knew it was a unique experience while it was happening. I knew you didn't always get to go to Broadway with shows that you wrote with your friends. I knew that you didn't always get to Broadway with shows that came out of a complete, shared, unwavering devotion to the stories you wanted to tell.

Since that time, I've known what it feels like to be a part of an actual dream come true.

And that's Broadway.

———————

2010: A Home For *The Scottsboro Boys*

Beowulf Boritt, Scenic Designer

Early on, we looked at the Sondheim Theatre as a possibility for *Scottsboro*.

I think everyone felt like being in an older theater was better. And oddly, the Lyceum is one of the few theaters that still has its "colored balcony," the upper balcony with a separate staircase for black people, which was bizarre. Our show just fit at the Lyceum.

———————

The Scottsboro Boys *received the most Tony nominations ever, of any musical that had already closed. With 12 nominations, the show also holds the record for most nominations ever with zero wins.*

———————

2010: Dust From Shakespeare's Ghost

David Loud, Musical Director and Supervisor/Conductor/Actor

Scottsboro Boys was in the Lyceum. That theater is truly like going back in time. That is *the* old theater. There is dust there from, like, Shakespeare's ghost. It is *old*.

It was absolutely wonderful to do a historical play in that house because it felt like there were many ghosts of many varieties in that house. Or memories. Or vibrations in the air. It's a great theater.

It's a difficult theater to have a hit in, because it's sort of on the wrong side of Broadway. You're not in the center of the hub. People don't— when they can't get into *Wicked*, it's not like they go next door to you. You're not next door to *Wicked* so you can't pick up the extra little eight-o'clock sales boost. We had a difficult run there financially but it was a magical place to do the show. It's set up differently than any other Broadway theater I've ever seen. It's a great house.

2010: You Did Good, Kids

Susan Stroman, Director/Choreographer

Going to the Lyceum with *The Scottsboro Boys* was perfect, because the theater really does feel like an old vaudeville house. It feels like it has ghosts in a way that no other Broadway theater does.

Every night, the actors would enter from the back of the house, so they would take a moment together, in the lobby of the Lyceum, to stand in a circle together and remember the real Scottsboro Boys. Then they would go charging down the aisles and the show would begin.

We originally did *Scottsboro Boys* at the Vineyard, and it was intended for a small space. But when there were producers who wanted to bring it to Broadway, it was great to be able to give the show that kind of presentation.

We closed quickly but were nominated for 12 Tony Awards, which I think was the community's way of saying: "You did good, kids! It wasn't commercial, but you did good."

2012: Part of My Early Theatergoing Experience

Walter Bobbie, Director/Actor

I have always wanted to work in the Lyceum Theatre.

When I started coming to New York as a young man, I saw many plays at the Lyceum when the APA Phoenix was in residence there. I thought it was such a mysterious place, and still do.

I learned we were moving *Venus in Fur* into the Lyceum and I was thrilled.   The Lyceum recalls such vivid memories of my early theatergoing experience.

2013: Beyond The Beaumont

André Bishop, Artistic Director of Lincoln Center Theatre

The logistics of doing a Lincoln Center show not at the Vivian Beaumont are different, because we're not all there on the spot. But the rest of it seems the same.

I love old-fashioned proscenium theaters, and quite frankly, they're easier to work in. They're easier to direct in, they're easier to design in. And they're easier to act in. So when we do go to another Broadway house, I welcome that. The thing about the Beaumont is that the choosing of plays is always an interesting task for anybody—but for me, here, it's also an architectural decision. I have this very strong belief—and not everybody shares it—that certain plays are not right for the Beaumont.

The Nance is a play about old-time burlesque, and half of it takes place in the theater. You can't really do it in a modern, architectural thrust stage. It wouldn't be right. So I love going to Broadway theaters. Because of the proscenium.

2013: From Another Time

Joanna Gleason, Actor

I just went to see *The Nance*, and that was at the Lyceum. Those theatres that are between 6th and 7th Avenue intrigue me. They're old, and quite beautiful. It's like they're from another time. It would be interesting to be in one of those someday.

A Way Back to Then

Jennifer Ashley Tepper, Theatre Historian/Producer

I may have only spent from June to October of 2008 in the Lyceum Theatre on 45th Street, but it was enough. No one could ever take it away from any of us: for a brief shining moment, we had been a part of Broadway. As much as any other show, from *Truckload* to *A Chorus Line*. We were a part of it all.

[title of show] has a song about finding your "way back to then," accessing the part of you that is hopeful and positive and excited and brave. And in some ways, writing this book felt like finding "a way back to then." I got to multiply the joy I felt when quizzing backstage employees at the Lyceum about their theatrical pasts in 2008, by getting to quiz the entire Broadway community about their theatrical pasts in 2013! *[title of show]* was my "then," and I found a way back indeed.

I discovered the Lyceum three times: once when I read about it in books, once when I lived inside it for five months, and once when I got to hear about it through the stories of everyone in this chapter.

Final Thoughts, Outtakes & What's Next

This is the first volume of a multi-volume work that will include all 40 Broadway theaters, as well as several Broadway theaters that are no longer.

*Here are some final regards to the **Winter Garden**, the **Richard Rodgers**, the **Marquis**, the **Al Hirschfeld**, the **Neil Simon**, the **August Wilson**, the **Mark Hellinger**, and the **Lyceum**; and a preview of tales from future volumes of The Untold Stories of Broadway...*

I want to do a show in the **Lyceum** someday, because it's so strange. It's really old, and it feels so lonely. I want to do a show there.

-Jason Tam, Actor

I've always wanted to know what it's like backstage at the **Nederlander**. I don't know why, it's just very quaint and nice. I want to know what it's like there.

-Brittnye Batchelor, Hair/Makeup Artist

I've never worked in the **Circle in the Square**, and I've always liked that space. I've auditioned there a few times. I'd love to work there someday.

-Daisy Eagan, Actor

I really want to work at the **Marquis** someday. That's the theater I saw my first Broadway show in. It's just right smack there in the middle of Times Square, and it's so visible. As a child, that theater was what I felt like Broadway was. It's in the middle of it all. There's a glittery sheen on that theater for me.

-Jay Armstrong Johnson, Actor

I've had the intimate experience, at the **Longacre**. I think it would be a fun challenge to do the **Gershwin**! What would that be like? You probably can't even see the front row because the orchestra pit is so big! What is that energy like? I wonder how much energy it takes to fill that space.

-A.J. Shively, Actor

I want to work at all of the biggest and most over-the-top theaters. And I really love the **Mark Hellinger**.

That's where they did the *Oliver!* revival in 1984. I was cast in that, but I didn't end up doing the show. And I always loved the Mark Hellinger. I thought it was just crazy and gothic and ornate. I can't believe it's not a theater anymore. But it lasted a long, long time.

-Jason Graae, Actor

The **Booth**! I love that theater. It's small, it's intimate, it's a jewel box. You can feel everyone, no matter where you're sitting.

-Evan Pappas, Actor

If you ask people what theater they want to work in someday, you probably get the same answer a lot from playwrights. The **Booth**. And just like all of them, I want the Booth so badly. It's just such a beautiful ratio of stage space to audience. It's a comfortable and beautiful space to experience a play in. One day, I hope I get the Booth. Who knows?

-Doug Wright, Writer

I almost got to work in the **Booth**. I almost did *Most Happy Fella*, but I ended up doing *Crazy for You* instead. I sat in the last row there and saw *Who's Afraid of Virginia Woolf?* And I felt like I was *in* it.

-Jessica Molaskey, Actor

People love the **Booth**. It's just a favorite theatre, of people who have worked in it, and even people who haven't yet. People say, "I want to work in the Booth."

There's just something very homey about it. At one point when I worked there, we had a Christmas party between shows. It was down in the lobby, with homemade food, and fresh-baked cookies, and Secret Santa. I have a really vivid memory of that party.

It was my first theater, and it just spoke to me. It wasn't a glamorous theater, and the dressing rooms were certainly not fancy. But you could just put it in the palm of your hands, that theater. You could just put your arms around it.

-Florie Seery, Press Agent

Everyone's going to say the **Booth** is the theater they want to work in someday. Everyone's going to say the Booth. I just know it.

I would actually have to say the **Music Box**. I think the Music Box is delightful. Magical. I think the acoustics are extraordinary.

And the **Belasco** because I love ghosts. And ghosts love me. I want to work there. Those two theaters... they've got good bones.

The most important thing to me is that in the best Broadway theaters, it's like you can tell they've been made with love. Kind of similar to the way you can tell a really good meal has been made with love. Not necessarily always the best ingredients, but totally made with love. Some of the theaters were really made with love; sometimes they were made *for* love. And those two, the Music Box and the Belasco, you just know they were loved when they were built. I actually think love went into almost everything in this part of town, but those two... they understand the point of a Broadway house. They've got good bones.

-Anne Bobby, Actor

I want to work in the **Booth**. I want to work in the **Imperial**. I want to work in the **Shubert**. I want to work in the **Music Box**, because it was Irving Berlin's theater.

I've worked in 13 Broadway theaters so far, and I want to work in every one I haven't gotten to yet. I'd like to hit them all. That's the plan. I'm putting that out into the ether.

I love love love Broadway. I love the theaters, I love the people in them, I love the community, I love being a member of the community. It's a close-knit group, where people look out for each other, as evidenced by Broadway Cares/Equity Fights AIDS. It is a community that takes care of itself, and looks out for itself, and is filled with wonderful people, who are not just tolerant, but open and giving. We're all different colors and races and religions and orientations, and we all support each other. It is a great, great community, and it's an honor to be a part of it. It's all I ever wanted as a kid, and I pinch myself every day because I get to be a part of it.

-Danny Burstein, Actor

Just like how the songs you write for a show are dependent on the characters, I think that the theater that we would want is dependent on the show. I feel like the space should always depend on the exact style of the show. Although I like the **Shubert**. That would be a great theater to do a show in. And I love the **Booth**.

-Benj Pasek, Writer

It's really difficult, because you always want the show you're doing to fit the theater. You have to get lucky, and hope that the theater that works best is available to you at the time. It doesn't always happen.

There's not a specific theater I want to work in, in the future, but I love the idea of getting to explore more Broadway buildings. I've mainly produced in Shubert houses, but recently I got to produce a show at a Nederlander house, and I want to work in a Jujamcyn house too. I just love all of those buildings. Every one of them is perfect, for different kinds of shows.

-Arielle Tepper Madover, Producer

I love the **Music Box**. I love the **Helen Hayes** and the **St. James**. Those are really beautiful theaters and they're fun to work in. They have a sense of intimacy to them, and yet they have all the opulence of a beautiful Broadway theater. The challenges are the **Marquis** and the **Minskoff**. I love *Lion King* in the Minskoff. I've done many shows there, and *Lion King* really fits! It's like *Wicked* and the **Gershwin**. They were perfect for each other. The show just fits there. It was wonderful to watch those two theaters have challenges met by shows that were just perfect fits for the space. The Marquis is an interesting place to work, and a different challenge. I love it. There's a certain modern feel to it, and the audience gets to come into a hotel and go up escalators into a theater. For people coming to Broadway from different parts of the world, that theater offers a totally different perspective. It's a challenge because it's not the traditional Broadway house everybody is used to working in, but it's a beautiful theater and I love working there. I love the **Lunt**, where you go backstage through the little secret passage door.

There's really no theater I can think of where I go: "Oh I hate that place." I like them all.

-Rick Sordelet, Fight Director

I love those old Broadway musical houses. There's an energy in those theaters that you can't recreate anywhere else. You're sitting there watching a big musical, and you hear the sound of the traffic or the subway. New York is all around them, and that makes them special.

I'm always curious when I'm in play houses where people aren't mic'd, because then the size of the theater and the acoustics really matter. And as an audience member, you really have to listen. You can't be picky though. You really can't be picky. I'd love to work on any of those stages.

-Jake Epstein, Actor

There are a lot of great theaters, and I haven't worked in all of them yet. But I'm mostly driven by the project, and not by the theater.

I love non-traditional spaces. Most Broadway theaters are old proscenium houses, and I'm looking forward to a new generation of different kinds of theaters. I think there are going to be more theaters that look for different ways of placing the audience's relationship to the stage. I admire and I love Broadway, but I also think that there's room for a new kind of architectural design within the theatrical experience.

-Julie Taymor, Director

The funny thing about the big musical houses is that none of them were built for the sound and technology that's there today. They were built so you'd have really good acoustics when you were hearing live voices—not voices through speakers. I remember the time of live voices particularly well, and I remember how shows used to sound. It's a bit of a crapshoot these days as a composer. Composers are often a little bit disappointed when everything starts to be mixed in the theater. You're hearing it through speakers, so everything gets a little bit homogenized, and it's never quite as good as it was with the orchestra in the rehearsal room. There, you hear every instrument, and you hear how the orchestration fits together. When you start hearing it through speakers, everything gets mushed together and you sometimes lose some of the definition of sound you had when it was just the orchestra.

I've worked in six Broadway houses. Out of all of them, the **St. James** was the best, just in terms of the way that the show sounded in that space.

-Mel Marvin, Writer/Arranger

I love going backstage and I love taking my kids backstage. When they were little, I wanted them to know what I did, and be part of it.

I think that what I do is so odd. It's so odd that "Mom" is a playwright. But I want them to see what I'm doing so I always take them, even if they can't see the play because it's too adult. I take them backstage, because it's so beautiful. It seems magical to me that you're behind the set and looking out onto where all the people would be, if the people were there.

When my daughter was ten, I took her to see *Dead Accounts* at the **Music Box**, and we went backstage. She was so enchanted by it. We took one of her drawings and stuck it on the refrigerator of the kitchen on the set.

It's wonderful when kids show up. Josh Hamilton brought his son too, and Katie Holmes brought in her daughter. There's so much press around that little girl that we could've all been like: "Wow, Suri's here." But you know, really it just felt like "Cool, another kid is here, someone brought their kid to the theater!"

-Theresa Rebeck, Writer

306

This is where I started. My father was a stagehand here at the **Jacobs**, years before I was. I was here from the time I was six years old, on. There was a show here that cut out a part of the ceiling, for machinery, and when the show closed, there was this perch left. My father put a chair up on the perch for me, and I'd sit up there and watch the show every night. I grew up in this particular theater.

-Mike Van Praagh, Stagehand

It was really cool to be a kid on Broadway, and it meant that I matured very early. I always knew that when I was around my friends at home—kids—I could be a kid. But when I was around adults on Broadway, I had to act like an adult.

I loved hanging out with adults, because I got to learn so much from them. They gave me advice. They taught me about theatre. I got to learn about different card games, and backstage traditions. I learned what homosexuality was at an early age, and my friends back on Long Island didn't. I'm not gay, but I was open to that world. I matured very early on, and always understood that people were all different, and that was great. That's what theatre at a young age teaches you.

During *Beauty and the Beast*, I was rotating back and forth with another Chip. So, I made sure to learn everything about the theater. I sat with the stage managers one time when they were calling the show. I sat with the sound mixer in the back one night. I sat with the conductor in the pit. I watched all the rigs one night. I wanted to know how it all worked.

I was a kid, and over the summer, I would go to camp during the day and then go do Broadway at night.

-Harrison Chad, Actor

The first time I saw a Broadway show, I saw four in four days. I saw *La Cage* at the **Palace**, *A Chorus Line* at the **Shubert**, *Big River* at the **O'Neill**, and *42nd Street* at the **St. James**. I was about six years old. I was amazed at the sets in *La Cage*. And my sister and I realized that they weren't all women on stage, because we saw how big their hands were. I was disappointed in *Big River*, because everyone had told me there would be water on stage, and it was just smoke. I was also confused by kids smoking cigarettes on stage, because I didn't realize they weren't real. I was excited by musicals, and I was just curious about everything going on, on stage.

-Andrew Leeds, Actor

The first Broadway show I saw was *Les Mis* five times. Through the late 1980s, during the first Broadway production of *Les Mis*, my family was there all the time. I was obsessed with it. I think most little girls my age who saw that show really wanted to play Cosette, and then later became obsessed with playing Eponine. That was exactly what happened to me, too. I was extremely cliché. My first show wasn't anything outside of the box. It was just straight up *Les Mis*.

We also saw *Les Mis* all the time in Boston, near where I'm from. Later, when I saw *Rent*, I thought: *This is amazing!* I was really struck by it, because I had only ever seen *Les Mis* 900 times and maybe *Phantom* once. I didn't grow up on musical theatre like a lot of people in the business did.

-Sarah Saltzberg, Actor

I moved here right after I graduated from high school—I don't know what my parents were thinking! When I first moved here, *Hairspray* was happening at the Neil Simon. I was good friends with some of the cast, and they brought me backstage. It was so cool. When I got to walk on the stage, I thought I'd died and gone to heaven.

I saw so much theatre. I saw everything I could. One of the first things I saw was *The Last 5 Years*, off-Broadway, starring Sherie Rene Scott. I thought: *That girl's good!* She ended up becoming a huge part of my life. I saw *Fosse*. I loved that. I saw *Take Me Out*, which was mind-shattering to me. I saw Bernadette Peters in *Annie Get Your Gun*, which was incredible.

There was not a Broadway show I went to that I wasn't enamored with. It was always: *I want this. I want to be a part of this business so badly.*

- **Lindsay Mendez,** Actor

I grew up on the other side of the world, in Western Australia. The first time I came to New York, I was in awe of every theater I walked into. Each one was my favorite. I had flown 26 hours to get here, so just being here was incredibly exciting.

Later on, my favorite theaters became the ones where I got to see my heroes, or the ones where I got to see someone live who I'd only ever seen on the back of a CD. But I wasn't fussy. A few years later, when I officially moved to New York, I would walk into each theater and think: *This industry is amazing and this art form is amazing and I just want to be part of it. In this city.*

-**Carmel Dean,** Musical Director/Arranger

It's always either very chill or completely crazy backstage. It's either you're sitting backstage watching *Lost* DVDs, or it's insane and you have to get out of the way or you'll lose a limb. I did *Women on the Verge of a Nervous Breakdown* at the **Belasco**, and if you were in the wrong place at the wrong time, it was dangerous. Then I did *Chicago* at the **Ambassador**, and we had a couple times when people missed their cues because they were really busy reading *Game of Thrones*.

-**Nikka Lanzarone,** Actor

I moved to New York in 1985 after working in Louisville, Kentucky. I was an actor, and then in grad school, my thesis was denied and they said, "But you're really good at public relations. So I made the move to New York and got a job working for a singing clown, and starting looking for jobs in PR. I would see shows and look in the back of Playbills and apply. When I was in Louisville, I thought that every Broadway theater had a publicist in it, sitting at a desk. I didn't know that everyone working on a show wasn't sitting in the theater. I didn't know this whole world existed! I thought you walked up to the fourth floor of the **Shubert** and there you'd see the *A Chorus Line* publicist and the advertising exec and everyone. I just had no idea!

-**Chris Boneau,** Press Agent

When you go first backstage on Broadway, you expect such glamour, and such hugeness. In touring houses around the country, the backstage areas are massive and very nice. You think that Broadway will be like that, or nicer—and then you come here, and you see pipes everywhere. You have to go underneath the stage to get across. You climb a bunch of stairs to get to your dressing room. You're surprised there isn't an elevator. Then you realize: *Oh. This has a charm about it. These people I idolize, these Broadway performers, don't need to work somewhere glamorous. This is legit. This is what it needs to be. This is all you need.*

-**Michael Mendez,** Actor

When I was a kid, I saw a picture in People Magazine of Matthew Broderick, when he was in *Brighton Beach Memoirs*, which was probably right before he moved to New York. He was on his bike, leaving the stage door of the **Alvin**, and it made a huge impact on me. I was a teenager from Illinois, and I thought: *That's the ultimate New York experience: to leave your stage door on your bike!*

Years later, during *Angels in America*, Stephen Spinella and I would each ride our bikes to the theater. After we did our show, we would leave the stage door of our theater, the **Walter Kerr**, on our bikes. I remember the feeling of the two of us riding down Broadway, after doing that play. It was springtime, and there was something so liberating about all of that energy: the rush of adrenaline from doing that play and then just getting on your bike and riding downtown, through New York City. I think seeing that picture of Matthew really embedded that my mind, and I thought: *That's what you do when you're on Broadway.*

-Joe Mantello, Director/Actor

One of the coolest things that's associated with Broadway is the stage door hat. When you're an actor and you put on that hat, it's like telling everyone in the world that you just did a two-show day. I have always been in search of the perfect stage door hat. I've never quite found it. I have some hats that are close, but no hat that's the perfect one, the one that says: I am an actor! I am a proud member of Actors Equity, I just did two shows, and I'm really tired. My friend Danielle wants me to get a stage door sombrero.

-Alex Wyse, Actor

My favorite thing about Broadway theaters is that feeling when you're in tech. The fun of hanging out in a Broadway theater—working so hard but also feeling like you're camping out. It's your home away from home. You bring a pillow and you sleep underneath the tech table. I love that feeling of being so involved.

The day that they take the tech tables away, you feel so naked. *Where are the board games? Where's my computer? Where am I going to put my snacks?*

- Amanda Green, Writer

When I was a junior in high school, I did *13*, and when I was a senior, I did *Bloody, Bloody Andrew Jackson*. Both of those shows were at the **Jacobs**. It's my favorite Broadway theater, because I grew up there. But I never knew that it connected to any other theaters! Apparently it does.

I do remember that on opening night of *Andrew Jackson*, *La Bête* was across the street at the **Music Box**, and David Hyde Pierce made a paper sign and hung it in his dressing room window that said, "Happy Opening."

-Charlie Rosen, Writer/Musical Director/Musician

I've always wanted to work in the theaters on 44th and 45th Street, like the **Shubert** and the **Music Box** and the **Imperial** and the **Golden**. Because I feel like *that's* Broadway. I love **Circle in the Square**, and I loved the energy of working there, but it doesn't feel like a Broadway theater to me, in the way that I grew up thinking that a Broadway theater was. Working at the **Brooks Atkinson** felt closer to my idea of Broadway, because it was so close to other theaters. We got to be across the street from the **Biltmore**. It was almost like 44th and 45th Street.

-Todd Buonopane, Actor

All of the theaters I've worked in have been on the outskirts of Broadway. They've been great, but I was on 52nd Street, and then 41st, and then back up to 52nd and then 51st. The one show that got me smack in the middle of the Broadway district was at the **Marquis**, and I was there for the shortest time of all, only two months.

When you're in a theater, it becomes your home and you really get to know the two or three block radius around it. There will always be a warm spot in my heart for that strip of land on 8th between 50th and 52nd. I worked there on multiple shows, and I really saw the turnover there. It used to be a mess, and now it's not. I was there for that. But I'd love to know what it's like to work in the heart of the Broadway district.

-Jose Llana, Actor

I've worked in Broadway theaters that are in Times Square, and ones that aren't. I did two stints in a show on 42nd Street and then a show on 43rd Street, and it's just too crowded to be in the center of the theatre district now! Times Square wasn't like that when I started working, but now, I so prefer the theaters that are out of the way, farther uptown, in their own nooks. You think: *Please, let me be on Broadway! But please, let me be at the* **Winter Garden***!*

-Ed Dixon, Actor

In the **Gershwin**, I've done nine shows. I've only done one in the **Winter Garden**. Then you go to the **Lyceum** and I've done six or seven. At the **Longacre**, I've done five. They all have their own personalities. They're all different. Some are more beautiful than others. Some are more well maintained than others. Some have better lighting positions than others. Some have better, or bigger backstages. Are there favorites? I don't know if there are. The favorite is the one that's closest to all the places where you hang out.

-Ken Billington, Lighting Designer

There are quite a few theatre hangouts that are gone. The neighborhood's changed an awful lot. Big hangouts for theatre people used to be Barrymore's and McHale's. They were really, really good places. There used to be a place next to what used to be the **Martin Beck**, on the other side, called Ted Hook's Backstage. There was a place called Curtain Up, on the bottom of Manhattan Plaza. They used to have a piano in there and everybody would go and sing. After all of the shows, everybody would meet in one place and have a great time. Those places are gone. It's really very sad. There are places that people go now, but it's not the same thing. I don't know. Everything changes.

-Diane Heatherington, Box Office Treasurer

It's great to return to a theater you've worked in, and a lot of the reason is the stagehands. There are guys who are there every time you are, and you know them until they retire. The door men at theaters, they go house to house more often, but it's similar. Box office people, they stay forever. It's always nice to go back and revisit. Whenever I return to **Circle in the Square**, I always say hello to the house carpenter. We ask, "How's it going?" "How's your son enjoying college?" It's interesting because you get to know them, but only for however long your show runs. You're always visiting them on their turf.

-Robert LuPone, Producer/Actor

The stagehands are all a lot younger than they were when I started. They're everybody's sons. Actually... it's always been everybody's sons. The stagehand community is really the stagehand community. My wife and some of the people I work with hate to walk up to a theater with me, because it takes a long time to say hello to people. This is my neighborhood. I've worked in every single theater, as a stagehand or a production manager. Each theater is so different. On some shows, it's really all about the people who are in the theater. Whenever Bill Haber, the producer, would do his first day with his cast of a new show on stage at a theater, he would read from the Playbill what shows had been in that theater, and who had been in those shows. That's something that I try to do, every time I go into a theater. I pick up an old Playbill and learn: Oh! I'm at the same theater that Laurence Olivier was in! That keeps you enthusiastic, and a little bit in awe of where you are.

-Gene O'Donovan, Technical Supervisor

I hop the bus. Then once I get off the bus in Manhattan, I thank God I got off the bus! I get over here to the **Majestic** Theatre. It's the same. I've been ushering here at *Phantom* for 25 years. I get here and seat the people. It's exciting to meet different people, from all over the world, who come to see *Phantom*. It's nice to meet stars when they come to the show too. It's nice to talk to the actors and to the ushers I work with. I'd be staying home, throwing things at the television if I didn't have this!

-Sylvia Bailey, Usher

When we went into the **Music Box** for *The Farnsworth Invention*, *Deuce* had played right before us and Angela Lansbury had written on her dressing room mirror in lipstick, "Break a leg, Hank" because she knew that Hank Azaria was going to go into her dressing room.

Hank decided that he didn't like that dressing room. But he had them bring the mirror up and put it in his new dressing room. For the entire run of the show, it said "Break a leg, Hank. Love, Angela" in lipstick on the mirror. I thought that was such a nice custom. So, at the end of *Guys and Dolls*, at the **Nederlander** underneath my dressing table, I left a note myself. Tituss Burgess and I wrote: "Steve Rosen and Tituss Burgess Lived Here." Someone from *Rent* had done it already too.

It was just like what we did at French Woods summer camp, where we would write on the walls where we did shows. Someday they will tear down the White House Studios at French Woods, and all the things you've written, your credits will be lost forever. That happens in Broadway theaters too. They replace tables in dressing rooms, and some names disappear, but it's just a way to get a brief sense of: *I claim that I was here too.*

-Steve Rosen, Actor

When I was performing *Memphis* at the **Shubert**, I absolutely loved learning what stars of the stage and screen might have used the dressing room called home for two years; Angela Lansbury during *Blithe Spirit* and David Hyde Pierce during *Spamalot*, to name a couple.

"Only Make Believe," an organization started by Dena Hammerstein, which exists to bring the magic of the theatre to children in need all over the world, was to perform an all-star benefit performance on our day off on our Shubert theater stage. I was asked by stage management if one of the guest stars might be able to use my dressing room on that day. My answer was an obvious yes. I asked who might be occupying my quarters: Ian McKellen. Sir Ian McKellen would be sitting in the same chair, using the mugs I left for him possibly for tea time.

I left him a note taped to my mirror, in marker. He wrote me back. I have it framed. The date written in British style, followed by a masterful missive: "Dearest Chad, thank you for the loan of your room. Enjoy your Triumph. XO, Ian McKellen". The next year, it was Jeremy Irons, and he wrote a note as well. In marker. On my mirror.

- Chad Kimball, Actor

The **Music Box** is my favorite. As a writer, it's special. It's literally a music box. It's a jewel box of a theater.

I've worked in the **Cort** and the **Longacre**. I worked in what used to be the **Biltmore**, during its last days. It was big and creaky and scary and absolutely wrong for the show we were doing. I spent a lot of time on the fire escape, bemoaning my fate. So about that place, I mostly remember the fire escape.

-John Pielmeier, Writer

The only theater that I've always been dying to work in is the **Vivian Beaumont**—and I'm about to do a show there this season! I'm going to do *Act One* for James Lapine, and I just started working on it.
The Beaumont was designed by Jo Mielziner, who's one of my heroes. It's so big. You have a lot of options. As a set designer, so often, you're fighting for space in Broadway theaters. It becomes a jigsaw puzzle backstage, trying to make it all fit. The Beaumont is huge, backstage.

Apparently, the Beaumont has different challenges. When I got the job there, I bumped into John Lee Beatty somewhere, and I asked, "Do you have any advice about the Beaumont?" He said, "Just remember it's big and if you have something tracking in, it would take ten seconds in another theater, it will take 25 seconds at the Beaumont, because it's covering so much more distance."

That was a great piece of advice. I'll have to see if I have heeded it well, or not. I'm excited to walk into the Beaumont and have that first visit.

-Beowulf Boritt, Scenic Designer

If you ask me what theater I'd like to go to... well, for ease, I'd say the **Schoenfeld**, right off the bat. Ground floor load-in, hemp house, you can do whatever you want, everybody there is great. I love the crew there.

I spend a lot of time at the **Richard Rodgers** too. Again, very easy theater, great friends. But you've got to go up four feet to get in the load-in door! That always adds a bit of drama to the load-in. Same thing with the **Marquis**. I'll go there any day of the week, but you have to load in with an elevator! Those both are tricky. But I love all three of those theaters. I love the crews at each of them. I go to the **Cort** all the time too. I've done many shows there. Love the crew. You have to go down a long alley.

We've built shows before where the theater changed, mid-planning. And that was a challenge! But on the whole, we try not to go down the road of building a show without a venue commitment because that's crazy. Suppose you're planning for the **Richard Rodgers**, 30 feet deep, and they move you to the **St. James**, 26 feet deep? You've got four feet of show that you don't have anywhere to put!

-Neil Mazzella, Technical Supervisor

I write very much knowing in my head what the space looks like in my head. Once you get to a certain point of production, you do know which Broadway house you could potentially go into. Your show is either too big or too small for certain houses, from the moment you have a good idea of what it's like. You can really start pinning down: this show isn't going to be at the **St. James** and it's certainly not going to be at the **Gershwin** or the **Shubert**, but it might be at the **Broadhurst** or the **Golden**. You start thinking about all that. There are a lot of theaters that have been out of commission for my entire career. I'll never get a show into the **Majestic**, and no one is ever getting a show into the Gershwin. Those theaters have been out of commission for a very long time now! I stopped thinking about them; I stopped worrying about those two places. Most of the shows I write are of an intimate nature. I think that's just sort of my personality and my writing style. I think I was unlikely to end up at the Gershwin with anything anyway. I think I'll generally end up in midsized theaters. I love the Broadhurst. I've been there twice now. That's my perfect-sized house.

-Jason Robert Brown, Writer

Every closing night, I actually kiss the stage of my theater. These days, I kiss my hand and I put it on the stage, but on my first show, *Flower Drum Song*, I actually put my mouth to the stage and kissed it! It's just to say "thank you" to the theatre in some way. I've always kissed every stage on closing night. Have I closed every show that I've been in? Yeah.

-Telly Leung, Actor

I have this fantasy whenever I'm working in a Broadway theater. When I'm getting dressed in my dressing room before the show, I imagine all the stage managers in all the theaters simultaneously calling "15 minutes." Making the announcement to everyone in the theater. We're all having exactly the same moment, but we're each in a completely different universe.

-Michael Berresse, Director/Choreographer/Actor

There's this phenomenon I've noticed where you remember theaters you've worked in very specifically—and then when you return, they surprise you. You remember where this person's dressing room was, or where the wig room was. You remember where the band hung out. You're working there and you go through the backstage on your routine for the evening, over and over and over. You sort of memorize the people and where they always are, and what's always happening.

Then, you come back to the same theater ten years later to do another show, and the stage manager made different choices about the space. What was once the star dressing room is now the laundry room, and the orchestra is in a different place, and it seems like a completely different theater.

I played the **Brooks Atkinson** twice, and I played the **Richard Rodgers** twice. I went backstage and it seemed completely different. The backstages are sometimes transformed by the shows that are in them.

-David Loud, Musical Director and Supervisor/Conductor

It's like any business. We're all coworkers. We're all trying to get the same thing up. It's never a smooth road, when you're putting up something as complex as a Broadway show. It's a giant machine with 40 actors inside of it. That is a complicated process, and it's fun, and there are always going to be little problems that happen, and you solve them. You let 1700 people in every night to see it. That's always fun too. People get angry, stuff happens, you move on. Most of my problems go home at the end of the night.

A lot of people these days come to shows because they say they loved the movie. That concept of seeing a movie vs. seeing a live show blends together—not just for kids, either. Some are used to seeing shows in arenas and theme parks. Then, other people are used to the respectful, old-fashioned viewing experience. People come to your show who don't have any previous experience going to the theater. I'm thrilled they're here and buying tickets. That's why we keep going. We're just here to walk that tightrope and keep everyone as happy as possible.

-Austin Nathaniel, House Manager

The surprising thing to me is that I ended up doing Broadway at all! I was really into jazz and rock-and-roll. Then I happened to run into a friend who knew Gerry Ragni and Jim Rado, and they were looking for a composer to write *Hair* with. It was just a fluke. I love all genres of music, but especially rhythm music. I was going to write that. But then I got to Broadway. And it stuck.

-Galt MacDermot, Writer

You always have to spell the actor's name right. If you don't you're in for a problem. And you never let the reporter plug in the lights. You never pick up the socks from a wardrobe person. Everyone is in their own union. Union rules. There are some people that are still my friends. But you don't think much about that as you go on. You're not the talent. You never think about yourself. I have a story about going to the *New York Times* in my hot pants... I remember that because it was my second day at work. But mostly, you weren't involved in yourself, if you were in publicity. They told you to go wash the windows or get a coffee from Philadelphia and bring back a cheesesteak too, you got on the train and you went. There was no dignity. You were a flunkie.

You had to get umbrellas for the critics on opening nights. Back when critics reviewed shows on opening nights, if it was raining when they came out of your show you'd have to hold the umbrella for them as they went to the *New York Times* office. Then you'd have to wait there for the review, and then run with it in the rain to the ad agency, late at night.

-Irene Gandy, Press Agent

Through the years, I've noticed the perception of people regarding backstage door men/women to be that of someone doing little more than sitting at the door, either letting people in or keeping them out. Not true. In addition to representing the theater, we must also represent the current production performing in it. My priority is keeping the backstage area at the **Shubert** Theatre safe for the cast and crew. It's important to protect the integrity of the show while maintaining the security of the theatre. No one gets in after half-hour. I have been called a "pit bull" by some, while others have found me to be "warm and welcoming." Ever present in my mind is representing the backstage area of the Shubert as well as the creative people in it. "The play's the thing"... always.

- Rose M. Alaio, Door Woman

During my early days in New York, right after I graduated from Yale, it took Richard Maltby and me a year to get our first off-Broadway show on, and it took a lot longer for us to be self-supporting as writers. Luckily, I was a good pianist and could eke out a living as a rehearsal pianist or an audition pianist.

In those days, pianists would go from theater to theater to theater. My first experiences with Broadway theaters was playing four or five auditions a day, all in different theaters. During my first five years in New York, I must have played an audition in every Broadway theater that did a musical, before I finally got a job playing in an actual Broadway pit!

Marvin Hamlisch was a rehearsal and audition pianist at the time too, and I would run into him at auditions. That's how we got to know each other. It was very exciting to get up every morning and walk into Broadway theaters and know that people like Jule Styne and Charlie Strouse were sitting out in the house. It was all very exciting for me. But I don't remember any specific auditions! I played so many of them. It was just one after another. There were usually four or five pianists at each, playing for different singers. We'd all wait in the wings, play our song, get $5 and then go off to the next one.

-David Shire, Writer

My father-in-law always says, "Everyone hated that show except for the people that came to see it." That really hits me. It's surprising how many people loved *Good Vibrations* at the **Eugene O'Neill**, for all that's said about it. My friend Dashaun Young, who was in *Lion King*, said the exact same thing to me that you did. He said, "Secretly, *Good Vibrations* was one of my favorite shows. I saw it so many times and I just loved it."
I hear stories like that from time to time, which is really cool. We had so much fun every single night. We were trying to be one of those beach blanket movies of the 1960s. We were trying to do a musical with that sense of fun and adventure and that dream of "Let's just go West." Maybe that dream doesn't exist anymore, but that's the kind of story we were trying to do.

We all knew we were going to close. We saw how small the audiences were. We ran 50 previews and 94 performances. It was sad. I remember the final performance, looking across the stage at Kate Reinders and singing "God only knows what I'd be without you." That moment just got me. What do you say? For half of us, it was our Broadway debut. And you don't ever get another one of those. That was it.

-David Larsen, Actor

I've always loved the **Majestic** and I've never worked there. I've auditioned there. *The Music Man* was at the Majestic so it's tied to my early childhood longing to be part of the theatre. I love the **Music Box**. Getting to do *A Few Good Men* at the Music Box was phenomenal. I've always had a soft spot for the **Broadhurst** because it's where we did *Godspell* and then coming back to do *Lennon* was great. They're all so incredible.

I've rehearsed plays in the **Ambassador**. I rehearsed a play at the **Henry Miller's** Theatre before they changed the name. I did a bunch of play readings in the theaters when they were gonna tear down the **Morosco** and the **Helen Hayes**. I played the **Booth** in a play called *My Daughter, Your Son*. I loved that.

When you play these theaters, it's like you live in them. They're like homes. I remember Tim Busfield replaced Tom Hulce in *A Few Good Men,* and he hadn't been on Broadway before. We had been rehearsing. On his first day moving into the theater, a couple of days before he started the show, I opened the doors and the windows of his dressing room on matinee day and I said to him, "Look up and down this block. Look at all these theaters. You are now part of this community. This is your neighborhood. This is your world now." It's just so vibrant and so alive and so magical.

-Don Scardino, Actor/Director/Writer

I love the **Booth** Theatre because it feels intimate. I love the **Richard Rodgers** Theatre, mostly because I like the setup of the audience, the way that the seats go. I will always love the **Broadhurst** because that was where my first Broadway show was, and I think the Broadhurst has character. The **Gershwin** to me has character in a different way, because there's this brilliance in the *Wicked* set design and how it envelops the theater. I love when theaters do that: become a part of the show. I remember there were topiaries in front of *Secret Garden* at the **St. James**. Now, there are fake gaslights in front of *Phantom* at the **Majestic**. I suppose that some people think that makes the show "theme park-y," but I sort of like the notion of that, especially with the bigger musicals. The **Shubert** is pretty cool, because of its geographic location, the way it wraps around the corner at Shubert Alley, and because growing up, it was always "the *A Chorus Line* theater" to me. I have a place in my heart for the **Martin Beck**, because even though I haven't done a show there, I've been close to many people who have, so I've spent a lot of time backstage. As for the **New Amsterdam**, I've only done benefit concerts there, but when you stand on that stage and look into the house, you can see all of the carvings and the beautiful restoration they did to that theater. It's beautiful and ghostly.

-**Julia Murney,** Actor

Each time you identify which theater you might want your upcoming show to go into, there are different questions that sort of bump up against each other. Which theaters are easiest to do well in? (Which don't have second balconies? Which have big orchestra seating sections?) Which theater feels like it will hold your show in the right way? (Is there a relatively subjective, emotional preference for a specific theater?) Can your show fit on the stage? (What are the technical elements and will they fit?)

I mix all three, but usually my heart goes to: Does this feel like the right theater to sit and watch this show in? Part of me would've loved it if *Smokey Joe's Cafe* could have been in a smaller house than the **Virginia**, because it was a relatively small show. I would have loved to have seen it in the **Walter Kerr** or the **Plymouth**.

I still think of the **Schoenfeld** as the **Plymouth** and the **Jacobs** as the **Royale** and the **Nederlander** as the **Billy Rose**. The theaters change their names, but when you've spent years working in them, they're always the first name you called them by. That shows how old I am. There are some people that still think of the **Eugene O'Neill** as the **Coronet** Theatre, and that changed 50 years ago!

-**Jack Viertel,** Creative Director of Jujamcyn Theaters

The first thing I ever ever did on Broadway was sub at *Brooklyn the Musical*. *Brooklyn* was at the **Plymouth** Theatre, which is now the **Schoenfeld**. The name change happened very shortly after I conducted there. So I haven't actually done anything at the Schoenfeld, but I've done something at the Plymouth.

-**Charlie Alterman,** Musical Director

There are a couple Broadway theaters I'd love to work in someday. I've never worked at **Circle in the Square**, but I'd love to. I'd love to do theatre-in-the-round on Broadway. I think that'd be exciting.

I've never worked at the **Gershwin**. I've played big theatres, but to really play a monster like that, I think would be great.

I love the houses that I remember going to as a kid. The **Imperial** and the **Music Box** were so special to me because of the things I saw there. The **Broadhurst** too, and I've played in there now. The old **Helen Hayes** is gone, but the **St. James**, the **Royale**, the **Golden**. The little, teeny, jewel box houses are so wonderful.

Because I'm really strange, I've always wanted to play the **Cort** Theatre. I want to see what it's like to be on the absolutely wrong side of Broadway. I was in the **Al Hirschfeld** when it was the **Martin Beck** and it was strange because we were on the far side of 8th Avenue. It was like we were Broadway adjacent. But the Cort! That's a whole other world. I want to be in the Cort Theatre just to see what it's like to be on Broadway, but not on Broadway all at the same time. That theater is sort of like the gateway to Broadway. You kind of have to sail through it in order to get to the real Broadway.

If you go to Bar Centrale, and they go, "Where are you playing?" and you go, "The Cort," then they go, "No, really, where you playing?" Nobody wants to be at the Cort Theatre, but I want to be there! I want to play the Cort just once, to say that I have done it and have lived to tell the tale. I want to brave that outlying post.

Everybody goes to Hawaii. I want to see what it's like in that little island that's a hundred miles to the north of Hawaii where the Bermuda Triangle starts.

-Jason Alexander, Actor

I'm not at all surprised that a lot of actors want to work in the **Music Box**. There's a magic in that theater that performers have always adored. And of course, a lot of actors want to work in the **Booth** because it's so cozy and comforting.

Sometimes I like to play the game of "What was the first show I saw in each Broadway theater?" That's always fun to try to remember, because there were some that I went to a lot, and some it took me a long time to get to. I still kick myself that I got sick the day my family was going to see *Anya* at the Ziegfeld Theatre in 1965. That was the last show there, so I never got to go to the **Ziegfeld**. I never saw a show at the **Hudson**, although there were several that I could have. I did get to see several at the **Henry Miller**. I saw *Grease* at the **Eden**, which was downtown and has since been chopped up into a film multiplex. I saw *The Rise and Fall of the City of Mahoganny* at the **Anderson** Theatre, and I hated that show but that theater was one of the old ones that had been neglected. There used to be a lot of those...

I saw shows at the **Playhouse**, which used to be across from the **Cort**. I saw *Pump Boys and Dinettes* at the **Princess** Theatre. I saw shows at the **Rialto**. Terrible shows ran there. The **Earl Carroll** Theatre was diagonally across from the **Winter Garden** for years, before they turned it into a Woolworth's and Capezios. Nick van Hoogstratten's great book on lost theaters made me realize if you looked above Woolworth's you could have seen the fly gallery and dressing room windows. But I never did look!

-Ted Chapin, President of The Rodgers & Hammerstein Organization/Past Chairman of the American Theatre Wing

I wish you had lived when I lived. Because you're a theatre bunny like I'm a theatre bunny, and theatre bunnies like us love hunting down the carrot. We love looking for the important thing there, and chasing it, we love that. You would have gotten a big kick out of those days, the 1980s and 1990s. You would have loved the smells. You would have cried like I did when the theaters were being torn down. I remember going into the **New Amsterdam**, before they renovated it. It was like *Follies*.

-Michael John LaChiusa, Writer

Last night, I got off the subway at 41st and Broadway. I was walking down 41st toward Port Authority, past the back of the **New Amsterdam**, with the **Nederlander** across the street. I stopped and actually touched the bricks on the back of the old building and said, aloud, "I love theaters." I love theaters. I love them.

-Craig Carnelia, Writer

Who's in the walls? Who's on the stage? I think you feel it. I think these Broadway theaters are such shrines and testimonies to the amazing talent in our industry. I get more sappy every year. I so appreciate all of the wonderful people who have worked at Manhattan Theatre Club. I've had a chance to work with so many of them and there's so many more I want to work with.

-Lynne Meadow, Artistic Director of Manhattan Theatre Club/Director

I used to live in midtown, on 49th Street. Then, I had to move away. But I'm moving back. A lot of people want to get away from midtown, because they don't want to live where they work, they don't want to be too "in it" all the time... but I always find myself in midtown when I don't need to be. I could be anywhere else in the city, but I just gravitate there because it's where the magic lives. I just want to be around it all the time.

I lived in this building, Elmsford Arms, which is very historic, and it's right across the street from Worldwide Plaza. John Bolton was my neighbor, and he taught me all about the history of the building and how Worldwide Plaza used to be the old Madison Square Garden, and I just flipped out. I looked it up, and found old photos of Madison Square Garden with *our* little building next to it! I remember I talked to my grandparents, who were here then, and I told them where I lived, and they told me some concerts and games they saw right next door. Here I was living where my grandparents had a date night when they were my age! That's another part of this town and these theaters. It feels like you're coming full circle. I feel such a connection with them, because New York is in my family. I just can't stay away. I lived in L.A. for a year, and all I could think about was midtown. I don't know if I'll ever leave midtown.

-Ben Rappaport, Actor

There are some theaters I wouldn't mind playing again. There's a strange, beautiful thing that happens to you when you walk by a theater, and it's sad. You pass the **Winter Garden** or the **St. James**, or the little **Helen Hayes**, on your way through New York City. Then you get to Sardi's, and you sit there and remember that you used to go in those places every night, and now you can't go in. It's somebody else's show now. You walk by there and it's verboten. The door men would probably say, "Hey John, how are you?" but it's not your place anymore. It's a curious sadness.

-John McMartin, Actor

Broadway is a great place to work, and it's always exciting, because we have something happening every night! There are a lot of big shows coming to town this year, and lots of shows waiting to come in, after that. We've never had more shows waiting for a theater than we have now.

-Robert E. Wankel, Co-CEO and President of The Shubert Organization

I'm sure you've heard this over and over again, but I remember my first time landing in New York. I remember taking the N/R train to the M60 bus and then being on that bus riding into Manhattan. I remember feeling a deep sense of belonging. *I am cut out for this. I feel so right about this city.*

To this day, I think that's such a lucky thing because I know there are a lot of people who are like: *This is where my job is. But I don't love New York.* I understand that, but I think I was very fortunate to feel a relationship so immediately. And I still feel that way. I still feel like this is my favorite place to live. When my family first moved to New York, I loved exploring the subways and figuring out the city and trying not to seem like a tourist. I was really, really, really excited about anybody in a show jacket, and all of the weird Broadway gift shops. In Detroit, Michigan, there was nothing. I ordered away for this magazine called *The Music Stand* that was filled with show memorabilia and little mugs with music notes and *Phantom* masks, and I would read that magazine over and over again. Then I got here and *The Music Stand* had a shop on every corner in Times Square! I would go in and look at the show memorabilia and think: *This is what I've wanted my whole life, a place that loves musicals and theatre as much as I do.* Those shops were such a big part of my first year being here.

Gavin Creel and I were roommates for years, and he made his Broadway debut in *Thoroughly Modern Millie.* I remember going to his dressing room, and he'd taken a couch from our old apartment to put backstage. I watched him pick out paint chips and I thought: *This is what people do. Your dressing room isn't just the place you get dressed. It's your home.* And I've felt at home in every single dressing room I've had, even my concrete block in the basement of **Circle in the Square**.

I love that tradition of making the theater your second home. It becomes your midtown apartment. It becomes the place that you go to drop things off during the day or change for an audition or put on makeup. I think people end up feeling so tied to the theaters that they've performed in, because of that relationship. You spend so much time in the theater. You form associations with the people who work there. You remember who came to visit you backstage and what you had on the walls and what things were there that made it feel like home. And as you grow up, the things all come with you. I have a little stone that an acting teacher gave me in college and a little egg that a dresser gave me when I did *Sweeney Todd* at the Kennedy Center. They both said, "This is for your dressing room." I have all these collections of things that come with me everywhere. Just like moving apartments, some of the things get thrown out as you move from place to place. It's an evolving process of making a home in each theater and thinking about all of the people who've made their homes in that theater before you.

What a beautiful legacy! The flops and the hits. The people who were there for a minute and the people who were there for years. Being a part of that legacy is something that I cherish, and that feels so unexpected. The dreams that you have of being on Broadway when you grow up, you don't know if those will come true. You don't know if you'll actually get to be a part of it. And then you do, and you want to carry every part of that with you.

When we were talking about what theater we were going to go into for *The Glass Menagerie*, Cherry Jones said, "The **Cort**! It just has to be The Cort!" That's where she did *The Heiress* and I understand that attachment to certain theaters. Each person has a different one where they get that feeling of: good things happen here, good work happens here. Whether that's actually true or not, you feel these connections with the actual buildings. You walk into these theaters and you know that people have put their blood, sweat and tears into them. That connection is a surprise and a gift, once you're in that place that you never really knew existed when you were a kid growing up in another state. The actual feeling of being on Broadway, that's just something no one can teach you until you're actually living it.

-Celia Keenan-Bolger, Actor

That was a nice walk down memory lane. I realize how lucky I am to have been in so many incredible theaters. It's such a lucky, lucky life.

-Christian Borle, Actor

Timelines

Shows featured in The Untold Stories of Broadway, Volume 1

2. Winter Garden

1911	La Belle Paree
1912	The Passing Show of 1912
1913	The Passing Show of 1913
1914	The Passing Show of 1914
1915	The Passing Show of 1915
1916	The Passing Show of 1916
1917	The Passing Show of 1917
1918	Sinbad, The Passing Show of 1918
1919	The Passing Show of 1919
1920	The Passing Show of 1921
1922	The Passing Show of 1922
1923	The Passing Show of 1923
1924	The Passing Show of 1924

1. Richard Rodgers

1925	The Greenwich Village Follies
1926	Is Zat So?

1934	Ziegfeld Follies of 1934
1936	Ziegfeld Follies of 1936
1938	Hellzapoppin

1943	Rosalinda	1943	Ziegfeld Follies of 1943
1947	Finian's Rainbow		
1948	Love Life		
1950	Guys and Dolls		

		1953	Wonderful Town
1954	On Your Toes	1954	Peter Pan
1955	Damn Yankees		
1957	New Girl in Town	1957	Ziegfeld Follies of 1957, West Side Story
1959	Redhead	1959	Saratoga
			Once Upon a Mattress,
1960	Tenderloin	1960	The Unsinkable Molly Brown
1961	How to Succeed in Business Without Really Trying		
		1962	All American, Nowhere to Go But Up
		1964	Funny Girl
1965	Do I Hear a Waltz?, Pickwick		
1966	Pousse-Café, I Do! I Do!	1966	Mame
1969	1776	1969	Jimmy
		1970	Georgy, Purlie
1971	No, No, Nanette	1971	Follies
		1972	Much Ado About Nothing
1973	Raisin		
		1974	Gypsy
1975	Chicago	1975	Doctor Jazz
		1976	Pacific Overtures, Fiddler on the Roof
		1977	Beatlemania
1978	Working, The Best Little Whorehouse in Texas		
		1979	Gilda Radner - Live From New York
		1980	The Roast, 42nd Street
1982	Nine	1982	Cats
1987	Fences		
1988	Checkmates		
1989	The Merchant of Venice		
1990	Accomplice; Oh, Kay!		
1991	Lost in Yonkers		
1992	Movin' Out		
1993	Laughter on the 23rd Floor		

1995	How to Succeed in Business Without Really Trying		
1996	Chicago		
1997	Steel Pier		
1998	Footloose		
2000	Seussical		
		2001	Mamma Mia!
2002	Movin' Out	2002	Once On This Island benefit
2006	Tarzan		
2007	Cyrano de Bergerac		
2008	In the Heights		
2011	Bengal Tiger at the Baghdad Zoo		
2012	The Gershwins' Porgy and Bess		
	Cat on a Hot Tin Roof, The Rascals: Once Upon A Dream,		
2013	Romeo and Juliet		
2014	If/Then	2014	Rocky

4. Hirschfeld

1924	Madame Pompadour
1927	Spread Eagle
1940	Lady in Waiting, Cabin in the Sky
1941	Watch on the Rhine
1942	My Sister Eileen
1943	A Connecticut Yankee
1945	On the Town
1946	The Iceman Cometh
1956	Candide
1960	Bye Bye Birdie
1964	The Physicists, I Had a Ball
1965	Oliver!, Drat! The Cat!, Baker Street, Marat/Sade
1967	Hallelujah, Baby!
1968	Man of La Mancha

		1972	Ring Around the Bathtub
		1973	No Hard Feelings
		1975	Habeas Corpus
		1977	Happy End, Dracula
		1980	Onward Victoria
		1981	Bring Back Birdie, The Little Foxes, The First
		1982	Come Back to the 5 & Dime Jimmy Dean, Jimmy Dean
		1984	The Rink

3. Marquis

1986	Me and My Girl		
		1987	Into the Woods
		1989	Grand Hotel
1990	Shogun, the Musical		
1991	Gypsy, Nick & Nora		
		1992	Guys and Dolls
1993	The Goodbye Girl		
1994	Damn Yankees		
1995	Victor/Victoria	1995	Moon Over Buffalo
1998	The Capeman, Forever Tango	1998	The Sound of Music
1999	Annie Get Your Gun	1999	Kiss Me, Kate
2001	A Christmas Carol		
2002	Thoroughly Modern Millie	2002	Sweet Smell of Success, Man of La Mancha
		2003	Wonderful Town
2004	La Cage Aux Folles		
2005	The Woman in White		
2006	The Drowsy Chaperone	2006	The Wedding Singer
		2007	Curtains
2008	Cry-Baby, Irving Berlin's White Christmas	2008	A Tale of Two Cities
2009	9 to 5	2009	Hair
2010	Come Fly Away	2010	Elf
2011	Wonderland, Follies	2011	How to Succeed in Business Without Really Tryin
2012	Evita	2012	Elf
2013	Jekyll & Hyde	2013	Kinky Boots

5. Simon

1927	Funny Face
1928	Treasure Girl
1929	Spring is Here, Heads Up
1930	Girl Crazy
1934	Anything Goes
1935	Porgy and Bess
1936	Red, Hot and Blue
1937	I'd Rather Be Right
1938	The Boys from Syracuse
1941	Lady in the Dark
1943	Something for the Boys
1954	The Golden Apple
1955	No Time for Sergeants
1962	A Funny Thing Happened on the Way to the Forum
1964	High Spirits
1965	Flora, The Red Menace
1966	"It's a Bird...It's a Plane...It's Superman"

6. Wilson

1925	Caesar and Cleopatra
1926	Garrick Gaieties
1930	Garrick Gaieties
1933	The Mask and the Face
1935	The Taming of the Shrew
1961	The Conquering Hero, A Man for All Seasons

1967	Rosencrantz and Guildenstern Are Dead		
1968	The Great White Hope		
		1969	Our Town
1970	Company		
1973	Tricks, Molly		
		1974	Cat on a Hot Tin Roof
1975	Shenandoah		
		1976	Bubbling Brown Sugar
1977	Annie		
		1978	A History of the American Film
		1980	The Stitch in Time
1981	Merrily We Roll Along, The Little Prince and the Aviator Little Johnny Jones, Do Black Patent Leather Shoes Really Reflect Up?, Seven Brides for	1981	Copperfield, Oh, Brother!
1982	Seven Brothers		
1983	Brighton Beach Memoirs		
1985	Biloxi Blues		
		1986	Wild Honey
1987	Breaking the Code		
1988	Ah, Wilderness	1988	Carrie
1989	Senator Joe	1989	City of Angels
1992	Jake's Women	1992	Jelly's Last Jam
1993	Cyrano - The Musical	1993	My Fair Lady
		1995	Smokey Joe's Cafe
1996	The King and I		
1998	A View From the Bridge, Swan Lake		
1999	The Scarlet Pimpernel		
2000	The Music Man	2000	The Wild Party, Gore Vidal's The Best Man
		2001	King Hedley II
2002	Hairspray	2002	The Crucible, Flower Drum Song
		2003	Little Shop of Horrors
		2005	Little Women, Jersey Boys

2009	Ragtime
2011	Catch Me If You Can
2012	Jesus Christ Superstar
2013	Big Fish

7. Lyceum

1905 | A Doll's House, Just Out of College

1907 | The Boys of Company "B"

1922 | The French Doll

1924 | Fashions of 1924

8. Hellinger

1934 | Calling All Stars

1941 | Banjo Eyes

1946 | Born Yesterday

		1951	Two on the Aisle
		1953	Hazel Flagg
		1956	My Fair Lady
		1964	Fade Out - Fade In
		1965	On a Clear Day You Can See Forever
		1966	A Joyful Noise
1967	You Can't Take It With You, The Show Off		
1968	Exit the King, The Misanthrope		
1969	Cock-A-Doodle Dandy	1969	Dear World, Coco
		1971	Ari, Jesus Christ Superstar
1972	The Great God Brown, Don Juan		
1975	Truckload		
1976	Something's Afoot	1976	1600 Pennsylvania Avenue
		1978	Timbuktu!, Platinum
		1979	The Utter Glory of Morrissey Hall, Sugar Babies
1980	Morning's at Seven		
1982	"MASTER HAROLD"...and the boys	1982	A Doll's Life
		1983	Merlin
1984	Whoopi Goldberg	1984	Oliver!
		1985	Grind
		1986	Rags
		1988	Legs Diamond
1993	Three Men on a Horse		
1995	The School for Scandal		

2000	Rose
2001	The Invention of Love
2002	Morning's at Seven
2003	I Am My Own Wife
2006	The Lieutenant of Inishmore
2007	Is He Dead?
2008	Macbeth, [title of show]
2010	The Scottsboro Boys
2012	Venus in Fur
2013	The Nance

Acknowledgements

The same today as it was in ancient Greece, theatre is still passed on from generation to generation. Skills and lessons and stories and techniques and passion are passed from person to person, and I have many people to be grateful to in that regard. In addition to the 200 interviewees, many other people contributed to making *The Untold Stories of Broadway* happen.

When I declared I would write this book, people began connecting me to others. Immediately, there was an outpouring of folks being generous with their time, their smarts, and their connections. I was blown away by the selflessness and helpfulness of the community. At one point, I "cold-emailed" Christian Borle and he said yes to an interview for the book. He then connected me with Rose M. Alaio, the stage door woman at the Shubert, who I interviewed as we walked around the set of *Matilda*. She connected me with James Woolley, a stage manager and usher who often works in the Shubert, who I interviewed weeks later in the lower lobby. This type of chain reaction happened all the time. Every step of the way, people were connecting me to their friends, calling and emailing on my behalf. I want to thank all of the people who opened up their hearts and their address books for me.

This book would not have been possible without the hard work and dedication of an indefatigable team of helpers, who transcribed, researched, co-interviewed, and gave invaluable insight as the book came together. Sierra Fox, whose sleight of hand made this book what it is, provided endless amounts of knowledge and heart. Julia Castellanos was a constant inspiration, always ready to shriek together at a new discovery. Anna Marie Ray always knew if the Brooks Atkinson had a broken window. Andrew Greenberg was always game to relate each story back to Jan Maxwell. Larry Owens provided a constant stream of positivity and passion. Allie Glickman shared tears and dreams of being a Broadway producer someday. Nathan Bell came to New York City from Ohio for his second time ever, and co-interviewed with me, perfectly exemplifying the spirit of this book. Drew Factor moved to the city in the middle of this book being written and inspired with his bravery and guts. Tess Harkin, a budding journalist in her own right, was helpful and animated. Jess McGinty was there for smart thoughts and stagedoor adventures. This book would not have been possible in any way without the skills and passion of the names above. Go back and read those names again, and remember them, because you're going to be hearing a lot from them in the future.

Thank you to those friends who jumped in to lend a special helping hand when needed: Andrey Patino, Angelica Nicholas, Anthony Stelmach, Ashley Melchiorre, Ashley Rodbro, Corey Brunish, Dyan Flores, Jeff Heimbrock, Jeffrey Vizcaino, Jerilyn McDermed, Jessica Genick, Kaitlynn Smith, Kali Ponzo, Keurim Hur, Matt Bur, Natalie Chernicoff, Olivia Gunderson, and Tarryn Steyn.

I also need to thank colleagues, family and good friends who were a constant source of support. First, Joe Iconis, for being the greatest friend I could ever ask to be opening doors with. Thank you for always inspiring me with your writing, your love for theatre, and your love for our family of friends. I cannot wait to be in one of these Broadway houses working on one of your shows together. Thank you to my "musical theatre Godmother" Mana Allen, for your wisdom, your kind heart, and your willingness to talk theatre for hours at the Cafe Edison, over a bowl of matzo ball soup! Thank you to Jeremy, Joe, Sean and everyone else at Sardi's, for carrying on theatrical tradition. Our whole community is lucky that you are here. Thank you to Richard Frankel, Tom Viertel, and Philip Geoffrey Bond who I am so honored to be working on theatre with, every day. Thank you to Matt Murphy, whose generosity as a person is matched only by his brilliance as a photographer. Thank you to Monica Simoes, who has been telling the stories of these theaters through photos for years, in the most beautiful way. Thank you to Justin "Squigs" Robertson, who I'm grateful to have known since the *[title of show]* days, who lent his own unique brand of creativity to this project. Thank you to my colleagues at 54 Below, and at Davenport Theatrical. Thank you to my friends who made a great deal of this work possible in so many different ways, from 3am rescues to technical triumphs: Aaron Simon Gross, Alexis Field, Amanda Taraska, Ben

Skinner, Blair Ingenthron, Caleb Hoyer, Danny Abosch, David Snyder, Dylan Bustamante, Emily Essig, Eric Price, Hunter Arnold, Jason SweetTooth Williams, Jenna Lloyd, Justin Braun, Kayla Greenspan, Kevin Michael Murphy, Lauren Marcus, Leah Harris, Max Blake Friedman, Michael Gioia, Nic Rouleau, Rachel Sussman, Steven Tartick, and Zack Zadek. Thank you to Michael Berresse, Jeff Bowen and Hunter Bell, who always knew. Always. Thank you to all of my life-changing teacher/mentors through the years, and especially to Zoraida Adams, Jacquie Hasko, Noel Levin, Larry Maslon, and Jeffrey Eric Jenkins. Thank you to my brother Zephrem Tepper, whose first Broadway show was *Good Vibrations*. Thank you to my sister, Jessica Kent, for your enthusiasm and sisterly love, and for letting me sit on your Times Square fire escape and write this book in my head. Thank you to Leigh-Ann Tepper for showing me the movie *Gypsy* and never letting me forget that I said, "This would make a great show!" Thank you to my dad, Larry Tepper, for your renditions of "Luck Be A Lady" and "Something's Coming" and for grinning with excitement, like a kid, every time we're sitting in theater seats together. Thank you to my mom, Janis Tepper, for sending me to theatre camp, for hunting down every cast recording I ever wanted, and for never missing a show.

Thank you to Brisa Trinchero and Roberta Pereira and everybody at Dress Circle Publishing, who were as excited about this project as I was, from my first pitch to the last draft, whose unwavering support, energy, and ideas made this book what it is. You are the reason that hundreds of people of Broadway, including me, got a platform to tell their stories, and I will always be grateful from the bottom of my heart.

Special thanks to all the people at the Shubert Organization, the Nederlander Organization, Jujamcyn Theaters, Lincoln Center, Manhattan Theatre Club, Roundabout Theater Company and Disney Theatrical Productions who are such excellent stewards of Broadway's iconic theater buildings.

Part of the proceeds of The Untold Stories of Broadway Volume 1 *will benefit Broadway Impact, a grassroots organization of theater artists and fans mobilized in support of marriage equality.*
www.broadwayimpact.com

Volume 1 Complete List of Interviewees

Deborah Abramson
Loni Ackerman
Lynn Ahrens
Rose M. Alaio
Jason Alexander
Mana Allen
Charlie Alterman
Michael Arden
Sylvia Bailey
Brittnye Batchelor
Bryan Batt
Damian Bazadona
Hunter Bell
Marty Bell
Brig Berney
Michael Berresse
Ken Billington
André Bishop
Susan Blackwell
Nick Blaemire
Corbin Bleu
Heidi Blickenstaff
Walter Bobbie
Anne Bobby
Chris Boneau
Beowulf Boritt
Christian Borle
Barry Bostwick
Jeff Bowen
Jared Bradshaw
Jason Robert Brown
Jeb Brown
Laura Bell Bundy
Todd Buonopane
Danny Burstein
Liz Callaway
Liz Caplan
Len Cariou
Craig Carnelia
Eileen Casey
Harrison Chad
Ted Chapin
Rey Concepcion
Nancy Coyne
Gavin Creel
Charlotte d'Amboise
Ken Davenport
Penny Davis
Carmel Dean
Robin De Jesus

Jamie DeRoy
Marilyn D'Honau
Ed Dixon
Christopher Durang
James Dybas
Daisy Eagan
Jill Eikenberry
Jake Epstein
Bert Fink
Terry Finn
Stephen Flaherty
Merwin Foard
Shannon Ford
Merle Frimark
Fritz Frizsell
Larry Fuller
Artie Gaffin
Jack Gale
Irene Gandy
Chris Gattelli
Joanna Gleason
Annie Golden
Jason Graae
Todd Graff
Randy Graff
Ilene Graff
Amanda Green
Harry Groener
Jonathan Groff
Julie Halston
Ann Harada
Diane Heatherington
Laura Heller
Tom Hewitt
Larry Hochman
Abe Jacob
Sally J. Jacobs
Jay Armstrong Johnson
Jason Kantrowitz
Doug Katsaros
Andrew Keenan-Bolger
Celia Keenan-Bolger
Steve C. Kennedy
Chad Kimball
Eddie Korbich
Perry Kroeger
Michael John LaChiusa
Nikka Graff Lanzarone

Liz Larsen
David Larsen
Andrew Leeds
Telly Leung
Caissie Levy
Peter Link
Margo Lion
Jose Llana
William Ivey Long
David Loud
Anna Louizos
Hal Luftig
Robert LuPone
Galt MacDermot
Arielle Tepper Madover
James Maloney
Richard Maltby Jr.
Joe Mantello
Josh Marquette
Kathleen Marshall
Mel Marvin
Tony Massey
Michael Mayer
Neil Mazzella
Elizabeth McCann
John McMartin
Lynne Meadow
Michael Mendez
Lindsay Mendez
Alan Menken
Joanna Merlin
Lin-Manuel Miranda
Jessica Molaskey
Eric William Morris
Ann Morrison
Randy Morrison
Christopher Murney
Julia Murney
Donna Murphy
Anne L. Nathan
Austin Nathaniel
Casey Nicholaw
Jack O'Brien
Gene O'Donovan
Kelli O'Hara
Brynn O'Malley
Laura Osnes
Evan Pappas
Joey Parnes
Benj Pasek

Justin Paul
Diane Paulus
Michon Peacock
Mary Beth Peil
Tim Pettolina
John Pielmeier
Tonya Pinkins
Hayley Podschun
Red Press
Lonny Price
Harold Prince
Anthony Rapp
Ben Rappaport
Theresa Rebeck
Fred Ricci
Krysta Rodriguez
Charlie Rosen
Steve Rosen
Daryl Roth
Michael Rupert
Alex Rybeck
Harvey Sabinson
Sarah Saltzberg
Don Scardino
Justin Scribner
Florie Seery
David Shire
A.J. Shively
Rick Sordelet
Louis St. Louis
Michael Starobin
Don Stitt
David Stone
Susan Stroman
Charles Strouse
Jason Tam
Julie Taymor
Bernie Telsey
Joe Traina
Michael Van Praagh
Jack Viertel
Donna Vivino
Frank Vlastnik
Jim Walton
Robert E. Wankel
John Weidman
Ira Weitzman
Jennifer Werner
Frank Wildhorn
Amy Wolk

James Woolley
Doug Wright
Nick Wyman
Alex Wyse
Maury Yeston
Brian Yorkey

In Upcoming Volumes of
The Untold Stories Of Broadway...

The Ambassador Theatre
The American Airlines Theatre
The Ethel Barrymore Theatre
The Belasco Theatre
The Booth Theatre
The Broadhurst Theatre
The Broadway Theatre
The Brooks Atkinson Theatre
The Circle in the Square Theatre
The Cort Theatre
The Criterion Center Stage Right
The Edison Theatre
The Eugene O'Neill Theatre
The Foxwoods Theatre
The George Abbott Theatre
The Gershwin Theatre
The Golden Theatre
The Helen Hayes Theatre
The Imperial Theatre

The Bernard B. Jacobs Theatre
The Latin Quarter
The Longacre Theatre
The Lunt-Fontanne Theatre
The Majestic Theatre
The Minskoff Theatre
The Morosco Theatre
The Music Box Theatre
The Nederlander Theatre
The New Amsterdam Theatre
The Palace Theatre
The Samuel J. Friedman Theatre
The Gerald Schoenfeld Theatre
The Shubert Theatre
The St. James Theatre
Studio 54
The Stephen Sondheim Theatre
The Vivian Beaumont Theatre
The Walter Kerr Theatre

Also From Dress Circle Publishing

Showbiz by Ruby Preston

Staged by Ruby Preston

Starstruck by Ruby Preston (2014 Release)

The Tour by Joanna Parson (2014 Release)

The Home For Wayward Ladies by Jeremy Scott Blaustein (2014 Release)

Broadway Academy by Ruby Preston (Young Adult – 2014 Release)

Founded in 2011 by Brisa Trinchero and Roberta Pereira, Dress Circle Publishing is the only publisher dedicated solely to producing books with Broadway themes. Dress Circle Publishing is eager to discover and promote new literary voices among new or established authors who are actively working in show business.